JONES & BARTLETT LEARNING   INFORMATION SYSTEMS SECURITY & ASSURANCE SERIES

Internet Security: How to Defend Against Attackers on the Web

MIKE HARWOOD

SECOND EDITION

JONES & BARTLETT
LEARNING

World Headquarters
Jones & Bartlett Learning
5 Wall Street
Burlington, MA 01803
978-443-5000
info@jblearning.com
www.jblearning.com

Jones & Bartlett Learning books and products are available through most bookstores and online booksellers. To contact Jones & Bartlett Learning directly, call 800-832-0034, fax 978-443-8000, or visit our website, www.jblearning.com.

Substantial discounts on bulk quantities of Jones & Bartlett Learning publications are available to corporations, professional associations, and other qualified organizations. For details and specific discount information, contact the special sales department at Jones & Bartlett Learning via the above contact information or send an email to specialsales@jblearning.com.

Copyright © 2016 by Jones & Bartlett Learning, LLC, an Ascend Learning Company

All rights reserved. No part of the material protected by this copyright may be reproduced or utilized in any form, electronic or mechanical, including photocopying, recording, or by any information storage and retrieval system, without written permission from the copyright owner.

The content, statements, views, and opinions herein are the sole expression of the respective authors and not that of Jones & Bartlett Learning, LLC. Reference herein to any specific commercial product, process, or service by trade name, trademark, manufacturer, or otherwise does not constitute or imply its endorsement or recommendation by Jones & Bartlett Learning, LLC and such reference shall not be used for advertising or product endorsement purposes. All trademarks displayed are the trademarks of the parties noted herein. *Internet Security: How to Defend Against Attackers on the Web, Second Edition* is an independent publication and has not been authorized, sponsored, or otherwise approved by the owners of the trademarks or service marks referenced in this product.

Microsoft, Internet Explorer, Windows, Microsoft Office, Microsoft Security Development Lifecycle, and Microsoft Baseline Security Analyzer are either registered trademarks or trademarks of Microsoft Corporation in the United States and/or other countries. (ISC)², CISSP, ISSAP, ISSMP, ISSEP, CSSLP, CCFP, CAP, SSCP, and CBK are registered and service marks of (ISC)², Inc.

There may be images in this book that feature models; these models do not necessarily endorse, represent, or participate in the activities represented in the images. Any screenshots in this product are for educational and instructive purposes only. Any individuals and scenarios featured in the case studies throughout this product may be real or fictitious, but are used for instructional purposes only.

This publication is designed to provide accurate and authoritative information in regard to the Subject Matter covered. It is sold with the understanding that the publisher is not engaged in rendering legal, accounting, or other professional service. If legal advice or other expert assistance is required, the service of a competent professional person should be sought.

Production Credits

Chief Executive Officer: Ty Field
President: James Homer
Chief Product Officer: Eduardo Moura
SVP, Curriculum Solutions: Christopher Will
Director of Sales, Curriculum Solutions: Randi Roger
Editorial Management: High Stakes Writing, LLC,
   Lawrence J. Goodrich, President
Copy Editor, High Stakes Writing: Ruth Walker

Product Manager: Rainna Erikson
Product Management Assistant: Edward Hinman
Production Manager: Tina Chen
Associate Production Editor: Kristen Rogers
Senior Marketing Manager: Andrea DeFronzo
Production Services Manager: Colleen Lamy
Manufacturing and Inventory Control Supervisor:
   Amy Bacus

Composition: Gamut+Hue, LLC
Cover Design: Scott Moden
Rights & Media Manager: Joanna Lundeen
Rights & Media Research Coordinator:
   Mary Flatley
Cover Image: © yienkeat/Shutterstock
Printing and Binding: Edwards Brothers Malloy
Cover Printing: Edwards Brothers Malloy

ISBN: 978-1-284-09055-0

Library of Congress Cataloging-in-Publication Data
Harwood, Mike.
   [Security strategies in Web applications and social networking.]
   Internet security : how to defend against attackers on the web / Mike Harwood, MCT, MCSE, A+, Network+, Server+, Linux+, Writer and Editor for the yoursecondfifty.com/magazine. -- Second Edition.
      pages cm
   Includes bibliographical references and index.
   ISBN 978-1-284-09055-0 (pbk. : alk. paper)
   1. Online social networks—Security measures. 2. Application software—Security measures. 3. Internet—Security measures. 4. World Wide Web—Security measures. I. Harwood, Mike. Security strategies in Web applications and social networking. II. Title.
   HM742.H38 2015
   302.30285--dc23
                              2015019892

6048

Printed in the United States of America
19 18 17 16 15   10 9 8 7 6 5 4 3 2 1

Contents

© Rodolfo Clix/Dreamstime.com

PART TWO　　Secure Web-Enabled Application Deployment and Social Networking　　75

CHAPTER 4　　**Mitigating Risk When Connecting to the Internet**　　**76**

© Rodolfo Clix/Dreamstime.com

Preface

Purpose of This Book

This book is part of the Information Systems Security & Assurance Series from Jones & Bartlett Learning (*www.jblearning.com*). Designed for courses and curriculums in IT Security, Cybersecurity, Information Assurance, and Information Systems Security, this series features a comprehensive, consistent treatment of the most current thinking and trends in this critical subject area. These titles deliver fundamental information-security principles packed with real-world applications and examples. Authored by professionals experienced in information systems security, they deliver comprehensive information on all aspects of information security. Reviewed word for word by leading technical experts in the field, these books are not just current, but forward-thinking—putting you in the position to solve the cybersecurity challenges not just of today, but of tomorrow, as well.

Part 1 of this book examines the evolutionary changes that have occurred in data processing and computing, personal and business communications, and social interaction and networking on the Internet and World Wide Web. It also covers relevant security considerations for small businesses and personal users.

Part 2 reviews the risks, threats, and vulnerabilities associated with Web-enabled applications accessible via the Internet. In addition, it covers the risks, threats, and vulnerabilities associated with social networking Web sites that allow perpetrators to plant malicious code and malware with widespread global impact. Web site and application security and best practices to help mitigate these risks are explored. Common sense and best practices for online privacy and securing your privacy data are presented, providing you with countermeasures to protect your privacy and privacy data.

Part 3 presents the next and greatest business challenge—securing the mobile user. With Web applications and social networking now being accessed remotely and from mobile wireless connected devices, these devices are at risk. This part of the book explores mobile communications security, given the rapid use of 4G wireless networking for mobile communication. You also learn about VoIP- and SIP-enabled applications, such as unified communications, and how they provide real-time communications for both personal and business use. Finally, Web-security organizations, standards organizations, education, training, and certification organization are presented to provide you with additional resources and planning strategies for a career in secure Web application design and development.

Learning Features

The writing style of this book is practical and conversational. Step-by-step examples of information security concepts and procedures are presented throughout the text. Each chapter begins with a statement of learning objectives. Illustrations are used both to clarify the material and to vary the presentation. The text is sprinkled with Notes, Tips, FYIs, Warnings, and sidebars to alert the reader to additional helpful information related to the subject under discussion. Chapter Assessments appear at the end of each chapter, with solutions provided in the back of the book. Chapter summaries are included in the text to provide a rapid review or preview of the material and to help students understand the relative importance of the concepts presented.

Audience

The material is suitable for undergraduate or graduate computer science majors or information science majors, or students at a two-year technical college or community college who have a basic technical background, or readers who have a basic understanding of IT security and want to expand their knowledge.

© Rodolfo Clix/Dreamstime.com

Acknowledgments

It takes the dedication and hard work of many people to create a book such as this. Fortunately, I was given a fantastic team with whom to work, and this book clearly reflects their professionalism and commitment to the project. I would like to thank Jeff T. Parker, the technical reviewer, for an amazing job reviewing and improving content. In addition I would like to thank Jeff for his writing touch-ups and additions to the content. He deserves a rest after this one. I would also like to thank Lawrence Goodrich and Ruth Walker for keeping the ball rolling and everything on track. Dealing with authors and timelines cannot be easy, but somehow they pull it off.

Finally, I would like to thank Paige Harwood not only for her ongoing support throughout the project but also for a terrific job of content editing and work on Chapter 3.

To summer, time off,
and time with family

About the Author

Mike Harwood has been working in IT for more than 13 years. He is currently the IT manager for a large manufacturer located in the Kootenay region of British Columbia, Canada. In this role, he researches technology trends and implements relevant solutions in a manufacturing environment. He holds several industry certifications and continues to author technical titles on a variety of topics.

© Rodolfo Clix/Dreamstime.com

PART ONE

Evolution of Computing, Risks, and Social Networking

© Rodolfo Clix/Dreamstime.com

From Mainframe to Client/Server to World Wide Web

IN THE WORLD OF NETWORKING AND COMPUTING, technologies come and go regularly. New protocols are developed; new media are introduced, as well as faster hardware. The cycle of improvement is continuous. Among this rapid growth and change, old hardware, applications, and systems are often replaced. In many instances, the actual technology is no longer useful, but the concepts behind the technologies remain important.

This chapter provides a brief history of computing, networking technology, and Internet developments. It looks at the evolution of modern data processing, the emergence of the World Wide Web, the growth of e-commerce, and the Internet developments that have changed the way people work and live.

After all, in order to know where you are going, you need to know where you have been. This is as true in technology as in any other field.

Chapter 1 Topics

This chapter covers these topics and concepts:

- What the evolution of data processing is
- Where mainframe computers are used and why
- What the nature of client/server computing is
- How distributed computing is used on a network
- How the transformation of brick-and-mortar businesses to e-commerce businesses took place
- How and when the World Wide Web revolution occurred
- What groupware and Gopher are
- What the changing states of the World Wide Web are

- What the Internet of Things (IoT) is, and what its particular security vulnerabilities are
- What virtualization is, and how cloud computing is used in modern networks

Chapter 1 Goals

When you complete this chapter, you will be able to:

- Identify the highlights in the evolution of data processing, and distinguish between information and data
- Identify the key points in Web development
- Understand the characteristics of Web 1.0, 2.0, and 3.0
- Understand the role of cloud computing, and identify the role of virtualization in modern networks
- Review the beginnings of e-commerce
- Understand the Internet of Things and potential security and privacy risks

The Evolution of Data Processing

Without a doubt, the emergence of high-speed data processing changed the world in profound ways. Data processing, the transformation of raw data into information, has opened new areas of communication and understanding. Many people assume that the developments in data processing are a product of the digital age, but data processors and computing devices go back hundreds of years. However, before you can appreciate the evolution of data processing, you need a clear definition of data and of information and how they are related.

Understanding Data, Data Processing, and Information

People often use the terms *data* and *information* synonymously. To understand the function of data processing, it is important to know one term from the other. Data are essentially facts, figures, or other forms of raw input from which conclusions are drawn. These conclusions become usable information. Data in its raw form has no real significance or application. It is merely the collection of observations, statistics, and recordings. The analysis of data transforms it into information. In other words, to have

FIGURE 1-1

Processing data into information.

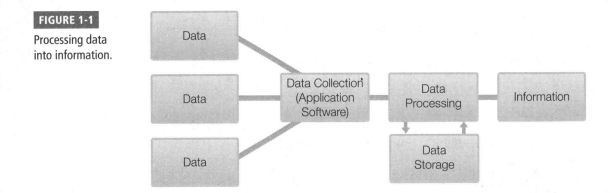

relevance as information, data needs to be recorded, organized, and interpreted within a specific framework. Data processing refers to the steps data goes through to become information. Figure 1-1 displays a simplified flow chart identifying how data transforms into information.

If the definition of data processing is the transformation of data from its raw form to understandable and applicable information, the evolution of data processing is traceable to long before the digital era. The abacus, for example, dates to ancient times and in its day was a complex data processing device. Using rows of beads, the abacus takes raw data input, calculates complex problems, albeit manually, and returns usable information. In addition to the abacus, a number of analog computing devices predicted astronomical events. As early as 150–100 B.C., a device known as the Antikythera mechanism was taking raw astronomical input and outputting applicable information.

> **NOTE**
>
> Interested in traveling back in data processing time? Check out the online virtual abacus at *http:// www.alcula.com/suanpan.php*.

These early technologies formed a knowledge base that was continually built upon over the centuries. The concepts of these early devices still can be found in data processors used today. The designers of these antiquated devices are the true data processing pioneers, making the abacus, sextant, slide rules, and other such devices the IBMs or Intels of their day.

Today you will not see an office full of accountants calculating tax returns on an abacus, but the function of data processors remains virtually the same. Figure 1-2 provides a snapshot of the history of modern data processing and those technologies that have led to the systems and processes used today.

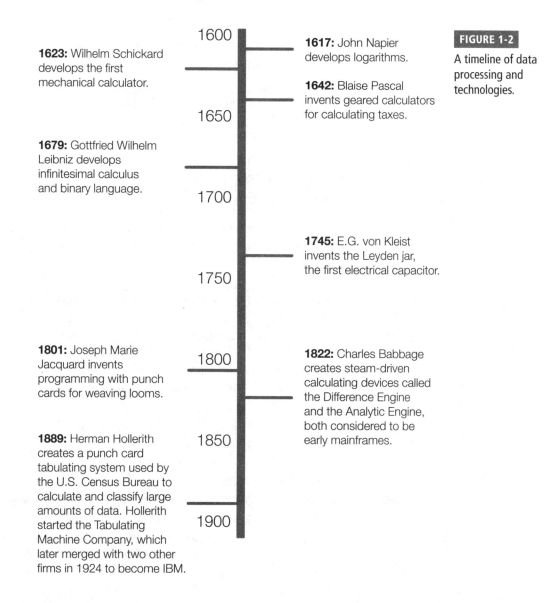

1600

1623: Wilhelm Schickard develops the first mechanical calculator.

1617: John Napier develops logarithms.

1642: Blaise Pascal invents geared calculators for calculating taxes.

1650

1679: Gottfried Wilhelm Leibniz develops infinitesimal calculus and binary language.

1700

1745: E.G. von Kleist invents the Leyden jar, the first electrical capacitor.

1750

1801: Joseph Marie Jacquard invents programming with punch cards for weaving looms.

1800

1822: Charles Babbage creates steam-driven calculating devices called the Difference Engine and the Analytic Engine, both considered to be early mainframes.

1889: Herman Hollerith creates a punch card tabulating system used by the U.S. Census Bureau to calculate and classify large amounts of data. Hollerith started the Tabulating Machine Company, which later merged with two other firms in 1924 to become IBM.

1850

1900

FIGURE 1-2

A timeline of data processing and technologies.

1900s and Rapid Growth

The second half of the 1900s saw remarkable developments in technology and data processing. Listing all the developments of the 1900s could fill books. Here are highlights:

- **1924**—Hollerith merges his Tabulating Machine Company with two other companies to form International Business Machines (IBM). IBM focused on developing calculators and machines for business and financial institutions.

- **1941**—Germany's Konrad Zuse invents four computing devices: Z1, Z2, Z3, and Z4. The Z3 was revolutionary and is believed to be the first fully functional, programmable digital computer. The Z1, Z2, and Z3 were destroyed during World War II.

- **1942**—American John Vincent Atanasoff and his partner Clifford Berry develop the first electronic computer system known as the Atanasoff-Berry Computer. The computer used vacuum tubes and regenerative capacitor memory modules, the forerunner of the dynamic random access memory (DRAM) used today.

> **NOTE**
>
> Who knew? Grace Hopper was a programmer working on the Mark I. During an inspection, Hopper discovered a dead moth in the Mark I that had actually brought the behemoth system down. Since then, the word *bug* has described computer glitches or other anomalies. Hopper also coined the word *debugging* to correct program anomalies.

- **1943**—During World War II, the U.S. military needs a calculator to help battleships more accurately fire long-range ammunition, taking into account wind resistance, distance, velocity, drag, and other factors. The military sends word that it needs a system to easily calculate trajectory and create accurate firing tables. The Harvard Mark I, built in partnership with IBM and Harvard, fills this need. The Mark I is the first large-scale, automatic, digital computer.

- **1946**—The British-made Electronic Numerical Integrator and Computer (ENIAC) is a 30-ton computer with more than 18,000 vacuum tubes. The ENIAC system can be programmed and reprogrammed to perform a variety of computing tasks. Its original purpose is to calculate exact military artillery firing tables for long-range ammunition.

- **1951**—Two ENIAC developers, J. Presper Eckert and John Mauchly, go to work on the Universal Automatic Computer (UNIVAC). The UNIVAC becomes the first commercially available computer system and is used by some of the largest corporations and the U.S. Census Bureau. In 1952, CBS News uses it to predict the results of the presidential election.

- **1964**—IBM releases a revolutionary new system, the IBM/360. The 360 is the first modern **mainframe** computer.

- **1971**—The release of the Intel 4004, a 4-bit central processor, is a huge step forward in personal computing. The 4004 is the first central processing unit (CPU) available on a single chip.

- **1973**—A sign of things to come, the Alto computer offers a simple **graphical user interface (GUI)**, an interface based on graphical elements as opposed to text only, and a mouse-type device for input. Developed by Xerox, the Alto is designed for offices with workstation systems.

The mid-1970s to the early 1980s introduced the **minicomputer** to large corporate networks. Minicomputers were mid-range systems between the new, low-powered microcomputers and the high-capacity mainframes. Minicomputers were significantly cheaper than mainframes, which allowed more companies to buy them. While not as powerful as mainframes, minicomputers could run full, multi-user, multitasking operating systems like the UNIX. Minicomputers took high-end processing away from the mainframe and made it accessible to any company that could afford it.

- **1975**—MIT's Altair 8800 takes the market by storm as the first widely marketed personal computer for both homes and offices. It is available as a completed computer and as a kit that budding computer hobbyists can build themselves.

- **1976**—Word processing is born with the release of Electric Pencil software.

- **1977**—The release of Apple II changes the desktop computer market forever. The Apple II displays color graphics and user-friendly navigation and input devices.

In the 1980s and early 1990s, the popularity of microcomputers exploded, putting a personal computer (PC) on the desks of more than two-thirds of office workers in the United States. New productivity tools were developed for the desktop PC.

- **1981**—IBM releases the PC, and the rivalry between Apple and the PC begins.

- **1984**—Apple introduces the first Macintosh. The easy-to-use Macintosh comes with a proprietary operating system and is the fist popular computer to have a GUI and a mouse.

- **1990**—Microsoft releases Windows 3.0, a very successful GUI interface built upon the DOS operating system. Windows 3.11 arrives as the networkable version of the OS.

- **2002**—The number of personal computers by all manufacturers shipped since 1975 reaches 1 billion, according to industry research firm Gartner Dataquest.

> **NOTE**
>
> Some people consider 1997 a turning point for computer and processing ability. IBM's Deep Blue computer beat world chess champion Garry Kasparov in a six-game match. Although it had been tried before, this was the first time a computer was able to beat a chess master.

Since 2002, technology and data processing machines have continued to grow rapidly. Manufacturers develop new and revolutionary processors, motherboards, and chipsets—and companies and standards bodies develop new **protocols** (defined policies or standards that users adhere to)—at a staggering pace. So where are things headed?

Many believe that the future is in the clouds. That is, today is a transition toward *cloud computing*, which provides distributed applications and services over the Internet. You'll learn more about cloud computing and distributed applications later in this chapter.

Mainframe Computers

April 1964 was notable for the release of the IBM/360 mainframe computer known as Big Iron. Before the IBM/360, computer systems had a single purpose as either a data processor or a computing device. Promoted as a multi-use mainframe, the IBM/360 was designed for a variety of applications.

▶ **NOTE**

Although computers that existed before the release of the IBM/360 technically resembled mainframe systems, industry experts consider the IBM/360 the start of the mainframe era.

The IBM/360 saw huge commercial success due to its versatility and programmability. It set the standard for business computing for years. The IBM/360 brought about a new networking model for corporations—the *centralized* or *mainframe computing model*. The idea was to tap into the resources of powerful, centralized computer systems.

So who uses mainframes? You do. If you use an automated teller machine (ATM), conduct business online, or work in finance, health care, insurance, or related industries, you likely use a mainframe somewhere along the line. Mainframes are largely hidden, working in the background, managing daily operations for the world's largest companies. The mainframe is the foundation of modern business, online and off.

Mainframes are the most robust systems available today with numerous disaster-recovery and fault-tolerant solutions built into their design. Because of their strength and processing power, mainframes maintain the most mission-critical applications in the world.

However, you are unlikely to sit directly in front of a mainframe to work. Rather, you use a Web browser or another application on your workstation as the interface between you and the mainframe. The mainframe manages the applications, all processing, and database storage. This configuration is known as **centralized processing** or *centralized computing*, in which the workstation is merely a gateway to the centralized system where all processing, computing, and storage takes place.

Key advantages of housing applications on a mainframe include:

- **Processing power**—The mainframe has more processing power than regular network servers and workstations, allowing for faster and more complex applications.
- **Database management**—You can store and access a central database with maximum efficiency. Mainframes can support huge databases, often on the scale of terabytes of information. Also, mainframes allow centralized management for security and backups of the database.
- **User-friendly interface**—Using the Web as an interface to the mainframe makes it easy and user friendly to access a remote mainframe. This also allows for "anywhere anytime" access to mainframe databases.
- **Application continuity**—Mainframes are built to last, and they have little or no downtime. Users can expect to have uninterrupted access to their database.

- **Application security**—Mainframe applications and databases are centrally managed, helping ensure that data is secure and safe from tampering.

- **Database backups**—Today's mainframes are designed for robust backups, ensuring that if a problem occurs, backups are available to restore lost data.

Mainframes are part of daily life. As you go online to Amazon, eBay, Barnes and Noble, and virtually any other large Web site, you likely are accessing a mainframe.

Client/Server Computing

Any computer on a network can have one of two roles or a combination of both: server and/or client. A **server** is a computer system designed to provide resources to other nodes on the network. It may provide central storage for files, access to printers, processing, and more. The server responds to client requests. For example, a Web browser sends a request to a Web server and the server responds with the requested information—a Web page. This interaction is the basis of almost all communication behind the **client/server** network.

Many of today's applications and protocols use the client/server architecture. Domain Name System (DNS), Dynamic Host Configuration Protocol (DHCP), **File Transfer Protocol (FTP)**, **Hypertext Transfer Protocol (HTTP)**, **Telnet**, **Simple Mail Transfer Protocol (SMTP)**, and Post Office Protocol version 3 (POP3) are examples of protocols that use a client/server model. All of these protocols rely on a server to answer requests from clients. A client/server networking model is less about hardware and more about how applications and protocols use the hardware.

Client/server networking is widely used today because of its advantages, which include:

- **Scalability**—It's easy to add workstations or other peripherals to an established network.

- **Centralization**—Consolidated control of the network allows for easier management of large networks, including both network resources and network user accounts.

- **Convenience**—Users can have single-password access to all the network resources they're allowed access to.

- **Efficiency**—Network data is easier to back up when it's stored in a single location.

- **Security**—Access to sensitive data is easier to monitor and secure.

> **NOTE**
>
> A potential drawback of a client/server network is a single point of failure. That is, if a server fails, its services are unavailable. Network administrators employ a series of fault-tolerant strategies to ensure that this does not occur.

The client/server network configuration grew from the need for easier administration after the proliferation of standalone computers. The complexity of managing hundreds or thousands of office computers, each with local storage and applications, is a nightmare for network administrators. The client/server model enables centralized management and greater administration efficiency. Administrators can manage applications, backups, and network security from one central location.

Networks use various types of application servers: Web servers, FTP servers, application servers, database servers, name servers, mail servers, file servers, and print servers. Most Web services are also types of servers. Each of these services may require a dedicated server, such as a single electronic mail (e-mail) server. A server may also provide several services at once, for example, both a Web and e-mail server.

The client/server is a form of centralized computing in that a central computer provides access to various network services, such as the Internet or databases. However, many client/server networks are a form of distributed networks because processing is not the sole responsibility of the server. Rather, workstations often have local applications installed and use local processing.

Distributed Computing on a Network

There was a time when computer networks were composed of a large mainframe computer and low-end workstations. Workstations had limited power, and all processing was the responsibility of the mainframe. Many of today's organizations do not use this model. Instead, they place powerful systems on the desktop. This allows processing to occur in a distributed fashion so that network resources and processing are located throughout the network and are not reserved for a handful of servers.

> **NOTE**
>
> *Client/server computing* refers to the way applications use hardware, and *distributed computing* refers to how and where application processing takes place.

For example, suppose an office uses a word processing program. In a distributed application model, a workstation handles the processing of the application while a server handles only centralized storage and administration of data. In this case, the word processing program is a **distributed application**. In a centralized processing model, a mainframe or server would manage all this.

Server clusters are an example of distributed networking. Server clusters are groups of interconnected servers. The cluster provides increased performance, load balancing, and fault tolerance. The processing of client requests is distributed to an array of servers.

Although sometimes complex and difficult to manage, distributed systems have these advantages:

- **Greater performance**—More servers and distributed processing equal more processing power. The servers in a distributed configuration can provide levels of performance beyond the scope of a single system by combining resources and processing power.

- **Shared workload**—Rather than having individual servers perform specific roles, a distributed system can perform a number of roles, assigning the appropriate resources to the best places. This approach maximizes the capacity of the systems by allocating tasks based on which server in the cluster is best able to service the request.

- **Business continuity**—If one server fails, another is there to take its place. A distributed configuration reduces a single point of failure and helps ensure continued operation.

Transformation of Brick-and-Mortar Businesses to E-commerce Businesses

From the beginning, the business potential of the **World Wide Web** was evident. The geographical location of businesses became irrelevant, and the reach of potential customers went global. However, in the mid-1990s, many offline businesses used Web sites simply as an advertisement or shop window.

> **NOTE**
> The term **e-commerce** refers to the buying and selling of goods and services over electronic systems such as the Internet.

The transformation of brick-and-mortar stores to e-commerce could not happen overnight. Although the World Wide Web was highly popular by the mid-1990s, technology was not available for fully integrated e-commerce. Many companies could see the potential of the Web as a marketing and business tool, but significant challenges in policy and protocols had to be addressed first.

Four key areas of concern for e-commerce included the following, which are still relevant today:

- **Integrity**—Assurance that a message has not been captured and tampered with in transit.

- **Nonrepudiation**—Assurance that neither party can refute the actions of the other. For example, the customer must be assured of the seller's identity, the seller must use a secure and trackable form of payment processing, and the seller must use a proof-of-delivery system so that neither party can later deny having processed the data or received the goods or services.

- **Authentication**—The ability to verify a person or system's identity.

- **Privacy**—The assurance that all information is stored confidentially.

> **NOTE**
> As good as the systems and protocols are, they aren't perfect. Confidence with online transactions is shaky due in part to fears of data theft and concerns over spam and identity theft.

Before businesses could turn to the Web and customers could feel comfortable purchasing online, these concerns had to be addressed. Fortunately, by the end of the 1990s, systems were developed to manage each of the four areas, which you'll learn about throughout this book. Important protocols that emerged during this period were Hypertext Transfer Protocol with Secure Sockets Layer (HTTPS) and Public Key Infrastructure (PKI), which helped to ensure secure online communications.

Now, many businesses either augment their brick-and-mortar stores with e-commerce or move their businesses completely online. This, however, is not an easy transition. The businesses that have successfully made the move have learned that Web sites do not automatically generate visitors; it takes hard work and dedication. The idea of "build it and they will come" does not apply to e-commerce.

E-commerce Today

Today, e-commerce is a big part of the Web with huge companies like Amazon and eBay leading the way. However, it's not easy to succeed online. Companies come and go on the Web just as brick-and-mortar stores always have on Main Street. The companies that survive do so by taking full advantage of e-commerce solutions and understanding the nature of online marketing.

Some common features of e-commerce sites include:

- **Catalog**—Contains detailed information about the store's products or services. Details include product or service name, description, shipping costs, and such information as size or turnaround time for services. This is similar to the concept of the storefront or catalog of a brick-and-mortar store.

- **Shopping cart**—In brick-and-mortar stores, customers use carts while shopping and to transport items to the checkout register. Online shopping carts enable a customer to add and remove items, change the quantity, and sometimes store the items so they can finish shopping and the check-out process later.

- **Transaction and payment processing**—When the shopper proceeds to the virtual checkout, software computes the cost of the goods or services sold and charges the shopper, using a an elaborate verification processes.

- **Fulfillment system**—Once the customer completes an order, systems ensure appropriate processing is completed. For example, systems monitor whether an order ships to the correct address, the item is removed from inventory, a customer notification is sent, and the customer is invoiced.

An online e-commerce presence is mandatory for most modern businesses, and with this comes a new world of security concerns. Protecting the virtual storefront is complicated, and keeping transactions records and customer data private is integral to success. Companies like Target, Sony, and other big merchants spend millions on security and still suffer data breaches. How can a smaller company with tight budgets hope to be secure?

The World Wide Web Revolution

The World Wide Web has changed how the world operates, communicates, and conducts business. For many, the terms *Internet* and *World Wide Web* (WWW, or Web) are synonymous, but these two technologies are not the same. The Internet (with a capital "I") is a large, global network consisting of routers, cabling, servers, and all the hardware that create the Internet network infrastructure. The Web is just one of the services deployed over the Internet. The Web is an interconnected system of interlinked **hypertext** documents accessed via the Internet. An example of a service using the Internet is e-mail, which exchanges messages using SMTP. Using FTP to transfer large files is another example. The infrastructure of the Internet was in place long before the Web was loading Web sites using HTTP.

FYI

In a packet-switching network like the Internet, entire messages are broken down into smaller pieces called *packets*. Each packet is assigned source, destination, and intermediate node addresses, which routers use to correctly send packets to their destination, much like an address and Zip code. Packet-switched networks use independent routing, which allows data packets to find their own way and avoid high-traffic or low-bandwidth areas. Independent routing also allows packets to take an alternate route if a particular route is unavailable.

Pre-Internet Era

As outlined earlier in this chapter, computers emerged toward the end of World War II and quickly began changing. New technologies made hardware smaller, faster, and more affordable. The advancements of system software and application software gave programmers and users open access to this new hardware. In the history of the Internet and the Web, this is called the *pre-Internet era*.

The first computer networking efforts emerged in the late 1960s and 1970s, and included the Advanced Research Project Agency Network (ARPANET) project. **ARPANET** was the first operational packet-switching network. **Packet switching** is now the predominant method for communication on the Internet.

In the 1980s, computers became small and inexpensive enough for widespread use in homes and offices, initiating the pre-Internet PC era. Computer network technologies developed quickly, including operating systems, protocols, media, hubs, and routers. Combining these technologies forms the infrastructure of networking and results in **local area networks (LANs)** and **wide area networks (WANs)**. The interconnectivity of LANs and WANs introduced a set of new network-wide services. Notable technologies include e-mail, file transfers between systems and between workstations and servers, **Internet Relay Chat (IRC)**, and the **Usenet** discussion forum. Original experiments in computer networking accelerated, and networks became faster and more robust. These technologies paved the way for modern applications used today, including the World Wide Web.

E-mail, a particularly significant development, is a technology for exchanging digital messages over a network. It was originally a text-only communication tool that exchanged messages between users logged onto one host. Later it extended to e-mail exchanges between hosts that use the same operating systems. The first LAN-based e-mail system emerged in the 1990s. SMTP is part of the Transmission Control Protocol/Internet Protocol suite and the protocol used for sending e-mail. Although e-mail was originally restricted to the LAN, over time it revolutionized digital communications across the Internet.

Usenet

Usenet was the first networked discussion service. It was born in the late 1970s when three machines were networked to exchange news using the **Unix-to-Unix Copy Protocol (UUCP)**, in addition to mail and file transfers.

Usenet was the first network application to categorize and organize the news items into specific newsgroups, as shown in Figure 1-3. These groups were a system of hierarchically organized articles by subject content. Users subscribed to a particular newsgroup, and the news server kept track of which articles were accessed with discussions organized by threads and sub threads. If this sounds familiar, it's because remnants of the Usenet approach still exist in many discussion mechanisms that learning management systems use in online courses and discussion forums.

Usenet users coined the terms *Frequently Asked Questions (FAQ)* and *spam*. The FAQ grew from the need to save space and minimize time to provide information users frequently needed. The FAQ started as a series of periodic posts on Usenet. As some users started posting unsolicited messages to the groups, the term *spam* began to denote excessive message posting of posting similar messages across newsgroups. Usenet was the predecessor of the **Bulletin Board System (BBS)** and Internet forums. Unlike them, however, Usenet did not have a central administration or server. Instead, it used a system of servers that stored and forwarded messages. This was a great advantage at the time of Usenet.

The technologies behind Usenet are rudimentary by today's standards. However, they used computer technology available at the time in a creative new way. They paved the way for applications you use today and were at least as exciting to users then as Facebook is today.

Groupware and Gopher

Two more significant developments on the road to the World Wide Web are *Gopher* and *groupware*. The University of Minnesota developed the Gopher system in 1991 to provide a simple-to-use method to search a file system. **Gopher** organized text files in a hierarchical way and enabled remote users to view this structure. **Archie**, a tool that Gopher used, was the first Internet search engine. Archie originated as a way to maintain and index file systems on remote machines. Archie worked via a client by telneting or e-mailing requests to a server that maintained the file hierarchies. Archie updated the contents of the file systems about once a month. **Veronica (Very Easy Rodent-Oriented Netwide Index of Computerized Archives)**, a search engine that Gopher later used, updated these lists more frequently. In addition to the Gopher resources, Veronica included references to other resources, such as Usenet archives.

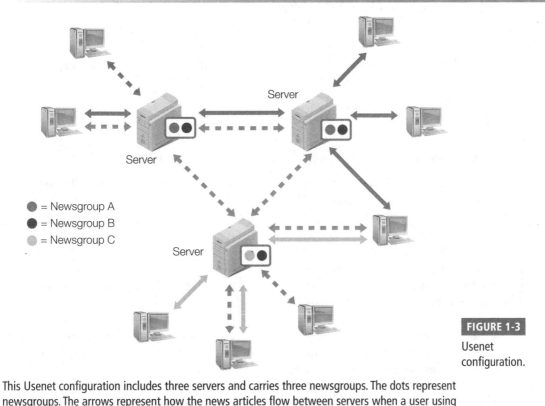

● = Newsgroup A
● = Newsgroup B
● = Newsgroup C

FIGURE 1-3

Usenet
configuration.

This Usenet configuration includes three servers and carries three newsgroups. The dots represent
newsgroups. The arrows represent how the news articles flow between servers when a user using
one news server wants to read articles from a newsgroup that resides on another server.

In offices, the need to work collaboratively with co-workers spawned a new direction
in software development. Various collaboration efforts set the foundation for new software
known as groupware. **Groupware** defines any collaborative software package or workgroup
support system. These tools enable groups to collaborate in a joint effort regardless of
where coworkers are located. Even the earliest e-mail systems can be considered a form
of groupware. Other new tools included electronic calendars (or **calendaring software**)
and instant messaging. Calendaring tools maintained individual and team electronic
versions of an appointment book and contact lists. Instant messaging systems enabled
synchronous chat between two individuals or synchronous, text-only conferencing.
The possibilities seemed endless.

Groupware tools are as important today as when the technologies arrived. Today,
groupware applications have created a "work anywhere" environment in which workers
have access to the same tools at home as they do in the office.

The stage was now set for the World Wide Web.

Emergence of the World Wide Web

The World Wide Web emerged in 1989 from the work of Tim Berners-Lee and Robert Cailliau at CERN, the European Organization for Nuclear Research. They introduced the concept of hypertext that would become a foundational concept of the Web. In their original World Wide Web proposal, they wrote:

> Hypertext is a way to link and access information of various kinds as a web of nodes in which the user can browse at will. Potentially, hypertext provides a single user-interface to many large classes of stored information such as reports, notes, databases, computer documentation, and on-line systems help.

In 1990, Berners-Lee designed several key tools needed to create the Web, including HTTP, **Hypertext Markup Language (HTML)**, and the World Wide Web's first browser. He also created the first Web pages and posted them to the Internet. Using the hypertext documents, the Web enabled users on one computer to access information stored on another through a worldwide network.

Building on the work of Berners-Lee, the Mosaic Web browser was introduced in 1993. Mosaic was the first graphical browser and its user-friendly interface made it more popular that its predecessor, Gopher and the WorldWideWeb browser. With that one search engine, the WWW became the most popular interface for accessing and searching the content on the Internet. Today, the ubiquity of the Internet and the rapid development of communication technologies have done away with geographical boundaries and created access to global commerce and trade.

The Changing States of the World Wide Web

The World Wide Web is dynamic and is in a constant state of change. The growth of the World Wide Web is categorized into three distinct phases, distinguished by the terms Web 1.0, 2.0, and 3.0. These terms define the state of the World Wide Web at certain periods and identify how it was used. The following sections provide a glimpse at Web 1.0, 2.0, and 3.0.

> **NOTE**
>
> The term *Web 1.0* was actually coined after the term *Web 2.0*. Web 1.0 describes the Web and its features between approximately 1990 and 2003.

Web 1.0

Web 1.0 is sometimes refererred to as *Static Web* because of the lack of user participation, that is, visitors would go to a Web site, gather information, and leave. There was little or no back and forth communication. The time of Web 1.0 was one of mostly dial-up Internet access, new and emerging protocol technologies, and limited user experience. The following are some characteristics of Web 1.0:

FYI

Beginning in the late 1990s, the first Web browser war occurred between Netscape and Microsoft. In an attempt to grab market share, the companies steadily introduced new browser features, including proprietary HTML tags. Unfortunately, the competition to introduce enticing new features took precedence over repairing software bugs. Netscape Navigator's <blink> tag is an example of a nonstandard HTML tag. It appeared to the user to be blinking. Microsoft Internet Explorer introduced the <marquee> tag. It caused enclosed text to scroll in different directions. Some modern browsers support the nonstandard HTML elements for legacy reasons, while others do not and instead adhere to HTML standards that were established later. The browsers of Web 1.0 were not always compliant to standards and contained bugs, which often rendered them unstable.

- **Static Web sites**—Web sites were non-interactive, displaying information but not much else. Web site content was updated infrequently compared to Web 2.0, where blogs and **social networking**, the use of online services designed to establish friendships and find like-minded people, are used frequently.
- **Sites are non-interactive**—Wikis did not exist; user-generated content was minimal. Sites were visited for information and left.
- **Limited open source software**—Much of Web 1.0 software was proprietary, meaning that users could not contribute to the development of the software. Web 2.0 uses large amounts of open source software where users can augment existing software or create their own application and features.

Web 1.0 pages often consisted of a single HTML document using frames to organize the presentation of the information. A *frame* is a portion of the Web page that users accessed. Each frame displayed a different HTML document. The use of frames came from the need to keep information normalized, reusable, and modular, so that when changes were needed, modifications in the code were minimal. For example, if a system of Web pages used a menu, it made sense to isolate the menu in a frame. When authors wanted to change only one item in a menu, they could make a single change in the frame where the menu's HTML code resided, rather than making the same change to every Web page.

Web 1.0 and Keyword Search

In the PC era, searches mainly looked through titles of documents in file repositories; it was a slow and arduous process to find information. Web 1.0 introduced browsers with a keyword search, which looked through the content of Web pages for specific words or phrases known as keywords. Newer search engines use a software agent, called a *spider* or *bot*, that crawls through the Web, visits Web sites on servers, and follows the links in documents. The information that spiders collect is used to index a Web page. Indices are used to retrieve information faster and to separate search results into categories.

This system spawned a new industry, that of search engine optimization (SEO). This refers to the strategies the spiders use to identify keywords on a site; these increase rankings on displayed search results. When you initiate a keyword query, like a Google search, the search engine goes through its index, finds the best matches according to a search algorithm, and provides hits. As search engines are based on different indexing techniques and search algorithms, the hits from various search engines may be different. Some search engines, such as Google, cache a portion of the Web page and provide it with the hit list.

With the massive growth of information on the Web, search engines are faced with the challenge of developing systems that are aware of the relevance of the hits to the user. Web 2.0-generation Web engines have tried to solve this problem. Google's system emerged out of the ranking of users. Nevertheless, as the amount of information on the Web grows, searching takes more time. Web 3.0, the Semantic Web, seeks a more intelligent and focused search.

Directory Portals

Similar to keyword search, directory **portals** began during Web 1.0 to add purpose or to group the information users retrieved. They are not search engines. They organize groups of links into a structure usually in categories and subcategories. Early instances of directory portals relied on human organization of the structures. In novel examples of directories, the structure emerged out of user tagging. It was common for early directories to charge for the inclusion of a Web page in the portal. They resembled the yellow pages in phone directories where the phone numbers of companies are organized by categories based on the service they provide. One example of a directory portal is Yahoo! Directory.

> **NOTE**
>
> The term *Web 2.0* has different meanings depending on whom you ask. Here's one definition from Dictionary.com: "The second generation of the World Wide Web in which content is user-generated and dynamic, and software is offered that mimics desktop programs." Web 2.0 examples include Wiki, Meebo, Digg, Twitter, Delicious, Squidoo, Facebook, and many, many more.

Web 2.0

From about 2003 to the present, **Web 2.0** has changed the online experience. Web 2.0 is not about infrastructure technology, although new high-speed technologies have helped facilitate Web 2.0. Web 2.0 is a new way for users to interact with the Web. On a personal level, Web 2.0 means blogging and social networking to establish online friendships and a sense of community. On a business level, it means using blogging and social networking to establish grassroots marketing efforts and business awareness. Web 2.0 has, to some extent, moved away from the technology to become an interactive part of daily life.

FYI

Epinions.org was an early service for exchanging product reviews between users, a predecessor of the modern, vertical-purpose social networking site. Founded in 1999, it was later acquired by eBay. It not only showed who was friends with whom, as some of its predecessors had, but it gave users more control over the content of the site while they shared opinions and rated consumer products.

Social networking is a big part of Web 2.0, enabling people to congregate based on similar interests in a user-friendly manner. Web 1.0 provided places for information dissemination on topics involved with hobbies, professions, religion, politics, and more. Web 2.0 took this to the next level. With the maturing of Web 2.0, sites started providing user-generated content with tools for content creation, collaboration, and communication. A good example is the Wordpress blogging software that is free and easy to use.

Web 2.0 applications include:

- **Facebook, Twitter, LinkedIn, Tumblr, Instagram, Google Plus**—Social networking Web sites. Social networks fit the criteria of Web 2.0 because they enable the connection and interaction between people who share personal or professional interests and other characteristics.

- **Delicious (formerly del.icio.us)**—A bookmarking distribution site used to store and share Web bookmarks known as social bookmarking. Delicious and other similar sites enable you to share, organize, search, and manage bookmarks of Web resources. These sites do not enable file sharing, only links to sites.

- **Flickr, Picasa**—Popular photoblogging Web sites. You can use photoblogging sites to store and display images for personal use or to display pictures for sale.

- **Wordpress, TypePad, Squarespace**—Free and open source blogging software. You use blogging software to quickly and easily create and maintain blogs on the Web. Many blogging packages restrict business use while paid options do not.

- **Wikipedia**—A user-generated information site. A key part of Web 2.0, Wikis allow user-generated reference content. If you are an expert in a particular subject, you can create a Wiki page to share your knowledge and information. Wikis are referred to as *dynamic documents* because the content is generally open to anyone's editing and changes.

- **Bloglines**—A **Really Simple Syndication (RSS)** reader. RSS feeds provide a way for people to distribute information, updates, notices, or content changes that occur on their Web sites. You subscribe to a Web site's RSS feed(s), and the Web site sends you information as it becomes available. RSS lets people know what's happening with a site and tries to get them to return. RSS readers like Blogline enable you to read the RSS feeds. Many Web browsers and e-mail clients include built-in RSS readers.

FYI

It is important to note that Web 2.0 has its detractors. One has to do with the information itself. With the prevalence of user-generated content on Wikis and blogs, the line between researched, peer-reviewed information and personal musing becomes blurred. Much of the information online today lacks authority, but it is used as if obtained from credible sources. To some, the extent of information gathering is limited to a simple Google search. Web 2.0 has given voice to all and may have obfuscated the boundary between the ramblings of the uninformed and true knowledge.

This is just a glimpse at the applications associated with Web 2.0. There are thousands more and new ones are added daily. One thing all Web 2.0 applications have in common is interactivity. Web 2.0 is about sharing, communicating, and revealing. Based on the success of Web 2.0, the future of the Web is clearly in the hands of users, not developers. A caveat with all Web 2.0 applications being interactive is the struggle to maintain security and data privacy. Before using any of these sites it is essential to read the terms of use and policies. You will likely be surprised how vulnerable you and your data actually are.

Web 3.0

With new, user-generated content, the amount of information on the Web is growing exponentially. The effectiveness of searching and search engines likely will decrease because it will become more difficult to differentiate between useful and trusted information sources and bad information. A solution is needed.

In 1991, Berners-Lee created the original World Wide Web. Now Berners-Lee has a new vision: **Web 3.0**, also known as the *Semantic Web*. You can think of the Semantic Web as the transformation of the Web into one giant, online database. The Web could then be searched and categorized like any other database. This would allow greater control of searching and manipulation of information.

technical TIP

HTML, as a technology and language, enabled presentation of content within Web 1.0 and 2.0. It linked and created relationships between documents. Web 3.0 needs a technology that will capture meaning and focus on the data, as opposed to the documents as entities. Researchers are examining Extensible Markup Language (XML), **Resource Description Framework (RDF)**, and **Web Ontology Language (OWL)**. Many see parallels between these efforts and the pillars of object orientation. As classes describe the entities in object-oriented programming, XML, RDF, and OWL define and describe the data (data attributes and behaviors).

Web 3.0 or the Semantic Web is all about information access, retention, organization, and categorization. On a practical level, Web 3.0 allows you to maintain all information from a calendar, documents, medical records, and more online and in a single, easily accessible database. Web 3.0 moves people closer to fully integrating their online and offline information, making the browser not only a search engine but a productivity tool.

Some believe Web 3.0 will enable our online information to be stored in a personal online database from birth until death. All personal information will be housed and accessed online—after, of course, security concerns are addressed.

Introducing the Internet of Things (IoT)

The thought of a completely interconnected world, where everything and everyone communicates automatically about location, status, and much more, may seem like the stuff of science fiction. But this technology is in use today and expanding rapidly. Enhancements to networking infrastructure, the relatively low cost of storage and computing power, networking protocol advancement (IPv6), and a lot of imagination and innovation have created the possibility of a highly interconnected world. This world has come to be known as the Internet of Things (IoT).

The concept of the IoT is straightforward; it is the connection of any IP-aware "thing" to the Internet. This could be anything from a fitness monitor to a car to a washing machine to even a pet dog. But why is all this interconnectivity needed? The purpose is to allow smart devices to self-report their status, allow for remote management, and automatically record data for analysis. How many devices may be connected? With the nearly limitless unique IP addressing capability of IPv6, the number of worldwide connected devices is in the billions.

Some of the fields where IoT technologies are in use today and expanding include the following:

- **Manufacturing**—In a manufacturing environment the future will see an increase in IP-aware components that can report on their current state. This may be a valve reporting on its state, motors reporting on bearing wear, or heavy equipment reporting on its location and service requirements. All of this self-diagnostic reporting serves to increase reliability and leads to a *predictive failure environment*. Machines can give warnings before they break down, in other words. Many manufacturers see this type of self-reporting environment as integral to their future viability and competitiveness.

- **Healthcare**—The healthcare field has many current and future potential uses for IoT. IoT devices can monitor patients' blood pressure, glucose levels, blood sugar, abnormal cellular growth in any part of the body, and much more. Smart devices such as fitness bands and heart monitors can be remotely monitored via wireless networks to report on patient conditions. Given the potentially sensitive nature of all of this personal data being monitored and remotely transported, however, security and privacy become critical concerns.

- **Transportation**—Logistics companies already use IoT technology today to collect data on vehicles and drivers automatically: their location and even their tire pressure. IoT enhances logistics by using sensors to report traffic delays and accidents and provide real-time tracking of equipment and products. Smart devices help with predictive and remote maintenance and even fuel management.

A world of interconnected devices seems to be an increasing reality, but what of the security considerations? It's bad enough if hackers gain access to your toaster and switch the setting for your raisin toast to "dark." But if they can gain access to the toaster, what about the car, the alarm system, the computers, and the cell phone? If everything is connected to the Internet, you must also be aware that everything connected to the Internet can be hacked. In short, any time access is authorized, you must anticipate the risk of unauthorized access. So the self-reporting heart monitor or the advanced manufacturing controls all may have vulnerability. The more is connected, the more widespread the security risk.

With literally billions of devices targeted for deployment in an IoT, infrastructure security becomes a significant concern. The challenge will be to keep security strategies and policies in step with the rapid expansion of interconnected devices. Unfortunately, many current IoT devices transport unencrypted data and may use a Wi-Fi network that's easily snooped on or hacked. Many of these devices are vulnerable to attacks such as cross-site scripting or denial of service.

For a system administrator in an IoT world, some of the key security concerns to address include the following:

- **IoT privacy**—With billions of interconnected devices each relaying a portion of data, privacy concerns become a significant issue. For example, medical information, daily habits, and other personal data may be compromised, allowing snoops and hackers to develop patterns and profiles of an individual's life. Depending on the device, data and personal information may be transferred without encryption. Maintaining personal privacy in a Web 3.0 world is difficult, and the expansion of IoT may make to next to impossible.

- **End-to-end encryption**—Many of the devices that may be connected with the IoT framework may not by default use end-to-end transport encryption. System administrators will need to determine the importance of particular data sets and ensure that critical data cannot be read during transport. This may include seemingly harmless data sent from a valve in a manufacturing environment or a heart monitor on an outpatient.

- **Authorization and authentication**—When securing IoT devices, it will be necessary to remember the basics. Authorization refers to access control permissions determining who is allowed to do what with data or a device. Authentication refers to passwords or other methods of identity verification. Securing IoT infrastructure will require both of these functions, including, wherever possible, the enforcement of password complexity rules.

- **Software updates/patching**—One other standard security consideration is the management of updates and patches. Developers may not be thinking security as they first bring their IoT devices to market. Patches will be needed later to plug any security holes. The system administrator managing IoT will need to ensure that all devices are patched securely.

With IoT endpoint devices predicted to number in the billons by 2020, security becomes a critical and alarming concern. The potential for a significant security breach seems a real possibility. As you continue to learn about Web security strategies, keep in mind the IoT. Securing IoT devices and communication is going to be difficult, and will be part of every system administrator's job in the future. Writing secure code for all of the devices in scope will not be easy, and testing procedures will be critical. However, manufacturers' desire to get products to market quickly may increase the risk of security threats.

Cloud Computing and Virtualization

Cloud computing and virtualization are growing in importance and popularity among individuals and organizations of all sizes. This section explains how consumers and organizations use them today.

Cloud Computing

In a broad sense, cloud computing builds on the idea of thin clients but on a more ambitious scale. **Cloud computing** is the accessing of resources or processing outside the local firewall. In a more narrow interpretation, cloud computing is the distribution of specific applications and services from dedicated Internet-based virtual servers.

With cloud computing, the processing of applications and services from local workstations and even the LAN is shifted to Internet-based server farms that manage the distribution of network functions. Cloud computing is the ultimate in centralized and distributed networking.

> ▶ **NOTE**
>
> Thin client computing requires no local storage, operating systems, or processing power. Rather, it is the job of the server to store files, run applications, and process all services and requests. Essentially, thin client PCs are dummy terminals. The advantages of a thin client architecture include: simpler administration, reduced hardware costs for upgrading, and single point of administration for applications and backup procedures.

Although it may seem that cloud computing is a relatively new technology, it has been around for some time. You've likely seen cloud computing in action. For example, e-mail accounts with providers such as Hotmail or Gmail require you to log onto a remote server to retrieve or send e-mail. The e-mail and data are stored remotely on a server and not on your local system. This is a simple example of cloud computing. Another is **Google Docs**, which provides users with word processing, spreadsheet, and presentation applications distributed through Google's cloud servers. All that's needed to access this form of cloud computing is a Web browser and Internet connection. The network servers distribute and maintain the applications, and you merely go online to use them.

The implications of this technology are significant. With the processing and distribution handled remotely, cloud computing levels the playing field for companies that lack the funds to constantly upgrade their network to accommodate new technologies and applications. In technical terms, cloud computing is the great equalizer. Companies can leverage their existing hardware and network infrastructure rather than continue a constant hardware upgrading cycle. A system running Linux with an 8 gigabyte (GB) universal serial bus (USB) disk drive can run modern applications as a thin client system as well as a high-powered desktop system can.

Types of Cloud Computing

Three types of clouds are **Software as a Service (SaaS)**, **Platform as a Service (PaaS)**, and **Infrastructure as a Service (IaaS)**, described as follows:

- **SaaS**—A software delivery method in which the cloud servers distribute specific applications or services to the client, typically through the client's Web browser. The applications can be distributed to hundreds or even thousands of clients simultaneously. This enables clients to access applications with limited licensing considerations, servers, and other hardware requirements. SaaS removes the need for a company to consider multiple installations, software updates, and other local administration requirements.

- **PaaS**—A method of distributing operating systems or platform applications over the Internet. These platforms are often used to run the SaaS. Not only do the client systems get the application from the cloud but they also get the platform on which the application is run.

- **IaaS**—A method of delivering an infrastructure, which includes servers, storage, and networking components, over the Internet. The owner of the cloud computing hardware is responsible for updating and maintaining that equipment to ensure the delivery of applications over the cloud. The client often pays per-usage for the right to use the equipment.

In the networking world, a pendulum is swinging between a preference for local computing and processing and centrally managed applications, distributed services, and administration. Today's technologies with high-speed networks, low-cost disk storage, and enhanced protocols create the perfect environment for cloud computing. The ability to accommodate growth and leverage the existing network infrastructure will no doubt be too attractive for many companies to ignore. For cloud computing, it seems the sky is the limit.

Virtualization

Virtualization provides another method of leveraging and maximizing current resources. Cloud computing is a form of virtualization. The generic term *virtualization* refers to using a resource for something other than its intended purpose. With virtual memory, for example, a portion of your hard disk is used to swap data between itself and the physical memory. In this way, the system can take advantage of unused hard disk space to increase performance of the physical memory.

You can apply this principle to other areas of IT, including network storage, operating systems, hardware, and applications. The term **virtualization** refers to the creation of a virtual version of actual IT services, applications, or resources. For example, you can build virtual software versions of systems that behave like their physical equivalents. A *virtual machine (VM)* is a software implementation that behaves like an actual physical machine, with which you can interact from your own computer. VMs can simulate a complete system or just one particular process. What happens in the VMs does not change the state of the computer the VM is "played" on. The VM is a guest on the host computer. It is used to execute functionalities that are not present on the host machine. One host can run multiple VMs at the same time.

Virtualization technologies are popular solutions for network, storage, and servers. When you virtualize a network, you split the bandwidth into more manageable channels assigned to servers or other devices in real time. When you virtualize storage, resources physically located on multiple servers appear as a single storage entity. Server virtualization uses multiple servers that appear as one on your computer without your having to manage their actual physical servers, processors, and operating systems. Grid and cloud computing are specific virtualization approaches and implementations.

CHAPTER SUMMARY

Today, networks and data processing provide a foundation for most businesses. The evolution of modern data processing, the emergence of the World Wide Web, and the growth of e-commerce continue to progress and evolve, making them an integral part of our workdays and lives. The Web continues to grow from yesterday's Web 1.0 to today's Web 2.0 and tomorrow's Web 3.0. Each new development brings with it more opportunities and shifting personal and business online practices.

KEY CONCEPTS AND TERMS

Archie
ARPANET
Bulletin Board System (BBS)
Calendaring software
Centralized processing
Client/server
Cloud computing
Distributed application
E-commerce
File Transfer Protocol (FTP)
Google Docs
Gopher
Graphical user interface (GUI)
Groupware
Hypertext
Hypertext Markup Language (HTML)

Hypertext Transfer Protocol (HTTP)
Infrastructure as a Service (IaaS)
Internet Relay Chat (IRC)
Local area networks (LANs)
Mainframe
Minicomputer
Packet switching
Platform as a Service (PaaS)
Portals
Protocols
Really Simple Syndication (RSS)
Resource Description Framework (RDF)
Server
Simple Mail Transfer Protocol (SMTP)

Social networking
Software as a Service (SaaS)
Telnet
Unix-to-Unix Copy Protocol (UUCP)
Usenet
Veronica (Very Easy Rodent-Oriented Netwide Index of Computerized Archives)
Virtualization
Web 1.0
Web 2.0
Web 3.0
Web Ontology Language (OWL)
Wide area networks (WANs)
World Wide Web

CHAPTER 1 ASSESSMENT

1. _____ refers to the ability to verify a system's or a person's identity.

2. You have been asked to reduce the number of applications you host on your internal network. You decide to use an online version of the company's accounting software. This may be an example of which of the following?

A. Virtualization and SaaS
B. Cloud computing and IaaS
C. Cloud computing and SaaS
D. Virtualization and IaaS

3. Which of the following best describe data? (Select two.)

A. Applicable information
B. Facts and figures
C. Collection of recordings
D. Processed information

4. Tim Berners-Lee, the original creator of the World Wide Web, envisions the future Web 3.0 more resembling which of the following?

A. A dynamic document
B. A database
C. A fully redundant network
D. A user-generated social network

5. Packet-switched networks use independent routing, which allows which of the following?

A. Networks to operate independently from each other
B. Packets to seek the lowest bandwidth route
C. Networks to better balance their bandwidth
D. Packets to take an alternate route if a route is unavailable

6. You have just installed a software patch without reviewing its intended purpose or understanding its potential effect. This is an example of _____.

7. _____ is the assurance that a message wasn't captured and tampered with during communication transit.

8. You have just installed a client/server network. Which is *not* an advantage of the client/server model?

A. Scalability
B. Eliminates a single point of failure
C. Centralized management
D. Centralized storage

9. The World Wide Web is technically the same as the Internet.

A. True
B. False

10. Which of the following has *not* been a factor in the development of the Internet of Things?

A. Enhancements to networking infrastructure
B. The relatively low cost of storage and computing power
C. Stringent federal legislation requiring use of encryption on all "smart" devices
D. Networking protocol advancement (IPv6)

Security Considerations for Small Businesses

© Rodolfo Clix/Dreamstime.com

E-BUSINESS IS NOT ONLY ABOUT making business processes available over the Web or designing and posting a Web site online. It is also about doing it securely, to ensure customer and business data is protected. E-business leverages up-to-date technologies and trends to turn a viable business into a viable online business. But if this is done incorrectly, the e-business can be compromised and customer data stolen. If this happens, the integrity of the business fails. This is a common occurrence not only with small businesses but also with the largest online vendors, who spend hundreds of thousands a year on security measures. For CEOs and small business entrepreneurs, e-business is all about testing and improving strategies to grow an e-business. For IT administrators, it is about understanding these business goals and at the same time keeping the online business secure.

E-commerce existed in a variety of forms before the inception of the Web. Money wire transfers, for example, were electronic fund transfers (EFTs) to exchange account information over private communication networks. Businesses also have been engaging in a form of e-commerce known as electronic data interchange (EDI) when transmitting computer-readable data in a standardized format to another business. The Web took the opportunities for electronic commerce to a new level and became a necessary element of most businesses.

With Internet and Web developments, e-commerce and e-business have taken a giant leap forward, and an online component to business is an expectation today. For those responsible for securing e-commerce interests, understanding business goals and objectives is the first step. This chapter explores the objectives of e-business and e-commerce, including what it takes to create, manage, and secure a successful online business.

Chapter 2 Topics

This chapter covers the following topics and concepts:

- How business evolved from brick and mortar to the Web
- What the process of transforming a business into an e-business is
- What highly available and secure Web site hosting is
- How e-commerce enhances customer-service delivery
- What the risks, threats, and vulnerabilities for business Web sites are
- What the risks of handling revenues online are
- How the risks inherent in unsecure systems can be managed
- How access for telecommuters and remote employees is secured

Chapter 2 Goals

When you complete this chapter, you will be able to:

- Identify the procedures for growing a business through the World Wide Web
- Understand the process of transforming the business into an e-business
- Identify the features of secure and highly available Web sites
- Identify the various forms of online revenue streams
- Review the process of building a Web-enabled customer service strategy
- Understand how to obtain new online customers
- Design a solid e-business marketing plan
- Enhance customer service delivery
- Understand the features of self-service Web sites
- Identify the function of VoIP/SIP enabled Web sites
- Understand how to develop secure telecommuting channels

The Evolution of Business from Brick and Mortar to the Web

Since its inception, the face of e-commerce has been rapidly changing with the introduction of new technologies. E-commerce has gone through three distinct phases that feature the adoption of trends from the respective developmental stages of the Internet and the Web. In this section, you will read about these three distinct stages of the e-commerce history with respect to the level of automation of the business processes: the brick-and-mortar model, the consumer-driven model, and distributed e-commerce.

E-commerce: A Brick-and-Mortar Model

Many early e-commerce sites offered catalog display systems essentially duplicating brick-and-mortar storefronts. One of the primary goals of e-commerce at this development stage was to get more information about products and services out to potential customers, but the emphasis was still on driving people to the actual physical store. In many cases, the e-commerce sites operated as display windows for the brick and mortar store. Many customers began to visit these sites, but for comparison shopping, not necessarily to buy online. Because the Web sites were informational and no financial transactions took place, nor was any customer data stored, security was not a huge risk.

The e-commerce business model of this time closely mimicked the policies, procedures, and practices of the physical store. Much of the software and infrastructure and many of the security protocols were in early stages of development. Over time, software advanced, allowing greater support for online transaction processing, supply-chain management, customer-relationship management (CRM), enterprise resource planning (ERP), ordering, inventory management, shipping and logistics, and data mining.

As technologies advanced, it become clear that e-commerce sites were more than electronic advertising for physical stores; they were themselves a viable storefront. As the focus shifted toward the Web, more businesses were marketing online and more consumers were shopping online; and an increased concern about security and **privacy**—the protection of individual rights to nondisclosure—emerged.

Customer-Focused E-commerce

Rather than merely presenting catalog offerings to the consumers, e-commerce applications then developed around the business semantics of the transaction. True Internet e-commerce shifted from general selling to focusing on the individual customer. Online marketing became critical, and whoever could do it best, made money. Many e-business owners could see that the focus had to move from a passive marketing strategy, whereby customers might stumble upon a Web site, to aggressive marketing strategies by which potential customers were sought out and brought to a Web site.

To do this, a strong emphasis was placed on demographic research and understanding everything possible about potential customers. Internet marketing leveled the playing field, so that anyone with a product or idea could easily put up a Web site and try online marketing. Many such entrepreneurs become wealthy overnight, while many more lost everything. The focus on tracking customers and on visitor demographics led to numerous strategies to acquire personal information. Getting Web visitors to sign up for newsletters, e-mail updates, and other giveaways was a strategy used to gather information on potential customers. The policy forms and protocols used to manage and ensure integrity of this personal data were largely immature and unregulated.

Today the World Wide Web is a marketing and advertising juggernaut with organizations scrambling to be a part of it. Advertising controls much of the Web today; virtually any Web site you visit displays a number of ads. Right now, in the background, people are scrambling to find personal information to profile potential customers and tracking visitors' surfing habits to see what sites they visit and why. Your Facebook account, for instance, reveals demographic information, and this information determines what ads appear when you check the site.

Understanding how Internet marketing works and the objectives behind it is an important part of developing a comprehensive security strategy.

Emerging Trend: Distributed E-commerce

Web 2.0 developments and the Web 3.0 paradigm have launched the next stage of e-commerce, where consumers can advertise their needs, and businesses or individuals can compete to meet them. With the promise of the Semantic Web, intelligent agents would assist you in finding businesses or individuals to fulfill your needs. The Web browser changes from a mere interface to an intelligent personal assistant or agent.

You have experienced significant advances on the market with wireless and embedded Internet-enabled devices. The desktop machine is predominantly used during office hours. Wireless technologies provide access to network computing anywhere. Smartphones and devices offer interaction quality comparable to that of the desktop. Embedded devices have been emerging in homes and businesses alike. These devices not only provide access to an entity on the Internet, they also enable local computing to gain access to certain activities. It is a distributed e-commerce model, where e-commerce occurs anytime and anywhere.

The convenience of anytime, anywhere shopping comes at a high price—complex security requirements. Every device, whether computer or smartphone, has to have secure access to the online business. This is not easy to provide. Many elements are needed, from secure protocols, authorization strategies, and authentication methods, to physical security of devices. The e-business, meanwhile, needs storage methods that keep customer data secure, including personal and credit card information. A hole in any security point can and will likely lead to a security breach.

The Process of Transformation into an E-business

Profitability and competitive edge are two important goals for all companies. Managers and CEOs continually look for ways to increase their customer base and improve their company's bottom line. In their pursuit of business goals, most business owners do not think of the security implications of their decisions. It is up to the IT department or security experts to understand the organizational objectives and apply the correct level of security measures to ensure that business goals can be met securely. This section explores common business drivers that spur companies to create a Web site or improve their existing Web sites, as well as the associated security concerns.

- **Growing the business through the Web**—A Web presence is a must for business today, even for companies that don't engage in e-commerce. Potential customers use the Web to find information about products and services they can buy online or locally. An easy-to-use and informative Web site can help expand a company's services.

- **Transforming your business into an e-business**—The Web makes some business processes easier and more efficient. For example, you can tie your back-end inventory database to a front-end Web interface for sales purposes. Real-time inventory updates streamline ordering and customer delivery. In addition, a Web presence can save on the cost of printing and mailing items that change often, such as sales flyers and product lists.

- **Building secure and highly available Web sites and e-commerce portals to expand revenue potential**—Reliability and availability are key considerations for e-business. Reliability refers to the robustness of the Web or e-mail server and its ability to continue service in the event of failure. Every e-business needs to have high availability, which allows it to be accessible 24 hours a day. Downtime often equates to a loss in sales and potentially a loss of customers.

> **NOTE**
>
> Each of these elements—interactive communications, customer databases, inventory records, transaction receipts—has an associated security risk. Throughout this chapter, you will review various security measures to address these business goals.

- **Building a Web-enabled customer service strategy**—Users today are accustomed to using Internet communication methods such as Web-chats, instant messaging (IM), forums, social networks, and e-mail. E-business customer service strategies must be able to adapt and use these forms of communications to meet the expectations of modern consumers. Such a strategy engages customers more dynamically and with the technologies they are accustomed to using.

- **Obtaining new customers**—In Internet marketing, acquisition is a critical consideration for every business. If you don't have visitors, you don't have customers. Today, acquisition is such a concern that companies of all sizes are now hiring *acquisition consultants* whose job it is to drive traffic to corporate Web sites.

Managing and Securing the Customer Life Cycle

Growing an online business and securing it also requires an understanding of customer life-cycle management (CLM) and how it pertains to online marketing. CLM refers to the relationship established with online visitors from when they first click onto a Web site to the time they leave. CLM is an essential part of the online marketing campaign and forms the foundation from which all marketing strategies are designed and applied.

There are three distinct stages involved with CLM:

- **Acquisition**—Getting visitors to the Web site. Leading a visitor to the site either by marketing, online or offline. Once the visitor arrives at the Web site, the next CLM stage begins.

- **Conversion**—Having visitors perform a desired action on the site, such as making a purchase or at the very least providing information. If there is a sale, secure transaction protocols need to be in place such as HTTPS to keep data secure. Collection of visitor data requires privacy policies and internal security measures to keep data secure.

- **Retention**—Having the customer return for future business. Typically customer data will be stored. The rules regarding the storage of customer data are often in policies available on the vendor's Web site. This includes what can be done with customer data and how long it can be kept. Before sharing your information online, it may be a good idea to review the data retention policy.

These stages flow sequentially, and one cannot happen without the other. There can be no retention without acquisition and no conversion without acquisition. Complicating CLM are those developers and marketing businesses that assert that e-business success is all about acquisition and getting traffic to the site. This statement is only partially true. Growing your e-business online involves getting *qualified* traffic to your site. This means that marketing strategies focus on the acquisition of visitors who fit your desired demographic.

Meanwhile, Web sites, smartphones, fitness trackers, personalized apps, and social networks and much more are working 24 hours a day to collect personal information. The level of concern about data security and privacy is at an all-time high.

FYI

If you operate an online business, if you are in charge of security for a company, or even if you simply frequent online businesses, it is a good idea to take the time to review Web policies. Web policies guide how data is secured and managed. To get an idea of a data policies and the potential vulnerabilities they address, check out the following policies:

https://www.facebook.com/policy.php

https://www.tumblr.com/policy/en/privacy

http://aws.amazon.com/agreement/

https://www.linkedin.com/legal/privacy-policy

Most large companies such as these have thorough data usage polices and rules. Smaller companies may not.

Highly Available and Secure Web Site Hosting

Most e-business contract with a Web hosting company to host their e-business site. Each of these companies utilizes several advanced methods to ensure availability. When you are choosing a Web hosting company, it is important to review the policies and procedures of the company has to ensure they employ availability measures. Some of the problems the Web hosting company is charged with protecting against include:

- **Hardware failures**—These are managed using redundant hardware configurations such as redundant arrays of independent disks (RAID) for hard disks, multiple memory, and failover servers. Hardware failures are the greatest threat to reliability and availability.
- **Software failure**—These are a constant concern. Applications should always be hardened with the latest service packs and patches.
- **Virus infection**—All Web-hosting companies require up-to-date virus checkers and constant updates on the checkers.
- **Denial of service (DoS) attacks**—A denial of service (DoS) attack works by flooding a server with service requests so that it shuts down. These threats can be managed using secure protocols.
- **Infrastructure failure**—Web hosting companies typically use high-end networking equipment, but even it can fail. Redundant infrastructure equipment is used in a failover configuration to manage any potential loss of availability.
- **Power outages**—These are commonplace and are managed using large uninterruptible power supplies (UPS). The UPS will manage brownouts, blackouts, and power spikes.
- **Natural disasters**—Fire, floods and other natural disasters have the potential of downing Web servers. Natural disasters are typically managed using remote network locations. Should the primary location be compromised, the second facility can take over.

Any good Web hosting company will be aware of these threats and take the necessary precautions to mitigate them.

FYI

Internet communications are based on the Transmission Control Protocol/Internet Protocol (TCP/IP) suite. However, several protocols within that suite offer only limited communication security. File Transfer Protocol (FTP), Hypertext Transfer Protocol (HTTP), and Telnet are examples of widely used protocols that are not secure. They send communications in cleartext, allowing anyone to easily capture and read the content. Ensuring that an e-business Web site maintains the integrity and confidentiality of communications is a key consideration. Fortunately, several secure Web communication protocols enable confidentiality between Web clients and servers and customers and e-businesses.

E-commerce and Enhanced Customer-Service Delivery

Just like offline stores, e-business have a number of customer service avenues available. Feedback forms, e-mail, phone, and visitor forums are all possibilities. The incorporation of customer service strategies will significantly change how well your online business is perceived and trusted, which will ultimately improve your conversion rates.

There are three levels of customer-service communication, each with its own advantages and disadvantages. These levels are one-way communication, limited two-way communication, and full two-way communication.

One-Way Communication

One-way communication is the most cost-effective form of customer service. With one-way communication, customer support and service materials are placed on the e-business site to communicate with customers. This may include a section for frequently asked questions (FAQs), support documents, and knowledge centers. The intent of one-way customer service communication is to have customers find answers to their questions before calling or e-mailing customer support. If done correctly, this can reduce customer-service costs while also addressing customer needs.

There are several key strategies you can employ to incorporate into one-way communication style site.

- Develop a comprehensive FAQs section. Many customer-service calls are repeat questions. Answering these questions in a FAQs section can reduce customer frustration and the time required to manage customer service calls.

- Develop downloadable manuals and product documentation to better inform customers of the product or service.

- Make sure your page layout is clear and displays your content well. A cluttered e-business site makes it hard to find relevant information.

- Develop a knowledge center or searchable database for answers to commonly asked questions.

- Record training videos or webinars for customers to watch.

- Many customer service calls concern checkout procedures. Streamlining and thoroughly testing checkout procedures can significantly reduce customer-service calls.

Limited Two-Way Communication

Most e-business Web sites will incorporate some form of limited two-way communication. This communication strategy moves more toward Web 2.0 seeking feedback from the visitor. The incorporation of this feedback into the site makes it better suited to address the needs of target customers. Some Web-enabled systems used for limited two-way communication include:

> **NOTE**
>
> The information received from these types of forms is incorporated into the Web site to form FAQs, and knowledge databases. The more feedback received, the better the e-commerce site becomes.

- Customer surveys
- Feedback forms
- "Contact us" forms
- E-mail support links
- Customer support request form
- A social networking site set up in association with the main site

Full Two-Way Communication

Full two-communication is the most time-consuming and costly form of customer support; it requires full dialog with the customer. This form of customer communication can quickly become unmanageable. Imagine 5,000 visitors to an e-business site per day, and 1 percent of those have a support question. That's 50 support calls each requiring 10 to 20 minutes. That could translate into eight-plus hours of customer support. For small and new e-business, this could be hard to accommodate.

Several technologies make full two-way communication for customer support possible. These include:

- Phone support
- E-mail communication
- Forums
- Instant messaging
- Web chats
- VoIP

Two-way communication strategies are essential for large organizations and require dedicated staff to manage large customer-service systems. Small to mid-sized companies may lessen the focus on two-way communication to reduce support costs.

E-business with Integrated Applications

E-commerce requires an infrastructure of technologies that starts with the Internet and World Wide Web and includes hardware, software and networking components, distributing computer environments, middleware, user-interface technologies, server-side facilities and services, languages, and software development methodologies.

The five layers you will observe are the foundation (bottom-most layer), internal applications, middleware, e-commerce application, and relationship layer.

- **Foundation Layer**—This is the basic operational platform, which consists of the hardware and system software on the local machines, as well as the networking hardware and software that enable computers to communicate.

- **Internal Applications Layer**—This layer represents the Enterprise Resource Planning (ERP), Customer Relationship Management (CRM), and legacy systems. It acts as an interface between the infrastructure and the e-commerce applications. ERPs are systems that enable a business to execute product planning, inventory management, and purchases. CRM systems manage the customer base. They collect data on the customers and potential customers and their buying habits. They use this information to set prices, negotiate terms, customize promotions, add features to the product, or extend services offered, all to customize the business's relationship with any individual customer. ERPs and CRMs have started to integrate solutions that support both the revenue and the administrative support functions of a business.

- **Middleware Layer**—This is the framework that enables distributed applications for common services. Examples of middleware frameworks are Java Remote Method Invocation (RMI) and the Common Object Request Broker Architecture (CORBA). Java RMI provides a framework for writing distributed applications in the Java environment. CORBA enables code written in various languages (including code written for legacy systems) to communicate and work together.

- **Application Layer**—E-commerce applications make up this layer. Software needs to be written for the commerce server and the Web server. The Web server is the interface of the commerce server to the applications requesting services from the commerce service by means of the Internet.

- **Relationship Layer**—This layer is the user interface to the e-commerce application. Two examples of entities that reside in this topmost level of the e-commerce architecture are e-commerce agents and wireless technologies providing user access to the e-commerce applications.

Risks, Threats, and Vulnerabilities for Business Web Sites

Because e-commerce sites manage money and sensitive client information, they are often targets of attack. Part of e-business is knowing this and maintaining strong security of the site.

E-commerce security has three main concepts: confidentiality, integrity, and availability. **Confidentiality** allows only authorized parties to read private information. **Integrity** emphasizes the need for the information to be delivered unaltered to the recipient. **Availability** enables access to the information.

While security features do not guarantee a secure system, they are necessary to build a secure system. Security features fall into one of the following categories: **authentication** (verification of the identity of the user), **authorization** (allowing manipulation of resources in a specific way), **encryption** (hiding information by making it not readily understandable to unauthorized users), and **auditing** (keeping records of operations and transactions).

Vulnerabilities of a system can exist in its components. Attackers usually target entry and exit points in a computer system.

Connecting to the Internet Means Connecting to the Outside World

In the networking world, there are two types of networks, public and private. The private networks are the local and wide area networks owned by organizations. Private networks are tucked in behind a firewall and secured. No user outside the organization is allowed entry into the network. Companies of all shapes and sizes have secured private networks.

Public networks are a different story. The Internet is the largest public network. It is unregulated and full of dangers. Each and every time you connect to the Internet, you are leaving the relative safety of the local area network behind and heading out to a very public place.

For personal use, the dangers of the public Internet are not as significant as they are for business. Before going online, a business should have a full understanding of what the potential risks to data are and how to protect that data on the Internet.

The Internet and the Web Never Sleep

Long after the lights go out in brick and mortar stores, e-commerce Web sites are open for business and will stay that way. Modern networking hardware is designed to last and to run thousands of hours without failure. In the event of failure, numerous strategies are in place to ensure that the Internet is open for business.

The Internet itself is a mass interconnected collection of computer networks. These networks are linked using routers and high-speed media such as fiber cabling. The Internet operates as a huge mesh network enabling multiple paths for data to reach its destination if one path is unavailable. Riding on these hardware technologies and fault-tolerant strategies is the most robust suite of protocols in use today, TCP/IP.

This all means that the Internet is built on solid ground and that it can be trusted to be up and running 24/7/365. E-businesses take advantage of the Internet by posting Web sites that are available anytime and anywhere. This also means that security concerns never sleep.

Virtual Businesses Run 24/7/365

The availability of the Internet allows e-business unrestricted access to everyday, all-day, business availability. This is a particular boon for those companies whose e-business uses a self-service form of e-commerce. With self-service Web sites, no interaction is required in the part of the business, all support, purchasing, e-mail responses and even shipping are automatically handled.

With this open access to a global market, it is no wonder that organizations are scrambling to be a part of this open marketplace. However, despite being available at all hours, many companies do not see an adequate return on their investment, and their Web sites generate very little interest. Here are a few reasons why an e-commerce site may fail even though it is available all the time.

- **No visitor tracking**—Tools such as Google Analytics provide e-business owners with a detailed look at the traffic flow to their site: who their visitors are, where they came from, and how long they stayed. Web analytic tools help track and trace visitors allowing e-business to watch for trends and patterns that help focus their site.

- **Poor site design**—An e-business site may be available at all hours, but if it is unappealing and difficult to work with, it will not see the required conversions.

- **Confusing checkout procedures**—If analytic software shows that visitors are leaving when they get to the checkout, you have a problem with checkout procedures. To streamline, visit other e-business site and get ideas from those you see.

The overall point is that if an e-business site is open 24/7/365, it should be enjoying some level of conversions. If not, it is time to go back to the drawing board and reevaluate the business strategy plan or make one for the first time.

Web Sites Are Prone to Attack and Scrutiny

Right now on the Internet, governments, defense industries, and companies in finance, power, and telecommunications are all subjected to a barrage of attempted cyberattacks. The threats are numerous and managing them is an arduous responsibility. The Internet is not a secure medium; it is unmonitored, unmanaged, and full of potential risks. However, this is where e-commerce sites reside, and that's where they have to be made safe. Listed below are a few security considerations to keep in mind.

There are numerous threats to be aware of, including:

- Denial-of-service (DoS) attacks, which, as described earlier, stop access to authorized users of a Web site, so that the site is forced to offer a reduced level of service or, in some cases, cease operation completely

- Data theft, which involves criminals gaining access to sensitive data such as price lists, catalogues, and valuable intellectual property, and altering, destroying or copying it

- Alterations to your Web site by criminals who would damage your image or direct your customers to another site

- Unauthorized access to financial information about your business or your customers, with a view to perpetrating fraud

- Viruses that may be used to corrupt your business data

Any of these threats could lead to a security incident that could have significant impact on a business and its reputation.

The Risks of Handling Revenues Online

Breaches of confidentiality and personal data theft will impact an e-business adversely. Therefore it is imperative, for the success of the business, to invest in mitigating the risks that can lead to loss of confidentiality.

Confidentiality, as defined by the International Organization for Standards in the ISO-17799 document, is "ensuring that information is accessible only to those authorized to have access." Unless it is clear that the information can be made public, what you disclose to a business or a party should be kept between you and the other party. In other words, confidentiality is the prevention of intentional or unintentional unauthorized disclosure of contents. Confidentiality is even more important in the case of customer information. Loss of confidentiality can occur in many ways, intentionally and unintentionally. For example, data may be exposed through intentional release of company data or a misapplication of network rights. To ensure confidentiality of customer data, e-commerce sites implement network security protocols, and network authentication services, as well as data encryption services.

In addition to security protocols, organizations have detailed policies identifying the handling of customer data. These include how long data is kept, how it is stored, and how it is disposed of. Some policies might be listed on an e-business Web site for customers to read.

Credit, Charge, and Debit Cards

When a customer pays by credit, charge, or debit card, payment acceptance and processing protocols go through the following four major steps:

1. The cardholder securely sends the card number to the merchant along, with shipping and billing information.
2. The online merchant seeks bank authorization, which requires the amount of the purchase to be reserved against the customer's fund availability.
3. The merchant's bank sends the request to the bank that issued the customer's card.
4. If cardholder funds are available, the issuing bank sends an approval message through a network. If the funds are not available, it denies the request.

Online transactions are typically settled when the authorization request is issued. When the transaction is settled, the fulfillment systems ship the product or deliver the service to the buyer. If the consumer is downloading digital goods, delivery of the product or the service can start immediately. The merchant's account receives a deposit at the time of settlement. This deposit equals the deduction of funds from the customer's account. Processing fees may also be charged against the cardholder's account.

Electronic Cash and Wallets

An **electronic wallet** is a device that stores electronic currency or information about the wallet's owner, such as name, address, phone, and credit card numbers. The electronic wallet resides either on the client's PC or on the e-commerce server. It automatically fills in data on Web forms. A smart card is a plastic card that contains a computer chip that stores electronic currency and information about the card user. The card needs to be inserted in a card reader in order for its data to be used.

Electronic cash is similar to the cash you carry in your wallet. You purchase electronic cash with a credit card, and then download it to your electronic wallet or to a card. No additional permissions are then needed to use this cash. This is an anonymous channel for payment online. The only restriction is the requirement that the merchant accept the particular electronic cash. Payment with electronic cash goes through these steps:

1. The consumer acquires electronic cash from an electronic cash broker.
2. The consumer purchases goods or services from a merchant.
3. The merchant sends a specifically coded invoice to the consumer's browser.
4. The consumer's electronic wallet interprets the invoice and sends it and the electronic cash amount to the broker.
5. The electronic cash broker interprets the invoice and validates the electronic cash.
6. The broker notifies the merchant that the transaction is valid and deposits the transaction amount to the merchant's account.
7. Then the merchant can fulfill the consumer's order.

Vulnerabilities of Web-Enabled Applications

Web applications are software entities that do not operate in a vacuum. Their code, usually large collection of programming commands that may or may not reside in a single place, provides vulnerabilities that malicious individuals may want to exploit. Once built, these applications reside and operate on a network and inherit the vulnerabilities of the networked environment. Malicious individuals exploit these vulnerabilities in a myriad of ways for a myriad of reasons. Most of the time, the attacks occur where the money is. Thus, e-commerce sites as well as social networking sites that typically involve some kind of financial transactions are of particular interest to malicious individuals. They may operate on their own, or build intricate networks of malicious individuals of various technical skills, and engage a network of hijacked computers to execute elaborate attacks, while able to cover their tracks. To mitigate these risks, you must consider several areas.

Firmware

In addition to the basic network security considerations, upgrading firmware is important. Firmware is a small software program that is stored on a piece of hardware. This may be a video card, motherboard, digital camera, or printer. Firmware is also used on the devices used to create the network infrastructure such as network cards, routers, or switches.

Hardware ships with one version of firmware already stored on the chips. However, firmware can be updated on each device. The reason firmware is updated is to add more functionality to a hardware device, correct a problem with a hardware device, or sometimes to address a security flaw.

In a secure environment, administrators must periodically check the manufacturer's Web site to check whether new firmware has been released for a particular piece of networking hardware. If new firmware has been released, the administrator should verify why the new firmware has been released and what it is designed to do. If new firmware has been released and includes a security fix, administrators should apply the firmware as soon as possible.

Operating Systems and Applications

▶ TIP

It is a security best practice to periodically check a software vendor's Web site for updates, service packs, and patches. You can be sure hackers are trolling these sites finding new vulnerabilities and using them before administrators apply a fix.

Both operating systems and applications require maintenance to ensure that they are secure. Today's applications and operating systems are complex, having to accommodate a dynamic environment while providing secure services to clients. This complexity makes it very hard to produce products that provide 100 percent security out of the box. Because of this, administrators must be diligent in ensuring that potential security holes are all plugged. This process is sometimes referred to as application or operating systems hardening.

The No. 1 way to harden applications is to ensure that they have the latest service packs and patches installed. These updates are designed to address the security flaws in applications and make them more robust and harder to exploit.

Coding and SQL Vulnerabilities

While it may be difficult for the end user to know, applications sometimes have inherent coding flaws making them vulnerable for attack. Remote code execution vulnerabilities, for example, are enabled by improper coding techniques, and let the attacker run code on a vulnerable server to gain unauthorized access to privileged information.

As with other forms of software, it is essential to check the developer's Web site periodically for updates to products. Once a coding error is found and a patch released, the patch should be tested and applied as soon as possible.

SQL injections allow an attacker to retrieve crucial information from a Web server's database by carefully crafted statements that an attacker can enter into the username or password fields of a Web site, and fool the system into allowing access. Query requests to databases in SQL can be crafted and sent to the server to expose information. Adding a condition "or '1 = 1'" to an SQL statement would modify a query that would execute in any case, by bypassing the restrictions of the original query constraint.

Some commands in programming languages accept unformatted user input. By sending unexpected input, attackers can crash an application, get access to a portion of the memory content on the victim machine, or forcibly execute attacker-supplied code. When an attacker provides more input than an application can store in the temporary memory (or buffer), the extra information has to go somewhere. This information can overflow to other memory entities, overwriting the code and application executes. This extra information, when carefully crafted, can make the function in an unexpected way, display private data, or crash the application. Buffer overflow is a frequently exploited vulnerability.

Managing the Risks Inherent in Unsecure Systems

Many of the technologies used today, from protocols to software applications, are not secure. Strategies must be in place to ensure that systems and communications are secure. It is not uncommon to hear of a new security flaw in a Web browser or application, and these security risks and threats are real. Those working within IT know that a function of their job is to try to mitigate the constant threat of security breaches. This involves using secure protocols and managing applications and operating systems from a security framework.

In a network environment, protocol security is of utmost importance. Therefore a through knowledge of all networking protocols and their function is essential for network administrators.

System and Protocol Security

In the late 1970s and early 1980s, the US Department of Defense Advanced Research Projects Agency (DARPA) needed a system that would allow it to share the resources of its expensive mainframe computer systems. From this the ARPANET, the forerunner of today's Internet, was developed.

The original ARPANET network used a communication protocol known as NCP, but limitations were soon discovered, and a new protocol was needed to meet the new networking demands. That new protocol was the Transmission Control Protocol/Internet Protocol (TCP/IP). TCP/IP soon became the unquestioned leader in the protocol arena; increasingly, networks of all shapes and sizes were using it. The TCP/IP protocol suite got its name from the two main protocols in the suite: TCP and IP. TCP is responsible for providing reliable transmissions between the systems, and IP is responsible for addressing and route selection of the individual packets of data.

Many of the technologies in use in the 1970s and 1980s have fallen by the wayside. Most have been replaced with faster and more robust options. TCP/IP has remained the exception, with all the major network operating systems including support for TCP/IP and networks and the Internet relying on it. The problem is, though, that TCP/IP was developed and used in a time before there were the security concerns of today. This leaves the most widely used protocol a potential security risk.

Although TCP/IP is often referred to as a single protocol, it is actually a protocol suite composed of many protocols, each with its own function on the network. Some of these individual protocols within TCP/IP are highly insecure. Secure options can be used as replacements. As an example, Table 2-1 lists some commonly used TCP/IP protocols, their functions, and their secure counterparts.

While a detailed discussion of the protocols within TCP/IP falls outside the scope of this chapter, it is important to note that administrators need to be aware of each of these protocols and their secure options. One in particular to be concerned with is IP itself.

Securing IP Communications

When data is sent over the network, it is assumed that it will reach its intended destination without being accessed and viewed by anyone it is not intended for. The problem is that basic IP transmissions lack security, and anyone with the motivation and know-how can access and modify that data. Many of the data transactions that occur every day do not need security, as much of the communication sent is not worth tampering with or stealing. However, for communications that do require security, Internet Protocol Security (IPSec) is often the answer. There are other methods to help secure data transmissions, however, such as Secure Sockets Layer (SSL). SSL provides Application Layer security, whereas IPSec operates at the IP Layer. Working at the IP Layer allows IPSec to encrypt transparently most network communications.

IPSec is an IP Layer security protocol designed to provide security against internal and external attacks. This is an important consideration, as the reasons for securing against attacks from outside the network are well documented, as are the methods for doing so. IPSec provides a way to protect sensitive data as it travels within the LAN. As you know, firewalls do not provide such security for internal networks, so a complete security solution will require both a firewall solution and internal protection provided by such security mechanisms as IPSec.

To create secure data transmissions, IPSec uses two separate protocols, Authentication Headers (AH), and Encapsulating Security Payloads (ESP). Briefly, AH is primarily responsible for the authentication and integrity verification of packets, whereas ESP provides encryption services. As they are independent protocols, when implementing an IPSec policy, you can use them together, or they can be used individually. Whether one or both are used will depend on the security needs of the network.

PROTOCOL	FULL NAME	DESCRIPTION
TABLE 2-1 TCP/IP protocols and functions.		
FTP	File Transfer Protocol	Protocol for uploading and downloading files to and from a remote host; also accommodates basic file management tasks. FTP transmissions, including the password, are sent as cleartext and at risk of interception.
SFTP	Secure File Transfer Protocol	SFTP combines FTP with SSH to provide a secure option for FTP communications.
HTTP	Hypertext Transfer Protocol	The widely used protocol on the World Wide Web used for the retrieving files from a Web server. Data is sent in cleartext. The protocol is not suitable for online transactions such as banking or e-commerce.
HTTPS	Hypertext Transfer Protocol Secure	Secure protocol for retrieving files from a Web server. HTTPS uses SSL for encrypting data between the client and the host. HTTPS should always be used for e-commerce or any online financial transactions.
Telnet	Teletype Network	Allows communication and management of remote systems. Telnet offers no encryption, and text and passwords are transmitted as cleartext.
RSH	UNIX utility used to run a command on a remote machine	Replaced with SSH, as RSH sends all data cleartext.
SSH	Secure Shell	Secure alternative to Telnet, which allows secure sessions to be opened on a remote host.
RCP	Remote Copy Protocol	Copies files between systems, but transport is not secured.
SCP	Secure Copy Protocol	Allows files to be copied securely between two systems. Uses Secure Shell (SSH) technology to provide encryption services.
SNMPv1/2	Simple Network Management Protocol v1/2	Network monitoring system used to monitor the networks condition. Neither SNMPv1 nor 2 is secured.
SNMPv3	Simple Network Management Protocol v3	Enhanced SNMP service offering both encryption and authentication services.

The purpose of implementing IPSec and data transmission security is to guard against attacks, but what attacks are you guarding against? There are several different types of attacks that you need to be aware of when configuring a security plan. Knowing the potential threats can help pinpoint the holes that need to be plugged. Some of the types of attacks you need to be concerned with include the following:

- **Eavesdropping**—When network communications occur in cleartext format, there is the danger that someone can intercept transmissions and read the data. Of course, once the data is accessed, it can be modified and forwarded. Imagine the impact if this were to occur in a bank. When sensitive data is being transmitted throughout the network, it must be encrypted to protect against eavesdropping.

- **Address spoofing**—IP address spoofing is a technique that allows the attacker to reroute data in transit. Essentially, IP spoofing involves convincing a sending computer that it is the intended recipient when it isn't. Network devices use IP addresses to determine the sender and receiver for a data transmission. In a spoofing scenario, the hacker either intends to conceal their computer's identity or is trying to impersonate another computer's identity.

- **Man-in-the-middle attacks**—This attack involves the attacker between the sending and receiving devices. With the ability to monitor and intercept transmissions, the attacker can modify data while the sender and receiver assume communication remains between them alone. Nonrepudiation is a countermeasure for this attack, meaning the sender and receiver validate they are who they say they are.

- **Denial-of-service attacks**—The intent of this attack is not so much to obtain data as it is to block traffic or deny legitimate services.

- **Sniffer attacks**—These are designed to monitor the network and attempt to access and then view data within a packet. Encryption can be used to encode the data within a packet reducing the vulnerability of the sniffer attacks.

This list represents only a few of the possible types of attacks you may encounter, but they provide enough motivation to secure those networks and understand how data can be accessed.

Managing Application and Coding Security

Protocols aren't the only security consideration on the network; there are many, including managing the inherent security flaws located in software such as operating systems and other applications. One of the keys to keeping systems and systems safe and secure is in the vigilant maintenance of the applications you use. The problem is, much of the software used today is released with security flaws right out of the box. Browsers, operating systems, and office applications are examples of software that has been released with significant security concerns. This is why network administration requires knowledge of service packs and patches.

A patch is a single software fix designed to fix a specific issue. For example, a patch may be released to plug a security flaw in a browser. Service packs, however, are collections of patches. A service pack is a major upgrade to an application. Service packs are periodically released for products such as Windows operating systems. These service packs are updated either manually or automatically, with each new release providing fixes, updates, and enhanced features for the operating system. Keep in mind that any software package without the latest service packs installed is at risk. To be as secure as possible you need to know when, why, and how service packs should be used on a server.

Using Service Packs

Using an operating system or another application right out of the box without applying updates is an unsafe practice, as most software has inherent security flaws. While all software is put through rigorous testing before it is released, all too often this testing fails to identify all potential security risks in real-world application. The result is that even before your new software package is on store shelves, work is under way to develop service packs and patches.

All companies will have identified policies highlighting best practices for updating and installing service packs. In a network environment, these polices are strictly enforced, as updating software, particularly a server operating system, can have unforeseen negative results. As best practice for installing service packs, consider the following:

- **Check the manufacturer's Web site**—Whether it is Microsoft Windows, Linux, or any other software vendor, their respective Web sites will list the latest service pack, instructions for installation, and any known compatibility issues. The manufacturer will also clearly identify the security issues that the service pack is intended to address.

- **Verify resources**—Does your system have enough hard disk space or memory to accommodate the new service pack? Service packs often represent a significant upgrade to the existing software. It is a best practice to verify resources before the installation.

FYI

While many home users have their systems set to update automatically, professional network administrators generally do not. At times the application of service packs can cause unexpected issues, and this is too risky on a live production server. The term given to updating software without first exploring what the updates are designed to do is *blind patching*. Blind patching is not recommended for server software upgrades. Instead, most IT staff will develop a patch management policy and procedures that govern time limits to understand, test, and roll out patches for production servers. Time to roll out a patch may differ according to how critical the patch is.

- **Back up the system**—If installing a service pack on a server, the system should be backed up beforehand. If something unexpected happens, it is possible to return to before the service pack was installed.
- **Take a performance baseline**—When working on live servers, many administrators choose to take a baseline to gauge performance before and after the service pack is applied. This makes it possible to verify that the service pack has not caused performance degradation in the server.
- **Reconfigure the system**—Some service packs may require some post-installation procedures, including restarting services, reinstalling protocols, or updating other resident software.

Service packs are released infrequently and are usually used to address numerous issues within an operating system. Patches, on the other hand, provide a quick fix for a program or feature and are more commonplace. Patches are designed to address a very specific problem. For instance, you would download a patch to fix a security hole in the operating system when downloading and installing an entire service pack may not necessary.

Whatever the purpose of the patch, you need to do a full backup before you patch, because patches invariably change system files. For patches directed toward applications on the server, it may be tempting to skip a backup, but this is not advised. If something goes wrong with the patch, it is important to be able to get back to the point you started from before the patch.

Telecommuting and Secure Access for Remote Employees

Remote access to the network and telecommuting is commonplace for today business environments. Naturally, it is impractical to use dedicated connections for each remote employee instead; secure remote communication channels need to be established over an untrusted network, the Internet. While the Internet provides the network infrastructure through which remote employees can access the corporate network, it opens up significant security concerns. To address these security concerns a virtual private link is established between the employee system and the remote network. This private link is known as a **virtual private network (VPN)**.

Secure Web communication protocols provide a way to authenticate clients and servers on the Web and to protect the integrity of communication between clients and servers. Three such protocols are:

- **Point-to-Point Tunneling Protocol (PPTP)** creates a secure communications tunnel between two points on a network. This tunneling functionality is the basis for virtual private networks (VPNs). VPNs are used to establish remote point-to-point connections over a public network such as the Internet. PPTP enables authenticated and encrypted transmissions between two end points such as a Web client and a server. PPTP competes with L2TP and IPSec as protocols for establishing a VPN.

- Layer 2 Tunneling Protocol (L2TP) is similar to L2TP in that it utilizes tunneling to deliver data. It authenticates the client in a two-phase process: It first authenticates the computer and then the user. By authenticating the computer, it prevents the data from being intercepted, changed, and returned to the user in what is known as a man-in-the-middle attack. L2TP ensures integrity, but does not guarantee confidentiality. L2TP does not provide encryption over a VPN, but that's where IPSec comes in.
- **Internet Protocol Security (IPSec)** is a protocol used to secure communication between systems within a network as well as securing communications that are transmitted outside of the local LAN. IPSec can be used to encrypt, authenticate and verify integrity of communications. IPSec is commonly used to secure VPN connections.

Each of these three protocols is for securing specific forms of communications via VPNs.

Any employee with access to the Internet can create a VPN link and access the corporate network as if he or she were sitting right at it. In this way, a VPN extends a LAN to include remote clients. Using secure protocols, the VPN provides a secure point-to-point dedicated link between two points over a public IP network.

Organizations use the VPN link as a secure, cost-effective, and convenient way to connect remote users to their networks. Many elements are required to establishing a VPN connection:

- **A VPN client**—The client is the remote user attempting to access the corporate network. The VPN client is the computer that initiates the communication.
- **A VPN server**—The VPN server responds to the client request and authenticates the connection.
- **Transmission media**—The one most often used is the Internet; however, private networks also support VPN connections.
- **VPN protocols**—A VPN is created and secured using specific protocols namely PPTP, L2TP and even SSL. PPTP and L2TP can create the VPN tunnel and enable authentication and encryption. Authentication allows VPN clients and servers to establish the identity of people on the network. Encryption allows potentially sensitive data to be guarded from the general public.

> **NOTE**
> Despite the advantages of using a VPN, there are two primary concerns: security and reliability. Security can be managed with proper protocol application; however, Internet connectivity can be unreliable, and it is hard to manage that.

CHAPTER SUMMARY

The Internet and the Web provide infrastructure and technologies for effectively conducting business transactions online. Companies today need to be online to expand their business and have it in operation 24 hours per day.

However, e-commerce attracts thieves because the possibility for illegal gain is much greater than in robbing brick-and-mortar stores. These attacks exploit vulnerabilities of the infrastructure, the software, and the people who participate in the online transactions. Any system is as secure as its weakest link. Therefore, understanding how these attacks work is crucial to developing security strategies. Data privacy, transaction confidentiality, and trust are essential to e-commerce, which becomes more complex as it expands globally.

KEY CONCEPTS AND TERMS

Auditing
Authentication
Authorization
Availability
Confidentiality
Denial of service (DoS) attack

Electronic cash
Electronic wallet
Encryption
Integrity
Internet Protocol Security (IPSec)

Point-to-Point Tunneling Protocol (PPTP)
Privacy
Virtual private network (VPN)

CHAPTER 2 ASSESSMENT

1. Denial-of-service (DoS) attacks stop access to authorized users of a Web site.

   A. True
   B. False

2. Which of the following are included in CLM? (Select three.)

   A. Acquisition
   B. Retention
   C. Suspension
   D. Conversion

3. Which of the following are required to establish a VPN connection? (Select three.)

   A. VPN client
   B. VPN server
   C. SSL
   D. Transmission media

4. You are designing a customer-service strategy for a large company. The client has asked that you incorporate full two-way communication between service staff and the customer. Which of the following methods would you suggest? (Select two.)

   A. E-mail support
   B. FAQ
   C. Customer feedback forms
   D. VoIP

5. Despite the overwhelming trend of companies having an online presence, some companies do not see an adequate return on investment from a Web site; or their Web site generates very little interest. Which of these following characteristics might *not* be a factor for poor performance by a Web site?

   A. Poor visitor tracking
   B. 7/24/365 availability
   C. Poor site design
   D. Confusing checkout procedures

6. Many security features are available for building a secure system. Which of the following describe categories of security features? (Select three.)

   A. Authentication
   B. Auditing
   C. Confidentiality
   D. Encryption

7. The most important single thing an organization can do to defend itself against network attacks and malware is to keep systems patched and updated.

   A. True
   B. False

8. "Contact us" forms are an example of which of the following?

   A. One-way communication
   B. Full two-way communication
   C. Limited two-way communication
   D. Full one-way communication

9. You have to connect three remote employees to the corporate network. Which of the following technologies would you use?

   A. SSL
   B. VPN
   C. One-way communication
   D. Remote acquisition

10. Which protocol is used by HTTPS for encrypting data between the client and the host?

   A. SSL
   B. SSH
   C. RSH
   D. TFTP

© Rodolfo Clix/Dreamstime.com

Security Considerations for Home and Personal Online Use

I N THE DIGITAL AND INFORMATION AGE, it's difficult to maintain privacy. Employers, advertisers, friends, doctors, and almost everyone else is looking to find your information online. As more of our data and personal information is stored online, security and privacy become hard to maintain.

Privacy breaches, Web vulnerabilities, and data theft are not a threat just to big business. Every day thousands of individuals are duped out of money, suffer identity theft, or find their data compromised. This chapter explores various privacy concerns for home users. It discusses how Web security and vulnerabilities are part of daily life at home and at work. Further, this chapter will explore some best practices for securing common online tasks.

Chapter 3 Topics

This chapter covers the following topics and concepts:

- What common security terms and threats are
- How to secure common online activities
- How to protect against e-mail scams
- What the OWASP Top 10 Privacy Risks Project is and what it includes

Chapter 3 Goals

When you complete this chapter, you will be able to:

- Understand common security terms
- Develop a secure online banking strategy
- Identify the security considerations for everyday online activities
- Review the process of social engineering
- Understand phishing attacks
- Review the OWASP Top 10 Privacy Risks
- Reduce the potential of identity theft
- Develop a list of best practices for online transactions

Common Security Terms and Threats

One of the best places to start when reviewing security threats is the terms and definitions used in security discussions. The following is a brief review of some of the core concepts of personal security.

Social Engineering

Social engineering is a form of attack that bypasses technical controls. It takes advantage of human kindness or the desire to be helpful. Social engineering is a threat from both outsiders and people within an organization. Social engineering is a means of tricking people into revealing sensitive data such as passwords or credit card information. This may include trying to get users to send passwords or other information over e-mail, shoulder surfing, or using any other type of method to trick users to get information. Social engineering is an attack that attempts to take advantage of human nature.

Social engineering takes many forms: shoulder surfing, dumpster diving, persuasion, and pretexting, to name a few.

Shoulder Surfing

Shoulder surfing typically involves an attacker literally looking over a user's shoulder to obtain username and password combination. This may happen in the office or in a public place such as a library or Internet café. Unfortunately, the problem is not only people looking over your shoulder but also hidden cameras well placed to record information. The increased use of laptop computers and remote computing has increased the shoulder surfing threat.

FYI

Some years ago a research project was conducted where numerous discarded hard disks were collected from dumps or secondhand shops. Each hard disk was scanned and run through software designed to retrieve deleted files. The result was a massive collection of personal data, including bank information and other sensitive documents. The best practice when discarding an old computer is to remove the hard disk and physically destroy it. This is often a policy in corporate environments, and a reputable company is contracted to destroy the hard drives. The same is true for old USB drives and backup devices.

Dumpster Diving

Dumpster diving is another form of social engineering. A lot of personal information gets discarded carelessly. It can easily end up in the hands of the wrong people. Dumpster divers go after not only old paperwork but also old hard drives. Many hard disks contain sensitive information that can be accessed and used. Even "deleted" information can be undeleted and used. The best policy is to completely destroy old hard disks that may contain sensitive data and to shred old documents. Larger corporations use disposal teams to shred and dispose of potentially sensitive data.

Persuasion

In a persuasion attack, the attacker pressures the user to divulge personal information. The user might be convinced the attacker is acting in the best interests of the user or company or that there will be consequences if the information isn't handed over. Also, the attacker may ask for logon information to update the user's computer. Or the attacker may otherwise seem to be doing the user a favor.

▶ TIP

The most effective guard against social engineering is educating users on types of attacks. Organizations should provide accessible documentation as to who can and cannot obtain personal information or username and password combinations.

Pretexting

Pretexting is essentially impersonation. It is a common social networking attack. With pretexting, the attacker pretends to be someone else to gain the trust necessary to get personal information. An attacker may claim to be a network administrator, a security staff member, or even a co-worker or friend.

The best way to prevent pretexting is to politely decline to give personal information before you have a chance to verify a person's credentials. Remember, most companies have policies outlining who can ask for personal information such as usernames and passwords.

There are other scams that are limited only by the imagination of the attacker. These attacks are particularly effective because they bypass traditional network security and focus on human factors.

Phishing

Many modern cyberattacks are very technical. They involve data capture, encryption weaknesses, and the manipulation of software vulnerabilities. But phishing attacks are not technical at all. Phishing attacks are based on the idea that "there is a sucker born every minute." Phishing attacks are all about tricking people into actions such as downloading malicious software or clicking links to spoofed Web sites. Phishing is a type of social engineering attack based on deception. Some phishing attacks are easily spotted. They don't look right. Others are not so easy to identify. The rule, then, is to never click suspicious links in e-mail, games, or other online communications. Phishing attacks appear to be on the rise—they are becoming increasingly elaborate and devious.

Phishing scams are also increasing on social networking sites. There, attackers attempt to acquire personal, sensitive, or confidential information, often by masquerading as friends or colleagues of their targets. The overall goal of the attack is to get information such as credit card numbers, username/password combinations, or bank account details. Some examples of phishing attacks are messages claiming to be from any of the following:

* An administrator asking you for your username and password
* A Web site, such as PayPal, asking you to reenter your bank account information
* A representative of your bank requiring personal and/or account information
* A company asking for confidential information
* A credit card company asking for personal information

Any such messages are likely to be phishing attacks. Such messages have become common in social networking, instant messaging, and e-mail. Regardless of where phishing is used, the intent is the same: to fake a Web site or identity to gain access to personal information.

In the world of network security, many attacks can be managed from an administrative level with secure protocols and firewalls. This is not the same for phishing, in which user education is the best line of defense. There are several preventive steps you can take to limit and reduce phishing attacks:

> **⚠ WARNING**
>
> The communications from a phisher look like the real thing. They may be hard to spot as fakes. Often, actual company logos, color schemes, and text are used to make the message or Web site look as legitimate as possible.

* Double-check any e-mail or message asking for any personal information.
* Don't click on links within e-mails that ask for your personal information. Instead, go directly to the site by typing in the uniform resource locator (URL).
* Don't type personal information in a pop-up screen.
* Protect your computer with up-to-date spam filters, antivirus and antispyware software, and a firewall.
* Open e-mail attachments only from trusted sources.

Identify Theft

Identity theft occurs when a cybercriminal acquires and then uses your personal information to effectively become you for conducting transactions. This may be using your personal information to secure loans, access accounts, gamble online, get a job in your name, rent a car, or open a credit card account. The types of information a cybercriminal is looking for include following:

- Your name
- Date of birth
- Home and work address
- Passport information
- Credit card numbers
- Social Security or social insurance number
- Bank account numbers
- Driver's license number
- Phone numbers
- Names of family members

Cybercriminals with only one of these pieces of information can't do much to hurt you. But if they have two or more of them, they may have enough to take your identity and use it online. Now you have to ask yourself how much of this information you willingly post online, and how much you send over unsecured public wireless access points.

The truth is that many people are putting enough data out there for their identities to be stolen. So just how can this happen? Here are some common methods that thieves use:

- Launching e-mail phishing attacks
- Exploiting unsecured social networking sites
- Taking advantage of unsecured dating sites
- Finding résumés posted online and searching them for personal data
- Scanning old computers
- Getting inside information from HR or IT departments
- Using spyware
- Using keystroke loggers
- Going dumpster diving

Unfortunately there are a number of creative ways cybercriminals can get your data one piece at a time until they have enough to steal your identity.

Protecting Your Identity

Maintaining your privacy and controlling your personal information are critical for staying safe online. Further, it's not just you but everyone in the household who must adhere to best practices when sharing sensitive data online. If a computer is shared in the home, a keystroke logger or other malware can affect everyone who uses that system.

FYI

Online bullying has become a significant problem for many people online. Online bullying, or cyberbullying, occurs when someone becomes a target of repeated negative actions by others. The intent is to humiliate, threaten, or harass. What's more, people of many ages are being bullied into divulging personal data such as logon credentials and credit card numbers.

To help prevent identity theft, consider the following:

- Be aware of the types of data a cybercriminal is after. Be very clear on what personal sensitive data is and how it can be used.
- Protect your Social Security or social insurance number at all costs. Very rarely will you need to put this number online. It should be safely tucked away most of the time.
- Monitor your credit report. Make it a habit to check your credit activity free of charge from the three credit bureaus.
- Create strong passwords. Weak and easy-to-remember passwords can cause data leaks.
- Use credit card numbers only on reputable sites. Verify secure transfers before entering credit card information.
- Guard your addresses and phone numbers closely.
- Clear the browser's cache if you are using a public computer.
- Do not use auto-fill forms on public computers.
- Restrict data sent over public wireless access.
- Use privacy controls on social networking sites.
- Use strong access passwords on laptops and mobile devices.
- Properly dispose of old computer hardware.
- Ensure your home wireless access point is using strong encryption.

This is just a partial list of some of the common strategies for keeping data secure and private. Many are just common sense, but people generally click too soon online and forget security basics.

Malware and Ransomware

Malware is an all-encompassing term referring to all forms of malicious software. Examples of malware include Trojan horses, spyware, worms, viruses, and adware. The various types of malware have different forms of mitigation and varying levels of consequence. For most forms of malware, an up-to-date virus scanner is effective at detecting and blocking and/or removing the malicious software. Malware is a moving target, constantly being altered to avoid detection. Of course, if the virus definitions on your system are outdated, they will not be able to detect and remove the newest malicious software from your system.

One form of malware that virus scanners are *not* effective against is **ransomware**. Ransomware is a particularly vicious form of malware. Ransomware refers to an attack whereby all the files and folders on a computer system are encrypted and held for ransom. Without the key for decrypting, users no longer have access to their own files and data.

▶ **NOTE**

Where does ransomware come from? Usually the attacks come from outside North America. Users might get this malware from sites offering free TV, movies, or free game offers. As users are tempted to click on these unbelievable offers, the ransomware is launched on the machine. Nothing is free—even on the Internet.

Once the deed is done, the computer user is informed using text files or messages. This might happen when attempting to access a document or other file, by pop-up window or an e-mail. The note informs the user that the files are encrypted and to gain access again, money will need to be sent to a particular address. The address is typically offshore, and if the money is sent, there is no guarantee the files will be released.

Ransomware attacks were once rare but over the past few years, they have become more common. They are a scary prospect for corporate IT administrators. Having a single computer system locked out with ransomware is bad enough, but having corporate servers and network clients locked out could mean a business outage. The financial impact from a loss of data could be significant to a company.

So what can you do if you are a victim of ransomware or similar malware? There are two options: pay the cybercriminals and hope they release the decryption key. Or format the computer, start with a clean installation, and recover from backups. The latter is strongly recommended, since there's no guarantee the malware won't simply re-encrypt the data at a later time. This is why you must always have recent backups of critical data. It is possible in a ransomware attack to lose all files, including your photos and other hard-to-replace items.

Cookies

A **cookie** is a very small data file that a Web site may write to your hard drive. It contains information such as when you visited certain Web pages, what you clicked on, and possibly even what your username and password are. Using the information in the cookies, Web browsers let the user bypass logon or other procedures in subsequent visits to the same Web page. Cookies are used to focus marketing according to what you've browsed before. Cookies make your access to certain Web pages more convenient, but they can be considered a privacy issue.

There are two types of cookies. *Persistent cookies* remain on your hard drive until they expire or are erased. *Session cookies*, on the other hand, help the browser store data for the duration of the session, so that for example, you don't need to enter a username and password to access each page where they are required within the same Web site. Or, when you place an item in a shopping cart, and move on to shop for other items, if it were not for the session cookies, your shopping cart would appear empty.

Wi-Fi Eavesdropping

One serious personal privacy concern is with data captured while traveling over wireless networks. By its nature, wireless network traffic is virtually impossible to confine, compared with traffic over the wire. Many people spend time at coffee shops or restaurants surfing over public wireless access. This is inherently insecure. It's very convenient to use a public wireless access point to get e-mail or check a Facebook status. However, the data traveling over the connection can be easily intercepted. The capture and reading of data in transmission is known as *eavesdropping*. Because this is a constant threat at public wireless access points, you must take steps to secure access by a network key, or to encrypt individual sessions. Best practice is not to push sensitive data such as passwords or banking data over public wireless networks.

> **TIP**
>
> A cybercriminal intent on capturing your data may set up a bogus connection, as in a hotel lobby, in the hopes that you'll mistake it for a network that is at least legitimate and maybe even somewhat secure. It is always best to be very cautious about all public access wireless points.

Without a session cookie, every time you open a new Web page, the server where that page is stored would treat you as a new visitor.

As they may contain accurate information (unless you falsified it), such as name, address, and credit information, cookies are a privacy threat. Depending on the Web site, cookies may contain information that specifies your preferences in airline seating or meals. Once a Web site collects this information about you, it may be sold to others or used in other abrasive practices, such as e-mail marketing campaigns or unsolicited sales calls. Consent to these practices is dubious at best, typically implied just by virtue of visiting the site. But browsers that support cookies also provide some mechanisms to partially block or completely disallow their local storage.

Securing Common Online Activities

Most people use the Internet daily to pay bills, book travel, shop, research, play games, or send e-mail. Because these activities are so common and well integrated into daily lives, it's no wonder that scammers and others with malicious intent would try to find vulnerabilities in each of these areas. Remember, everything you do online has security considerations. This does not mean that you should quit writing e-mails and send correspondence using paper and envelopes again. But it does mean you need to understand the lurking potential threats to your day-to-day online transactions. This section explores some common online activities and the potential threat associated with each.

Banking and Investing

One of the most common questions asked is whether online banking is safe. Many people continue to use telephone banking or regular mail to pay bills because of the uncertainty. Online banking can be safe, but there are still some risks. Some of those risks are possible to mitigate and control, while others are not.

Hypertext Transfer Protocol (HTTP) is the protocol that allows text, graphics, multimedia, and other material to travel between your computer and an HTTP or Web server. HTTP defines what actions can be requested by clients and how servers should answer those requests. In a practical implementation, HTTP clients (Web browsers) make requests in an HTTP format to servers running HTTP server applications (Web servers). Files, created in a special language such as HTML, are returned to the client, and the connection is closed.

HTTP uses a uniform resource locator (URL) to determine which Web page should be downloaded from the remote server. The URL contains the type of request, as in http://; the name of the server being contacted, such as www.pinterest.com; and optionally, the page being requested, such as /login. The result is the syntax that most Internet-savvy people are familiar with: *http://www.pinterest.com/login/.*

One of the downsides of using HTTP is that traffic is sent in cleartext. This is not suitable for online banking or shopping. A more secure method is needed. The solution is **Hypertext Transfer Protocol Secure (HTTPS)**. HTTPS uses a protocol known as the Secure Sockets Layer (SSL), which encrypts the information sent between the client and the host.

For HTTPS to be used, both the client and server must support it. All popular Web browsers support HTTPS, as do Web server products that provide sensitive applications. When accessing an application that uses HTTPS, the URL starts with HTTPS rather than HTTP, for example, *https://www.mybankonline.com.*

> **NOTE**
>
> Recently, while traveling and waiting to check into a hotel room, a couple were arguing with the hotel clerk about their reservation. They felt they had made one, but the hotel had no record of it. Unfortunately, the couple learned their reservation was made on a spoofed travel reservation site. They were forced to find a room elsewhere.

Online Banking Threats

Not all online bandits are clever or sophisticated enough to intercept encrypted transmissions. There are other forms of attacks, however, that are not as technical but often even more effective. Three of the more common types of attacks include spoofing (pharming) and phishing.

- **Spoofing**—Spoofing or pharming attacks involve creating fake Web sites equipped with forms to capture user information. Imagine entering your username/password, credit card information, or investment account numbers into a fake Web form. This type of attack is not as successful as it once was, because users are more adept at spotting fake sites. But cybercrooks keep trying it, and they sometimes succeed.

FYI

Anyone who has e-mail has likely seen a phishing message. These often involve fake prompts to reset one's password on (supposed) bank sites or PayPal, or to follow other links to fake Web forms. Financial institutions are highly unlikely to ever send e-mail alerts to change information. You may be able to verify an embedded link by checking the browser status bar while hovering over the link. Additionally, banks and other financial Web sites sometimes list recent phishing schemes, although these lists can be quickly outdated.

- **Phishing attacks**—As noted earlier, these attacks often involve e-mails that try to trick users into performing a particular action—for example, clicking on a link that will take users to a spoofed Web site with a form to capture their credentials or deliver malware. A popular phishing attack is the e-mail scam notifying you about your right to millions of dollars from a deposed prince. Phishing attacks are often easy to spot, but for the cybercriminal, it's a numbers game. If the scammer sends thousands or millions of phishing e-mails, only a small percentage of people need fall for the scam for it to succeed.

Mitigating Online Banking Risks

Online banking is here to stay. It is easy, flexible, and accessible around the world. However, as long as there is online banking, there will be cybercriminals who try to get at your banking data. Using a few best practices, though, it's possible to increase your online banking security and keep your data secure.

- **Authentication security**—First and foremost is password management. Use strong passwords that are very difficult for password cracker applications to figure out. Develop a password rotation policy so that you change passwords periodically. Finally, keep your passwords secure, not attached to the side of the monitor or kept in a wallet.
- **Site encryption**—When conducting an online transaction such as banking, make sure you see the "https" in the URL Web address and a tiny lock symbol located in the URL bar.
- **A dedicated computer**—It is often a good idea to use a dedicated computer for online transactions. It is probably not a good idea to use a shared computer that your kids use to play online games, or watch downloaded movies.
- **Virus scanning**—Keep the virus definitions in your antivirus software up-to-date to identify and remove the most recent malware that may have been downloaded onto your system.

FYI

When it comes to banking security, there is one thing to keep in mind—convenience is not always your friend. This means that using easy-to-remember passwords, using the same password for everything, or storing credentials in your smartphone may make life easier, but will also make it far less secure. Security is a nuisance and a hassle, and if that's how your own security practices feel to you, you are probably doing things right.

- **Private computers**—It is best never to use public computers, as in libraries or other shared areas, for online banking. If this is necessary, be sure that the auto-complete form option is disabled and that you completely log out of any site before leaving the computer. Also, take the time to delete the browsing history just to make sure.
- **E-mail requests**— Don't reply to requests from banks or other financial institutions asking to reset passwords. Likewise, don't click links within the e-mail that want you to download a product or service. It is best to go to the bank's or institution's Web site directly from your browser to ensure it's a valid site and not a phishing attempt.

Shopping Online

Over the last few years the popularity of shopping online has grown significantly. With this growth, the types and sophistication of threats aimed at online shoppers has also grown. The encryption and protocols used are the same as those discussed above in the online banking section. That is, the transactions are secured using the HTTPS protocol.

However, right now online there are countless fake e-commerce sites waiting to steal your information. Many fake e-commerce sites don't look fake at all. Instead, they appear to be legitimate sites with great offers and great products and services. Malicious e-commerce sites are often well designed and cleverly implemented, making them that much more dangerous. The potential threat for online shopping can be loss of money and personal information, as well as identity theft.

Listed below are a few tips for keeping online shopping secure:

- Verify the security of your connection. As with any financial transaction, ensure that the checkout for the shopping site has a secure connection. An indicator that a Web site should be secure is the lock icon or an unbroken key in the bottom right corner of the screen, or a Web site address that begins with https://.
- If the price seems to be too good to be true, it probably is. Many people have been fooled by $100 iPads or free trips. Save your money and get the best deal possible from a reputable vendor.

- As with other transactions, don't conduct financial or transfer sensitive data over public wireless access points.
- Read the privacy policy on the sites you are visiting. If no policy is visible or accessible, this could be a giant red flag.
- Periodically check your financial statements for unusual or unexpected charges.
- Don't use auto-fill for online forms, especially when using public computers.

E-Commerce Scams

One of the factors that limit the growth of e-commerce is the prevalence of online scams. These serve to undermine confidence and create an atmosphere of fear for those conducting business online. Many of these scams are not new, having been used by mail and over the phone for years. The World Wide Web has given these scams a new medium in which to operate. And with the relative anonymity of the Internet, it's hard to track those operating such scams.

The list of online scams is almost endless; being aware of them is the only protection. The following are some of the common ones:

- **Product offers**—Many Web sites offer products or services free or at extreme discounts. Sometimes when the credit card information is supplied, the product is not delivered, and the number is used fraudulently elsewhere.
- **Fake auctions**—Some sites offer auctioned material, but the products are not delivered. As with fake product offers, once the credit card information is obtained, the product is not shipped. There are many fake auctions. The key is using trusted and proven auction sites.
- **Online lotteries and giveaways**—There are thousands of Web sites promoting online lotteries and free giveaways. Although some may be legitimate, many are scams. Online lotteries are particularly suspect. A best practice is to carefully review the company before placing any confidential information on a lottery Web site.
- **Online contests**—Fake online contests are all over the Web. Many visitors are informed that they have won a prize and just need to enter personal information to collect. Such contests look legitimate and can easily fool the gullible visitor.
- **Mimic sites**—Some sites mimic well-known sites in order to gather personal information. They may appear as a banking site, with all the company colors and logos in place; a well-known e-commerce site; or a site such as PayPal. You often arrive at mimic sites by clicking the links in fraudulent e-mail messages widely sent as spoofing attacks, as mentioned earlier.
- **Donations**—In recent years, cybercriminals have taken advantage of natural disasters, such as earthquakes or tsunamis, to create illegitimate "charities" to help the survivors of these events. These can be particularly effective, preying upon people's goodwill. Many times, fraudsters send out messages and e-mails that link to a legitimate-looking Web site designed to gather personal banking information.

Cybercriminals spend millions of dollars a year developing products that can trick users into providing personal information. Their targets are both personal users and business and very convincing. Here are a few things you can do to protect against online scams:

- Be wary of unsolicited e-mail messages from a charitable organization, auction sites, banks or others asking for money or personal information.
- Ensure that your antivirus software scans attachments for possible malware.
- Do not click links from unsolicited e-mail, as they may link to a mimic site.
- If you receive an e-mail request from a charity you'd like to support, make sure the request is legitimate. Instead of clicking a link in the message, manually type the charity's Web address into your browser's address bar and look for instructions on how to donate.
- Keep alert on sites pressuring you into providing sensitive information. Phishers like to use scare tactics to create a sense of urgency.

Social Networking

Social networks are moving away from strictly personal communication and are increasingly embraced in corporate environments. As the popularity of social networking and personal communication grows, so too does the number of attacks and risks associated with it. Unfortunately, spammers, hackers, phishers, and others see a medium that they can exploit in an attempt to gain confidential information.

Despite the risks, social networking sites offer a number of communication benefits for both business and personal application. For business, social networking allows another avenue for employees to maintain contact with clients, find new customers, establish training groups and more.

Perpetrators

When discussing the risks and threats of the Web and social networking, it's important to highlight the many different types of perpetrators involved. Each type has its own attack methods. Knowing what these perpetrators intend is the first step in preventing their attacks. Some common perpetrators include:

- **Scammers**—They can be found sending out fraudulent e-mails, trying to gather personal information or creating false business sites attempting to get credit card or other financial information. Scamming has become commonplace on the Web, and it has hurt people's confidence in online shopping.
- **Blackmailers**—Blackmailing takes many forms online. Often, blackmailers find personal information about a person online, then threaten to release that information if demands are not met. In a recent case, a blackmailer gathered information from a Facebook user's posts and threatened to tell the person's boss that the employee had faked sick days. Mitigating the risk of blackmail requires limiting the amount of personal information posted to the Web.

- **Sex offenders**—Unfortunately, many sex offenders use the Web to find victims. Sex offenders can use social networking sites, discussion boards, forums, chatrooms, and other public Web spaces to find their victims. It is critical to withhold personal information from anonymous Internet contacts. In public Web spaces, those who do mean to do harm are searching for vulnerable or unknowing people to take advantage of.

- **Cyberstalkers**—Cyberstalking and the electronic tracing of people has become a huge problem online. Many people don't even know that someone is tracking them.

- **Online bullies**—Cyberbullying online has unfortunately become increasingly common. Bullies track and harass other users, posting hateful messages either directly or in public forums. With a little personal information, bullies can trace the steps of people online and electronically harass them. In some cases, bullying is an extension of what happens in schools and workplaces. In other cases, bullying occurs as a result of broken relationships. Bullying online is a serious issue that can require police intervention. Most recently, legislation is being drafted and adopted to combat cyberbullying.

Keeping Your Private Data Secure

In one form or another, social networking is here to stay. Therefore, being able to network securely is crucial. Fortunately, it's not complicated for you to protect yourself and enjoy the experience by keeping these safety tips in mind:

- Review all security settings. Who can see your posts? Your pictures? Your updates? Security on these sites can often be complex, and failing to set security features, or setting them incorrectly, can have significant consequence. It is a best practice logging on with another account to test your social network site to verify what contents can be seen and by whom.

- Take the time to get to know a Web site's rules. Read the privacy policy, data retention policies, advertising policies, and anything else you find. There are always unexpected elements in policies, and you don't want to agree to anything before you understand it. Do you own your posts? Your pictures? What happens to the data if you disable or delete your account?

- Keep personal information to a minimum. This includes travel plans, work schedules, phone numbers, children's school information, and anything you think someone may be able to use against you. When it comes to social networking, an ounce of paranoia is never a bad thing.

- Make sure you actually know the people you add to your social networking sites. Keep in mind that sometimes the person wanting to friend you is not who he or she claims to be. It could be someone posing as a friend or colleague. This happens very frequently.

- Do your pictures reveal too much? Is there a license plate or your house number in the background? Pictures can be tricky, as they sometimes reveal more than intended. Take the extra time to consider your pictures' content before posting.

- Use strong passwords. Many passwords are too easy to guess and others can be obtained using simple social engineering strategies. A best practice is to use strong passwords that mix numbers and letters. Additionally, changing the password periodically is always a good idea.

- Check terms of use. Social networking sites will post these. The terms-of-use policy identifies what can be done with your pictures and other content. Who owns a picture once it's posted? It is very important to know what can be done with your data.

- Use and maintain antivirus software. This is one of the fundamental rules for online security. For this type of software to be effective, it must be kept current with updates.

- Be aware that today's smartphones and cameras can track when and where a picture was taken. Often this information, if posted with the picture, can reveal more than expected.

Common Social Network Scams

Like any other form of online activity, social networking has its share of scams and threats. Anyone who has used social networks has no doubt seen a variety of social engineering and phishing attacks. Most people are aware of the potential dangers and avoid unnecessary risk. The word of an attack often spreads quickly. However, as scams become increasingly complex, attacks become harder to avoid.

Here are some of the most popular scams to be aware of:

- **Chain letters**—You probably know the pitch: "Forward this letter and good things will happen." Many chain letters on Facebook are merely annoyances. But others can be phishing attacks or attempts by someone to acquire more "friends."

- **In-app purchases**—Many popular apps and games are in theory "free" but offer the possibility of what are known as *in-app purchases*. Players of certain games find that they advance more easily if they spend money—for instance, $25 for a barrel of Smurfberries for players of the popular Smurfs' Village. In the case of Apple devices, at least, no credit card is required, because the device is already connected with the iTunes store. Irate parents have discovered their children were racking up hundreds of dollars, in some cases, on in-app purchases. Apple responded with a software change that at least requires the device password to be reentered for an in-app purchases. Critics countered that too many parents share their device passwords with their children for the software change to be much help.

- **Clickjacking**—Some of the catchy headlines that appear on social networking sites are not what they appear. Following these links can lead to fake forms and downloads for malware. Inserting such links onto a page is known as **clickjacking**.

Recently, a cybercriminal was able to dupe an elderly woman out of $6,000 over the phone in a matter of minutes. He called her, claiming to be a lawyer representing her nephew, who she knew was traveling abroad. The supposed lawyer explained that the nephew had gotten into some difficulty at his destination and urgently needed his aunt to wire him a sum of money. It all seemed a little unusual to the woman, but the "lawyer" sounded legitimate and clearly knew a lot about the family. And so she immediately arranged to transfer the money—which ended up in the account of the cybercriminal, not the nephew.

The attack was possible because too much personal family information was available on two separate Facebook pages. The sites listed family members, including pictures of one who was traveling. So the cybercriminal was able to piece together a believable story involving the traveling family member. That's how easy it's to lose money to scams.

- **Fake friends**—At some point you may receive a friend request from someone who seems familiar or whose name you know. Sending fake friend requests and getting inside someone's social networking sites are often first steps in an attack.
- **Phishing attacks**—It is not uncommon for a link to a fake site be used to capture authentication credentials.

These are just a few of the attacks that appear on social networking sites everyday. Most of these can be managed with awareness and common sense. However, it's important to educate friends and family of the risks to ensure that everyone knows the threats and management strategies.

Online Gaming

Over the last few years, the popularity of online gaming has exploded and with it a new host of potential online security breaches. Online games and entertainment are hard to control from a security perspective, as software publishers are continually offering (legitimate) updates and modifications to games that can be downloaded to enhance play. It is possible for malware to hide in these gaming updates, as many children are not thinking about security when viewing an link promising spectacular game enhancements.

Not all threats from games are from software or malware. Many online games offer a chat feature, and while the majority of those chatting are simply fellow game players, some are malicious users intent on gathering personal data. Online predators are one of the risks of online gaming chatrooms, forums, instant messages (IMs), and discussion groups. The anonymity of the Internet allows predators to troll the Internet looking for unsuspecting victims. Young adults and children are at particular risk from these predators.

3

Security Considerations
for Home/Personal Use

Typically, predators initiate contact with their victims by misrepresenting themselves as peers or understanding adults to develop relationships. As the relationship builds, the predator gains and then exploits the trust of the victim. Often the predator will try to get personal information from the victim or engage in sexually explicit conversation. Many countries have laws pertaining to the luring of children online. Prosecution can be difficult, however, and often the best defense is educating children about the dangers.

Securing online games can be difficult, as it's hard to monitor game play all of the time. To make game play in the home more secure, consider the following:

- Use a dedicated computer system for gaming. In this way, if the system is compromised by the latest Minecraft mod, banking credentials or other private data will not be exposed.
- Verify all game-related downloads. Many links offer enhanced features, invulnerability, and other fun modifications. If these mods are not sanctioned by the game developer, they can pose a serious risk.
- Keep the virus definitions of your antivirus software up to date on the gaming system. Out-of-date virus definitions may fail to protect you from a virus.
- Educate all users on the privacy risks associated with online gaming and the dangers of divulging personal information on game chats.
- Pick a game alias that does not identify you in any way.
- Do not use the same passwords when playing online as you use on other sites such as social networking or banking.
- Keep the game software patched and up to date.

Protecting Against E-mail Scams

E-mail remains perhaps the most convenient and effective method of personal and business communication. Not only does e-mail provide an easy way to contact and keep in touch with friends, colleagues, and clients, it also lets you save and archive content for future reference.

E-mail communication will continue to have personal and business applications, but it will bring with it a significant level of risk. These risks are not only from the outside but also from employees, who may either maliciously or unintentionally release sensitive information. Despite all of the risks associated with e-mail, there are no tools poised to replace it, so security remains a critical consideration.

To reach e-mail security, you need a combination of policies and procedures. *Policy* refers to the documented practices that outline acceptable e-mail usage. The function of these polices is to prevent the misuse of e-mail by employees and to educate the user to help prevent e-mail scams. *Procedures* such as firewalls, security protocols, and physical security measures are used to help secure e-mail communication.

It is important to remember that these procedures are put into practice because of the unrelenting attacks on e-mail communications. Many companies go as far as monitoring all outbound as well as inbound mail. The reason is not necessarily to check up on employees but to ensure the integrity and confidentiality of corporate information.

There are many different types of e-mail scams. Some are designed to steal information, others are hoaxes, and some carry malware. A great many others are simply annoying. Corporate environments use e-mail filtering software to help detect and reject e-mail threats and spam. To a lesser extent, many Internet service providers offer the same sort of feature to household customers.

Despite these efforts, e-mail scams have a way of sometimes getting through, including the following:

- E-mail suggesting monetary windfalls
- False giveaway e-mails
- Charity contribution e-mail hoaxes
- "Sudden emergency" e-mails
- E-mails warning of false virus claims and solutions
- E-mail petitions and protests
- E-mail chain letters

E-mail scams are an ever-present concern. For the best defense, monitor e-mails carefully, don't reply to suspicious ones, don't click links, and don't open unknown attachments.

The OWASP Top 10 Privacy Risks Project

One of the more critical exposure areas for home users is that of data leakage and privacy.

The Open Web Application Security Project (OWASP) is a global not-for-profit community of companies, people, and educational centers. It reviews top security threats and publishes those findings online. One of the threat areas regularly reviewed is the top 10 threats to online privacy. This section explores the top 10 list and highlights what these threats may mean for protecting personal privacy.

> **NOTE**
> The evolution of e-mail security is leading to more intrusion on employee e-mail privacy. Policies are becoming more rigid to better protect the company from e-mail scams.

> **TIP**
> To help manage e-mail scams, use technology such as e-mail filtering and vetting software to screen out phishing attacks and e-mails that spread malware. For both personal and business use, be very careful when using e-mail to convey sensitive and confidential information. It is a best practice to follow up on the e-mail to ensure it's in the right place.

> **WARNING**
> Never submit confidential information via forms embedded within e-mail messages.

> **NOTE**
> Not only you, but everyone in the household should be familiar with the OWASP top 10 list. It raises awareness, which should motivate everyone to adopt best practices for maintaining online privacy.

3

Security Considerations
for Home/Personal Use

1. Web Application Vulnerabilities

Everyone uses a variety of applications every day. These range from Word processors, Internet browsers, virus scanners, and games, to Web apps and much more. You must maintain and update all the programs you use. Security flaws are often discovered in applications, and unless these programs are patched and updated, cybercriminals can take advantage of these flaws. **Web application vulnerabilities** are data leaks resulting from out-of-date or unpatched applications. To prevent this, it's a good idea to keep a list of the programs you use and then check the vendor's Web site regularly for updates. Further, in a home environment, it's good to use automatic updates to keep your applications patched and current.

2. Operator-Sided Data Leakage

There are many people online trying to get to your personal data. Often they don't need to try to hard if you are leaking your own data. **Operator-sided data leakage** refers to the accidental or neglectful release of personal information. Often operators (including individual users like you) do this by unknowingly sharing personal information with malicious users. They may divulge too much on a social networking site or perhaps on an online dating site. The trick to preventing this is to have a clear understanding of which data is sensitive and then safeguard that data.

3. Insufficient Data Breach Response

If you discover your home computer has, or probably has, been hacked, you should assume there might be a data breach. Your data and that of other users might be compromised. The responsible reaction is to inform other users of that computer. You should also help them recover from the data breach. **Insufficient data breach response** refers to the risk you run if you fail to take these steps.

4. Insufficient Deletion of Personal Data

Knowing where your sensitive data is at any given time is important to be able to manage it. Is your personal data stored on an old hard disk, on a backup tape, in an online Web form, social network site, cached online? It is important to know where sensitive data is in order to properly delete and remove it from potential threat. If there are multiple computers in a household, there may be personal data on multiple systems if they have been used to access social networks or bank accounts, or to chat online. **Insufficient deletion of personal data** refers to failure to remove sensitive data after its intended purpose has ended.

5. Non-transparent Policies, Terms, and Conditions

All Web sites that allow input of data and online forms and collect personal information should have clear policies that outline how data will be used, stored, and retained. Often these policies make clear that your information may be shared with a third party. By signing up, you agree to this policy. Social networking sites, online dating sites, banks, investment sites, and online shops will typically have policies and terms and conditions. Often these will be available on a site. It's very rare that people will actually read these lengthy policies, though, since the actual document will be difficult to read and understand. This is the risk known as **non-transparent policies, terms and conditions**. Be careful, read the fine print, and make sure you know what you are signing up for before going onto a site and posting personal information. It is very common for people to freely give information without really knowing what can be done with their data.

6. Collection of Data Not Required for the Primary Purpose

Suppose you list your graduation date on a social networking site, or the ages of your children or their gender: All these types of data can be used to create demographic information. You may not have intended for data to be used this way, but companies can put all of this data together to form a profile and use this to target advertising or other initiatives based in the data you provided. You may be giving out personal data for one purpose, such as finding a partner online. The site, though, is using it for another reason. This is the risk known as **collection of data not required for the primary purpose**. Targeted advertising works by developing demographic profiles based on users' browsing habits and history. The ads are then matched to these profiles. Advertisers are always looking for your personal data. Do they have it? Next time you are online at a social networking site, check to see if the ads match your surfing history or are targeted to you in any way.

7. Sharing of Data with Third Party

One of the common issues with providing personal information online is the **sharing of data with a third party**. Some sites will share with another company for money the data you assume will be kept private. Other sites openly state that they reserve the right to share your data with a third party. There is a very active online market for personal data and information. This information is used primarily for advertising.

8. Outdated Personal Data

Back in 2010, a case was before the courts in which Google was being asked to remove **outdated personal data** from search engine results. The case was initiated by a Spanish man whose was name published in a newspaper in 1998 as the owner of a property to be auctioned off because of debts. This history followed him to 2014 in the Google search results. The man was trying to convince the courts that outdated personal information could be harmful to his reputation and a breach of privacy.

After years of court battles, the summary conclusion was that under European Union law, an Internet search engine operator "is responsible for the processing that it carries out of personal data which appear on its Web pages"—including material that has already been published in the media.

"This information potentially concerns a vast number of aspects of [an individual's] private life," the court wrote, adding, "Internet users may thereby establish a more or less detailed profile of the person searched against." This interferes with a person's fundamental rights, the court found, adding that people should be able to request the removal of links to "inadequate, irrelevant or no longer relevant" information.

This case brings up interesting concerns and some significant privacy issues. Is it possible in the information age to escape your past decisions, and how could this impact your life in the future? What if an employer, spouse, or child finds outdated personal information cached online? It is a serious threat to an individual's privacy and one difficult to fix.

9. Missing or Insufficient Session Expiration

Many people access social networking, financial, or other sensitive sites from public computers or shared computers at work or in the home. Privacy issues arise when their sessions on these sites are not properly closed or discontinued. That is, users need to log off and ensure that passwords and usernames are not stored in auto-fill forms. This is the risk known as **missing or insufficient session expiration**. In the past, a simple and effective cybercriminal attack involved people lurking at local libraries or other public computer sites and setting the browsers to remember credentials. Criminals would wait until legitimate users left and then simply use the auto-filled usernames and passwords those users left behind to access various sites.

10. Unsecure Data Transfer

Private and personal data travels over networks all the time to and from thousands of Web sites and millions of homes. Much of the data is sent over secure networks using encryption protocols and secure links. However, data continues to be sent over unsecured public wireless networks. **Unsecure data transfer** is a serious threat to online privacy but one that can be managed.

If nothing else from this chapter, it's important to understand the top 10 threats to your data privacy—not only for you, but for everyone in your household. Understanding these threats will go a long way toward protecting your privacy and the privacy of your friends and family.

CHAPTER SUMMARY

Maintaining the confidentiality and integrity of personal data in the information age is very difficult. Cyber criminals have a range of attacks designed to acquire your personal information. Social engineering attacks, including phishing, are increasing both in frequency and complexity. Even seasoned IT professionals are falling victim to the new range of attacks. Once a social engineering attack is successful, users may fall victim to identify theft, which in turn may result in a privacy breach and perhaps a loss of money and reputation. Multiple scams involving social networks and e-mail also threaten the unwary user.

OWASP outlines the top 10 online threats to privacy. Understanding these threats and ways to mitigate then is essential to protecting your privacy online. To successfully conduct transactions securely online, such as shopping, banking, gaming and more, you must understand the potential threats inherent in each of these activities. Maintaining security online means that all users must familiarize themselves with security policies, protocols, and best practices.

KEY CONCEPTS AND TERMS

Clickjacking

Collection of data not required for the primary purpose

Cookie

Hypertext Transfer Protocol (HTTP)

Hypertext Transfer Protocol Secure (HTTPS)

Insufficient data breach response

Insufficient deletion of personal data

Malware

Missing or insufficient session expiration

Non-transparent policies, terms and conditions

Operator-sided data leakage

Outdated personal data

Pretexting

Ransomware

Sharing of data with third party

Social engineering

Unsecure data transfer

Web application vulnerabilities

CHAPTER 3 ASSESSMENT

1. Missing or insufficient session information is no longer a privacy concern with modern browsers.

   A. True
   B. False

2. Kathleen is an avid user of social networking sites. She continues to post detailed information about upcoming trips, personal photos showing children, and her phone number and contact information. Which of the following OWASP privacy threats refers to her situation?

   A. Operator-sided data leakage
   B. Web application vulnerabilities
   C. Outdated personal information
   D. Insecure data transfer

3. Small files containing information you enter on some Web pages, including username and password combinations, are called which of the following?

   A. Malware
   B. Phishing
   C. Cookies
   D. Viruses

4. Anita has recently logged on a shopping site to purchase a new bicycle and bike shorts. She is concerned that the communication link is not secure. Which of the following could she check to verify a secure link?

   A. Contact the vendor via e-mail for a purchase policy
   B. Verify that HTTPS is being used in the URL
   C. Verify that HTTP is being used in the URL
   D. Uncheck the auto-fill option in the browser

5. Which of the following can be used in a social engineering attack? (Select three.)

   A. Dumpster diving
   B. Shoulder surfing
   C. Trojan horse
   D. Persuasion

6. Marco is using a public computer in an Internet café to update personal information. Which of the following are steps he can take to ensure his privacy? (Select two.)

   A. Ensure no one is shoulder surfing
   B. Bookmark the site for faster retrieval
   C. Erase the browser history when finished
   D. Make sure auto-fill is enabled

7. Banking online on a public wireless network is secure if a modern browser is used and if a strong username and password combination is used.

   A. True
   B. False

8. Mary recently received an e-mail that included a link to reset her PayPal password. This is likely a form of which of the following?

   A. Malware
   B. Phishing
   C. Cookies
   D. Insecure networks

9. Joe has recently discovered that all of the files and folders on his laptop are encrypted. He is a victim of a ransomware attack. Which is the best way for Joe to get access to his files?

   A. Pay for the decryption key.
   B. Hire tech support to create a decryption key.
   C. Format, reinstall, and use backups.
   D. Buy a new laptop.

10. Mimic sites are examples of which of the following?

    A. Phishing attacks
    B. E-commerce scams
    C. Malware
    D. Cookies

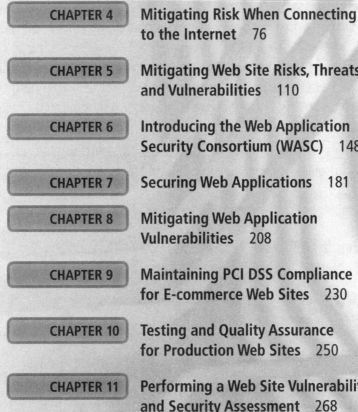

© Rodolfo Clix/Dreamstime.com

PART TWO

Secure Web-Enabled Application Deployment and Social Networking

© Rodolfo Clix/Dreamstime.com

CHAPTER
4

Mitigating Risk When Connecting to the Internet

I N JUST A FEW YEARS the Internet and the use of online resources have become an integral part of daily life for almost everyone, it seems. Many businesses are so dependent on the Internet that they would actually cease to exist without it. In addition to business, individual users rely on the Internet as an essential communication, information, and educational tool. For many people, it would be hard to imagine life without online access at their fingertips.

Dependence on the Internet and its services, however, does leave people somewhat vulnerable. The Internet is an insecure public network. While the majority use the Internet each day for legitimate purposes, a significant few use it every day for cybercrime, bullying, cyberstalking, data theft, and other nefarious activities. Some of these malicious users are random groups of opportunists looking to take advantage of any weakness on a small scale, while others are massive coordinated collectives looking to perpetrate significant crippling security attacks against large organizations and even countries. Expanding use of the Internet also means that online crime is growing in scope and complexity. Those using the Internet—and that is just about everyone—must take steps to mitigate the risks.

This chapter explores the Internet's risks and threats, along with the policies and procedures that can mitigate those risks.

Chapter 4 Topics

This chapter covers the following topics and concepts:

- Which threats exist when connecting to the Internet
- What Web site hosting is
- What the seven domains of a typical IT infrastructure are
- How to protect networks in the LAN-to-WAN Domain
- What best practices for connecting to the Internet are

Chapter 4 Goals

When you complete this chapter, you will be able to:

- Identify the common Internet risks and strategies to mitigate those risks
- Review common network vulnerabilities
- Understand the options for Web hosting
- Understand the function of DNS
- Identify features of perimeter security
- Identify common ports and their function
- Review the features of firewalls and identify the role of IDS and IPS systems
- Understand the purpose of a proxy server
- Review some best practices for connecting to the Internet

Threats When Connecting to the Internet

The Internet is an insecure and unregulated environment. Those who connect to the Internet without taking steps to secure their connection and who lack a fundamental understanding of common Internet risks expose themselves to danger. This danger can take the form of viruses, data theft, identity theft, cyberbullying, phishing, or other attacks.

Many users ignore security, believing that their computers hold no interesting information and therefore are not targets. This is untrue. Unguarded systems can be turned into zombie computers and, under the control of remote users, can be used to stage attacks against other systems or as repositories for offensive content. There is no way to avoid it; today's Internet users must understand the risks of connecting to the Internet and take appropriate steps to mitigate those risks.

Risks and Threats

As a public network, the Internet is full of risks. Some of these risks are easily removed with virus checking and software updates, but others are difficult and even impossible to predict and manage. Some security risks and threats are aimed at data and privacy, others at availability. Threats to data target application vulnerabilities, unsecured protocols, fraudulent e-mails, and poor Internet practices. Availability threats are due to bandwidth overuse, denial of service attacks, and hardware malfunctions. These threats aimed at both data and availability are just a sample of what network users are up against.

There are several categories of risks on the Internet; some are mitigated using software, others with secure protocols or common sense and policies:

- Hackers or malware (viruses, Trojan horses, worms)
- Personal attacks (harassment, fraud, identity theft, data theft)
- Offensive and inappropriate material
- E-mail attacks (phishing, spam, e-mail viruses)
- Predators

Hackers and Malware

The term **hacker** is commonly associated with cybercriminals who attack and exploit weaknesses in systems. This is not completely accurate. Historically, hackers are programmers who spend hours tampering with programs and applications, trying to figure out how they work. They don't mean or intend any harm to users or systems. Hackers often make programs better. A **cracker**, on the other hand, tries to gain access to computer systems or applications for illegal purposes. Today, *hackers* is the accepted term for those who attempt to harm computers, users, or software. The term *crackers* has largely fallen out of favor.

Hackers can harm or gain unauthorized access to a computer system or network in several ways. These methods include:

- Targeting and exploiting known vulnerabilities in software applications
- Installing and using malware
- Exploiting poorly managed networks where security protocols are not used or incorrectly applied
- Abusing people's trust through social engineering or identity theft

Types of Malware

Malicious software, or malware, is a serious problem. It's often assumed that malware means only viruses. There are many other forms of malware that are not viruses but are equally undesirable.

Different types of malicious software include the following:

Viruses. These are programs or pieces of code that are surreptitiously loaded onto your computer without your knowledge and performs undesirable actions on the system. Viruses are a constant threat on the Internet. The damage from viruses varies greatly, from damaging applications on a single system to disabling an entire network. Regardless of the impact, viruses can be very destructive, causing irreplaceable loss of information and hours of productivity.

Viruses have been with us almost as long as computers have existed. Like any other part of the IT industry, viruses have evolved and today are sophisticated, difficult to detect and very dangerous. To be considered a virus, the malware must possess the following characteristics:

- A virus must be able to replicate itself.
- All viruses require a host program as a carrier.
- Viruses must be activated or executed in order to run.

An important category of virus to be alert to is the **macro virus**, designed to infect, corrupt, and damage file formats that employ macros, such as Microsoft Office documents. To help minimize the impact and spread of viruses, use trusted antivirus software and a firewall configured for filtering. Since new viruses are generated every day, software of this nature is not foolproof, but it will reduce the risk of contaminating your computer.

Worms. These are programs designed to propagate automatically and silently, without modifying software or alerting the user. Once inside a system, they can carry out their intended harm, such as damaging data, embedding malware, or relaying sensitive information. The malware known as a **worm** is different from viruses and has the potential to spread faster than any other form of malware. Worms are similar to viruses in that they are able to replicate. However, worms don't require a host or user intervention to propagate. Worms spread at an alarming rate because they exploit security holes in applications or operating systems and automatically replicate and spread, looking for new hosts with the same vulnerability.

Properly configured firewalls and up-to-date antivirus programs are essential to protect against worms. In addition, you should take care when opening unknown applications and e-mail.

Trojan horses. These are designed to trick the user into installing them. Trojan horses appear as helpful or harmless programs but when installed carry and deliver a malicious payload. By definition, a Trojan horse program installs a *backdoor* or opportunity for unauthorized access. The backdoor is typically for communication from a hacker but could also be used to install additional malware. Just like the wooden horse of Greek mythology, Trojan horse malware is all about hiding. A **Trojan horse** comes hidden in a program, for example, in a shareware game. The game looks harmless, but when downloaded and executed, the Trojan operates in the background, altering or damaging the system.

A Trojan horse is different from a virus in that a Trojan horse does not replicate itself and does not require a host program to run. The main purpose of a Trojan horse is to install backdoors. The Trojan horse may send a small message to a controller to alert it to successful installation of the backdoor.

Trojan horses are most easily spread by being embedded in files on P2P sharing networks. Trojan horses also spread through the sharing of such programs using e-mail communications or removable media. In the past, many of the executable jokes sent through e-mail, such as cartoons and amusing games, were the front end of a Trojan horse.

4

**Connecting
to the Internet**

Malware or Annoyance?

Not every unwanted program that passes between computer systems is malware. Some of it is annoying but not designed to steal or corrupt information. However, such programs can and do tie up system resources, frustrating users and making the system difficult to use. Items that fall into the category of annoying software that's not necessarily malware include malware hoaxes, phishing, and spam:

- **Malware hoaxes**— A **malware hoax** preys upon the fear of malware. Basically, malware hoaxes are illegitimate announcements of new malware. A user receives an e-mail, for example, claiming that a new malware type has been released and the user has to perform some action to prevent the impending threat. This is a type of social engineering in that it attempts to trick a user into performing an action. If users perform the action, they may inadvertently damage or otherwise corrupt their own systems. In addition, hoaxes can waste administrator and user time and tie up resources and network bandwidth.

- **Phishing**—This is a form of social engineering. A message appears to come from a reputable, trusted source, such as a bank or system administrator. Users are tricked into divulging personal information, such as credit card numbers, bank account information, or credentials. This unsolicited e-mail is referred to as *phishing* (wordplay on "fishing"). Basically, someone sends a bogus offering to hundreds of thousands of e-mail addresses. The strategy plays the odds: For every 1,000 e-mails sent, perhaps one person replies.

- **Spam**—Spam has become one of the biggest nuisances of e-mail communication, frustrating users and administrators. Spam is messages—typically ads—sent en masse to e-mail addresses. Spam pollutes your e-mail inbox, causing a loss in productivity. Another problem stems from e-mail filtering, a countermeasure intended to stop spam. Some legitimate e-mails are filtered out by mistake and never read.

- **Adware**—In software applications called **adware**, advertising banners or pop-up ads are displayed while a program is running or a Web page is visited. Many types of adware track your Web browsing habits and report your behavior back to the adware sponsor. This data helps the company create more targeted marketing campaigns. The justification for adware is that it helps recover programming development costs and helps to hold down the cost of applications for the user. The disadvantages are that the ads continue to display until the application ceases, or until you close the ad's window. You typically also experience a slower system.

Spyware. **Spyware** is software that gathers system information through the user's Internet connection without his or her knowledge, usually for advertising purposes. Spyware applications are typically bundled as a hidden component of freeware or shareware programs that can be downloaded from the Internet.

Ways to Spread Malware

In order to be effective, malware requires a method to get from one computer to another. The Internet provides a great mechanism for malware to spread. Some of the common malware delivery types include:

- **Peer-to-peer (P2P) sharing networks**—P2P sharing networks have become very popular and are widely used to download everything from music to games and applications. The problem is that many of the applications and downloads carry malware.

- **Network shares**—A network share is a file, folder, or resource that is made available to the network. Malware can use network shares to propagate itself from system to system over the network. Poorly implemented security on network shares allows malware to replicate to a large number of computers connected to the network.

- **E-mail**—One of the most widely exploited technologies is e-mail. With the click of a button, malware can be sent to hundreds of thousands of users. Most malware attacks through e-mail require the recipient to activate the attack either by opening an e-mail or downloading something from the e-mail, assuming it's from a trusted source.

- **Web browsing**—Not all Web site administrators are equally prepared to protect against the above threats. If a Web site or a component of a Web site is compromised, malware may spread to all subsequent visitors of the site.

These are some examples of how malware can be transported from system to system. Those who write and export malware are always thinking of new ways to transport their software, such as through instant messaging (IM) and social networking. Keeping track of new and existing transport mechanisms is a key part of securing the network.

To protect your network from hackers and to prevent malware from harming a system, it's important to ensure that your software is up to date and all patches and service packs have been installed. This helps prevent hackers from taking advantage of vulnerabilities in the software. You also must ensure that trusted antivirus software is installed and up to date.

Table 4-1 compares various forms of malware.

4

Connecting
to the Internet

TABLE 4-1 Types of malware.

MALWARE TYPE	REPLICATE	HOST REQUIRED	USER INTERVENTION REQUIRED
Virus	Able to self-replicate	Needs a host program to propagate	Needs to be activated or executed by a user
Trojan Horse	Does not replicate itself	Does not need a host program	User must execute program in which the Trojan horse is hidden
Worms	Self-replicate without user intervention	Self-contained and does not need a host	Replicates and activates without requiring user intervention

Personal Attacks

Many online attacks seek to obtain personal information that can be used for identity theft, stealing data, harassment, and much more. Protecting against personal attacks and attempts at data theft are often more about personal browsing best practices than technical solutions. Personal attacks are battled best with skepticism and caveat emptor ("let the buyer beware").

Fraud. E-commerce is prevalent on the Internet and so are those who use e-commerce to defraud. Many sales and auction sites are legitimate businesses. Unfortunately, it's not always easy to tell the good from the bad. E-commerce fraud is a growing problem with losses measured in the hundreds of millions of dollars. Online fraud causes not only monetary loss but also an atmosphere of fear about online purchasing.

Combating fraud requires education and knowing what to look out for. Well-designed e-commerce sites incorporate trust elements to help build buyers' confidence. E-commerce trust elements include:

- **Client privacy agreement**—Before giving personal information to a Web site, review its policy for client privacy. The **client privacy agreement** outlines what can and cannot be done with your personal data. It's a contract between you and the site. The agreement often outlines how your personal data will be stored and for how long. It may also describe how and whether it will be shared. This is an important consideration.

- **Trust icons and logos**—These are used to associate a Web site with a known and trusted site. Examples of trust icons and logos are an icon for Secure Sockets Layer (SSL), which shows secure protocols are being used, an icon for the Better Business Bureau, icons or logos associated with trusted anti-malware companies. There are terms of use for displaying a logo and icon, but if a site qualifies, it can build trust. Of course, a fraudulent site also may display such logos to build trust. A wise buyer will exercise skepticism.

- **Customer comments and testimonials**—Customer comments and testimonials are a great way to build visitor trust.
- **Contact Us form**—An e-commerce site should display a way to contact the company for assistance. An e-mail should be provided at a minimum. A telephone number and address also provide assurance.
- **About Us page**—The About Us page of a Web site showcases the company. If you're purchasing online, it's a good idea to read about the company and its policies.
- **Return policy**—All e-commerce sites should display a return policy. Reputable companies offer a return policy or guarantee that fosters confidence.

If you are concerned about online fraud, pay close attention to the elements listed above. Legitimate e-commerce sites take the time to build customer trust and make the site look and feel legitimate. If you suspect a site, move on.

Harassment and cyberstalking. E-mail, IM, and social networking are designed to make it easy to stay in touch with colleagues and friends. Unfortunately, they also make it easy to harass or stalk someone online. **Cyberstalking** refers to repeated electronic communication with someone who does not desire the communication. It causes distress. Cyberstalking is a form of harassment. With more people using social networking sites, incidents of cyberstalking are increasing.

> **NOTE**
> Many technologies that facilitate cyberstalking are fairly new, and laws are slow to catch up to protect users. Many of the laws for offline stalking don't apply to online cyberstalking.

Cyberstalking and online harassment come in many forms. These include repeated offensive e-mails, tracking on social networking sites, IM spamming, tracking others on virtual sites, impersonating trusted friends or colleagues, constantly signing someone up for newsletters, creating online groups and forums that reflect negatively on someone, creating hate sites about someone, and creating fake sex ads. Harassment also can be done via mobile phones and handheld devices, so it can be a significant issue.

Preventing cyberstalking and harassment is not easy. Some harassment and cyberstalking tips include:

- Don't give out personal information except to a known contact.
- Use filtering features in e-mail and firewalls to block contacts from the harasser.
- Contact the police if it becomes a serious problem.
- Stop all communication with the harasser.
- Block the cyberstalker from social networking sites and only add trusted friends.

Identity theft. One of the fastest growing crimes is that of **identify theft**. Identity theft goes beyond fraud by assuming someone's entire identity. This is done by obtaining personal information, such as Social Security number, driver's license, passport, and credit card numbers. There are many ways a criminal can get personal information: dumpster diving, e-mail phishing, discarded hard disks, and spyware, to name a few.

Protecting against identity theft online involves exerting extreme care over whose personal information is given to whom and why. If buying online, be sure to verify the site's terms-of-use policy that identifies how personal data will be used and stored. Look for companies that encrypt data while in storage and offer safe disposal procedures.

E-mail Attacks

E-mail is an essential tool for business and has become the primary business communication medium. E-mail provides a fast, cheap, reliable universal method of global communication. While e-mail has opened worldwide communication, it has also brought a range of security concerns because it provides a gateway directly into the network through the network's users.

Preventing e-mail attacks and disruption require both technical and non-technical methods. Non-technical methods include not opening unsolicited e-mail, not opening unwanted attachments, not sending personal information that could be used against you, not giving your e-mail address to everyone who asks, not replying to spam, and not forwarding chain letters.

For technical solutions, use up-to-date virus scanners that check incoming and outgoing e-mails. Many companies also use **e-mail filtering** software, which performs the following:

- **E-mail tracking**—Administrators track the e-mail habits of network users, including whether attachments are sent and how often and to whom e-mails are sent.

- **Keyword filtering**—It's possible to provide network wide e-mail vetting. E-mail vetting software searches through e-mails using a list of keywords. Once the software finds a matching keyword, the software sends an alert to the administrator.

- **Legal disclaimer**—Besides searching for and quarantining e-mails with offensive words and phrases, e-mail-filtering programs allow an organization to add disclaimers to outbound e-mails. The intent of the disclaimer is to reduce liability. While a company is ultimately responsible for the actions of its employees, the disclaimer shows that the employees are bound by e-mail policy.

- **E-mail blocking**—E-mail filtering software can block both internal and external e-mails based on e-mail policy. A message may be blocked due to undesired content, including e-cards, gambling, and chain letters. Also, a message may be blocked due to unauthorized attachments, such as video and sound types, visual basic attachments, and executable files. With keyword-matching, the software can actively block e-mail from being sent to an intended recipient. For example, a company may wish to prevent its new sales strategy from being shared outside the company. E-mail filtering would not guarantee it, but it could block e-mails that contain the sales strategy as well as send an alert that someone attempted to send it.

- **Message priority**—Non-essential e-mails with large attachments can quickly tie up network resources. In response, e-mail filtering software can flag such messages and either block them altogether or mark them to be sent in non-peak network hours. This saves significant bandwidth.

- **Message archiving**—Increasingly, government regulations dictate that e-mail messages be retained as a record of an organization's e-mail communications. E-mail software programs allow archiving to easily retain copies of e-mails in a centralized and secure location.

Managing Online Risks and Threats

Reviewing the risks and threats of the Internet can seem overwhelming, but there are some common strategies that help mitigate online risks. These include:

- Keep applications and operating systems updated.
- Use trusted antivirus/antispyware applications. Ensure the applications are up to date.
- Protect portable devices such as cell phones, personal digital assistants (PDAs), and portable PCs.
- Password protect and encrypt data on the laptop. Should it be stolen, it can't be read.
- Secure the wireless access point.
- Use perimeter protection, such as firewalls, intrusion detection systems, and intrusion prevention systems.
- Encrypt data to ensure integrity and confidentiality.

Vulnerabilities and Exploits

Historically and even today, software developers create many applications and protocols with security as only a secondary consideration. Equally, network and system hardware are vulnerable by default. If not carefully managed, both hardware and software are easily exploited. In addition, regular users also present risk. Administrators and users should be aware of:

- **End-user vulnerabilities**—End users can be vulnerable if they are not educated in company policies and best use practices. Many companies offer employees security training to help mitigate breaches. With a little education and a better understanding of the risks, end users are less likely to open a network to potential threat.

- **Security vulnerabilities**—Many organizations don't use network perimeter security measures. If they do, some organizations don't ensure that security measures are properly configured. Network firewalls, for example, are useful only if properly configured.

- **Port vulnerabilities**—Your computer and operating system has 65,535 ports. These ports operate like windows or doors that allow access to the system. By default, most ports are left open, "listening" and ready to receive communication. These open ports may be exploited and should be shut. A firewall closes all the doors you don't need, thus minimizing the chances of a hacker entering.

> **▶ NOTE**
> You'll learn about port vulnerabilities in more detail in the "Port 80: Open or Closed?" section later in this chapter.

4

Connecting to the Internet

- **Software vulnerabilities**—Many software packages, from applications to operating systems software, can be exploited due to vulnerabilities in the software. All software must be monitored and upgraded when vulnerabilities are discovered and a patch is available.

- **Malware vulnerabilities**—Malware is an ever-present threat. Today, systems require anti-malware applications. Malware applications require maintenance and constant updates to address new threats.

In many cases, vulnerabilities are a result of inadequate policies and procedures. It's no secret that the Internet is dangerous, yet many home users and network administrators don't adequately prepare for the risks. Attacks are growing in both frequency and complexity. Systems left unsecured will at some point be attacked. At the time of this writing, an unsecured system put on the Internet takes between 15 to 30 seconds before becoming infected or compromised.

> **TIP**
>
> As a best practice, consider visiting the vendors' Web sites of your applications periodically. If you use Microsoft products, for example, check periodically for news on new patches and security threats. In addition, it's best to leave automatic updates on to keep your system as current as possible.

Perpetrators

Thousands of people wake up each day and go online for no other purpose than to commit cybercrimes. These can range from an ex-partner trying to stalk someone online to cyberterrorists aiming to down the power grid or disrupt the Internet's economic structure. Many people don't consider that when they are checking Facebook, there is a cyberwar going on. Internet perpetrators may include:

- Sexual predators
- Cyberterrorists
- Cyberstalkers
- Identity thieves
- Data thieves
- Malware developers and distributors
- E-mail spammers

There are specific measures designed to mitigate the actions of each of these perpetrators. The types of attacks these predators may use are included in the following sections.

Common Perpetrator Attacks

The following list is a sample of attacks that perpetrators may use:

- **Password attacks**—One of the most common types of attacks involves passwords. Usernames are easy enough to obtain or guess. If an attacker can get the user's password as well, the intruder can gain the level of system access associated with that user. This is why protecting administrator passwords is so important. A password with administrator privileges provides an intruder with total unrestricted access to the system or network.

- **Cyberstalking**—Cyberstalking and the electronic tracking of people has become a huge problem online. Many people don't even know that someone is tracking them through social networking or other means.

- **Social engineering**—It can be used both by outsiders and by people within an organization. Social engineering is a hacker term for tricking people into revealing their passwords or other privileged information. This includes trying to get users to send passwords or other information over e-mail, shoulder surfing, or other tricks. Social engineering takes advantage of people's natural tendency to be helpful.

- **Eavesdropping**—As it sounds, eavesdropping involves an intruder trying to obtain sensitive information, such as passwords, data, and procedures for performing functions, by intercepting, listening and analyzing network communications. An intruder can eavesdrop by wiretapping, using radio, or using auxiliary ports on terminals. It's also possible to eavesdrop using software that monitors packets sent over the network. In most cases, it's difficult to detect eavesdropping but fairly easy to stop. Using secure communication such as encryption assures important and sensitive data is not sent over the network in clear text.

- **Backdoor attacks**—A backdoor attack refers to the ability to gain access to a computer or program that bypasses standard security mechanisms. Many malware applications can create backdoor access to a system. This is the method of a Trojan horse program.

> **NOTE**
> Wireless communications are particularly susceptible to man-in-the-middle attacks. Key to preventing this type of attack is encrypting data while in transmission using protocols such as Internet Protocol Security (IPSec) or SSL.

- **Man-in-the-middle attack**—In a man-in-the-middle attack, the intruder places himself between the sending and receiving devices and captures communication as it passes by. The interception of the data is invisible to those sending and receiving data. The intruder is able to capture the network data and manipulate it, change it, examine it, and then send it on.

- **Spoofing**—In spoofing, the attacker fakes the real source of a transmission, file, or e-mail. This strategy enables the attacker to misrepresent the origin of a file in order to trick users into accepting a file download from an untrusted source, believing it came from a trusted source.

- **Dictionary attack**—Most of the passwords used today are chosen because they are easy to remember. This leaves them open to a dictionary attack. In this type of attack, a program scans through the entries in a dictionary data file, attempting to guess a password. This attack type is ineffective where password policies require inclusion of numbers and symbols in passwords.

- **Brute-force attack**—A brute-force attack attempts to crack a cryptographic key or password with little to no knowledge or advantage. It involves programs designed to guess at every possible combination until the password or key is cracked. Of course, the more complex a password is, the harder it is to crack and the less likely a brute-force attack will be successful.

4

Connecting
to the Internet

Denial of Service (DoS) Attacks

DoS attacks focus on key areas including network bandwidth, memory, CPU time, and hard-drive space. They are designed to overwhelm a resource until it becomes unavailable. The threat is against availability—with a resource overloaded, it becomes unusable. Types of DoS attacks include:

- **Ping flood**—A ping request packet is sent to a broadcast network address where there are many hosts. The source address is shown in the packet to be the Internet Protocol (IP) address of the computer to be attacked. If the router to the network passes the ping broadcast, all computers on the network will respond with a ping reply to the system. The attacked system will be flooded with ping responses which will cause it to be unable to operate on the network for some time and may cause it to lock up.

- **Fraggle**—A Fraggle attack sends spoofed User Datagram Protocol packets to a network's broadcast address. These packets are directed to specific ports such as port 7 or port 19. Once connected, the packets flood the system.

- **Smurf**—A Smurf attack is similar to Fraggle except that an attacker sends a ping request to a broadcast network address with the sending address spoofed, prompting many ping replies to the victim. This will overload the victim's ability to process the replies.

- **Distributed denial of service (DDoS)**—DDoS attacks involve a coordinated attack from hundreds or thousands of computers across the Internet. An attacker first breaks in, installs DDoS software and gains control. The attacker can then control all of these computers and launch coordinated attacks on victim sites. These attacks exhaust bandwidth, router processing capacity, or network stack resources, breaking network connectivity to the victims.

There are many other types of DoS attacks and they all seek to exploit a weakness and overwhelm a resource.

Web Site Hosting

An important part of protecting a Web site against many forms of attack is the care with which you arrange for its hosting. Once the decision is made to create a Web site and the site is designed, a Web hosting solution is needed. *Web hosting* refers to the placement of a Web site on a Web server, making it available to the Web. Web hosting companies provide storage, connectivity, security, access protocols, and other services necessary to serve files for a Web site.

Web hosting, both free and paid, is available from many different companies. Additionally, it's possible to outsource the placement of hosting services or provide that service internally within the network. Web hosting is essentially the placement of your Web site on the Internet through a server.

External Web Hosting

Thousands of companies offer Web hosting services. The cost varies by a company's needs. For example, hosting companies offer both dedicated and shared hosting services. Dedicated means a dedicated server is used to provide hosting services; shared has multiple companies using the same Web server. Naturally, a dedicated Web server is much more costly than a shared server.

All Web hosting providers offer packages that provide hosting services including:

- Disk storage space
- Available bandwidth
- Technical support
- Post Office Protocol version 3 (POP3) e-mail accounts
- E-mail forwarding
- E-mail auto-responders
- E-mail aliases
- File Transfer Protocol (FTP) access
- Password protection

When creating an e-commerce site, choosing the right Web hosting company and package features is critical. Among the many factors to consider:

- **Disk space and bandwidth**—If you have a large site that generates significant monthly traffic, you need a hosting plan that matches your space and bandwidth needs. Hosting companies charge extra if your bandwidth and space requirements are exceeded.
- **Flexibility**—Some hosting companies are rigid in their packages while others are flexible and adjust to changing business needs.
- **Technology**—Larger hosting companies have the financial resources to purchase the latest software and hardware to provide cutting-edge services. Choosing a hosting company that has the technology and expertise is worthwhile.
- **Pricing**—Prices of Web hosting companies vary greatly, but more expensive companies are not necessarily better. It's important to take the time to research different pricing options.
- **Guaranteed uptime**—In choosing a Web hosting company, it's critical to consider policies around uptime and backups. Guaranteed backup refers to the mechanism a company has in place for continuation of service in the event of hardware or software failure. Many Web hosting companies list their approach to uptime and the steps they take to ensure that Web sites are available.

4

Connecting
to the Internet

- **Backups**—Consider what the hosting company offers in terms of backups, frequency, and storage of backups. Does it offer offsite backup storage? It's critical to know where and how backups are used and stored.

- **Security**—Your Web site is operational 24/7, so you must know what steps and procedures are in place to ensure its security against internal and external attacks. This includes protocol usage and logical and physical security measures.

- **Dynamic service**—A Web hosting company should adapt as new technologies are introduced.

- **Support**—Most companies want a hosting company that offers quality customer support. This includes frequently asked questions (FAQ), e-mail, phone, and forum support.

You can avoid the inconvenience of changing hosting companies if you take the time to research and choose the right one initially. Additional hassles may arise if the hosting company allows you less flexibility and control than you'd have with an internally hosted Web site. A well-thought-out service level agreement (SLA) can help ensure that any problems are handled as if the infrastructure were controlled internally.

Internal Web Hosting

Internal Web hosting refers to maintaining your own Web server and not outsourcing to an external company. There are some advantages to this approach. First, it allows you complete flexibility in terms of Web site modifications. It allows administrators to manage their own security, backups, and uptime. It takes away reliance on an external company and shifts it in-house.

If a company Web site is mission critical, that is, downtime has a serious impact on business functioning, internal hosting has a few snags. Ensuring increasingly high levels of uptime is difficult to achieve, requiring redundant hardware and expertise to manage that hardware. Many companies start out hosting their own site to save costs but, once the company grows, shift to external hosting.

If you choose internal hosting, there are many elements you need to host your site:

- Web server with redundant drives and hardware to ensure uptime
- High-speed Internet connection to handle bandwidth requirements
- Adequate disk storage to hold the site
- Physical and logical security measures including locked doors and protocols
- Available IT personal who can manage the programming, maintenance, and security of the site
- Strong backup procedures including considerations for offsite backup storage

Many smaller companies don't have the technology infrastructure and personnel to adequately manage their own Web server. However, for some, the benefits of internal hosting outweigh the costs and hassles of external hosting.

Whois (Private or Public)

If you have a Web site, you are likely familiar with the need for a domain name such as *www.google.com* or *www.mybusiness.com*. When you sign up for a domain, whether it's a *.org*, *.com*, *.edu*, or any of the other domain suffixes available, you use an authorized domain registrar.

The governing body for all domain names is called the Internet Corporation of Assigned Names and Numbers (ICANN). Its Web address is *http://www.icann.org*. ICANN holds a record of every domain name, who owns it, and how and where it's being used. This is often referred to as Whois data because you can search for a domain owner and contact information from ICANN. For example, type `whois <domain>.com` in a search engine, and then click the Whois link that appears in order to view the information on the domain and owner.

> **NOTE**
> Most hosting companies provide a link to the Whois database on their Web sites. You can also visit *http://www.icann.org* to access links to the Whois Search Web page.

A Whois search can return a lot of information. It may reveal the domain owner's home address, work address, phone, e-mail address, and more. You can also find information on how long an individual or company has owned the domain.

Whois is not without problems. When it was first available, people used it as a way to find e-mail addresses for spamming purposes and to find new startups even before their Web sites were live. For these and other reasons, registrars started to offer private settings.

Private Whois settings provide more protection of personal data. Often, just the information from the hosting company is provided. However, authorities such as police can request your registrant information, private or not.

The choice of using private settings or public Whois information depends on whether you want personal contact information released. In some cases, it's good to allow people to see your information to be able to contact you. However, you should use private settings if you don't want personal information to be exposed.

> **TIP**
> Check your Whois information to make sure the information is accurate and up to date. This is the official record of ownership and contact information for domain transfers and other domain management needs, as well as protecting your property from fraud or theft.

Domain Name Server

Domain Name System (DNS) servers perform a relatively basic, but very vital, role for the Web and its users. The function of a DNS server is to provide name resolution from domain names to IP addresses. This means it maps the domain name, such as *google.com*, to its IP address. The DNS server follows a systematic process. The DNS server consults its own databases for the requested information. If need be, a DNS server will also contact other DNS servers as needed to get the necessary information. This process may involve a large number of queries.

As you may know, each endpoint network device, such as a server or workstation, requires a unique IP address. A device's IP address is similar to a physical mailing address for snail mail in that it helps data get routed to the proper recipient. Because people cannot be expected to remember hundreds of IP addresses, they rely on a hierarchical system of domain names. In terms of hierarchy, domains read right to left, with the first being a special top-level domain (TLD). Examples are *.com*, *.net*, *.aero* or *.edu*. These represent a group or type of domains. For example *.aero* is for registered airline companies or pilots, while *.edu* is strictly for educational institutions. The next domain after the TLD provides an easy-to-remember host name, such as *google.com*, to access the hosts. When you type *google.com* into a Web browser, your configured DNS server takes the request and searches through a system of servers to find the correct Transmission Control Protocol/Internet Protocol (TCP/IP) address that relates to *google.com*. After the DNS server discovers the correct IP address, the DNS server returns the address to the client. The client can then communicate to the IP address, i.e., your browser can then browse to the Web server.

To assist subsequent requests for the same address, the DNS server adds the address to its cache. This includes requests from workstations as well as requests from other DNS servers searching to resolve the same domain name. For a workstation to send requests to the DNS server, the IP address of the DNS server must be known to the workstations.

Split and Dynamic DNS

In many instances, organizations maintain their own internal DNS servers to resolve internal queries. This provides added security in two aspects. First, by using a *split-DNS*, an organization can hide internal server addresses from external queries. Second, a company can maintain a unique, internal domain name that isn't resolvable by external DNS servers. For example, *google.com* employees may perhaps browse internal sites on the domain *our-google.edu*. Even if this internal domain name existed, any attempts to browse it from outside Google would not resolve to an actual host.

DNS is designed to experience few changes per IP address. However, some hosting providers and platforms support Dynamic DNS (DDNS). DDNS as a service provides IP address resolution just as standard DNS does, but DDNS handles resolution for domain names whose IP addresses change frequently. Normally, an IP address is associated with a domain name for weeks, months, or even years. However, consider a person whose personal PC is also a Web server. The IP address assigned from the Internet service provider to the home PC may change frequently, for example, every time the PC is shut down for the night. In this case, Dynamic DNS will change its cache in near real-time, resolving the home-based domain name immediately. Normal DNS servers can take between hours and a few days to propagate new information, but Dynamic DNS avoids these delays.

This can be provided manually, or Dynamic Host Configuration Protocol (DHCP) service also can include the DNS server address when providing an IP address.

Before DNS was used, resolution of host names was performed through static text files. These text files are called HOSTS files and are still the first source for attempting domain name resolution by default for many operating systems today. However, HOSTS files normally hold very little information and the client must rely on DNS.

To ensure that DNS servers are not overwhelmed with requests, the domain name space is divided into a hierarchy of subdomains, each of which has a number of servers providing name resolution services. Other domains are then listed as subdomains of the sub-domains, and so on. To avoid overwhelming the domain servers, a DNS administrator can designate a DNS server as a DNS authority for a subdomain. This authority server handles all resolution requests for that subdomain.

> **NOTE**
> Most common operating systems provide the ability to act as a DNS server. Some implementations are more sophisticated than others, but the basic principle of host name-to-IP-address resolution remains the same.

The amount of computing power required by a DNS server is proportional to the number of DNS requests that it will handle. Within an organization, records might be configured for only a relatively small number of hosts, and there might be only a small number of client requests. In such an environment, it would be unlikely to have a server dedicated to DNS functions. In contrast, a DNS server for an Internet service provider would need to be powerful enough to accommodate perhaps millions of requests per hour.

Although servers running DNS are likely to have fault-tolerant measures implemented, DNS itself has mechanisms that can deal with server downtime. In addition, most DNS clients can be configured with multiple DNS servers' addresses should the first-choice server be unavailable for any reason.

Working with DNS

The **Domain Name System (DNS)** is the standard name resolution strategy used on networks today. DNS is non-proprietary, meaning that it works on all operating system platforms from Linux, to UNIX and Windows operating systems. The function of DNS is to resolve host names such as *http://google.com,* to an IP address. In this case, google.com resolves to 74.125.39.103, one of many different IP addresses for Google, depending on your location. Host names make it easier for people to remember Web addresses rather than their IP address.

DNS operates in the DNS namespace. The **DNS namespace** is an organized, hierarchal division of DNS names. At the top level of the DNS hierarchy is an unnamed DNS node known as the root. For the entire Internet there are 13 root servers. All other nodes in the DNS hierarchy are known as labels. Together they form the DNS tree.

4

Connecting to the Internet

TABLE 4-2 Common top-level domain names and their intended purpose.	
TLDS	**DESCRIPTION**
.com	Used by commercial organizations
.gov	Government organizations
.net	Network providers
.org	Nonprofit organizations
.edu	Educational organizations
.mil	Military
.ca (for example)	Country-specific domains

Perhaps the best example of a DNS tree can be seen using the Internet. At the top level are domains such as .com, .org, or .edu as well as domains for countries such as .ca (Canada), or .de (Germany). These are in fact called TLDs or top level domains. Table 4-2 shows some of the more common top-level domain names and their intended purpose.

Below these top-level domains are the subdomains associated with organizations, for example, Microsoft.com. In many of the TLDs in Table 4-2, any individual may register a subdomain. However, some TLDs restrict who may register a subdomain. For example, the TLD ".aero" is available only to organizations and people in the aviation industry. Figure 4-1 shows a sample of the DNS organization of the Internet.

Understanding the DNS Name

The DNS naming structure can be confusing. Consider the following DNS name for a server:

bigbox.support.acme.com

When reviewing a DNS naming system, whether for an internal DNS or Internet DNS, the left-most part identifies the machine name, in this case *bigbox.* Moving to the right, *support* is a child domain of *acme.com.*

Continuing to the right you have *acme.com* that is a child domain of the top-level domain *.com.* In this case, whoever wanted to create the domain *acme.com* had to contact an established domain registrar. For the *.com* domain, there are several commercial registrars available for individuals and organizations to create subdomains.

Most internal networks and the Internet use DNS naming. This means that you will need to plan and design the DNS namespace that will be used. You should consider your organization's functions or internal divisions, such as *shoes.xyz.com* and *support.xyz.com.* Perhaps it's important to identify by geographical location, such as *prague.xyz.com* or *peoria.xyz.com.*

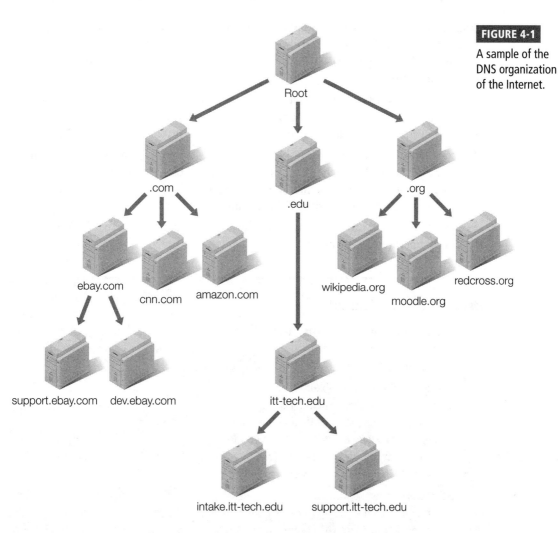

FIGURE 4-1

A sample of the DNS organization of the Internet.

The first step is to choose the top-level domain name that will be used to host the organization's name on the Internet. Although *.com* is the most popular, a nonprofit organization may opt to use *.org,* and a university may use *.edu.* Next, choose the second-level domain name that identifies the actual organization, *google.com,* for example. This is often referred to as the parent domain name and is the domain name used on the Internet.

To develop a namespace, many organizations map out the namespace according to how it will best suit the organization.

Common DNS Attacks

DNS is a fundamental service for networks and therefore has to be secured. There are many different strategies to secure DNS servers, many of which involve verifying that the DNS server is correctly installed. Before looking at ways to protect the DNS service, let's take a quick look at the types of attacks that are used against DNS systems:

- **DoS attacks**—DoS attacks attempt to overflow the DNS server with recursive queries or queries it must forward to another DNS server. The intended result is to tax the resources of the original DNS server, leaving it unable to handle legitimate name resolution requests.

- **Footprinting**—In this type of attack, the attacker attempts to obtain DNS zone data which may provide the domain names, computer names and even IP addresses of network systems. This is an early form of reconnaissance before a targeted attack.

- **Address spoofing**—Essentially, IP spoofing involves convincing a sending computer that the attacker is the intended recipient when it isn't. Network devices use the IP address to determine the sender and receiver for a data transmission. In spoofing, the hacker assumes the identity of a legitimate IP node.

- **Redirection**—In a redirection attack, the attacker attempts to redirect DNS queries to servers operated by the attacker.

Troubleshooting Client DNS

When a client system is unable to use name resolution services (DNS), there are three key areas on which to focus troubleshooting efforts: physical connection to the network, local systems network settings, and database consistency.

Common causes of not being able to access DNS services can be directly traced to clients' physical network connectivity. Such things as a hardware failure or cabling issue could cause this. To test, you need to verify that the client system is connected to the local network. This can be done by browsing the network or trying to PING the DNS server. Once you know that the client system is physically connected to the network, you can move to the next troubleshooting area.

The next step is to check that the DNS client computer has a valid IP configuration for the network. This includes the subnet mask, IP address, and the IP address of the DNS server. You can use the `ipconfig/all` command on Windows systems and the `ifconfig` command on Linux-based systems to verify these settings. It may be a good idea to PING the DNS server to ensure that the client system can see it on the network. If confirmed, it begins to look like the DNS problem may rest on the server itself.

One more problem on the client end is when client computers receive incorrect or stale information from a DNS server. A few things can cause this problem but most likely it's related to the DNS database. For instance, if the client computer is getting its zone information from a secondary server, that server may not have up-to-date information. The trick for testing this is to manually update the zone information to secondary servers.

The Seven Domains of a Typical IT Infrastructure

This chapter has mentioned *domain* in several different contexts. You learned about domain names for Web sites, the Domain Name System, DNS servers, and DNS attacks. This section focuses on one of seven domains in a typical information technology (IT) infrastructure that plays an important role in mitigating risk when connecting to the Internet—the LAN-to-WAN Domain.

To provide some background, there are seven domains in a typical IT infrastructure, as follows:

- **User**—This domain refers to any users of an organization's IT system. It includes employees, consultants, contractors, or any other third party. These users are called *end users.*
- **Workstation**—This area refers to the computing devices used by end users. This includes devices such as desktop or laptop computers.
- **LAN**—This domain refers to the organization's local area network (LAN) technologies. A LAN is two or more computers connected together within a small area.
- **WAN**—A wide area network (WAN) is a network that spans a large geographical area. The most common example of a WAN is the Internet. Organization's with remote locations use a WAN to connect those locations.
- **LAN-to-WAN**—This domain refers to the organization's infrastructure that connects the organization's LAN to a WAN.
- **Remote Access**—This domain refers to the processes and procedures that end users use to remotely access the organization's IT infrastructure and data.
- **System/Application**—This domain refers to the equipment and data an organization uses to support its IT infrastructure. It includes hardware, operating system software, database software, client-server applications.

Figure 4-2 shows the seven domains of a typical IT infrastructure. Because the LAN-to-WAN Domain figures prominently in regards to Web-related security issues, the next section focuses on this domain.

Protecting Networks in the LAN-to-WAN Domain

The administration of local area networks and wide area networks is a complex task. Not only must administrators concern themselves with the day-to-day user end operations, they must also be vigilant about the constant threat of attack. Many network administrators are highly paid to ensure that network communications, hardware, and the entire network is secure. Any security breaches are the responsibility of the administrator. This can be a stressful position.

This section explores some of the methods commonly used to protect networks.

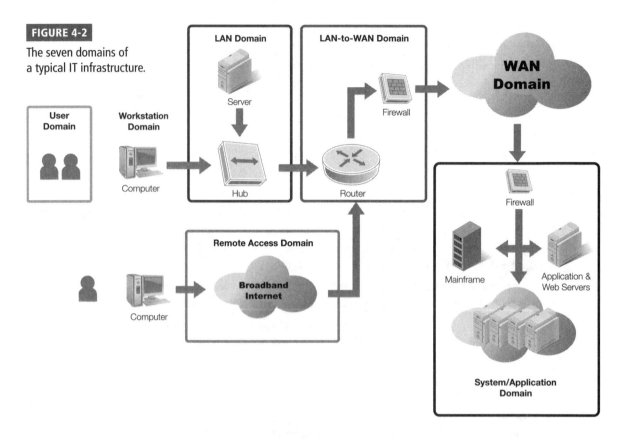

FIGURE 4-2

The seven domains of a typical IT infrastructure.

Perimeter Defense Strategies

Perimeter defense strategies refer to security measures on the edge of the network that protect the internal network from external attack. No one perimeter security mechanism is enough to protect the network. Instead security is achieved from a combination of properly executed security strategies. It's a cliché but true that security is only as strong as the weakest link. So the administrator must consider all possible threats and practice sound risk management.

Perimeter security strategies employ both hardware and software controls:

- Antivirus/spyware/spam/phishing software
- Intrusion detection systems
- Intrusion prevention systems
- DoS/DDoS defense
- Firewalls
- Application control and bandwidth management
- Demilitarized zones
- Port management

The following section explores some of the more common perimeter security strategies and how they are used in a network environment.

Port 80: Open or Closed?

When configuring network security and using secure protocols such as IPSec or restricting unused network services, it's important to understand ports and their purposes. Each protocol within the TCP/IP suite has a port association. During communication, the target port is checked to see which protocol or service it's destined for. The request is then forwarded to that protocol or service. As an example, HTTP uses port 80, so when a Web browser requests a Web page, the request is sent through port 80 on the target system. If port 80 is shut, the HTTP service will be unavailable.

A system has 65,535 ports available, numbered from 1 through 65535. These are broken down into three distinct designations: well-known ports (1–1023), registered ports (1024–49151), and dynamic ports (49152–65535). The dynamic ports are also sometimes called the ephemeral or private ports.

Table 4-3 presents some of the most familiar services and their respective port. The table also specifies whether the service relies on the TCP or UDP method of sending.

TABLE 4-3 Protocols, port assignments, and services.		
PROTOCOL	**PORT ASSIGNMENT**	**TCP/UDP PORT**
File Transfer Protocol (FTP)	21	TCP
Secure Shell (SSH)	22	TCP
Telnet	23	TCP
Simple Mail Transfer Protocol (SMTP)	25	TCP
Domain Name System (DNS)	53	UDP
Trivial File Transfer Protocol (TFTP)	69	UDP
Hypertext Transfer Protocol (HTTP)	80	TCP/UDP
Post Office Protocol version 3 (POP3)	110	TCP
Network News Transfer Protocol (NNTP)	119	TCP
Internet Message Access Protocol version 4 (IMAP4)	143	TCP
Simple Network Management Protocol (SNMP)	161	UDP
Hypertext Transfer Protocol Secure (HTTPS)	443	TCP

Transmission Control Protocol (TCP) and User Datagram Protocol (UDP) are two protocols in the Transport layer of the Internet Protocol Suite. Of the 65,535 ports available, a service may use either TCP or UDP for communication. The primary difference between TCP and UDP is in guarantee of delivery. UDP sends information and assumes it was delivered, while TCP checks to ensure delivery.

When securing a network, it's recommend to shut down unused ports to help prevent unwanted access. Be warned, however, that once the port is shut, the associated service is not available.

Firewalls

As previously mentioned, the Internet can be a dangerous place unless proper security measures are taken. Security is an essential consideration for today's networks. When it comes to perimeter network security, the name of the game is firewalls. However, many organizations and home owners see the firewall as the only needed perimeter security measure. While it's important, it's not the only measure needed.

The ability to protect data and to stop intruders from accessing internal networks is becoming increasingly important to organizations and individuals alike. This protection, from a network connectivity perspective, comes in the form of a firewall. Firewalls are not a new technology, and as more organizations connect their networks to the Internet, firewalls have become commonplace.

Basically, a firewall controls, prevents, and monitors incoming and outgoing network access. It's the job of the firewall to prevent unauthorized network access, both from outside and inside network users. Depending on the type of firewall, data packets sent to and from the network pass through the firewall, and all this data can be checked for whether it's allowed for transfer. Figure 4-3 shows how a firewall system typically fits into a network.

FIGURE 4-3

A standard network
firewall configuration.

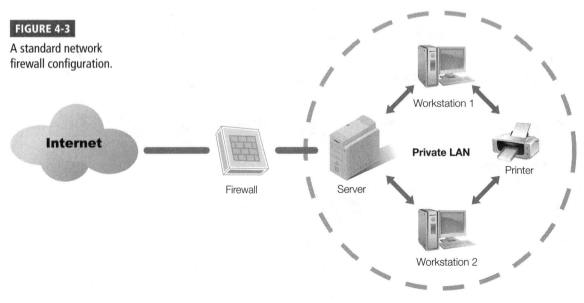

Internet

Firewall

Server

Private LAN

Workstation 1

Printer

Workstation 2

In essence, the simplest type of firewall is a router in that it makes forwarding or blocking decisions based upon given criteria. The difference between a firewall and a router is that a firewall can make the decisions based on a wider variety of criteria than a router can. Firewalls that perform essentially as a router decide by simple routing information whether to allow or deny network traffic. These *packet filtering* firewalls are fast and cheap. The next type of firewall is called a circuit gateway firewall, and it will better hide the network behind it. These firewalls can make decisions based on both TCP and IP information. Those cost a bit more but are still not as intelligent as an application-layer gateway firewall. These firewalls, also called proxies, can allow or deny traffic based on application commands. The most complex and costly firewall of all is the stateful multi-layer packet inspection firewall. These firewalls combine the qualities of the previous three. Although the most common use of a firewall is to protect the boundary of an organization's network, some companies use firewalls internally as well to protect network areas containing sensitive data, such as research or accounting information.

Today's advanced firewall systems provide many security services on incoming communications:

- **Content filtering**—Many firewalls can be configured to check the content leaving and entering the site and flag it if it appears to be a threat. Content blocking involves allowing or denying transmissions based on content.

- **Virus scanning services**—A firewall server can use anti-malware software to check all incoming and outgoing transmissions for malware. This provides centralized, network-wide malware scanning and vetting services.

- **Network address translation (NAT)**—To protect the identity of machines on the internal network, and to allow more flexibility in internal TCP/IP addressing structures, many firewalls (and proxy servers, which are covered in the next section) translate the originating address of data into a different address, which is then used on the Internet. Network address translation is a popular function because it works around the limited availability of TCP/IP addresses.

- **Signature identification**—All applications have unique signature identifiers. In the antivirus world, a signature is an algorithm that uniquely identifies a specific virus, worm or Trojan horse. Firewalls can be configured to detect certain signatures that are associated with malware or other undesirable applications and block them from entering the network.

- **Address filtering**—Firewalls can be configured to filter by Web address. This is an excellent way to exclude known malware and undesirable sites.

Many of these functions are not considered initially. However, because the firewall sits at the perimeter of the network, it's an ideal place to combine security services that closely monitor network traffic and access.

Demilitarized Zones (DMZs)

Also at the perimeter of the network is something known as the demilitarized zone (DMZ). Some network servers need to be accessible to both internal and external users. It's possible to put such servers into the internal network but that gives a level of access that may not be wanted. Therefore, these servers are put in the DMZ. The DMZ is part of a network on which you place servers that must be accessible by sources both outside and inside your network. However, the DMZ is not connected directly to either network, and it must always be accessed through the firewall. This means that external users don't gain access to the internal network at all.

A DMZ creates additional security for the internal network by placing publicly accessed servers outside the local network. You can create an additional step that makes it more difficult for an intruder to gain access to the internal network.

There are different ways to deploy a DMZ depending on the organization's security needs. Two common DMZ strategies include the N-tier and the three-homed firewall configurations. With the three-homed configuration, the firewall filters traffic between the two network segments. An N-tier configuration uses two firewalls with the DMZ sandwiched in between. In this configuration, an attacker would need to pass through two firewalls to access the internal network. Figure 4-4 shows an example of three-homed firewall and Figure 4-5 shows the N-tier firewall design.

FIGURE 4-4

A DMZ using a three-homed firewall configuration.

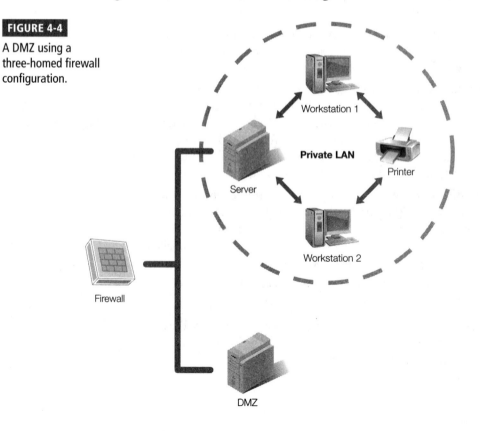

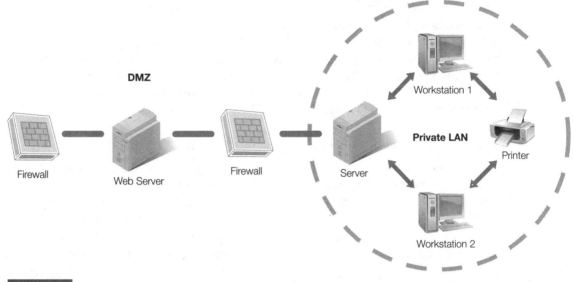

FIGURE 4-5

A DMZ using an N-tier firewall configuration.

Proxy Servers

Proxy servers and firewalls go hand in hand in networks. The proxy server sits between the client computer and the Internet, monitoring Web page client requests. If a client wants to access the *google.com* Web site, the request is first sent to the proxy server rather than directly to the Internet. The proxy server identifies whether the requested page is in its cache and if so returns the page to the client.

Retrieving pages from the proxy cache is faster than going on the Internet to retrieve the page and also reduces usage bandwidth by limiting client requests that actually have to go online. If the requested page in not in the proxy cache, the client request is forwarded to the appropriate Web site and the information is returned to the client. The transaction between the proxy server and the client is largely transparent to the user with no apparent lag time.

FYI

Proxy servers themselves are not security devices, but they do sit at the edge of the network and improve overall network performance. They can be configured to do some content and Web filtering to help secure the types of Web sites that are accessed. Proxy caching can greatly increase the response time to the client and can significantly reduce the bandwidth needed to fulfill client requests.

One issue that has plagued proxy services is stale content. When a Web page is retrieved from the cache, it may not be the most recent site update. This may not matter for some sites, but for others with more dynamic content, the cache would be stale. To combat this, the proxy server is configured to periodically revisit commonly accessed sites and retrieve the most current data for the cache. This is an automatic process, but the frequency with which proxy servers update their cache can be configured by administrators. Figure 4-6 shows an example of a proxy server.

Intrusion Detection Systems and Intrusion Protection Systems

Two other perimeter security defense mechanisms are the **intrusion detection system (IDS)** and the **intrusion prevention system (IPS)**. The IDS device actively monitors the data packets that travel the network and compares traffic against its parameters of known threats. The IDS will pinpoint any traffic that falls outside the secure parameters. All potentially dangerous traffic is flagged and logged. It's up to the administrator to review the log file and take appropriate actions to manage the potential threat.

FIGURE 4-6

A proxy server.

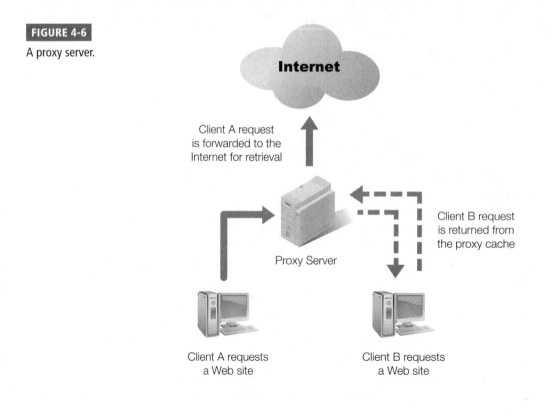

Client A request is forwarded to the Internet for retrieval

Client B request is returned from the proxy cache

Proxy Server

Client A requests a Web site

Client B requests a Web site

False Positives and False Negatives

When a device such as an IDS incorrectly identifies network traffic as suspect, it's called a *false positive*. Another example of a false positive is when a legitimate e-mail is incorrectly sent to your spam folder. If the device also actively blocks traffic because of a false positive, this can mean blocking traffic essential to business.

The opposite also happens when a device fails to stop malicious traffic. Spam that appears in your e-mail inbox and was not caught by your spam filter is called a *false negative*. False negatives can be damaging since users come to trust their spam filter and open what should be legitimate traffic.

False positives and false negatives add workload to the administrator and annoyance to users. But in both cases, they are far better than no filtering at all. Both false positives and false negatives can be greatly reduced by spending time tuning the security device. Tuning will save time, result in fewer lost e-mails, and possibly avoid disrupting business.

The IDS is a passive security measure in that it only monitors the network and doesn't take steps to mitigate the risk. In addition, many IDS systems are prone to a "better safe than sorry" security approach. When the IDS device encounters network traffic which may be suspicious, it logs that traffic along with all suspicious traffic. Thus, IDS devices generate numerous false reports in an attempt to perform a thorough job. This causes the administrator to weed through many false security reports, which can be time consuming. To reduce the administrator's time reviewing logs, the IDS device must be tuned. By spending the time necessary to tune the IDS, the organization will save much more time in the long run.

The IPS systems device goes one step beyond the IDS in that it flags potentially harmful traffic and also attempts to prevent that traffic from harming the network. IPS systems can automatically block suspicious traffic. In this way, IPS systems are known as a reactive security measure.

IDS and IPS systems are not a replacement for a firewall system as they provide different services. They are used in conjunction to help create a comprehensive security plan.

> **NOTE**
>
> Many perimeter security defense mechanisms such as the firewall, IDS, and IPS can be host-based or network-based. Host-based security systems are installed on the local system and provide security services for a single host. Network-based systems monitor an entire network.

4

Connecting
to the Internet

Data Leakage Prevention

A primary focus of network security is to guard the perimeter of the network to keep out external threats. Anti-malware software, firewalls, IDS, IPS, and e-mail filtering software were designed to address the external threat. These mitigating strategies neglected the threat from inside the network.

Security measures have evolved in recent years and now protection within the network and data protection are as important as managing external threats. Internal threats come from many sources: disgruntled employees, stolen laptops, captured network data, stolen backups and hardware, to name a few. These threats have pushed security strategies focusing on data leakage protection.

Data leak prevention, also known as data loss prevention, focuses on efforts to control what information leaves the network and in what form. It focuses on the confidentiality and integrity of information. Data leakage can happen in a variety of ways including:

- **Stolen hardware**—Laptops stolen with company information can be a disaster. All company laptops need to have data encryption and passwords in case they fall into the wrong hands.

- **Misplaced backups**—Backups, if stolen, can be restored and the data stolen. Most companies use both physical and logical methods to secure data backups.

- **E-mail**—E-mail is one of the biggest sources of data leaks both by intentional and unintentional methods.

- **Non-secure transmissions**—It's a good practice to encrypt sensitive data on the internal network and if it's sent externally. Use secure protocols such as IPSec to help ensure data is safe in transmission.

- **Undeleted files**—Files are often recoverable even when they appear deleted. Software used for undeleting files is commonplace and easy to use. Policies should be developed to manage the disposal of computer equipment to prevent possible data loss.

- **Portable devices**—Flash drives, thumb drives, and CDs/DVDs offer more ways for data to be purposefully leaked. Prevention has become very challenging. Some practices for organizations include disabling universal serial bus (USB) ports and including read-only CD/DVD drives in users' workstations.

The prevention of data loss requires a multifaceted approach of non-technical solutions, such as end-user education, and a variety of security strategies, including protocols, physical security, and encryption strategies.

Best Practices for Connecting to the Internet

Regardless of threats on the Internet, people will go online. The trick is to do so safely and to reduce the risks to yourself and the network. The following is a list of best practices when connecting to the Internet:

- **Keep all applications current**—Look for updates to software including productivity software, virus and operating systems.
- **Use trusted anti-malware software**—Antivirus software includes mitigation strategies for known malware. Keep this software installed and current.
- **Use perimeter security**—Home users and corporate networks need to incorporate strong perimeter security strategies. This includes the firewall, IDS, and IPS. In addition to installing them, take the time to use them properly. For home users, IDS and IPS functionality is sometimes included in full-featured antivirus software.
- **Secure backups**—Backups on removable media such as tape sets and USB needs to be secure in the event of theft.
- **Use secure passwords**—Choosing hard-to-guess passwords goes a long way to securing many online transactions.
- **Report cybercrime**—If you suspect that you or someone you know is a victim of cybercrime such as stalking or bullying, report it to the police.
- **Personal information**—If using social networking sites, use caution when divulging personal information.
- **Use data encryption**—The ability to encrypt data is built into operating systems. It's a best practice to encrypt data to prevent it from being read if stolen.

Best practices for Internet connectivity follow a series of commonsense strategies and technical solutions. Never assume you are anonymous or secure on the Internet. It's a best practice to assume someone is trying to access your system and act accordingly.

CHAPTER SUMMARY

Because the Internet is insecure and unregulated, there are many risks associated with online connectivity. These include hackers, malware, personal attacks, and e-mail attacks. End users, hardware, and software all have inherent vulnerabilities. Perpetrators are working night and day using a whole range of methods to exploit these vulnerabilities.

Despite these risks, businesses and personal users will continue to use the Internet. Therefore, they must employ strategies to mitigate the risks. These strategies require a combination of non-technical and technical methods—including careful consideration of Web site hosting, policies to protect local area and wide area networks, and using best practices for connecting to the Internet.

KEY CONCEPTS AND TERMS

Adware	E-mail filtering	Macro virus
Client privacy agreement	Hacker	Malware hoax
Cracker	Identify theft	Spyware
Cyberstalking	Intrusion detection system (IDS)	Trojan horse
DNS namespace	Intrusion prevention system (IPS)	Worm
Domain Name System (DNS)		

CHAPTER 4 ASSESSMENT

1. Worms are able to self-replicate.

  A. True
  B. False

2. You have created a Web site and need to increase visitor trust. Which of the following methods are used to build trust? (Select two.)

  A. Logos
  B. Testimonials
  C. Color choice
  D. Font size

3. IDS and IPS systems are a replacement for a firewall system.

  A. True
  B. False

4. Which of the following attack types is based on faking the real source of a transmission, file, or e-mail?

  A. Backdoor
  B. DDoS
  C. Spoofing
  D. Front door

5. To increase network security, you have decided to block port 21. Which of the following services is associated with port 21?

  A. FTP
  B. HTTPS
  C. DNS
  D. SFTP

6. A(n) _____ is a passive network monitoring and security system.

7. Servers within the DMZ sit outside of the local network.

  A. True
  B. False

8. Port _____ is used by the HTTP protocol.

9. A _____ sits between the Internet and the client systems responding to client requests for Web pages.

10. Which of the following best describes the function of the DNS server?

  A. Uses Media Access Control addresses to locate network systems
  B. Provides host name-to-IP resolution
  C. Provides IP name resolution
  D. Encrypts host names

11. A DoS attack is designed to overwhelm a particular resource making it unavailable.

  A. True
  B. False

© Rodolfo Clix/Dreamstime.com

Mitigating Web Site Risks, Threats, and Vulnerabilities

PERIMETER NETWORK SOLUTIONS—firewalls, intrusion detection systems (IDSs), intrusion prevention systems (IPSs), and demilitarized zones (DMZs)— are all needed for network security, but they manage only part of the risk. Today's networks require much more than perimeter security. Internal services such as e-mail, File Transfer Protocol (FTP), Hypertext Transfer Protocol (HTTP), and Telnet operate 24/7 and are a security battleground. These protocols and Web applications form the basis of the modern business economy, and that makes them a target for hackers.

In some respects, managing Web application security is more difficult than other traditional network areas. Among the many facets to Web application security are controlling visitors, securing site feedback mechanisms, and plugging code-related security holes. Today's network administration requires a complete security strategy encompassing all aspects of internal and external security strategies. This chapter explores some of the threats associated with Web security.

Chapter 5 Topics

This chapter covers the following topics and concepts:

- Who is coming to your Web site
- Whom you want coming to your Web site
- How to accept user input on your Web site
- What the Open Web Application Security Project (OWASP) Top 10 threats are
- What some additional Web threats are
- What best practices for mitigating known Web application risks, threats, and vulnerabilities are

Chapter 5 Goals

When you complete this chapter, you will be able to:

- Identify who is coming to your site
- Review who you want to come to your site
- Manage user input
- Work with OWASP
- Understand XSS
- Manage injection flaws
- Prevent malicious file execution and cross-site request forgery
- Manage information leakage
- Prevent unsecure communications
- Implement best practices for Web application security

Who Is Coming to Your Web Site?

Many companies don't give a second thought about who is visiting their sites. This is fine if a company manages a non-interactive information site. However, a company with an e-commerce Web site needs a clear understanding of the types of traffic visiting the site. This is important for two reasons: security and marketing.

Many companies don't take the time to track visitors. This can be because they fail to see the importance or, more likely, are unaware how and why Web tracking software works. One of the common methods organizations use to track customers is known as Web analytics software. There are several types of analytics software available; some are free and others require licensing. The types of information that Web analytics software can provide includes:

> **NOTE**
>
> To manage and grow a corporate Web site without gathering information sacrifices a lot of valuable information, particularly information on visitors and visitor trends. Information is key to this, and analytics software is a must for any company wishing to expand its online presence.

- **Visitor location**—Analytics software can help you learn your visitors' geographical location by country, state, or city. This helps you pinpoint where much of your traffic is coming from and allows you to tune your page for location. Or you may wish to develop location-specific pages.

- **Visitor sources**—It's possible to identify where your visitors come from before landing on a site and which search engines brought them there.

- **Visitor type**—Are visitors repeat visitors or is this their first time? Analytics software allows administrative and marketing staff to find trends in visitor behavior.

- **Visitor navigation**—Analytics software allows administrators to know exactly how visitors are navigating the site. This includes how long they stay on a page and the links they select.

- **Average time on site**—What is the average time spent on a page? Analytics software allows administrators to pinpoint exactly how long visitors stay on the site.

- **Leave (bounce) rate**—With analytics, it's possible to identify how long visitors stay. It also identifies from which pages most visitors leave. This helps identify ineffective pages that need improvement to hold visitor interest.

> **NOTE**
>
> A detailed discussion of analytics software and Google Analytics falls outside the scope of this book. However, tracking visitors is an important consideration for network administration. For more information on Google Analytics and its use, refer to *http://www.google.com/analytics/*.

As mentioned, many companies offer analytics software. A common Web analytics software package is Google Analytics. This package uses an easy-to-navigate graphical interface to generate and display statistics. Figure 5-1 shows a portion of the main screen of the Google Analytics tool and the results for a live Web site.

This screen, known as the Google Dashboard, provides quick links to a variety of visitor information and gives a clear idea who is visiting a site. The following list identifies some features of Google Dashboard:

- **Visits**—This area provides a quick glimpse of how many visitors the site receives per day.

- **Site Usage**—The site-usage area provides several key visitor-information statistics, including the number of visits per month, page views, bounce rates, average time on site, and percentage of new visits.

- **Visitors Overview**—This section provides visitor statistics, including Web browser used, Internet access method used (cable, DSL, dial-up), time on site, and language used. The links from this section provide a quick look at who exactly is coming to your site.

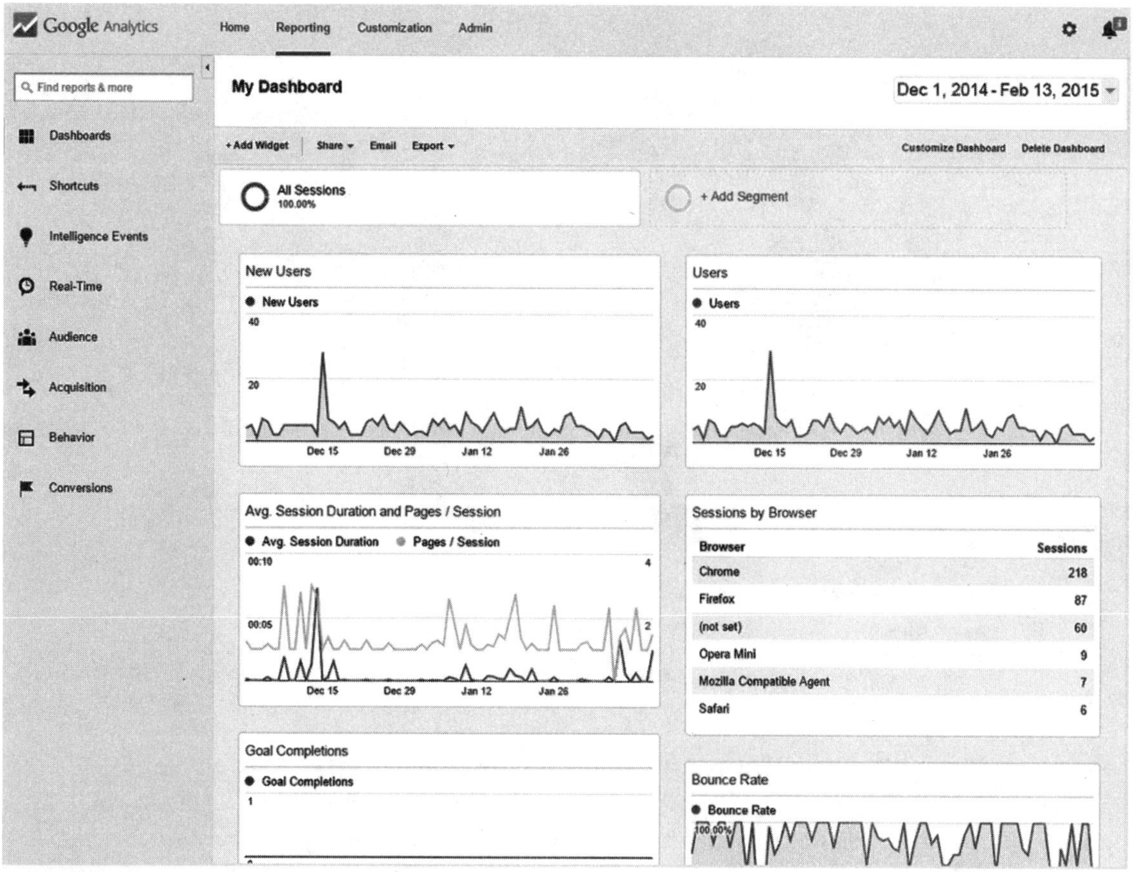

Google and the Google logo are registered trademarks of Google Inc., used with permission.

FIGURE 5-1

Reviewing Google Analytics results.

- **Map Overlay**—This section provides a visual representation of visitors geographically. The map shows the frequency of visitors from worldwide locations. Figure 5-2 shows a portion of the Map Overlay summary screen. The shades of gray in the figure represent the approximate number of visitors per geographic location.

- **Content Overview**—This section displays how visitors access the content on a page. This includes which links visitors click and how long they view a page. The content reports identify how visitors interact with each page.

Google and the Google logo are registered trademarks of Google Inc., used with permission.

FIGURE 5-2

Google Analytics map overlay statistics.

Whom Do You Want to Come to Your Web Site?

Driving quality and qualified traffic to a Web site does not happen by accident. Rather, it's a strategic process. The first step is to clearly identify whom you want to come to your site. This is the process of isolating the Web demographic. If an organization does not take the time to clearly identify the ideal demographic, it will have difficulty focusing the look, feel, and content of the site. In marketing, the characteristics of the demographic determine the design of the site. For example, a site intended for snowboarders would certainly look different than one designed for avid poker players.

One of the first steps in creating a site for a specific demographic is to create a customer profile. The profile is a description of your customer based on various criteria. The customer profile identifies characteristics of the people you want to come to your site, by gender, age, geographical location, income, education, and more. Once a clear customer demographic is established, it's possible to design a site that appeals to that demographic, and the site will be more effective.

Demographics are the statistical characteristics of a segment of the population. For an organization's Web page, demographics are the specific characteristics of your customers that enable you to segment your visitors.

> **NOTE**
>
> The customer profile provides a framework from which to create a Web site that meets the needs of desired visitors. The customer profile is reviewed periodically to ensure that it still meets the needs of the organization.

Identifying the demographic for a Web site is important to:

- Help create a focus for the site based on visitor need.
- Create a design suited for a specific group.
- Pinpoint characteristics of your ideal customer.
- Identify the geographical area with the highest number of ideal customers.

Establishing a customer profile is important when deciding who you want to come to your site and the mechanisms you will use to drive traffic to the site. When pinpointing a demographic, several characteristics may be included:

- Age range
- Gender
- Marital status
- Geographical location
- Occupation
- Income range
- Online/offline shopping habits
- Spare-time activities
- Club memberships, such as a book club or cooking club
- Participation in sports leagues
- Approximate disposable income
- Ownership of rental properties
- Years of college attended
- Level of education, including vocational or trade

These are some of the characteristics that make up a customer profile. A completed customer profile will give you a clear understating of whom you want to come to your site and how to prepare the site for them.

Accepting User Input on Your Web Site

Web 1.0 was non-interactive and primarily relayed information. Web 2.0 introduced more interaction between Web site and visitor. A Web site may have any number of interactive elements, each designed to engage visitors so they will return to a site. Having interactive elements is a great addition to a site, but they may introduce security considerations including phishing, bullying, and cyberstalking.

Despite the risks, today's corporate sites provide various forms of user input including forums, surveys, feedback forms, and e-mail. Each of these input mechanisms is designed to increase interactivity and communication to visitors.

Market Segmentation

Market segmentation provides a method of dividing visitors by group. Instead of looking at visitors to a Web site as a whole group, it's divided to help focus marketing efforts. It helps you see who is going to a site and who you want to visit the site.

There are many ways to segment a Web site's visitors, including:

- **Customer location**—Analytics software can segment visitors according to their location. Administrators can group visitors by country, state, city, territory, province, and more.
- **Customer demographic**—Visitors can be segmented according to their unique demographic characteristics—age, education, income level, or more.
- **Customer behaviors**—Visitors can be grouped and segmented according to their behaviors, such as surfing habits, online-spending trends, forum participation etc.
- **Customer lifestyle**—It's possible to segment visitors by their beliefs, values, and attitudes. They may be more willing to become customers if they believe you share their beliefs.

Forums

Forums are discussion boards that provide a place on a Web site for visitors to chat and meet. Forums enable communication between visitors. Such interaction improves the overall value to all visitors. Information can be monitored and used to better the site, products, or services. Additionally, visitors engaged in forums are likely to return to a site for continued discussion and responses.

Forum advantages include the following:

- **Repeat visitors**—Visitors will return to check on posts and respond to questions or comments.
- **Increased keyword exposure**—Search engines search forums. When valuable keywords are repeated, this can increase a site's search engine optimization (SEO) position.
- **E-mail address acquisition**—Often, forum membership requires an e-mail address. This allows a company to continue marketing to visitors and customers.
- **Opportunities to gather demographic data**—It's possible to track forum users by isolating demographic information, such as location and interests.
- **Support for online relationships**—By participating in forum discussions, corporate employees and visitors can get to know each other.

Along with the advantages of including forums on the Web site, there are some potential downsides, such as:

- **Requirement for technical expertise**—Creating and supporting the forum requires technical experience and occasional maintenance.

- **Requirement for content monitoring**—Sometimes content in forums becomes inappropriate and can reflect poorly on the organization. The content monitor must ensure that the content remains appropriate and professional. This can be automated but if it is, it will be less effective against motivated spammers.

- **Need to police for bullying and stalking**—Unmonitored forums can be a haven for cyberbullies and cyberstalkers. Cyberstalking or cyberbullying reflects very poorly on the organization.

- **Risk of ad flooding**—Unmonitored forums can be flooded by ads and other non-related content. Once the forum is set up, it should be monitored to ensure that automatic content is not spamming the forum.

Web Site Feedback Forms

Another form of user input used on a site is feedback forms. A site may use a variety of feedback forms, each with a unique purpose. Feedback forms can be used to obtain specific information about a Web site and how visitors use and access the site:

- **Contact Us forms**—The Contact Us form enables visitors to ask questions and leave comments for the organization.

- **Customer support forms**—Customer support forms are dedicated to helping visitors who encounter problems with the product or service provided. These forms are another way for visitors to interact with the site and the organization. The information you can obtain includes delivery and shipping issues, hard-to-follow instructions, navigation problems, confusing checkout procedures, and more. Customer support forms help identify whether there is a problem, as well as offer an interactive solution.

- **Signup forms**—Signup forms are commonly used to enable visitors to sign up for newsletters or other features of a Web site.

Online Surveys

Web site surveys provide another great way for visitors to communicate. Surveys gather information from the visitor and provide a method to interact with the site. Surveys should be brief and require only a few minutes to fill out. Questions must be carefully chosen to draw out the type of information you are seeking.

The Open Web Application Security Project Top 10 Threats

Dynamic Web pages and Web applications are commonplace. And so are the risks and threats to these Web applications. The **Open Web Application Security Project (OWASP)** is an organization that researches and publishes known security threats to Web applications and Web services. Periodically, OWASP publishes the Top 10 list of the most critical Web security vulnerabilities. Prudent Web administrators need to be well aware of the OWASP Top 10 list. This section explores the OWASP list and briefly outlines the attacks and vulnerabilities to Web applications and Web services.

You can read more about the Top 10 list at *http://www.owasp.org/index.php/ Category:OWASP_Top_Ten_Project.*

1. Injection

Most of today's Web applications use databases to store the data needed for the Web sites and application retrieval. This information may include user credentials, financial information, contact information, invoices, and inventory. These databases are usually safe. However, if the information were to fall into the wrong hands, your data may be compromised and used.

There are many forms of **injection flaw attack**. In general, an injection flaw enables the attacker to bypass access controls and create, change, delete, or read any data the application can access. The result is compromised data. One of the most common forms of injection flaw attack is the **SQL injection attack**. SQL injection attacks are designed to break through database security and access this information.

As the name suggests, an SQL injection attack "injects" or manipulates SQL code. SQL stands for Structured Query Language. By adding unexpected SQL to a query, it's possible to manipulate a database in unanticipated ways. The result is that SQL injections allow an attacker to retrieve crucial information from a Web server's database by carefully crafted statements that the attacker enters in the username or password fields of a Web site, fooling the system into allowing access.

Mitigating Injection Flaws

Injection flaws are dependent on the hacker's being able to access the database with invalid input. Therefore, the first line of defense is to ensure that input is validated. **Input validation** refers to the verification of all data that is received to help prevent malicious data from entering an application. All input must be validated before being used. Input validation is a form of filtering in which unexpected or unwanted input is automatically rejected and the underlying database remains inaccessible. The keys for reducing injection flaws are to validate all input and to perform validation on the Web or hosting server. Client-side input validation is easier to exploit.

2. Broken Authentication and Session Management

Authentication and session management are also vulnerabilities for Web applications. They include all aspects of handling user authentication and managing active sessions. Authentication is critical for all network services, from logons to network resource to access of Web applications. User authentication on the Web typically involves the use of a user ID and a password. There are alternate authentication methods available from biometrics to cryptography tokens, but such strategies are too complex and costly for most Web applications.

Username/Password Authentication

In establishing a connection between a client and a server, a username and password is the most common authentication method used. Authentication is the process of determining if the person trying to make the connection is supposed to have access to the network. Dictated by the network administrator, usernames are easily accessed and freely distributed. They are traditionally unsecure, leaving passwords as the only security measure.

Creating secure passwords is essential in a secure network solution. Passwords have long been the security hole in networks. To help plug this hole, here are password guidelines to keep in mind:

- **Minimum length of password**—This sets how many characters must be in the password. It's recommended to use at least eight.
- **Password duration**—This specifies how long a password can be used before a new one must be set. Depending on the network, this can range from a day to a month.
- **Password reuse**—It's possible to prohibit the use of the same password repeatedly. This ensures that users create new passwords, which are more secure.

Password considerations include:

- Passwords should contain at least eight characters. The more characters, the stronger the password.
- Refrain from using simple, easy-to-guess passwords, such as your name or birthday. Oddly, many passwords are chosen for their ease in remembering rather than their difficulty in deciphering.
- Use case-sensitive characters and mix up the letters. Strong passwords take advantage of case sensitivity.
- Passwords are a lot harder to guess or crack by brute force if symbols and numbers are mixed in with letters. Unfortunately, they might also be harder to remember.
- A useful tip for creating a strong, but memorable, password is to use the first letter from a movie quote or song lyric. For example: "I'm going to make him an offer he can't refuse" becomes "Igtmhaohcr." Add a number or a symbol, and "Igtmhaohcr!" becomes a very strong password.

If authentication credentials are compromised, attackers may get access to all resources associated with the authentication credentials. This is referred to as **broken authentication**. Social engineering is a common way to obtain user IDs and passwords.

A **session** refers to the tracking of requests and communications between the Web server and the user. HTML is stateless by design and does not provide this capability, so Web applications must create and manage the session themselves. Two popular ways that Web sites arrange a session are by creating cookies and by creating a random string of characters in the URL or Web address. Both methods create a unique identifier for you that can be passed on as you browse and use the Web site. However, the string of characters in the Web address is vulnerable to eavesdropping.

Web applications use a session token. The session token is a unique identifier generated and sent from a server to a client to identify the current interaction session. The client usually stores and sends the token as an HTTP cookie or browser cookie. If the session tokens are not properly protected, an attacker can hijack an active session and assume the identity of a user. Also, unless all authentication credentials and session identifiers

---

Authorization Versus Authentication

When talking about access control and resource security, it's important to understand the difference between authentication and authorization. Although these terms are sometimes used interchangeably, they actually refer to distinct steps that determine whether a request for a resource will result in the resource actually being returned.

Authentication is any process by which you verify someone's identity. This usually involves a username and a password, but it can include a smart card, biometrics, voice recognition, fingerprints, or an assigned piece of hardware. Authentication is a significant consideration for network and system security.

Authorization is finding out if the person, once identified and authenticated, is allowed to have access to a particular resource. The person may have access as an individual or as part of a particular group. To have access, the person was granted rights or privileges or has a certain level of security clearance.

A bank transaction at an automated teller machine (ATM) is a good example of authentication and authorization. When a bankcard is placed in the ATM, the magnetic strip is read, and it's apparent that someone is trying to gain access to an account. If the process ended here and access was granted, it would be a significant security problem. Instead, once the card is placed in the bank machine, a secret code is required to authenticate the client, ensuring that the owner of the card is seeking access to the account.

With the correct code, the client is verified and authenticated, and access is granted. Authorization then would be what that user is allowed to access, for example, access to funds in a specific checking or savings account.

are protected with Secure Sockets Layer or other encryption methods, an attacker can hijack a user's session and identity.

Mitigating Broken Authentication and Session Management

Several strategies can be used to help mitigate the impact of broken authentication and session management. Many require the establishment of policies and procedures, while others are more technical. Consider using the following policies to reduce broken authentication and session management.

- **Strong passwords**—Password policies dictating how passwords are formed should require a minimum password length and a mixture of uppercase, lowercase, numbers, and symbols.

- **Password rotation**—Password policies dictate when a new password is required, typically within weeks to six months.

- **Encryption of password storage and transmission**—It's a common practice to ensure that passwords are encrypted both in local storage and as the password is transmitted over the network.

- **Session ID protection**—Typically, Secure Sockets Layer encryption is used to secure information sent over the network during a session. This includes all credential and ID information.

- **Caching and back button**—Limit session caching to prevent potential attackers from simply hitting the browser's Back button to reopen a session.

3. Cross-Site Scripting (XSS)

A well-known Web application vulnerability is **cross-site scripting (XSS)**. In an **XSS attack**, malicious scripts are applied to the Web server but run on the client browser. With XSS, attempts are made to execute malicious code by injecting it and running it on the client browser. If the script code can be executed, the attacker may have access to data, financial information and more.

> **NOTE**
>
> Why XSS and not CSS? The CSS acronym is often used for cascading style sheets. To prevent confusing the two acronyms, cross-site scripting uses the XSS acronym.

The overall purpose of the XSS attack is to obtain client browser cookies, security tokens, or any other personal information that can identify the client with the Web site and the Web server. With client credentials in hand, the attacker can assume the client's identity and impersonate the user's interaction with the site. Now the attacker has access to all client information including credit card information, addresses, passwords, and more.

The XSS attack takes advantage of the vulnerabilities of a Web site. The Web site itself is not harmed nor is it the real target of the attack. The intent is to attack the client browser and gather personal information and to impersonate the user. The target is the client browser's cookies and personal information.

5

Web Site Risks, Threats, and Vulnerabilities

There are two common types of XSS attacks, reflected and stored. **Reflected XSS attacks** "reflect" user input back to a user. An attacker most often uses social engineering to complete the attack. These are the general steps involved in a reflected XSS attack:

1. The user receives an error message, search result, password update request, or Hypertext Markup Language (HTML) e-mail spam message in which a response is required. The message contains at least one link with malicious code embedded in it.

2. When the user clicks on the malicious link, the program gathers the user's context or credentials and passes the information in the form of a request to a vulnerable XSS Web site server.

3. If the Web site server does not parse incoming requests for a reflected XSS attack, the attack continues. A malicious script is embedded in the response to the client and returned to the victim's Web browser.

4. The browser runs the script.

5. The attack is complete when the desired information is sent to the attacker.

> **NOTE**
>
> A user's *context* is a user's identity, usually stored as a value in a cookie.

Figure 5-3 shows an example of a reflected XSS attack.

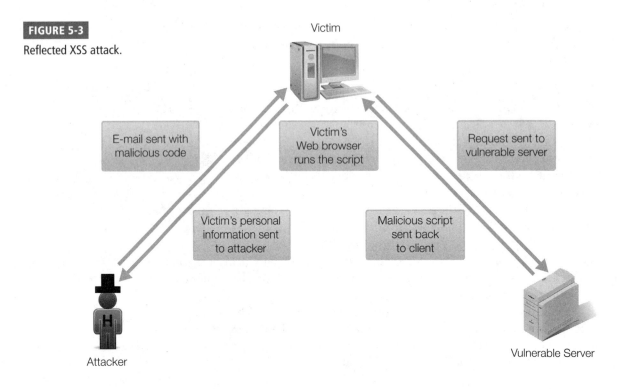

FIGURE 5-3

Reflected XSS attack.

Victim

E-mail sent with malicious code

Victim's Web browser runs the script

Request sent to vulnerable server

Victim's personal information sent to attacker

Malicious script sent back to client

Attacker

Vulnerable Server

Stored XSS attacks are also known as persistent XSS attacks. They are much like reflected XSS attacks with one notable difference. Reflected XSS uses a malicious script that is embedded into a uniform resource locator (URL) link and targets a single victim. The stored XSS attack embeds the script into a page that permits and stores user-supplied content, such as a social networking site or an online forum, where it will be accessible to multiple potential victims. The victim then retrieves the malicious script from the Web server when it requests the stored information.

Mitigating XSS Attacks

XSS vulnerabilities are caused by a failure in the Web application to properly validate user input. Because XSS attacks rely on user input and social networking, the strategies to mitigate XSS attacks revolve around the end user. Guidelines for preventing successful XSS attacks include the following:

- **Educate the end user**—Attackers often perform XSS exploitation by crafting malicious Web site URLs and tricking users into clicking on them. Therefore, you should train users to spot signs of fake sites and links. Let them know they should not enter input into suspect e-mail or Web site communications, for instance.

- **Secure your site**—Use a combination of policy and procedure to prohibit access to high-risk sites such as peer-to-peer (P2P) file-sharing sites, pornography sites, software-pirating sites, and other related sites.

- **Use a firewall**—A firewall system can restrict inbound and outbound connections reducing the overall risk of attack.

- **Be wary of links**—Don't trust links to other sites on e-mail or message boards. They may contain malicious code with damaging potential.

4. Unsecure Direct Object References

An **unsecure direct object reference vulnerability** occurs when administrators fail to secure directories and folders in a server. This attack, sometimes referred to as *directory traversal*, happens by adjusting URL input and accessing a site. This vulnerability can lead to the access of sensitive resources and data leakage.

Unsecure direct object reference vulnerabilities enable attackers to traverse the Web server's directories. For example, attackers can browse from the parent or Web root directory to other branches within the directory tree as if browsing their own file directories. If permissions on directories are not effectively set, attackers can navigate through the structure and look for any sensitive data.

Mitigating Unsecure Direct Object Reference

Server administrators need to anticipate if users modify the URL path and verify directory permissions. Additionally, a Web administrator can properly check for valid user input and monitor the site navigational structure. It's necessary to prevent jumping though folders and other system objects. Even if the attacker doesn't know the exact number of jumps necessary to arrive at the proper location in the directory tree, it isn't difficult to play with the character string input to figure it out.

Some of the common strategies used to reduce the threat of unsecure direct object reference and directory traversal include:

- Use input validation strategy to ensure that only expected input is accepted, also called *taking the known good approach*. Watch out for unneeded use of the "/" and "\" characters.
- Use permissions to lock down objects on the server. Ensure permissions are applied to each layer of directory traversal.
- Test the permissions and structure to ensure there isn't a traversal weakness.

5. Security Misconfigurations

Most applications and hardware devices have a default security setting when shipped. These include devices such as a home router or a network switch, or any of the myriad applications used everyday, such as an operating system or a database. Part of the role of responsible administrators is to understand the default configuration of their devices and to know which settings must be changed for secure operation. This is known as *system* or *application hardening*. It's the process of reviewing system configurations and removing non-essential functions and features. For example, this may mean removing certain roles from a server or blocking ports that are not in use.

Hardening is an essential security practice, as many system and application attacks take advantage of default settings such as accounts, unpatched known flaws, or unsecured or improperly shared data. **Security misconfigurations** can happen on any of your environment's servers, such as your database server, domain servers, applications servers, or firewall servers. Each type of server on the network has a large number of settings and configurations, and a misstep in any one can lead to a security breach.

Mitigating Security Misconfigurations

Mitigating security misconfigurations is an integral part of a security strategy. Administrators can take several steps to ensure that default settings or misconfigurations don't lead to a security breach.

- **Security audits**—Internal administrators commonly conduct periodic security audits on systems. They also arrange for third-party security experts to conduct more rigorous security checks. In corporate environments, for example, external audits might be conducted annually to ensure all appropriate security measures are in place. Audits will also require a change log, which identifies changes to any system that may negatively impact security, including system changes and a review of all user access. These audits can be very grueling and time consuming, but can be made easier with clear documentation and accurate change logs. Such documentation is essential to pass such audits.

- **Keeping operating systems current**—This means not only updating the operating system (OS) with the most current service packs and patches but also not letting the OS itself get too old. It's not smart, for example, to keep using Microsoft Server 2003, even though it may seem to work for your business. New operating systems are designed to meet current security demands.

- **Keeping databases current**—Like the OS, the database needs to be kept current with the latest patches and services packs. Also, the version of a database needs to be within the acceptable life cycle for a product. The life cycle is listed on each vendor's Web site, including end-of-support timelines.

- **Reviewing the life cycle of the products you use**—All applications and software have a life cycle, and it's important to know the rules. In the Microsoft world, for example, there is both *mainstream* and *extended* support. When a product is still in mainstream support, customers can request product changes or developments, and security and non-security updates are available. Once a product is out of mainstream support, it enters the extended support phase. New product developments cease, including non-security updates and service packs. However, security patches will still be released. In the Microsoft world, there are five years of mainstream support. Extended support continues for five years or for two years after two successor products (N+2) are released, whichever is longer. Then the product is retired. Once a product reaches the end of mainstream support, many administrators start planning the replacement of the application. All vendors have end-of-life polices, and managing security will require an understanding of life cycle management.

FYI

It's not just the OS and database that have a life cycle; service packs do as well. For Microsoft products, when a new service pack is released, Microsoft will provide either 12 or 24 months of support for the previous service pack. If you call support, you will often be required to have the latest service pack before you can receive assistance. It's important to know the rules and life cycle of the software you use in order to plan a security strategy.

- **Understanding the function and role of the system**—In order to comfortably switch off unused settings, it's important to first have a clear understanding of what the server or database is designed to do. It's difficult, for example, to close a port on a system or stop a service on the firewall without a clear idea of what it does. With a clear understanding of the server and its role, it's easier to start removing unnecessary features and functions.

- **Training and research**—Finally, it's important that administrators stay curious and constantly research the latest news on breaches or potential security flaws. You can be sure that the hackers are keeping an eye on the latest developments. Further, ongoing training on security strategies and hardening techniques is important.

6. Sensitive Data Exposure

Most companies have some form of sensitive data and therefore a risk of **sensitive data exposure**. Information such as credit card numbers, research secrets, student records, personal information, medical records, banking data, and employee records are forms of sensitive data. These businesses are trusted with this data and users expect that their information is secure and managed correctly. However, it seems that every time you turn on the news, another major security breach is announced. Protecting sensitive data is by no means easy, because there are always people out there trying to get access to it.

When it comes to protecting sensitive data it's important to know three things: which data is sensitive, where this data is located, and who should have access to it.

- **Which data is sensitive?**—Before security professionals can secure sensitive data it's important to know what constitutes sensitive data. An organization may be collecting terabytes of data, but not all data is equally important. Once it's understood what the critical data is, you can ensure a security strategy is in place to secure it.

- **Where is sensitive data located?**—Sensitive data is often stored on the file server, but what about in the cloud? Or perhaps on tape backup? Or in transit? In a manager's e-mail? Knowing where the data is will determine the security measures applied to it. All sensitive data in transit must be encrypted to prevent man-in-the-middle attacks or eavesdropping. This would include all data traveling outside the local network, but it may include even some data traveling within the local network, depending on what the data is.

- **Who needs access to the sensitive data?**— Access to sensitive data can be carefully limited to only those who need access, and at only the right level of access. This will help prevent attacks or data leaks from within an organization. In a business environment for example, there may be 20 accountants who need access to the network. However, not all accountants will have access to the same information. The controller may have access to the company's long-term plan and forecast data, and other accountants may not. Similar data strategies are found in other areas, such as research and development and human resources. Determining who needs access to what is an important consideration for security administrators.

Mitigating Sensitive Data Exposure

Mitigating exposure to sensitive data is critically important to administrators. A leak of sensitive data can have significant financial implications, can damage the reputation of the organization, and hurt its competitive advantage. Therefore, understanding what is sensitive data and how to secure it's essential.

- **Data storage**—Sensitive data, like any other types of data, needs to be stored somewhere. This may be on file servers, in the cloud, or even on a tape backup. Each of these locations requires a form of security to ensure data is stored securely. For example,]a company recently required the executive assistant to take a backup tape home every Friday as part of the tape rotation policy. Company data was unencrypted on the disk and kept in an unsecured location. This is not a great approach to maintaining secure data. Data stored on tape backup must be encrypted and the tape must be maintained in a secure location. Data stored on a disk or on the cloud must also be encrypted and protected using authentication and authorization strategies.

- **Data in transit**—Secure data does not just sit in storage; often it's on the move. This may be passwords to bank accounts, for instance, or credit card information entered into a Web server. Data in transit must be secured using appropriate protocols (such as IPSec, HTTPS, or FTPS) both in the LAN and the WAN.

- **Data authentication**—Authentication is a security measure whereby access to a system, file, or device is controlled by acceptable credentials. For instance, in a common network users will have a username and password to authenticate them and allow them access to the network. Without these credentials they will not be allowed on the network. It isn't always a username and password combination; it can be biometrics such as a thumbprint or a swipe card. The type of authentication used must be secure and managed. This is a common security problem as simple usernames and passwords can be easily obtained. Attackers can do this by using either password-cracking utilities or social engineering strategies.

- **Data authorization**—Once a user is authenticated to a network, *authorization* refers to the files someone has access to. So you can authenticate to the network using your username and password and have read access only to the accounting folder. Incorrect authorization can easily lead to security breaches—accidently or carelessly allowing access to sensitive data is fairly common.

- **Data polices**—Retention and use polices govern how sensitive data must be accessed and stored. All reputable organizations have publicized data and privacy use policies, including how data is stored, how it's used, and how it's kept. Note the box that follows, which shows excerpts from the U.S. Department of Education's privacy policy.

Excerpts from the Privacy Policy of the U.S. Department of Education

1. Privacy Policy Summary

Thank you for visiting the U.S. Department of Education (ED) website and reviewing our privacy policy. Our policy is simple: We collect no personal information about you unless you choose to provide that information to us. We do not give, share, sell, or transfer any personal information to a third party.

Some of our web pages (such as online publication order forms, conference and training registration forms, web discussion forums) let you voluntarily submit personal information. In those cases, we will provide a specific notice before you begin submitting any personal information, explaining how your information will be safeguarded.

2. Non-personal Information We Record

If you do nothing during your visit but browse through the website, read pages, or download information, our website's operating system will automatically record some general information about your visit.

During your visit, our web operating system will record:

1. The **Internet domain** for your Internet service, such as "xcompany.com" or "xcompany.net" if you use a private Internet access account, or "yourschool.edu" if you connect from a college or university domain.

2. The **type of browser** (such as "Netscape version X" or "Internet Explorer version X") that you are using.

3. The **type of operating system that you use** (such as Macintosh, Unix, or Windows).

4. The **date and time** you visit our site, and the **web pages that you visit** on our site.

5. The **address of the previous website** you were visiting, if you linked to us from another website.

We use this information for statistical analysis, to help us make our site more useful to visitors. This tracking system does not record information about individuals.

3. Cookies

The Office of Management and Budget Memo M-10-22, Guidance for Online Use of Web Measurement and Customization Technologies allows Federal agencies to use **session and persistent cookies**.

When you visit any website, its server may generate a piece of text known as a "cookie" to place on your computer. Placing cookie text allows websites to "remember" visitors' preferences, surfing patterns and behavior while they are connected.

The cookie makes it easier for you to use the dynamic features of Web pages. Cookies from ED.gov Web pages only collect information about your browser's visit to the site; they do not collect any personal information about you.

continued

Excerpts from the Privacy Policy of the U.S. Department of Education, *continued*

There are two types of cookies, **single session (temporary)**, and **multi-session (persistent)**. Session cookies last only as long as your Web browser is open. Once you close your browser, the cookie disappears. Persistent cookies are stored on your computer for longer periods.

Session Cookies: We use session cookies for technical purposes such as to enable better navigation through our site. These cookies let our server know that you are continuing a visit to our site. The OMB Memo 10-22 Guidance defines our use of session cookies as "Usage Tier 1-Single Session." The Guidance states, "This tier encompasses any use of single session web measurement and customization technologies."

Persistent Cookies: We use persistent cookies for two reasons: 1) to enable Google's Universal Analytics to differentiate between new and returning visitors to our site, and 2) to block repeated invitations to take the ACSI survey.

1. A Google's Universal Analytics (a third-party analytics provider) persistent cookie remains on your computer between visits to ED.gov for six months. Knowing if a user visited ED.gov within the past six months tells us the difference between visitors and "unique visitors" or those who visit our website more than once during this time period). This is an industry standard and provides high-level information on the breadth of traffic to and content usage of our given digital services. It is a powerful, invaluable metric because it's the only measure that accurately calculates how many individual users visited ED.gov website in a given time. Combined with total visits, it tells a more comprehensive story about ED.gov users and their visit patterns.

2. We also use persistent cookies to block repeated invitations to take either the ACSI (American Customer Satisfaction Index) or iPerceptions survey. Based on your usage pattern, you may be asked if you would like to complete a customer survey of our website. The persistent cookie is set to block repeated survey invitations, and it expires in 90 days. Simply put, if you say you don't want to participate in the survey, the cookie will remember this, and will not allow you to be asked again. We feel it is important and respectful to our users not to ask them the same question more than once. The ACSI or iPerceptions survey are customer satisfaction survey tools used by multiple federal agencies and organizations in the private sector. We use these surveys so we can compare ED.gov results to other government agencies and top commercial websites. These surveys enables ED.gov to: measure program performance; identify targets of opportunity; efficiently leverage scarce resources; obtain valuable feedback from our users; focus management's attention on outcomes; and report customer satisfaction results.

The OMB Memo 10-22 Guidance defines our use of persistent cookies as "Usage Tier 2-Multi-session without Personally Identifiable Information (PII)." The Guidance states, "This tier encompasses any use of multi-session Web measurement and customization technologies when no PII is collected."

continued

Excerpts from the Privacy Policy of the U.S. Department of Education, *continued*

If you do not wish to have session or persistent cookies stored on your machine, you can opt out or disable cookies in your browser. You will still have access to all information and resources at Department websites. However, turning off cookies may affect the functioning of some Department websites. Be aware that disabling cookies in your browser will affect cookie usage at all other websites you visit as well.

ED.gov uses a third-party analytics provider (Google's Universal Analytics) to analyze the data collected through the session and persistent metrics cookies. The third-party analytics provider does not receive personally identifiable information through these cookies and does not combine, match, or cross-reference ED.gov information with any other information. Please review the third-party analytics provider's privacy policy for additional information.

Pursuant OMB Memo 10-22 Guidance Attachment III, V, these cookies collect information similar to that automatically received and stored on the servers hosting ED.gov; they do not collect personally identifiable information. ED.gov does not access or store the raw information collected through these cookies. We do view aggregate statistical analyses prepared by our third-party analytics provider, but these analyses do not include any personally identifiable information. We do not sell, rent, exchange, or otherwise disclose this information to persons or organizations.

Reproduced from U.S. Department of Education privacy notice. Retrieved from *http://www2.ed.gov/notices/ privacy/index.html*

7. Missing Function Level Access Control

The security concern called **missing function level access control** is closely related to incorrect authorization assignment. Whenever a user is authenticated to a network or system and has general access to almost any area or a wide range of functions, there is a security issue. When applying authorization strategies and permissions, the principle of least privilege applies. This means that a user should have the least amount of permissions required to do their job. Additional privileges are added incrementally as business needs arise. These changes in permissions should be tightly controlled using change management procedures.

If users can access additional resources or application features beyond what their roles require, however, access controls have failed. This can result from careless permission assignment or a developer mistake. As an example, a corporate intranet site will often have public and private areas. The intranet site functions much like the Internet site using URL navigation. It's possible for someone to gain access to restricted or forgotten pages using a different URL. For example, a user may routinely navigate to *http:// myintranet/Reports.aspx*. This Reports page may be allowed, but the user might learn a management reports page exists as well. Upon trying *http://myintranet/managers_Reports. aspx* the employee could gain unauthorized access to manager reports. Controlled access to that specific function is missing.

Mitigating Missing Function Level Access Control

Mitigating access control can often be a difficult task. Managing authorization and permissions in a Windows server environment is straightforward. However, when business gets busy, when there is a large turnover of users or when a large number of changes in business practices take place, mistakes can be made. This is why periodic audits are often performed to ensure that all permission assignments are correct. One often-employed method of controlling access is using role-based permission assignments. This means that permissions are not set on an individual basis. Rather, they are assigned to a specific role or task that person performs in the organization. For example, teachers, assistants, and the school principal might all be assigned the same permissions and access to various network resources.

Permission assignment can be tricky, but you can control security breaches through permissions access with standards, audits, and policies. Perhaps a bit more difficult is tracking down access control to areas you may not consider. In every environment there is at least one user who spends time clicking and navigating through applications, looking for areas that he or she may be able to get into. If you are an administrator in a school environment for example, this is all but guaranteed. This includes navigating through the file server clicking every file and folder to see what available. The way to prevent users gaining access to secure files or unauthorized system functionality is to test and retest your systems. This must be done using a variety of user accounts, to ensure it's not possible from any of them, and by using the mindset of a hacker.

FYI

Some environments have a number of applications developed in house. In this case it's important that an application-development process policy be in place. Such a policy outlines the software development cycle and required testing procedures and security checks. In publicly traded companies, such a document is often reviewed as part of the Sarbanes-Oxley (SOX) testing. Essentially, SOX audit and testing is a rigorous process that you, as an IT professional, don't want to fail.

8. Cross-Site Request Forgery (CSRF)

Similar to a form of XSS attack, a **cross-site request forgery (CSRF) attack** creates links that take the visitor to a malicious destination URL. But while XSS attacks exploit a user's trust in a site, CSRF attacks exploit a Web site's trust of the user's browser. This can occur because once a visitor is authenticated and logged into a particular Web site, that site trusts all requests that come from the browser. This trust is exploited with CSRF.

So how does CSRF work? After a visitor logs in, the Web site issues authentication tokens within a cookie to the browser. Each subsequent request sends the cookie back to the site to let the site know that you are authorized. To the site, possession of the cookie means the user is trustworthy. Now, if the visitor were to leave that site and end up on the malicious site, the previous session may still be valid and authenticated. This is where the attacks happen. The attacker can now use the open session to access the previous site with already-approved authentication.

These attacks can be used to transfer money from your bank account and purchase products online. Fortunately, many banking, social network, and other sites log visitors off automatically after a set time period, limiting the danger.

Mitigating Cross-Site Request Forgery

The CSRF relies on an existing trusted session with the target site or the presence of an auto-logon cookie on the victim's PC. If a trusted session is available, the exploit commands are run on the site server within the victim's security context.

The end user can defend against a CSRF attack by doing the following:

- **Log off of all Web sites as you leave**—All Web sites that require you to log on also have a way to let you log off. Do so when you've finished with a secure site.

- **Don't store usernames and passwords unless you are sure**—It's convenient for sites to know you, so you don't have to type in credentials each time, but this can lead to a security breach.

- **Periodically delete cookies in the local browser**—Deleting cookies will help prevent misuse of cookies and authentication records.

- **Ensure browsers are up to date**—All end users should keep browser patched and current to prevent known security flows.

- **Be wary of unknown sites**—Be careful when clicking on unknown links in e-mail or those that pop up. It's difficult to predict if such a link will take you to a malicious site. If following an unknown link, ensure all sessions are closed.

> **NOTE**
>
> Have you been frustrated to be logged off a Web site after a short period of not typing? Part of the strategy of developers is to set a short time period for trusted user sessions. This helps prevent CSRF attacks.

FYI

Many years ago now, the author and a colleague were installing a new firewall on a Linux variant. They had very little experience at the time in Linux, so they installed it with the default settings and went to lunch. By the time they returned, their new server had been taken over and was largely out of their control. A call was waiting from their ISP, advising them that the server was possibly being used as a staging point for hacker attacks. They seemed to be the last two people on the planet unaware of a very common vulnerability. That's how fast security concerns can arise. From then on, they researched vulnerabilities before installing—and as an extra precaution, took shorter lunches.

9. Using Components with Known Vulnerabilities

Many companies use software that has exceeded it life cycle. Others use unpatched applications, and still others may use open-source software solutions with well-known vulnerabilities—well known at least to hackers. The Internet is full of documentation on how to exploit known vulnerabilities within applications or hardware devices. These sites often include not only the documentation but also the tools required to gain access.

Your job as an application user is to try and know as much about vulnerabilities in the applications you use as hackers do. This is not an easy task. Vulnerabilities are not known right away and it can take days, months, or even years before they are discovered. By then the damage is already done.

Mitigating Components with Known Vulnerabilities

So how do you know if an application has a "known" security vulnerability? This is not always easy to discover. Vendors don't typically hide the fact that there is a vulnerability, but most people don't think to go to a vendor's Web site periodically to review the latest security risk for an application. All users, whether network administrators for large companies or home users, must take steps to ensure they are not at risk from a well-known vulnerability. The list below highlights some common sense strategies to help mitigate this risk.

- **Keep applications up to date**—The constant revision and short life cycle of some of your favorite applications make it tempting to stay on older versions for both familiarity and cost reasons. However, vendors will stop patching old versions of software, and when this happens, you are largely on your own.

- **Do your research**—The best time to find a vulnerability is before you even install the application. Whether you are installing a new application at home or rolling out an application business wide, spending time researching and reviewing known security vulnerabilities will almost certainly save you a great deal of trouble.

- **Keep your patches current**—Most applications can provide automatic updates. Operating systems, virus checkers, word processors, and many more apps will automatically log on to the vendor's Web site for the latest patches. This is a great strategy for client systems. In the server world, patching is typically scheduled and tested before patches are installed. Either way, patching your systems to address known and recently discovered vulnerabilities is essential.

- **Remove unused functionality**—The less you have complex applications do, the easier they are to safeguard. Removing unused functionality, plugging ports, and limiting services is all part of hardening applications to help prevent unwanted access.

10. Unvalidated Redirects and Forwards

Suppose you are a Web developer, and many users access a page on your site using a well-known URL. For instance, say they commonly navigate to *www.mysite.com/books.htm* or have a bookmark to go directly to that address. In your development you have created a new page for the books landing page, perhaps *www.mysite.com/books_library.htm*, and want people to go there instead of the old URL. Perhaps you want only a certain region or IP range going to the new URL. In such as case, a developer may use a redirect as a method of taking users where they need to go.

Suppose, however, that it wasn't the developer controlling this redirect but rather someone with malicious intent. Then they could redirect to a site without the user really knowing and be able to capture password information and other information from users who assume they are on a legitimate site. This is a very simplistic explanation of the dangers of redirects and forwards. These essentially take your browser on a journey where you don't want to go. This is known as **unvalidated redirects and forwards**—links from trusted sites that take users to an unauthorized site to gain sensitive information from them or to install malicious software on their machines.

As a practical example of using redirects, suppose you need to change the preferred domain of your site. A preferred domain is the one targeted by search engines for indexing pages. If you are receiving an error that your site is not being indexed, it may be that the preferred domain is not correctly set. As Web administrator, you have set up your preferred domain. For example, maybe it's currently *http://mysite.com* now and you need it to have the "www" as *http://www.mysite.com*. If the preferred domain is not set as the correct one, you may need to redirect engines to the desired site for indexing. You can set the preferred site using Google Webmaster Tools.

1. On the Webmaster Tools Home page, select your site.

2. Select the option Site Settings.

3. In the Preferred domain section, select the option you want, as shown in Figure 5-4.

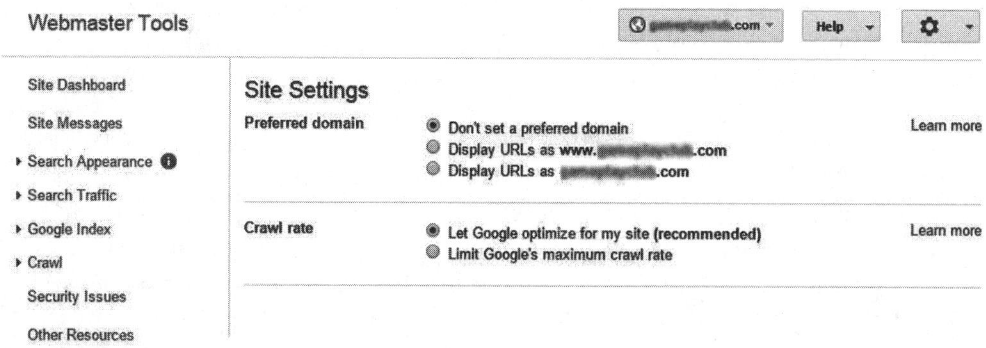

FIGURE 5-4

The Web developer tool screen used to set a Web site as the preferred domain.

In this case maybe *http://www.mysite.com* becomes the indexed preferred site. As Web developer, you may need to use a **301 (permanent) redirect** to move traffic from your non-preferred domain (*http://mysite.com*) to the desired site (*http://www.mysite.com*). In the HTTP world, there are a number of status codes generated and written to a log file located on the Web server. It's likely that you have seen some of the more common codes such as: HTTP Error 401—Unauthorized Access, HTTP Error 400—Bad Request, HTTP Error 404—Page not found, and HTTP Error 500—Internal server error. When a Web page is redirected, one of the common status codes used is 301. A developer may also use a **302 (temporary) redirect**.

Permanent redirects using 301 codes are common if you are merging two domains together, setting a preferred domain, changing domain names, or want to maintain a familiar domain for visitors. Temporary redirects are a little bit different and can be used by spammers or other malicious users. They can take advantage of temporary redirects to capture data and destroy the integrity of a trusted site.

Another common strategy used for redirection is to use the buttons found on Web sites that promise a download or another desired function but which when clicked give a completely different result. The download buttons may look valid. They may apparently be offering updates to common applications such as multimedia or antivirus programs.

FYI

The author and his colleagues had to stop a user on the network from attempting to download Minecraft mods onto a company computer. Processes were in place to prevent this. When asked why he was downloading mods at work, he replied that he was afraid of getting a virus on the family's *home* computer.

5

Web Site Risks, Threats, and Vulnerabilities

However, these buttons may really be links to downloads of malware or adware. Gaming sites are a common place to put such links, which attempt to trick children into downloading various types of malicious software.

Mitigating Unvalidated Redirects and Forwards

Mitigating redirects is somewhat straightforward. If you are a Web developer, the best way to prevent issues with redirects traffic is simply not use them. If you do use them, it's important to use them as intended. For example, restrict the use of temporary redirects and use permanent ones wherever possible. It's also possible to use a whitelist that automatically blocks all pages from any website that is not in your list of allowed Web sites.

Additional Web Threats Not in the Top 10

OWASP identifies the top 10 threats to Web security, but they are not the only threats. The following section details some additional threats that have been on the list in the past and remain a threat.

Malicious File Execution

Malicious file execution is a vulnerability caused by unchecked input into the Web server. Because of unchecked input, the attacker's files can be executed or processed on the Web server. Essentially, the application is tricked into executing commands or creating files on the server. The ability to execute commands on the server can have huge implications including a complete takeover of the server, access to the data on the server, site defacement, and XSS attacks.

Any application that does not adequately restrict or prohibit execution of uploaded files is at risk of a malicious file execution attack.

Mitigating Malicious File Execution

Many of today's newer applications try to manage and prevent the ability to launch malicious file execution attacks. However, it's important to test any application's ability to mitigate malicious file execution. Malicious file execution can be mitigated

---

FYI

Web site defacement is a type of attack in which the attacker changes the appearance of a Web site. The attacker might replace a company's home page, for example, with a Web page that displays messages from the attacker.

using input validation and denial of certain file extensions. Additionally, access control mechanisms, account management, and specific firewall configuration all reduce the chances of a successful execution of a malicious file.

Some strategies that help prevent and manage malicious file execution include:

- Strongly validating user input using only expected, known, good input
- Configuring the firewall to restrict Web servers from making new connections to external Web sites
- Use network segmentation to increase security for sensitive systems and data

Information Leakage and Improper Error Handling

When an error occurs, whether related to the network, operating system, or a Web application, error logs are generated to help programmers isolate the cause and work towards preventing the error in the future. Many error messages are designed to be thorough and include as much information as possible to help troubleshooters. Unfortunately, error messages are not always secured, and an attacker can exploit the information provided within one. This situation is referred to as **information leakage**.

Some of the information that may be included in error messages includes:

- **Error tracing**—Error messages include detailed information about how and when the error occurred. This information is meant to be helpful for debugging and support calls. But it's also helpful for the cybercriminal, providing details on application vulnerabilities and other information that can be used to design an attack against the application.

- **Network and name information**—Administrators take steps to remain anonymous and unknown to attackers. Many error messages can undo these efforts by including such information as server name, IP address, and network services used. This information can provide attackers with the ability to pinpoint network locations.

- **Verification of the existence of a file**—If a user who is not authorized to access a file attempts to do so, the error message returned often says the user is not authorized to access that resource. For an attacker trying to locate files known to contain sensitive information, the error message has just provided a positive hit.

- **ID or password login failure**—Failed logon attempts often generate an error message. These error messages can help pinpoint the correct logon credential and compromise a system. Some even provide helpful examples of correct naming conventions, such as You must enter "Smith.John" not "John.Smith".

- **Database details**—Many database error messages include information on database names and other seemingly harmless information. However, attackers can use this information to access database vulnerabilities.

An attacker can use virtually any information in error messages. Attackers try hard to elicit errors to provide them this information. Corporate policies regarding the handing of error messages are critical.

Mitigating Error Message Handling Errors

Of the vulnerabilities listed so far in this chapter, mitigating error messaging is one of the easiest to manage. However, it takes constant vigilance by the administrator to ensure confidentiality. To prevent error messages from being excessively helpful to attackers, consider the following:

- **Policies and procedures**—Develop network-wide policies and procedures dictating who has access to error messages. The fewer people who have access to error messages, the better.

- **Error message storage**—Develop procedures for how error messages should be stored. Many error messages are immediately reviewed and then kept for future reference. They need to be kept securely.

- **Assume the worst**—Many error messages are cryptic and seem unreadable; however, they may contain information that can be used against you and your applications. Treat the material as confidential, assuming it is valuable to an attacker.

- **Apply adequate permissions**—Applications logs contain error messages. It's important to ensure that the logs on a server are closely guarded and controlled.

Unsecure Cryptographic Storage

Cryptographic storage involves the encryption of data so it cannot be captured and read. *Encryption* refers to the conversion of data in clear text to cipher text that cannot be read without known decryption keys. *Unsecure cryptographic storage* refers to sensitive data that is stored without appropriate encryption. This includes the storage of passwords, sensitive information, financial records, and credit card information. Finding unencrypted information is all too easy for attackers.

Encryption is the best way to protect stored data in a business environment. However, encryption carries a new set of security considerations.

Mitigating Unsecure Cryptographic Storage

There are many publicly available cryptographic algorithms. Nearly all have been tested extensively and proven to have suitable strength or shown to have weaknesses. Therefore, an application developer need not create a new algorithm. When choosing among publicly available algorithms, take care to choose a strong one.

Storage of the keys is of the utmost importance. It's bad practice to store the private keys where they are always accessible; rather store private keys offline and accessible only when needed.

More information on security protocols and cryptography is covered in the next section.

Unsecure Communications

As soon as data begins to travel through any media, it is susceptible to data theft and other forms of tampering. Security measures are deployed to ensure that communication is secure from the sending point to the end. This includes LAN and WAN communications, Web applications, and those communications that travel through the public network. This section explores some of the strategies used to secure communications.

Mitigating Unsecure Communications

Before two systems on a network can securely exchange data, they must agree on a security agreement. This agreement is the **security association (SA)**. For communication to occur, both the sending system and receiving system must agree on the same SA.

A system known as the **Internet Key Exchange (IKE)** manages the SA negotiation process for Internet Protocol Security (IPSec) connections. IPSec is a protocol used to ensure confidentiality and integrity of data communications. IKE is an Internet Engineering Task Force (IETF) established standard method of security association and key exchange resolution. IKE performs a two-phase operation; the first ensures a secure communications channel and the second negotiates the use of SAs.

Phase I SA negotiation. In Phase I SA negotiation, the two computers establish a secure and authenticated connection. IKE provides the initial protection during this phase. There are several negotiations during the main mode phase including:

- **Encryption method used**—The encryption methods include DES and 3DES. Encryption methods are discussed later in this chapter.

- **Integrity algorithm**—Phase I negotiation uses one of two integrity verification methods, the Message Digest 5 (MD5) and Secure Hash Algorithm (SHA).

- **Authentication method**—Authentication methods include Kerberos V5, certificate, or pre-shared key authentication.

- **Diffie-Hellman**—The Diffie-Hellman represents a base keying strategy. There are three Diffie-Hellman groups: Group 1 (768 bits of keying material), Group 2 (1,024 bits), and Group 2048 (2,048 bits).

Once these factors have been negotiated between systems, IKE will generate a master key that protects authentication. Without this authentication, the communication will fail. Each of these elements is discussed later in this chapter.

Phase II SA negotiation. Phase II negotiates which SAs will be used. There are three steps to complete Phase II:

- **Step 1**—Systems exchange requirements for securing data communications. This includes the IPSec protocols, Authentication Headers and Encapsulating Security Payloads, integrity and authentication methods (MD5 or SHA1), and encryption methods (3DES or DES). Once an agreement with these elements is achieved, the SA is established. Actually, two SAs are established, one for inbound traffic and one for outbound.

- **Step 2**—The security key information between the two systems is updated. In this process, IKE is responsible for refreshing keying material and for creating new or secret keys for the authentication and encryption of packets.

- **Step 3**—In the final step, the SAs and keys, along with the Security Parameters Index (SPI), are passed to the IPSec driver.

Internet Security Protocol (IPSec)

IPSec is an IP layer security protocol designed to provide security against internal and external attacks. This is an important consideration as the reasons and methods for securing against attacks from outside the network are well documented. IPSec provides a way to protect sensitive data as it travels within the LAN, including session communication between the Web server and the client. Firewalls don't provide such security for internal networks, so a complete security solution will require both a firewall solution and internal protection provided by such security mechanisms as IPSec.

To create secure data transmissions, IPSec uses two separate protocols, **Authentication Header (AH)** and **Encapsulating Security Payload (ESP)**. AH is primarily responsible for the authentication and integrity verification of packets while ESP provides encryption services. They are independent protocols and can be used together or individually. Whether you use one or both depends on your network's security needs.

Authentication Header. Before using AH, it's important to understand what its function is and what it can and cannot do. AH provides source authentication and integrity for data communication but does not provide any form of encryption. AH is capable of ensuring that network communications cannot be modified during transmission. However, AH cannot protect transmitted data from being read.

AH is often implemented when network communications are restricted to certain computers. In such an instance, AH ensures that mutual authentication takes place between participating computers, which in turn prohibits network communications between non-authenticated computers.

Encapsulating Security Payload. Encapsulating Security Payload (ESP) provides encryption services to network data; however, you can also use it for authentication and integrity services. The difference between AH authentication and ESP authentication is that ESP includes only the ESP header, trailer, and payload portions of a data packet. The IP header is not protected as with AH, which protects the entire data packet. For encryption services, ESP provides encryption with the Data Encryption Standard or triple DES encryption algorithms.

IPSec authentication protocols. To establish IPSec communications, two hosts must authenticate each other before SA negotiations can take place. The three different ways systems can be authenticated are:

- **Kerberos**—Kerberos provides the primary security protocol for authentication within a domain and verifies both the identity of the user and network services. Advantages of Kerberos include its ability to provide mutual authentication between user and server as well as its interoperability.

- **Public key infrastructure (PKI)**—PKIs authenticate clients that are not members of a trusted domain, non-Windows clients, or computers that are not running the Kerberos authentication protocol. The authentication certificates are issued from a system acting as a certification authority (CA).

- **Pre-shared keys**—In pre-shared key authentication, computer systems must agree on a shared, secret key to be used for authentication in an IPSec policy. Pre-shared keys are used only where certificates and Kerberos cannot be deployed.

IPSec encryption protocols. IPSec offers three primary encryption methods. The one chosen will depend on the security needs of an organization. The encryption methods are:

- **Data Encryption Standard (DES) (40-bit)**—This encryption method provides the best performance but at a cost: encryption security is lower. It can be used in environments where data security is a little lower.

- **DES (56-bit)**—Through your IPSec policies, you can implement DES as the encryption method. The DES algorithm is a 56-bit encryption key. Published in 1977 by the U.S. National Bureau of Standards, this algorithm allows the ability to frequently regenerate keys during a communication. This prevents the entire data set from being compromised if one DES key is broken. However, its use is considered outdated for business use, and should only be used for legacy application support. Specialized hardware can crack the standard 56-bit key.

- **Triple DES (3DES)**—IPSec policies also allow the choice of a strong encryption algorithm, 3DES, which provides stronger encryption than DES for higher security. 3DES uses three 56-bit encryption keys, creating in effect a 168-bit key. However, due to several demonstrated attacks since its creation, 3DES's effective strength is equal to an 80-bit key. Still, it's used in such high-security environments as the U.S. government.

FYI

HTTPS is the protocol within the Transmission Control Protocol/Internet Protocol (TCP/IP) suite used for accessing a secure Web server when authentication and encrypted communication is possible. With HTTPS, the client request is forwarded to a secure port number (443) rather than to the default Web port number 80. Once established, HTTPS manages and secures the entire protocol. HTTPS encrypts the session data using the SSL protocol.

Secure Sockets Layer (SSL)

Secure Sockets Layer (SSL) is the standard security technology for establishing an encrypted link between a Web server and a Web browser. This link ensures that all data passed between the Web server and browsers remain private and integral. SSL is an industry standard and is used by millions of Web sites to protect their online transactions with customers.

To create an SSL connection, a Web server requires an SSL certificate. When you choose to activate SSL on your Web server, you will be prompted to answer questions about the identity of your Web site and your company. Your Web server then creates two cryptographic keys, a private key and a public key.

Failure to Restrict URL Access

The **failure to restrict URL access attack** overlaps with unsecure direct object reference. Information on a Web server is not sufficiently protected when direct links aren't present. A user, whether persistent or fortunate, can and will find hidden URLs. Web application developers must implement access control for each function. The Web user must be authorized explicitly to operate that function. Otherwise, it's only a matter of time before unauthorized users discover sensitive data.

Mitigating Failure to Restrict URL Access

Removing the risk of attacks requires careful planning. Because a skilled attacker can skip simple validation steps, Web application developers need to plan from the design stage to implement protection throughout the application. Likewise, Web site administrators must anticipate an attacker's actions. Penetration testing, which mimics an attacker, is most effective for identifying vulnerabilities.

Table 5-1 summarizes the OWASP Top 10 threats and the additional threats discussed in this chapter. The table also summarizes a description of the threats as well as the mitigating strategies.

TABLE 5-1 Summary of the OWASP threats discussed.

OWASP TOP 10	THREAT	THREAT DESCRIPTION	MITIGATING STRATEGY
1	Injection	Injection flaws enable the attacker to bypass applications' access controls and create, change, delete, or read any data the application can access.	Input validation, verifying all data that is received, helps prevent malicious data from entering an application.
2	Broken authentication and session management	Compromised authentication strategies lead to data loss.	Develop strong password policies and secure session ID management.
3	Cross-site scripting (XSS)	Malicious scripts are applied to the Web server but run on the client browser. With XSS, attempts are made to execute malicious code by injecting it and running it on the client browser.	Educate users about questionable links and restrict access to high-risk sites.
4	Unsecure direct object references	Attacker can access and abuse object references, unprotected files, or folders.	Ensure the ability to traverse folders and files is locked down.
5	Security misconfiguration	Applications or hardware with settings and configurations that create security risks.	Harden applications by removing or controlling access to non-essential functions and features.
6	Sensitive data exposure	The accidental release or capture of sensitive data such as credit card numbers, research secrets, student records, personal information, banking data, employee records.	Understand what is sensitive data, where it is stored, and who has access to it.
7	Missing function level access control	Potential security issues when a user is authenticated to a network, system, or application, but individual function access is not controlled.	Test systems to ensure the right levels of permissions are set to each system and applications.

continued

TABLE 5-1 Summary of the OWASP threats discussed, *continued.*

OWASP TOP 10	THREAT	THREAT DESCRIPTION	MITIGATING STRATEGY
8	Cross-site request forgery	CSRF attacks exploit the trust a Web site has in the user's browser.	Log off of Web sites when finished and store usernames and passwords effectively.
9	Using components with known vulnerabilities	Known application vulnerabilities that, when attacked, have exploits running with system privileges.	Keep up to date with vulnerabilities and keep all applications and hardware current within the identified lifecycle.
10	Unvalidated redirects and forwards	Modifying trusted URL domain with unvalidated URL data, using links to redirect a user to a malicious site. Once the redirect has occurred, the attacker may steal user credentials or have users download a malicious application.	Limit the use of redirects, especially 302 temporary redirects. Use a whitelist to control where redirects can go.
Additional Web Threat A	Malicious file execution	Execute applications on the Web server or remote system.	Ensure appropriate input validation.
Additional Web Threat B	Information leakage and improper error message handling	Attackers gain information from error logs and messages.	Secure error messages and develop policies restricting access to error reports.
Additional Web Threat C	Unsecure cryptographic storage	Sensitive data are stored in plaintext.	Use encryption protocols to ensure any captured data cannot be read.
Additional Web Threat D	Unsecure communications	Network communications are sent in cleartext. All captured data can be captured and read.	Use security protocols to secure transmissions in transit.
Additional Web Threat E	Failure to restrict URL access	Similar to unsecure direct object reference. An attacker may browse unprotected areas and data.	Lock down files, folders, and directories to ensure unauthorized viewers cannot access them.

Best Practices for Mitigating Known Web Application Risks, Threats, and Vulnerabilities

As shown in this chapter, there are a number of risks and threats aimed toward Web applications. Mitigating these risks requires a combination of policy, procedure, and technical strategies. Attack strategies include:

- Authentication and authorization attacks
- Client-side attacks, including XSS and CSRF attacks
- Command execution attacks, such as malicious execution and SQL injection attacks
- Information disclosure attacks, such as directory traversing

A number of best practices can be deployed to help mitigate and manage these attacks. These include:

- **General network security procedures**—To help protect Web applications, harden the network to ensure it's secure by establishing perimeter defenses, such as IDSs, IPSs, and firewall systems. This also includes establishing strong physical and logical security measures.

- **Network security procedures**—Procedures are used as a rulebook for network security implementations. Who is allowed to see error logs? Who is responsible for ensuring encryption? Who enforces password policies? Network-wide security procedures are documented and must be followed.

- **Deploy encryption strategies**—Encryption of stored data and moving data is critical. All sensitive data needs to be encrypted and secure.

- **User education**—Many attacks rely on social engineering strategies. The best defense is to educate users on the potential dangers of clicking on links, giving out personal information, and other things users may do without realizing how dangerous they are.

- **Preventive mitigation tools**—To stay ahead of attacks, software is available that scans systems for potential Web application vulnerabilities.

CHAPTER SUMMARY

Many forms of attack aim at Web applications. Some rely on social networking and others use technical scripts. Regardless of the type of Web application attack preventative and mitigating strategies can help manage the risk.

OWASP lists the top 10 Web application vulnerabilities. Administrators must be aware of what the risks are and how they can harm a system. Today's network administration requires a complete security strategy that encompasses all aspects of internal and external security strategies. All sensitive data, whether stored on a disk or in transmission, must be secured using protocols such as SSL, HTTPS, and IPSec.

KEY CONCEPTS AND TERMS

301 (permanent) redirect
302 (temporary) redirect
Authentication Header (AH)
Broken authentication
Cross-site request forgery
    (CSRF) attack
Cross-site scripting (XSS)
Encapsulating Security
    Payload (ESP)
Failure to restrict URL
    access attack
Information leakage

Injection flaw attack
Input validation
Internet Key Exchange (IKE)
Missing function level
    access control
Open Web Application
    Security Project (OWASP)
Reflected XSS attack
Secure Sockets Layer (SSL)
Security association (SA)
Security misconfigurations
Sensitive data exposure

Session
SQL injection attack
Stored XSS attack
Unsecure direct object
    reference vulnerability
Unvalidated redirects
    and forwards
Web site defacement
XSS attack

CHAPTER 5 ASSESSMENT

1. Reflected and stored are types of XSS attacks.

A. True
B. False

2. An attack has occurred on your network. An attacker was able to traverse several files and folders, looking for sensitive data. What type of attack has occurred?

A. Unsecure direct object reference
B. XSS
C. CRFS
D. Injection flaw

3. AH is the protocol within IPSec used for encryption services.

A. True
B. False

4. As network administrator, you are concerned with the plaintext transmission of sensitive data on the network. Which of the following protocols are used to help secure communications? (Select three.)

A. IPSec
B. HTTP
C. SSL
D. IKE

5. To increase network security, you have decided to use HTTPS on your shopping cart site. Which of the following ports does HTTPS use?

A. 80
B. 53
C. 443
D. 51

6. _____ and AH are used to secure IPSec transmissions.

7. CSRF attacks exploit the trust a Web site has in a user's Web browser.

A. True
B. False

8. Kerberos is a(n) _____ protocol.

9. To increase overall communication security, you decide to implement 3DES encryption. Which of the following statements is true of 3DES?

A. Its key length is 168 bits.
B. It cannot be used in a Windows-based environment.
C. It uses 128-bit encryption.
D. It has to be used with Kerberos.

10. You are concerned about a cross-site forgery attack. Which of the following can you do to help prevent such an attack?

A. Ensure antivirus protection is up to date.
B. Log off of Web sites when finished.
C. Use stronger passwords.
D. Encrypt stored passwords.

11. To establish IPSec encryption, two hosts must create a shared key with each other before SA negotiations can take place.

A. True
B. False

© Rodolfo Clix/Dreamstime.com

Introducing the Web Application Security Consortium (WASC)

THE WEB APPLICATION SECURITY CONSORTIUM (WASC) is a nonprofit organization dedicated to promoting the best practices of application security. The participants are both experts and beginning students of application security—individuals, academic institutions, and corporations from all over the world. It's important to realize that anyone can participate and cooperate with WASC.

It is important when managing applications and services to understand their weaknesses and how they can be exploited. The function of WASC is to help identify these weaknesses and best practices for mitigating these threats.

Chapter 6 Topics

This chapter covers the following topics and concepts:

- What the threats to Web application security are
- What the common Web site attacks are
- What the common Web site weaknesses are
- What best practices for mitigating Web attacks are
- What best practices for mitigating weaknesses are

Chapter 6 Goals

When you complete this chapter, you will be able to:

- Understand the function of the WASC threat classification
- Review WASC threat types
- Identify the hazards of user input
- Understand the various injection attacks
- Understand common Web site attacks
- Manage injection flaws
- Review proper input and output handling
- Understand the role of authentication and authorization in Web attacks
- Review directory security
- Review best practices for Web application security

The Threats to Web Application Security

Security is a top priority for today's Web sites and Web applications. The computing world struggles to ensure that security keeps pace with expanding e-commerce and online business opportunities. Old vulnerabilities are commonly exploited while new ones are discovered. News of exploits, identify theft, and other security breaches shakes consumer and end-user confidence.

Despite the risks, people continue to shop, bank, and post personal data online. With each transaction, they send credit card information, names, addresses, passwords, and more over the Web. This information is constantly at risk. In the past, perimeter security measures were deployed to help address the risks as were security protocols such as Secure Sockets Layer (SSL) and **Transport Layer Security (TLS)**; however, these measures are not enough to secure all data.

The **Web Application Security Consortium (WASC)**, a nonprofit group dedicated to improving application security practices, identifies 34 classes of Web attacks and 15 different Web site weaknesses. Web sites and Web applications face these attacks every day. Some attacks seek to capture data, others to overwhelm the system and applications. Further, many of these attacks cannot be addressed with traditional perimeter security measures. New security and policy measures need to be incorporated into an organization's security strategy.

Common Web Site Attacks

Phishing schemes, denial of services, stolen credit card numbers, identify theft—the threats to Web sites and Web applications seem overwhelming. The first step in protecting Web applications and Web services is having a clear understanding of the current threats that can affect an organization's network and Web services. Attacks result in loss of data, identity theft, loss of brand integrity, and loss of money.

Web site and Web applications are a target for today's hackers and cybercriminals. As people become more integrated into the Web—with online banking, online health-care information, online purchasing, and the posting of confidential data—securing Web applications and services becomes increasingly critical. Unfortunately, every online transaction is a potential security risk with cybercriminals patiently waiting to exploit Web site and Web application vulnerabilities. Organizations today must design and implement strategies to address Web site vulnerabilities. The WASC outlines 34 threats to Web applications and processes. These risks are discussed next.

Abuse of Functionality

Today's Web sites offer many interactive features and provide a range of services and functionality. In normal operation, the functions that a site provides are a harmless addition to the Web site, but in the hands of the hacker, these functions become a security threat.

The abuse of functionality attack takes advantage of the features of a Web site or a Web application to launch an attack. An abuse of functionality attack can access an application or Web site with the intention to defraud, launch a denial of service attack to consume resources, modify the site, or damage the Web application.

The abuse of functionality problem occurs with interactive Web sites. When Internet visitors are given access and interactive privileges, such as using the search feature or uploading files, some people find ways to turn these features into attacks. There are several forms of interactive content that may be abused:

- Password/username recovery forms
- E-mail forms, which can be used for spam
- A Web site's search feature, which can be used to navigate through unrestricted areas of the Web site directory
- A Web site's file upload system, which can be used to upload malicious content or to replace key configuration files
- Username-and-password forms, which can be abused to flood a Web site in a DoS attack

Brute-Force Attacks

A **brute-force attack** attempts to crack a **cryptographic key** or password simply by guessing. The cryptographic key is the confidential component of a cryptographic system. A brute-force attack involves programs designed to guess every possible combination until the password or key is guessed correctly. Of course, the more complex a password is, the harder it is to crack and the less likely brute force will be successful. This is why choosing passwords that are difficult to guess is so critical.

For Web applications, the most common forms of brute-force attacks are launched against user logon credentials. Many users choose passwords that are easy to remember and they change them infrequently. A brute-force dictionary attack uses an exhaustive list of words attempting to guess at a password or username. This includes trying common misspellings of words, uppercase and lowercase words and guessing at common strategies such as replacing the capital letter "O" with a zero (0) and the number 1 with a lowercase letter "i." Although it may sound very time-consuming, a brute-force attacker can process millions of name and password combinations per second.

A successful brute-force attack may allow the intruder to assume the identity of the broken account and:

- Access confidential and sensitive data intended to be protected behind user credentials.

- Provide access to administrative areas of applications, Web servers, or operating systems. Once there, the intruder may have unobstructed access to change, modify, copy, or delete data and sensitive information.

- Place **malicious code**, such as Trojan horses, worms, and other malware into Web servers or applications. Among the brute-force attack types that can be launched are:

    - **Logon credentials**—Today's users have username/password combinations for everything from social networking sites to online banking and system logons. Brute-force attacks can be launched at each of these areas.

    - **Credit card information**—Some hackers brute-force credit card information. This includes getting the security CVV number on the back of a card.

    - **Files and folders**—Many files on a system are protected using a "security by obscurity" principle, meaning the directory location is secret. Brute-force attacks that keep guessing at directory locations can eventually find them. The directories may hold sensitive data such as usernames and passwords or company information.

> **NOTE**
>
> One way to verify if a system has been attacked by a brute-force attack is to check the log files periodically. A log file registering numerous logon failures may be an indication of a brute-force attack.

These are a sample of the types of brute-force attacks that can be launched. Essentially, anywhere credentials or user input is required, an attacker may use a brute-force attack.

Authentication Account Lockout Policy

Account lockout policies are used to configure how a system will respond to invalid logon attempts. All operating systems use some sort of authentication lockout procedures. In this section, you will review those available in Microsoft Windows operating systems in editions intended for organizational or enterprise use.

The danger of not having an account lockout policy in place is that it's possible for intruders to keep guessing usernames and passwords in an attempt to gain access to the system. An example is programs that run through a dictionary of words and characters trying to access an account. To prevent these brute-force attacks, you can use account lockout policies that shut the account down after a preset failed number of logon attempts.

There are many options for configuring account lockout options. Table 6-1 summarizes account lockout options in Windows operating systems.

A lockout policy is designed to secure the authentication process. Without such a strategy in place, the authentication process is easily compromised.

TABLE 6-1 Account lockout options in Windows.	
ACCOUNT LOCKOUT POLICY	**DESCRIPTION**
Account lockout duration	The lockout duration defines the number of minutes that an account remains locked out. Once the time has been exceeded, the account will automatically be enabled. The available range is 0 to 99,999 minutes. You can also specify that a locked-out account will remain locked out until an administrator explicitly unlocks it by setting the value to 0. The default is 30 minutes when the account lockout threshold is set to 1 or higher.
Account lockout threshold	The threshold policy sets the number of failed logon attempts that must be exceeded before a user's account is locked out. The value can be between 1 and 999 failed logon attempts. The default is 0.
Reset account lockout counter after	This policy specifies how long the counter will remember unsuccessful logon attempts. The available range is 1 minute to 99,999 minutes. The default setting is None; this policy is enabled only if the account lockout threshold policy is set to something other than 0.

Developing Password Policies

Passwords represent one of the biggest security concerns for both networks and Web site access. Once a password is compromised, access to the system is an easy logon process. To help make system passwords more secure, organizations of all types develop and enforce password policies. Table 6-2 shows some of the password policies that may be used.

For many environments, the default password policy settings are sufficient. For those systems that require additional security, configuring the password policy is one of the first steps to take in securing the system.

Buffer Overflow

A **buffer overflow** occurs in an application when more information is stored in the buffer than the space reserved for it can hold. A *buffer* is a temporary data storage area. When a buffer's storage area is exceeded, it can cause data in other areas to be overwritten, which can corrupt stored information. Buffer overflows have been a form of attack since the 1980s and are a result of application programming that fails to test and consider the potential problems with buffer overflow attacks.

An attacker can launch a buffer overflow attack to:

* Crash an application or process.
* Modify the application or process.
* Take ownership of an application or process.

In a common form of buffer overflow attacks, an interactive session or shell is initiated on the victim's machine. If the program being exploited runs with a high privilege level (such as root for UNIX/Linux or Administrator for Windows), the attacker gets elevated privileges to that machine.

Buffer overflows are not easy to protect against. In fact, most people must rely on well-written code to prevent buffer attacks. Unfortunately, many programs that are tested thoroughly still have potential buffer security flaws. Many people, to prevent buffer overflow security risks, rely on traditional security mechanisms, including maintaining up-to-date service packs and patches for all software applications.

Content Spoofing

Content spoofing involves creating a fake Web site or Web application and fooling victims into thinking it's a legitimate one. One of the goals of content spoofing is to lure victims to an authentic-looking but illegitimate Web site. The next step is to steal logon credentials, credit card information, or other forms of personal data.

Content spoofing tactics often include spam e-mail links, forum links, and chat room links. These links have the same goal, which is to lure victims to the fake Web site. At a content-spoofing site, if someone enters personal data, the attacker can read and use it.

> **NOTE**
>
> Content spoofing attacks combine with phishing attacks to lure victims to a site. Mitigation strategies employ the same strategies as those used with phishing.

TABLE 6-2 Password policies.	
PASSWORD POLICY	**DESCRIPTION**
Enforce password history	The password history policy sets the number of unique new passwords that must be associated with a user account before an old password can be reused. This prevents the same password from being used over and over, increasing the difficulty in obtaining the password. The value must be between 0 and 24 passwords.
Maximum password age	The maximum password age sets the number of days that a password can be used before the system requires the user to change it. You can set passwords to expire after a number of days between 1 and 999, or you can specify that passwords never expire by setting the number of days to 0. The default setting is 42 days.
Minimum password age	The minimum password age sets the number of days that a password must be used before the user can change it. You can set a value between 1 and 998 days, or you can allow changes immediately by setting the number of days to 0. The default setting is 0.
Minimum password length	Passwords using more characters are typically more secure than those using fewer characters. The minimum password length allows you to set the least number of characters that a password for a user account may contain. You can set a value between 1 and 14 characters, or you can establish that no password is required by setting the number of characters to 0.
Passwords must meet complexity requirements	Many users choose a password based on the ease of remembering the password. This policy ensures that the passwords chosen meet a certain complexity requirement making them harder to guess.
Store passwords using reversible encryption for all users in the domain	This password policy supports applications that use protocols requiring knowledge of the user's password for authentication purposes. Storing passwords using reversible encryption is essentially the same as storing plaintext versions of the passwords. Don't enable this policy unless application requirements outweigh the need to protect password information.

Many content spoofing attacks today use phishing as a mechanism to lure victims to an illegitimate site. For example, a recent e-mail campaign alerted e-mail recipients that a Christmas package was due to arrive and needed verification for delivery. The e-mail provided a link that, when clicked, took users to a legitimate-looking delivery site. Users were asked for an address, credit card information, and other personal data. These forms of attack are very effective, particularly when the original phishing e-mail appears to come from a trusted source.

Credential/Session Prediction

In computing terms, a *session* is an information exchange between two or more computing devices. The **session ID** identifies previous users to a Web site and stores user-specific information about a session. Credential/session prediction is an attack that involves impersonating the Web site user and then using the rights and privileges of that user on the site. Specifically, the session prediction attack tries to obtain the session ID of an authorized user. For example, if a Web site creates sessions using easily guessable methods, such as adding the date plus the first five characters of the last name, an attacker could easily generate valid session IDs while posing as a real user.

Session IDs allow for user tracking on a Web site, including automatic authentication for future visits. This means users don't have to reenter data and authentication credentials each time they log onto a Web site. If the session ID is compromised, the attacker can hijack a session or replay a session. In either case, your credentials are being used. It's impossible for the Web site to tell if a trusted source or an attacker is using the credentials.

The term *session hijacking* refers to an attacker obtaining a valid session ID and then using it to access the victim's sessions. With the session ID, the attacker can access the session and Web communication and pose as the owner of the session ID. Session IDs are usually kept in cookies or form fields on the client system.

> **▶ NOTE**
>
> One issue with session IDs is insufficient expiration time. If a session stays active too long without timing out and requiring renewed authentication, an attacker can reuse an old session and session ID. To mitigate, always log off Web sites when you're finished with them.

Cross-Site Scripting

The main purpose of the cross-site scripting (XSS) attack is to obtain client browser cookies, security tokens, or any other personal information that can identify the client with the Web site and the Web server. With client credentials in hand, the attacker can assume the identity of the client and impersonate the user's interaction with the site. Now the attacker has access to all client interaction information including credit card information, addresses, and passwords.

The XSS attack takes advantage of the vulnerabilities of a Web site, but the Web site itself is not harmed. The Web site is not the target of the attack. The intent is to attack the client browser, gather personal information by exploiting the Web server, and impersonate the user. The target is the client browser's cookies and personal information. The goal is to steal the identity of the cookie's owner.

Cross-Site Request Forgery

Similar to a form of XSS attack, a cross-site request forgery (CSRF) attack creates links that take the visitor to a malicious destination uniform resource locator (URL). While XSS attacks exploit the trust that a user has for a site, CSRF attacks exploit the trust a Web site has for the user's browser. This can occur because once a visitor is authenticated and logged onto a particular Web site, that site trusts all requests from the browser. This trust is exploited with a CSRF attack.

After a visitor logs onto a Web site, the site issues authentication tokens within a cookie to the browser. Each subsequent request to send the cookie back to the site lets the site know you are authorized to take whatever action is taken. The site has absolute trust in the browser's credentials. If the visitor were to leave that site and go to the malicious site, the previous session may still be valid and authenticated. Here is where the attack happens. The attacker can now use the open session to access the previous site with already-approved authentication.

Denial of Service

Denials of service (DoS) attacks are designed to prevent legitimate use of a network service. Attackers achieve this by flooding a network or Web application with more traffic or data than it can handle. This type of attack is not designed to gain network access but rather to overwhelm a system and tie up its resources to the point that it becomes unusable. A DoS attack can prevent a service from being available to users by completely overwhelming the application or system. For example, some attackers flood a Web server with so many requests that it cannot continue to function as a Web server. DoS attacks are often difficult to trace. Because attackers have no need to receive information back, it's common to spoof or fake the source of the attack. This makes it more difficult to trace the origin.

The impact of DoS attacks include:

* Saturating network resources, which then render that service unusable
* Flooding the network media, which prevents communication between computers on the network
* Causing significant downtime because users are unable to access required services
* Creating huge financial losses for an organization due to network and service downtime

Fingerprinting

A fingerprinting attack is used to gather as much information as possible about a target system, including the operating system used, Web application and version in use, database information, and network architecture. Gathering this type of information is critical for attackers because many of the attacks they use, whether XSS, buffer overflows, or others, are dependent upon certain versions of Web applications or software. This makes it important for administrators to ensure that fingerprinting attacks cannot pinpoint potentially revealing information to an attacker.

With fingerprinting, the attacker may be looking for the following information:

- **Web server version**—Knowing the Web server version allows the attacker to be aware of any associated vulnerabilities and mitigation steps patching them.
- **Network architecture**—Some fingerprinting attacks reveal the general outline of the network, including overall layout and perimeter security used.

From a security standpoint, any information that an attacker can get is too much information. If your company has a Web presence, it's likely that the firewalls permit Hypertext Transfer Protocol (HTTP) traffic over port 80. However, the firewalls don't need to permit, for example, a request to resolve a Domain Name System (DNS) request for a resource for internal use only, especially if the request originates from outside. Web servers can leak information through this port in HTTP that an attacker can use.

Format String

Format strings and buffer overflow attacks share a similarity in that both attacks exploit user input. With a format string attack, user input is interpreted as a command by the application. Although both the buffer overflow and the format string attack take advantage of available user input, format string attacks are successful because user input is not validated. Buffer overflow attacks are successful because the buffer boundaries are exploited.

Unfiltered user input employs format string parameters found in programming languages such as C and C+. The attack occurs when a malicious user uses string input for specific C or C+ functions. Common string function commands include:

- **Fprint**—Prints to a file
- **Sprintf**—Prints to a string
- **Printf**—Output of a formatted string

There are many different command string functions. The following is a list of parameters that can be used with these commands to complete the attack:

- **%s**—Reads character strings from the memory of the process
- **%n**—Writes an integer to locations in the memory of the process
- **%x**—Reads data from the stack

FIGURE 6-1

HTTP communication
process.

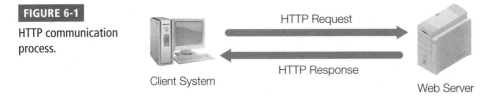

If the input string is entered with a valid parameter, the attacker may be able to:

- Run commands on the server.
- Read information within the stack.
- Cause segmentation faults and/or software crashes.

HTTP Response Smuggling

HTTP is the protocol used for transferring documents over the World Wide Web.
HTTP works on a client/server model with the client system requesting information
and resources from a Web server. This process is shown in Figure 6-1.

Figure 6-1 shows the request and response nature of the HTTP communication.
However in real-world application, the client usually does not communicate directly
with the Web server. Rather, the communication goes through intermediary points
such as firewalls and proxy servers. Figure 6-2 shows the HTTP request traveling
through intermediary points.

There are a number of intermediary points through which the HTTP request
may travel, including:

- Local browser cache
- Proxy server (onsite)
- Intrusion detection system (IDS)
- Filtering firewall
- Web application firewall
- DMZ

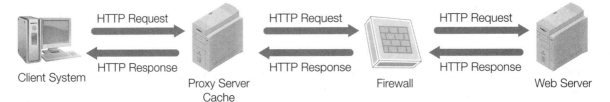

FIGURE 6-2

HTTP communication through intermediary points.

HTTP Response Splitting

This is a specialized attack. The attacker needs familiarity with the target Web application and the end-user agent or browser. As the name implies, the idea of the attack is in splitting something. The split object is the HTTP header or an error message sent back as a response. This relies on two criteria to be successful. First, a Web application must be vulnerable to the attack. Second, the attacker sends a specially formed HTTP request that makes the application return what is interpreted as two responses.

The attack is very similar to the HTTP request splitting attack. The attacker achieves the split by sending the carriage return (CR) and linefeed (LF) characters. Neither character actually shows up onscreen. However, when encoded within a string of information, the result can cause unintended consequences.

The threat created by this attack is the use of unexpected carriage returns. If successful, the attacker can interact directly with the Web server, instead of the application layer. The way to mitigate the risk is to screen for CR and LF characters at the application layer.

> **▶ NOTE**
> Sending a carriage return (CR) or linefeed (LF) character is essentially the same as pressing the Enter key on a keyboard.

HTTP Request Smuggling

This attack is effective whenever Web proxies or Web application firewalls are in use between a Web server and the end user. In other words, this attack is used when one server handles an HTTP request and then passes it on to another Web server. Requests by proxies are often parsed in different ways than the intended destination Web server. The proxy may parse only part of the request, if not just enough to know where it's intended to go. The request may include malicious commands or special characters to obtain new, sensitive information. When this attack proves successful, an attacker will leverage it to launch more malicious attacks.

HTTP Request Splitting

The attack is very similar to the HTTP request smuggling attack. The effect is similar to an HTTP response splitting attack. In an HTTP request splitting attack, the object being split is the initial HTTP request. The attacker forms a malicious request. This request is interpreted by most browsers as a single request. However, the Web server receiving the special request interprets it as two requests. The request is split by inserting special characters within the body of the primary request. The effectiveness of the attack depends on whether the Web application parses requests for CR or LF characters. If successful, the attacker can take advantage of the vulnerability to send longer lasting attacks.

Integer Overflows

An *integer* is a whole number, one that is not a fraction. Integers may be 0, 1, 2, 3, and so on, and their negative equivalents $-0, -1, -2, -3$, and so on. Integer-related vulnerabilities typically arise when an application performs some arithmetic on an integer and exceeds the integer's intended size. For example, in computing, an 8-bit integer is often used. The 8-bit integer has a value of -128 to 127. The integer overflow attack pushes the integer beyond this boundary. If 1 is added to 127, an integer overflow occurs.

The result of exceeding the integer boundary can lead to undefined and unpredictable outcomes such as crashes. Additionally, integer overflows can result in buffer overflows and can be used to execute malicious code.

LDAP Injection

The **Lightweight Directory Access Protocol (LDAP)** is a protocol that provides a mechanism to access and query directory services systems. Directory services include systems such as Novell Directory Services (NDS) and Microsoft Active Directory, database servers, Web servers, and Web application servers. Although LDAP supports command-line queries executed directly against the directory database, most LDAP interactions are via utilities such as an authentication program (network logon) or locating a resource in the directory through a search utility.

LDAP injection is an attack technique that exploits Web sites that allow LDAP statements from supplied input. If an attacker modifies an LDAP input statement, the attacker may be able to gain database access with full privileged permissions. LDAP injection vulnerability occurs due to weak input validation prior to processing LDAP statements.

Preventing LDAP injection requires monitoring and allowing only valid input for LDAP queries. This means utilizing both client-side and server-side validation to ensure the authenticity of the input. This validation should ensure that only authentic input is accepted.

Mail Command Injection

Another form of input validation attack is the mail command injection attack. The mail command injection is designed to attack mail servers and applications that use the IMAP and SMTP protocols. The Simple Mail Transfer Protocol (SMTP) protocol defines how mail messages are sent between hosts. SMTP uses Transmission Control Protocol (TCP) connections to guarantee error-free delivery of messages. SMTP is not overly sophisticated, and it requires that the destination host always be available. For this reason, mail systems spool incoming mail so that users can read it later. **Internet Message Access Protocol (IMAP)** is a Transmission Control Protocol/Internet Protocol (TCP/IP) protocol designed for downloading, or pulling, e-mail from a mail server. IMAP is used because although the mail is transported around the network via SMTP, users cannot always read mail immediately, so it must be stored in a central location. From this location, it needs to be downloaded, which is what IMAP allows you to do.

Many Web sites and Web applications allow users to submit forms, feedback, or other content using e-mail and the SMTP protocol. If attackers are able to place malicious input into the SMTP or IMAP conversations, they may be able to take control of the messages being used by an application.

SMTP injection vulnerabilities are mitigated by implementing strict validation of any user-supplied data that is passed to an e-mail server and in SMTP and IMAP conversations.

> ▶ **NOTE**
>
> SMTP and IMAP injection vulnerabilities are often exploited by e-mail spammers who obtain e-mail addresses and generate large numbers of nuisance e-mail messages.

Null Byte Injection

This attack is successful in part because of the diverse languages used for creating Web sites. For many Web sites, a Web page is created using a high-level language such as PHP, ASP, or Java. Sometimes the Web page processes information at a lower level language such as C or C++. A subtle difference between the former and latter languages is how they handle null byte characters. Examples of null byte characters are `%00` or `0x00` in hexadecimal.

In the case of high-level languages, a null byte character does not affect processing of information. In fact, with input validation, the null byte character is likely ignored. However, the lower, system-level languages act differently. They interpret a null byte character as the end of a string of information. This abruptly ends processing. How this affects the system can be unique per Web page. This abrupt end causes unknown behavior to the Web site and perhaps even the system. Even worse, whatever happens will be run with system-level privileges.

OS Commanding

Operating system commanding is an attack aimed directly at a system's operating system. In this attack, user input launches unauthorized commands on the operating system, including those on a Web or database server. In a successful OS commanding attack, the attacker can execute commands on the server through a browser or other input mechanisms. With OS commanding, executed commands by an attacker will run with the same privileges of the component that executed the command, (e.g., database server, Web application server, Web server, wrapper, application). Because the commands are often executed with elevated privileges, an attacker can gain access or damage parts that otherwise are unreachable (e.g., the operating system directories and files).

As with other forms of input attacks, the attack can be minimized by restricting character input, restricting forms of input, using permissions to lock down access and disabling unused commands. To help protect operating systems and network servers, security systems must be in place to maintain tight controls over acceptable user input.

Path Traversal

Path traversal attacks can occur on any server or system where files are stored. In a **path traversal attack**, the attacker attempts to circumvent acceptable file and directory

> **NOTE**
>
> A common path traversal attack uses the . . / syntax sequence to attempt to locate restricted areas on a server.

areas to access files, directories, and data located elsewhere on the server. This can be done by changing the URL address to point to other areas on the server.

Many attackers know the names and default locations of key files and directories in various applications and Web servers. Knowing the locations allows attackers to try a traversal attack directly to where they want to go. In a common path traversal attack, the attacker uses . . / to navigate the directory tree to access files in other directories.

Predictable Resource Location

Similar to the path traversal is the predictable resource location attack. Every system has numerous default system files and directories that are often forgotten but may hold sensitive data. Using a brute-force attack or even an educated guess based on default file locations, the attacker can potentially gain access to unauthorized areas.

Every operating system has default resource and system directories and files, which may include backup files and folders, log files, temporary files, download files, and update files. Any and all of these file and folder locations may contain information about network resources, Web applications, network topology, passwords, and sensitive data. Much of this information can be used to launch another attack and enable unauthorized access to sensitive locations. There are several predictable resource location attacks. The syntax to access them looks similar to the following:

* /backup/
* /logs/
* /system/
* /admin/
* /temp/
* /logs/

Preventing path traversal and predictable resource location attacks may involve removing old files and folders that contain sensitive data, securing files and folders that contain sensitive data, controlling user input, and establishing security filtering software that monitors access to files and folders.

Remote File Inclusion (RFI)

With injection attacks, attackers want to place their code and input on a target system. This is the intent of the remote file inclusion (RFI) attack. RFI attacks commonly attempt to take advantage of weaknesses in the PHP programming language. The PHP language is a scripting language commonly used to create dynamic Web pages. If attackers are successful in injecting files and code into a PHP-created Web site, they can access anything on that site, such as the database, passwords, and credit card information.

Once the attackers inject code, they can run malicious code on the target system. The results of an RFI attack range from errors to system crashes to complete system compromise.

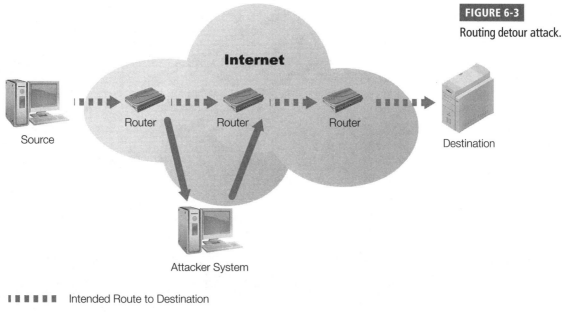

FIGURE 6-3

Routing detour attack.

■ ■ ■ ■ ■ ■   Intended Route to Destination

▬▬▬▬▬▬▬   Route Detour Attack

Routing Detour

Routing detour attacks are a form of **man-in-the-middle attack** in which an intermediary attacker reroutes data to an alternate location. (A man-in-the-middle attack involves eavesdropping on communication between the sender and receiver.) Routing is an important concept for networks and the Internet. All online transactions are routed to a destination based on information within the HTTP header. A message traverses the Internet from one router to the next until it finally reaches its destination.

The routing system used on the Internet can be a security threat in that an attacker may be able to reroute data away from its intended destination to one the attacker chooses. In some cases, the data can be routed and then rerouted back to the original destination and the theft goes completely unnoticed. This can be particularly damaging if the detoured data is sensitive, such as banking information or passwords. Figure 6-3 shows how a routing detour may occur.

Session Fixation

There are many types of session-based attacks; most are a form of impersonation. **Impersonation** refers to an attacker's attempt to use the session credentials of a valid user. A session fixation attack allows an attacker to steal and use a valid user session. A *session* is a communication between systems on a network. This attack can be successful when an authenticated user's session ID does not immediately expire, allowing an attacker to capture and use an existent session ID. During the attack, the attacker entices a user to authenticate to a Web server then hijacks the valid and trusted session ID.

FIGURE 6-4

Session fixation attack.

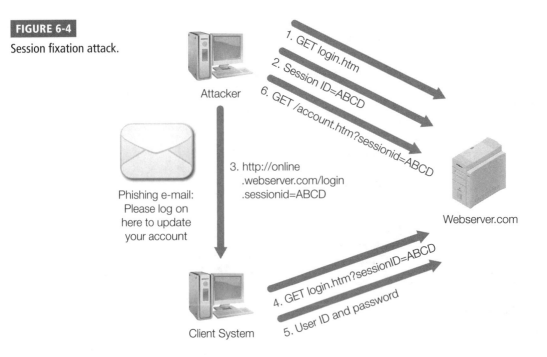

There are at least three ways in which an attacker can obtain a valid session identifier:

- **Prediction**—With prediction attacks, the attacker simply guesses at the session identifier often using a brute-force attack.

- **Capture**—Capturing a valid session identifier may involve obtaining a cookie that is used to store the session identifier or exploiting a browser's vulnerability.

- **Fixation**—Session fixation is an attack in which the victim is tricked into using a session identifier chosen by the attacker.

Figure 6-4 shows how this attack may occur.

SOAP Array Abuse

> **NOTE**
>
> Simple Object Access Protocol (SOAP) is an XML-based protocol that lets applications exchange information, commonly over HTTP.

Simple Object Access Protocol (SOAP) is a general method for communicating **Extensible Markup Language (XML)** over networks. XML is a set of rules for encoding documents electronically. XML was chosen as the standard message format because of its widespread use and open source development. Additionally, a wide variety of freely available tools significantly eases the transition to a SOAP-based implementation. SOAP is commonly used for browser-accessed Web applications and in communications occurring between back-end application components.

SOAP communications may be exploited using user-injected code similar to other injection attacks. XML syntax using characters such as <> and / can be inserted into SOAP communications, allowing the attacker to interfere with the data message.

SSI Injection

Server-side include (SSI) injection is an injection attack that occurs on the server and not on the client system. In an SSI attack, malicious code is placed in a Web application, which is then stored on the server. When the Web application is executed locally on the Web server, the malicious code carries out its function. The SSI injection attack is successful when the Web application is ineffective in filtering user-supplied input.

To defend against SSI injection attacks, an application must be configured to assume that all input is potentially harmful and take steps necessary to secure and filter all user input. This includes filtering the types and numbers of characters that are accepted by Web servers from users.

SQL Injection

Most Web applications use a database to store sensitive client or other information. This may include:

- User accounts and personal data
- User passwords
- Client financial information
- Credit card information

The Structured Query Language (SQL) is used to communicate with these databases and can be used to add or modify content, or to update or delete information from the database. Sometimes, if SQL is not properly deployed, configured, or updated, attackers may be able to exploit SQL.

Web applications use SQL statements that incorporate user-supplied data. If this user-supplied data is unsafe and unfiltered, the Web application may be vulnerable to an SQL injection attack. A successful attack will allow the attacker to access, read, delete, and modify the information within the database and even take control of the server on which the database is operating.

URL Redirector Abuse

URL redirecting points a Web page to another URL of your choice. That is, a visitor clicks on one URL and is then taken to another. URL redirecting is commonly done for a variety of reasons. For example, if a company changes its URL, a redirector takes customers and clients to the new site automatically. URL redirecting may be used for Web server load balancing, or to link updates or make navigation easier. In itself, URL redirecting is not a security risk.

URL redirectors can be misused by attackers, however, to redirect visitors to a malicious site. For example, a normal redirection link such as:

```
http://www.homepagexyz.com/login.php?redirect=
```

may take you to:

```
http://www.homepagexyz.com/home.php
```

This is a simple URL redirection. However, consider a slight variation. In the following sample:

```
http://www.homepagexyz.com/login.php?redirect=
```

may take you to:

```
http://www.h0mepagexyz.com/home.php
```

In the second example, the letter "o" has been replaced with the number "0", and the URL redirection may point to a malicious site. The malicious site may look authentic but will in fact be an imposter site. This very simple example shows how redirecting may catch users off guard.

XPath Injection

As previously mentioned, Web applications use databases to store and access information. Some of these databases store and organize data using the XML language. The **XML Path (XPath) language** is used for navigating XML documents and for retrieving data from within them. User input and queries are used with XPath to access the XML information. With **XPath injection attacks**, attackers are able to inject data into an application so that it executes user-controlled XPath queries. When successfully exploited, this vulnerability may allow an attacker to bypass authentication mechanisms and access XML information without proper authorization.

> **▶ NOTE**
> Strategies to ensure proper input validation are covered later in this chapter.

As with other injection attacks, input validation is an important part of the defense strategy. Input validation helps to ensure that malicious input is filtered out and does not execute and enable access to the XML database. Detailed input validation strategies include **sanitization**, accepting known good input only, and filtering. Sanitization is the inspection of user input for potentially harmful code and modifying the code according to predetermined guidelines.

XML Attribute Blowup

DoS attacks are commonly used to overwhelm network resources, hardware, Web applications, and more. DoS attacks are some of the oldest forms of attack, dating to the mid-1990s. The XML attribute blowup is a form of DoS attack aimed at exhausting the system's resources.

XML DoS attacks are extremely asymmetric: To deliver the attack payload, an attacker needs to spend only a fraction of the processing power or bandwidth that the victim must spend to handle the payload. Worse, DoS vulnerabilities in code that processes XML are also extremely widespread. Even if you're using thoroughly tested parsers like those found in the Microsoft .NET Framework System.Xml classes, your code can still be vulnerable unless you take steps to protect it.

XML External Entities

This attack relies on a Web application that employs an XML parser to parse untrusted data from the end user. The application's parser runs at system level privileges and does not filter what was provided to it before running. For example, an application expects XML structured data, but an attacker instead provides a command and path to a desired file on the local Web server. The application, instead of returning XML output, returns the password file on the local Web server.

The paths to many system files are known because a well-known structure is created upon installation. Some of those files could provide sensitive knowledge of that system, even revealing vulnerabilities. Further, some files specific to a certain user may also be revealed.

XML Entity Expansion

This attack is essentially a DoS attack. The attacker takes advantage of the ability to create XML-related macros, also called *entities*. Normally, a created entity is resolved by an XML parser. These entities are created with care that they don't loop endlessly. An attacker, however, may create sets of entities that recursively try to resolve themselves. This exercise would quickly exhaust a system's resources. The result would be a denial of normal operation and availability.

XML Injection

The XML injection attack takes advantage of the trusting nature of an XML application. Success of this attack follows the "garbage in, garbage out" rule of data processing. If unintended or malicious XML content is fed into a XML message, the result will likely also be malicious. The challenge for the attacker is gaining the intended effect. For example, imagine that an organization's XML application expects specific content to produce a letter to customers. The attacker instead sends content that the application successfully utilizes to create the customer letter. The letter's meaning is changed for the worst. You can imagine the customer's response when the organization claims the letters are all created automatically.

XQuery Injection

An SQL injection attack hijacks an SQL query, and an XQuery injection attack does the same for XQuery commands. In both cases, an attacker attempts to send data which may be acceptable to start, but is malformed to interrupt a query. The ending portion of the sent data will be malicious, sending a command or trying to elicit information or queries. All these are unauthorized to the attacker, but would be executed by the system with its own privileges, on behalf of the attacker.

> **NOTE**
>
> An XQuery injection attack is the same as the SQL injection attack in concept and method. The only difference is the setting, similar to a car hijacking versus a plane hijacking.

As shown in this section, there are numerous attacks that can be launched against Web server and Web applications.

Common Web Site Weaknesses

Many organizations are unaware of the types and large number of attacks that can be launched against their corporate sites. Administrators must be prepared to identify and protect against the variety of attacks that cybercriminals use. WASC highlights 15 well-known Web site attacks and identifies what they are designed to do. This section looks at the various Web attacks and how you can mitigate them.

Application Misconfiguration

Applications can be one of the more difficult elements to secure on a network due to their complexity and their ability to accept user input. Application misconfiguration attacks focus on identifying and exploiting weaknesses found within Web applications. Unfortunately, many Web applications have vulnerabilities out of the box and additional features enabled by default. This may mean hidden accounts, open security features, and more. The default configuration of most applications is typically not sufficient in terms of security. Application misconfigurations are common, and so too are the attacks aimed at exploiting them.

> **NOTE**
>
> Many administrators assume that all applications are flawed and have inherent security risks. This assumption is a good way to approach network application security.

Key to managing application misconfigurations is application hardening. **Application hardening** is the process of securing applications in use on a network. This involves clearly understanding how applications operate to ensure no unused or unsecured features are being used. For example, in the case of operating systems, it may be necessary to block or disable any unused services or ports. Additionally, it's necessary to ensure that all applications are updated with the latest service pack or patch.

Directory Indexing

Web sites have a directory structure. A URL takes you to a specific page within the directory index of the Web site. In normal operation, a user enters a URL address such as *http://www.xyz.com/page1/* and the page is retrieved and presented to the user. However, many sites use a feature known as automatic directory listing. **Automatic directory listing** identifies all of the files within a given directory if the base file is not found. The base files refer to such files as *index.html, default.htm, index.php,* and so on.

When these files are not found, a directory listing is sent to the client system. When a list is presented to the client, it may contain directories or files that were never intended to be seen or accessed. Directory indexing is often harmless, but revealing these files provides attackers with information.

Some of the files that may be included in the directory listing include:

- Backup files
- Temporary files
- Hidden files
- User accounts
- Configuration files
- Administrator documents
- Personal client folders

Improper File System Permissions

Effectively managing files and folders on an operating system will certainly involve assigning and managing the permissions required to access them. Permissions allow administrators to decide who can and cannot access particular files and folders and what they can do with them when they are accessed. If your system is configured with NTFS partitions, you have the option of controlling file and folder access on a per-user or per-group basis. If you are using a system with FAT partitions, you are out of luck. FAT partitions offer no local security functionality.

In a Windows environment, there are six basic NTFS permissions available: Full Control, Modify, Read & Execute, Read, Write, and List Folder Contents. Table 6-3 describes each of these.

TABLE 6-3　NTFS permissions.

NTFS PERMISSION	DESCRIPTION
Full Control	Gives the user complete control, including changing permissions, taking ownership, and all other access given by the other NTFS permissions.
Modify	Allows the creation of new files and folders, viewing and changing a file's attributes, listing and viewing the contents of a folder, and deleting files. The Modify permission does not allow the user or group to take ownership of a file or to change the permissions for files and folders.
Read & Execute	Allows users to traverse folders and execute files within those folders. It allows users to view the attributes of a file or folder, list the contents of a folder, and read the data in a folder's file.
Read	Allows users to list the contents of a folder, read the data in a folder's file, and see the attributes of a file or folder.
Write	Allows users to change the attributes of a file or folder, create new files and write data to those files, create new folders, and append data to the files.
List Folder Contents (for folders only)	Allows the user to traverse folders, list the contents of a folder, and see the attributes of a file or folder.

Inherited Permissions

Folders and files on a Windows-based system are often stored in a hierarchal fashion, meaning that folders are likely to contain additional folders and subfolders. Normally, when permissions are assigned to a parent folder, each of the subfolders (child folders) inherits the permissions of the parent folder. Inherited permissions can make the administrator's job easier, as it's necessary to assign permissions to only one folder instead of to numerous subfolders.

There are situations, however, where you will not want to have inherited permissions filtering down to subfolders. In such a case, you can establish explicit permissions, which will override any inherited permissions.

In Windows desktop system, for example, changing the inheritance setting for a file or folder is done through the Security tab of a folder's Properties dialog box. From the Security tab, click Advanced to open the Advanced Security Settings dialog box. Click the Edit button at the bottom of the box, and then deselect the Inheritable Permissions from this Object's Parent option. Once deselected, the file or folder's permissions can be explicitly set independent of any inherited permissions.

Advanced NTFS Settings

The six basic NTFS permissions discussed above are composed of several more specific NTFS permissions. Knowing the individual NTFS permissions allows an administrator to fine-tune permission settings and give more control over what users can and cannot access. Table 6-4 shows the advanced NTFS file permissions.

Improper Input Handling

As mentioned earlier in this chapter, many applications rely on external input from sources such as end users and browsers. External input provides a potential security risk as attackers aim to exploit input as part of an attack. In security terms, input handling refers to the validation, sanitization, storage, and filtering of user input. Most security experts suggest that it's a best practice to treat all user input as potentially harmful. Applications that accept user input are potentially vulnerable to injection attacks, overflow attacks, DoS attacks, and others.

TABLE 6-4 Advanced NTFS file permissions.

PERMISSION	DESCRIPTION
Traverse Folder/ Execute File	Allows or denies permission to move through folders. Traverse Folder takes effect only when the group or user is not granted the Bypass Traverse Checking user right in the Group Policy snap-in. Execute File allows or denies running program files.
List Folder/Read Data	List Folder allows or denies viewing file names and subfolder names within the folder. Read Data applies to the files only and allows or denies viewing the data in the files.
Read Attributes	Allows or denies the ability to view the attributes of files or folders.
Read Extended Attributes	Allows or denies the ability to view the extended attributes of files or folders.
Create Files/ Write Data	Create Files allows or denies creating files within a folder. Write Data allows or denies making changes to a file and overwriting existing content.
Create Folders/ Append Data	Create Folders allows or denies permission to create folders within folders. Append Data allows or denies the ability to make changes to the end of files.
Write Attributes	Allows or denies the ability to change the attributes of files or folders.
Write Extended Attributes	Allows or denies the ability to change the extended attributes of files or folders.
Delete	Allows or denies permission to delete file or folders.
Read Permissions	Allows or denies permission to read files or folders.
Change Permissions	Allows or denies the ability to change permissions of the file or folder, such as Full Control, Read, and Write.
Take Ownership	Allows or denies the ability to take ownership of files or folders.
Delete Subfolders and Files	Allows or denies the ability to delete subfolders and files.

FYI

Blacklisting and whitelisting define what's unacceptable or acceptable, respectively. This practice is useful for Web sites, user input, e-mail, or even phone calls. In this chapter, a whitelist might include numbers as acceptable content when prompting for a phone number. A blacklist might include letters for the same user input. Regardless of the strategy used, validation should include scans for certain characters and correct syntax usage.

When handling user input, there are a few security approaches to consider:

- **Sanitization**—When user input is sanitized, it's inspected for potentially harmful code and modified according to predetermined guidelines. Sanitization often involves identifying and disallowing specific characters and syntax sequences.

- **Reject known bad input**—Certain syntax and characters are banned from input. If they show up in a query, the entire input stream is rejected. With a **blacklist** strategy, a catalog of known banned input is referenced and updated as needed. Rejecting known bad input can be effective; however, attackers are quick to find new and improved ways to exploit Web sites. This means that a blacklist strategy may always be one step behind.

- **Accept only known good input**—An opposite approach to the blacklist is a whitelist strategy for managing user input. A **whitelist** approach allows only code that matches a set of acceptable inputs. All other input is blocked. This can be a highly effective way to manage user input as the administrator dictates what input is and is not allowed.

Improper Output Handling

Output handling refers to the way applications control their output data. Output data from the application may take the form of logging, printing, coding, error messages, or raw data to be passed on to another application. The risks of improper output handling occur when the application produces unintended or sensitive information, such as overly informative error messages. Another example would be if a malicious user purposefully provoked the application to reveal sensitive information.

Information Leakage

Information leakage occurs when a Web site or Web application discloses sensitive information unknowingly. For example, error messages can reveal information about the server, the application, and network topology that an attacker can use to exploit the system. Information leakage can come from a variety of sources, such as stolen laptops, unsecured backups, log files, error messages, employee e-mails, HTTP headers, and unencrypted data transfers. Any data leakage can assist an attacker in isolating and planning an attack.

There are many strategies to help reduce the risk of data leakage. These include:

- **End-user education**—Inform network users of the threats and impact of data leakage and how they can help prevent the problem.
- **Filtering systems**—Use filtering systems to help identify information heading into and out of the network and network servers.
- **Authorization**—Use permission to help secure local files, folders, and directories. Apply the principle of least privilege to help reduce who has access to key areas of the server.
- **Monitoring error messages**—Check whether error messages, which seem cryptic and unreadable, actually give out potentially sensitive information about the network.
- **Policies and procedures**—Develop strong networkwide policies and procedures to govern how data is to be handled and stored. This includes error messages and log files.

> **NOTE**
>
> When it comes to authorization, the concept of least privilege is often applied. The **principle of least privilege** refers to providing users with as few privileges as possible, just enough to fulfill their network needs. It's a security measure that ensures users are not granted more permissions than needed.

Unsecure Indexing

All Web pages must be indexed by search engines to be listed in search results. **Indexing** is an automatic process in which software programs known as spiders or bots examine Web sites, collecting data and analyzing the Web sites' keywords. The results are stored and indexed in the search engine's database. When a user performs a search, the search engine looks through the database and returns the results.

In the process of indexing, the spiders and bots may collect sensitive or unwanted information. This indexed information may be retrieved from the index database by an attacker who uses a series of queries to the search engine.

> **NOTE**
>
> How well is your site being indexed? There are many reasons why a site may not be indexed properly. To test indexing in Google, type the following in the Google search bar:
>
> *Site:yourdomainname.com*
>
> The results from this query will display the index results from your domain. This site search works equally well for all top-level domains, such as *.edu, .net,* and *.org.*

Insufficient Anti-Automation

Many Web applications require manual user input, such as filling out various Web-based user forms. Anti-automation attacks occur when processes that should be done manually are automated by the attacker. Automated attacks fill out forms and overload the system or take advantage of vulnerabilities. An example is an automated application that fills out forms for new accounts or continually posts to message boards.

FIGURE 6-5

An example of
CAPTCHA.

Type the code shown [   ]   🔊 Need audio assistance ?

Try a new code

Anti-automation strategies are used to prevent these forms of attack. **CAPTCHA (Completely Automated Public Turing Test to Tell Computers and Humans Apart)** refers to mechanisms used to protect against automated attacks. The function of CAPTCHA is to provide a challenge/response mechanism to help ensure that a form is being filled out by a human and not an automated process. A common type of CAPTCHA requires users to input letters or number combinations from a distorted image on the screen. Others strategies may be a simple math question, a logical question, or a required response to an audio message. Figure 6-5 shows a distorted text CAPTCHA.

Insufficient Authentication

For a client to gain access to a network, network resources, or many Web sites, both authentication and authorization are required. *Authentication* is any process that verifies identity. This usually involves a username and password but can include any other method of demonstrating identity, such as a smart card, biometrics, voice recognition, fingerprints, and codes. Authentication is a significant consideration for network and system security and one that administrators battle with regularly.

Authorization is finding out if the person, once identified and authenticated, is allowed access to a particular resource. This is usually determined by finding out if the person is a part of a group that provides the correct permissions or has a particular level of security clearance.

Insufficient authentication occurs when a Web site permits an attacker to access sensitive content or functionality without having to properly authenticate. Web-based administration tools are a good example of Web sites providing access to sensitive functionality. Depending on the specific online resource, these Web applications should not be directly accessible without requiring users to properly verify their identity.

Insufficient Authorization

In Web application terms, insufficient authorization happens when the application does not adequately ensure that authorization polices are being used and enforced. This means that after users are authenticated, they are limited to access based on their authorized privileges.

Many applications grant different application functionality to different users. The security trick is to balance the user permissions, granting enough access to use the application but not enough to allow access to protected areas.

Insufficient Password Recovery

Many Web applications and Web sites require password authentication. Unfortunately, passwords and usernames are often forgotten, and password recovery mechanisms are required. Typical password recovery requires users to provide secret information that only they should know, often in the form of a hint or response to a secret question that jogs the memory. The recovered username and password is sent to the user's registered e-mail address.

> **NOTE**
> When creating password and username combinations, do so with the assumption that an attacker may test password recovery mechanisms. If banking online or maintaining sensitive data on a Web site, verify that password recovery procedures are strong.

In many instances, the password recovery procedures are sufficient, but sometimes an attacker may pose as the one who forgot the password and recover it. With the username and password combination, the attacker then can lock out the legitimate user and use the account at will. In some cases, a legitimate user may not notice the attack for months, and the attacker has all that time to access the resources as the legitimate user.

Insufficient Process Validation

Each process used for a Web application follows certain logic and structure. For instance, a user purchasing an item from a Web site follows orderly steps. These include selecting the item, adding it to the shopping cart, entering credit card information, and so on. Web sites and Web applications often use similar logical flows to complete various transactions. **Process validation** refers to the correct sequence of steps in a transaction or online process. Insufficient process validation occurs when the attacker skips steps in the process and generates errors or unforeseen results.

> **NOTE**
> Insufficient process validation attacks are closely aligned with abuse of functionality attacks in which the function of the Web site is exploited.

Preventing insufficient process validation may involve carefully testing all Web processes in and out of their logical flow. Additionally, in development it's important to outline and create a logical process flow.

Insufficient Session Expiration

When devices on a network want to communicate, they do so by creating a session between them. This session is established using protocols and security mechanisms, and these security mechanisms set up trust in the session. Insufficient session expiration can occur when this trust is exploited by an attacker who captures the session ID and impersonates the valid user.

> **▶ NOTE**
>
> Any potential Web application with sensitive data should use a default timeout system that identifies when a site is inactive and automatically logs out. This helps prevent inadvertently leaving a session open to attack.

Many Web sites commonly use cookies to store session IDs, and once a cookie is captured, it may be used for an active session. One of the strategies used to prevent an attacker using a session ID is to end the session or log out. Once the session has expired, this attack cannot occur. Some applications have no expiration time set on a session and some have session expirations that are too long. Decreasing the session expiration time will help prevent an attacker from using an unexpired session.

Insufficient Transport Layer Protection

Insufficient transport layer protection refers to failure to encrypt or secure communications at the Transport Layer of the Open Systems Interconnection reference model. In the communication between a Web server and a client, if the link is not secured, all information is sent back and forth in cleartext. This makes the communication susceptible to a man-in-the-middle attack in which the integrity and confidentiality of the data in transit are threatened.

Today, administrators use the Transport Layer Security (TLS) protocol and the Secure Sockets Layer (SSL) protocol. TLS is used to secure communications between client/server applications. When a server and client communicate, TLS ensures that no one can eavesdrop and intercept or otherwise tamper with the data message.

The SSL protocol is similar to the TLS protocol in that it's used to secure connection between a client and a server, over which any amount of data can be sent securely.

Server Misconfiguration

The servers used by an organization are critical for daily operations, providing key services to both internal and external users. This includes authentication services, proxy services, firewall, data repository Web, e-mail, file server management, and much more. Given their importance, it's little wonder that they are often the target of attack.

Perimeter defenses are an important part of server security, but firewalls, IDS, and IPS are only part of the solution. The proper administration of servers is critical to overall security. There are many forms of attacks that may be launched at servers including:

- Exploiting bugs or security flaws in the operating system itself
- DoS attacks aimed at overwhelming server resources
- Injection attacks designed to corrupt the system or access sensitive data
- Launching a man-in-the-middle attack aimed at intercepting unencrypted data
- Malware attacks, including Trojan horses and viruses designed to disrupt server functioning

Open Systems Interconnection (OSI) Reference Model

In the networking worlds, there is a theoretical communication model known as the Open Systems Interconnection (OSI) reference model. This conceptual model, created by the International Organization for Standardization (ISO) in 1978 and revised in 1984, describes a network architecture that allows data to be passed between computer systems. In a nutshell, the functions of the seven layers of the OSI model are:

- **Application Layer**—Provides access to the network for applications and certain end-user functions. Displays incoming information and prepares outgoing information for network access.
- **Presentation Layer**—Converts data from the application layer into a format that can be sent over the network. Handles encryption and decryption of data.
- **Session Layer**—Synchronizes the data exchange between applications on separate devices.
- **Transport Layer**—Establishes, maintains, and breaks connections between network devices.
- **Network Layer**—Provides mechanisms for the routing of data between devices across single or multiple network segments.
- **Data Link Layer**—Performs error detection and handling for the transmitted signals and identifies how the network media is accessed.
- **Physical Layer**—Defines the physical structure of the network, such as the network topology.

Each device on a network, from switch to router, and each protocol operates at one or more levels of the OSI reference model.

These are only some of the types of attacks that can be launched against network servers. Each attack has its own strategy to get to the server and, therefore, security strategies aim to reduce the threat.

Many of the attacks launched against a server can be mitigated using perimeter defense mechanisms while others need to be done directly on the server. One mitigation strategy that cannot be overlooked is addressing server misconfiguration errors.

All operating systems ship with a default configuration. That is, they are preconfigured for use. Each organization has different security needs, however, making the default configuration ineffective for many organizations. Out-of-the-box server operating system software needs to be hardened and customized.

Strategies to properly configure the server include:

- Keeping the server current with the latest service packs and patches
- Hardening and configuring the operating system to address security adequately, potentially shutting down unused services and address ports. Installing and configuring additional security systems, such as filtering software and malware scanners

▶ **NOTE**

As previously mentioned, one common configuration problem is the handing of error messages. A server that is not configured to properly manage and store error messages can leak information.

- Using third-party companies to help test the server, looking for vulnerabilities
- Researching common server threats and how to configure a server to address them
- Regularly monitoring logs to search for potential breaches

It's important to remember that improperly configured server operating systems are a threat to an organization. Predictable accounts and passwords, limited local encryption, and known directory structures can lead to a breach in data confidentiality and potential server downtime.

Best Practices for Mitigating Web Attacks

This chapter provided descriptions of 34 potential attacks on a Web site. This is not an exhaustive list, but after reading through the 34 attacks, you should have a greater appreciation of the vast range of possible attacks. The attacks range in many factors, including technique, skill involved, and dependencies for success. Some attacks are the attacker's end goal, while others merely open a door for other purposes. Lastly, the attacks range in the damage that results if an attacker succeeds.

How do you mitigate all these attacks? With each attack comes certain ways to detect, prevent, or even reverse its effects. Further, new attacks are born continuously. Fortunately, you don't need to enact an exhaustive list of "just in case" controls for every new possible attack. The proper way to mitigate attack risks is to implement a best practices approach. This starts with being security conscious as early as possible. Your ability to protect against attacks is far more effective when security is considered from the earliest stages of design. The second step is knowing your infrastructure from each front-end Web application to each back-end database. You are more capable of understanding risks and how to mitigate them when you fully understand what is at risk. Lastly, being proactive is necessary to gaining support at all levels for seeing mitigation steps through to the end. You need senior management to appreciate the need for security. This comes primarily from exercising a proactive attitude. Let senior management witness how proactive you must be in order to sufficiently protect the Web sites. If security is not seen as important to you, how can it be perceived as important to those who may not understand it?

Best Practices for Mitigating Weaknesses

In addition to the 34 possible attacks, you read through 15 distinct weaknesses for
a Web site. The 15 are mostly deficiencies in authorization, data handling, or configuration settings. Just as you follow best practices for mitigating attacks, you must practice
due diligence for mitigating weaknesses. Awareness of these vulnerabilities is key.
If an administrator is not concerned about sufficient privileges, then weaknesses
get introduced. If a developer is not attentive to secure coding practices, weaknesses
get introduced. In all cases where weaknesses are introduced, attackers potentially
benefit. It's only a matter of time until they discover a weakness.

CHAPTER SUMMARY

Web applications and Web sites are the new security battleground. In this chapter,
you learned that WASC identifies 34 specific threats to Web application security.
Administrators need to be aware of and prepare for each of these types of attacks.
Many types of attacks employ user input to inject code or other malicious input
into a server or application. User input validation is the best weapon for ensuring
that only acceptable input is received.

You also learned that WASC outlines 15 Web site weaknesses that may be exploited.
Each of these threats has mitigation strategies to help reduce the vulnerability risk.

KEY CONCEPTS AND TERMS

Application hardening
Automatic directory listing
Blacklist
Brute-force attack
Buffer overflow
CAPTCHA (Completely
    Automated Public Turing
    Test to Tell Computers
    and Humans Apart)
Content spoofing
Cryptographic key
Extensible Markup Language
    (XML)

Impersonation
Indexing
Internet Message Access
    Protocol (IMAP)
Lightweight Directory Access
    Protocol (LDAP)
Malicious code
Man-in-the-middle attack
Output handling
Path traversal attack
Principle of least privilege
Process validation

Routing detour attack
Sanitization
Server-side include (SSI)
    injection
Session ID
Transport Layer Security (TLS)
Web Application Security
    Consortium (WASC)
Whitelist
XML Path (XPath) language
XPath injection attack

CHAPTER 6 ASSESSMENT

1. One way to verify if a system is attacked by a brute-force attack is to periodically check the log files.

A. True
B. False

2. Content spoofing tactics often include which of the following?

A. Spam e-mail links
B. Forum links
C. Chatroom links
D. A and C only
E. All of the above

3. How do XSS attacks differ from CSRF attacks?

4. Which of the following attacks involve the use of CR and LF characters? (Select two.)

A. HTTP request smuggling
B. HTTP response smuggling
C. HTTP request splitting
D. HTTP response splitting

5. A common path traversal attack uses which syntax sequence to attempt to locate restricted areas on a server?

A. ../
B. *.*/
C. CR
D. LF

6. During a session fixation attack, in which ways can an attacker obtain a valid session identifier? (Select three.)

A. Prediction
B. Capture
C. Fixation
D. Spoofing

7. Which attack allows the attacker to access, read, delete, and modify information held within a database and even take control of the server on which the database is operating?

8. Which of the following are actual XML-related attacks? (Select two.)

A. XML attribute blowup
B. XML internal entities
C. XML entity expression
D. XML injection

9. Which of the following are Web site weaknesses discussed in this chapter? (Select three.)

A. OS commanding
B. Improper file system permissions
C. Insufficient authentication
D. Fingerprinting
E. Server misconfiguration

10. Applications hardening is the process of securing applications in use on a network.

A. True
B. False

11. To avoid improper input handling, which approaches can you use when handling user input? (Select three.)

A. Stripping
B. Sanitization
C. Rejecting known bad input
D. Accepting only known good input

12. Which of the following is a strategy for reducing the risk of data leakage?

A. Sanitization
B. Strong firewall controls
C. Authorization
D. Encryption

© Rodolfo Clix/Dreamstime.com

Securing Web Applications

I N TODAY'S NETWORK AND COMPUTING ENVIRONMENTS, security is the name of the game. Securing Web applications has become an integral part of an organization's overall security strategy. As people's personal and business lives are increasingly integrated with the Web and Web applications, Web application security moves front and center. Web application security is the battleground for IT security and will be for the foreseeable future.

Web application security encompasses many elements from end-user education to stronger programming and development. One of the first considerations when designing strong Web application security strategies is to know what the threats are, where they come from, and how to mitigate them. This chapter examines one of the more commonly exploited areas of Web application security: end-user input. It looks at the dangers of cleartext communication and explains how to encrypt data as it travels throughout the network.

Chapter 7 Topics

This chapter covers the following topics and concepts:

- What issues arise with user input into a Web site
- What technologies and systems are used to make a complete functional Web site
- What the software development life cycle (SDLC) is
- How to design a layered security strategy for Web sites and applications
- How to incorporate security requirements within the SDLC
- When to use secure and unsecure protocols
- How Secure Sockets Layer (SSL) works
- How to select an appropriate access control solution
- What best practices for securing Web applications are

When you complete this chapter, you will be able to:

- Review the types and dangers of user input
- Understand how to lessen the risks of user input
- Review SQL security measures
- Understand how the SDLC impacts security
- Design a layered security strategy for Web applications
- Review the usage of Hypertext Transfer Protocol (HTTP) and Hypertext Transfer Protocol Secure (HTTPS)
- Work with SSL
- Understand access control designs
- Understand Web application security best practices
- Prevent insecure communications

When Your Application Requires User Input into Your Web Site

In the beginning, Web sites were non-interactive and mainly information portals with information flowing only one way. The early Web was a communication stream from the server to the client browser. Because each visitor to a site was given the same information and the same rights, there was no need to authenticate or validate users.

Today's interactive Web sites and applications provide two-way communication with menus, lists, forms, radio buttons, and uniform resource locator (URL) links all allowing interaction between the client browser and the Web application. This interactivity and potential user input allow a variety of attacks, including:

- Cross-site scripting (XSS)
- SQL injection
- Directory traversal
- URL redirector abuse
- Extensive Markup Language (XML) injection
- XQuery injection

Improperly validated and untrusted user input remains one of the larger security risks with Web applications. To combat input attacks, input validation methods are deployed both on the client side and on the server side.

Input validation is challenging, but it remains a key defense against validation attacks. Input validation is difficult because it's not easy to determine what constitutes valid input across numerous Web applications and processes. Although there's no single uniform answer to managing user input, general guidelines and practices include:

- **Don't rely solely on client-side validation**—On the client side, validation mechanisms are accomplished using the client browser. **Client-side validation** is adequate to catch mistakes such as typos or input errors from reaching the server but cannot be relied on as a strong security measure. It's likely that malicious users can bypass client-side validation mechanisms. The clear benefit of client-side validation is in increased performance by reducing unnecessary validation trips to the server.

> **NOTE**
>
> With most Web browsers, client-side validation can be easily bypassed by turning off JavaScript in the browser.

- **Ensure server-side validation**—Unlike client-side validation, server-side validation cannot be easily circumvented by malicious users. The server will verify the integrity of all user input to ensure that it's valid and trusted. Often, the server search validation will search for string lengths, characters, and any other syntax it can flag as potentially dangerous.

- **Use whitelisting and blacklisting**—One method to help validate user input is to employ a blacklist. The blacklist identifies strings and characters that are known to be potentially dangerous. All data in the blacklist are rejected; however, harmful data not listed in the blacklist are allowed. In this way, the blacklist must be updated and monitored regularly to ensure that threats are identified. Blacklists don't adapt quickly to new threats. Often whitelisting is the preferred method of input validation. With whitelists, only known good input strings and syntax are allowed; everything else is rejected. Whitelists are better suited to managing new threats because new threats will not match the known good data identified by the whitelist.

> **NOTE**
>
> One primary disadvantage of blacklists is that they become obsolete when a new attack is discovered.

- **Assume all input is malicious**—A key concept of input validation security is the underlying assumption that all input is potentially harmful or malicious. In essence, validation is guilty until proven innocent. Client-side and server-side validation mechanisms should adopt this approach. All input, regardless of source, is a potential risk.

- **Sanitize your input**—When user input is sanitized, it's inspected for potentially harmful code and modified according to predetermined, acceptable guidelines. Sanitization often involves identifying and disallowing specific characters and syntax sequences.

Get to Know Your Syntax with Request for Comments (RFC)

A **Request for Comments (RFC)** is a formal document from the Internet Engineering Task Force (IETF), which is the result of committee drafting and revisions to a technical document. Many RFCs are intended to become Internet standards and, as such, hold important information. When reviewing acceptable syntax for e-mail addresses, URL input, XML input, and more, it's advisable to review the RFC to verify the syntax used. Consider the following examples:

> **NOTE**
> Transmission of non-text objects in messages raises additional security issues. These are outlined in RFCs 2047, 2049, 4288, and 4289.

- **Validating e-mail address syntax and usage**—To help prevent malicious code being used in e-mail, verify correct e-mail usage procedures and syntax in RFC 5322.

- **Validating URL input**—RFCs define the rules and syntax for URL usage and access. Defend against canonicalization attacks by ensuring that the resource paths are resolved before applying business rules for validating them. A **canonicalization attack** involves backtracking up a directory path using "../" or dot, dot, slash to access areasnot intended to be accessible.

- **Validating HTTP input**—To find out all about HTTP formats and technical details, review RFC 2616.

Reviewing RFCs is a great way to become more familiar with the correct usage and characteristics of a trusted and used technology. Visit the Internet RFC/STD/FYI/BCP Archives Web site at *http://www.faqs.org/rfcs/* to search more than 5,000 RFC entries. The following are some RFCs that are important to the topics in this book:

- RFC 821, "Simple Mail Transfer Protocol"
- RFC 2396, "Uniform Resource Identifiers (URI): Generic Syntax"
- RFC 793, "Transmission Control Protocol"
- RFC 2045, "Multipurpose Internet Mail Extensions (MIME) Part One: Format of Internet Message Bodies"
- RFC 1738, "Uniform Resource Locators (URL)"
- RFC 822, "Standard for the Format of ARPA Internet Text Messages"
- RFC 1122, "Requirements for Internet Hosts — Communication Layers"
- RFC 2046, "Multipurpose Internet Mail Extensions (MIME) Part Two: Media Types"
- RFC 1157, "Simple Network Management Protocol (SNMP)"
- RFC 1866, "Hypertext Markup Language—2.0"

Technologies and Systems Used to Make a Complete Functional Web Site

Web sites use an array of technologies and systems to make a complete functional site. These technologies cover everything from the protocols, programming languages used, database systems, and more. Each of these elements must be secured individually to ensure the security of the entire Web site.

This section explores some common Web elements—HTML, CGI, JavaScripting, and SQL database back-ends—and discusses potential security risks of each.

Hypertext Markup Language (HTML)

HTML is the predominant language for creating Web pages. HTML provides an easy method of programming structural semantics for text such as headings, paragraphs, lists, links, and quotes. HTML allows programmers to embed pictures and interactive forms within a Web document. HTML was not created with security in mind; it was created as an online development tool.

HTML is known as a markup language that uses code for formatting a Web site within a text file. The codes used to specify the formatting are called tags. HTML tags are keywords surrounded by angle brackets like <body> that normally come in pairs, such as <body> and </body>, with the first tag at the start of the formatting and the second tag at the end. For example:

```
<html>
<body>
<h1>This is my Web site heading</h1>
<p>This is an introduction paragraph.</p>
</body>
</html>
```

In this example, the <html> and </html> tag pair identifies the Web site itself, the <body> and </body> tag pair identifies the visible text on the Web site, <h> and</h> identifies the heading, and <p> and </p> identifies the paragraphs.

In normal operation, HTML is a powerful markup language. Unfortunately, malicious HTML scripts can be used to attack a Web site. As an example, HTML pages can use forms that require user input:

```
<form>
First name:
<input type="text" name="firstname" />
Last name:
<input type="text" name="lastname" />
</form>
```

These HTML tags would create two simple boxes in which visitors to the Web site can enter their first and last names. What happens when a malicious user doesn't enter the proper, expected input but enters malicious scripts instead? If the user input is not properly sanitized and validated, the attacker can alter the page, insert unwanted or offensive images or sounds, and change content to damage the site's reputation.

If malicious users can insert their own <form> tags, they can create interactive content designed to steal information from the user, such as credit card information and bank account information. Malicious HTML tags can be placed in a message posted to an online forum or message board using the <script>, <embed>, <object>, and <applet> tags. When these tags are snuck into messages, they can run automatically on the victim's browser.

If a Web site is hacked, the maliciously entered tags may do damage. This may include setting up false forms, redirecting to other Web sites, or running a malicious script whenever the browser goes to the home page.

To help prevent such attacks, interactive Web elements such as discussion groups must be monitored to identify which data input is untrustworthy when it's presented to other users. Today, Web servers either will not accept non-validated input or will encode/filter it before sending anything to other browsers. All HTML forms and interactive user elements must ensure input is validated to prevent malicious HTML from being presented to the user. It's critical to check the HTML code periodically to see if malicious code has been added. One quick way to check is to verify the size of the file. If the file size has changed, there may be a problem. It's important to keep the Web site, Web server, and HTML code secure. If the source can be viewed and changed by anyone, there is a problem.

Common Gateway Interface (CGI) Script

CGI is a standard that defines a method by which a Web server can obtain data from or send data to databases, documents, and other programs, and present that data to viewers via the Web. CGI programs are commonly written in a language such as Perl, C++, or ASP. A CGI program is accessed by the Web server in response to some action by a Web visitor. This might be something simple, like a Web page counter or site form, or complex, such as a shopping cart and e-commerce elements.

> **NOTE**
>
> One of the rules for all interactive Web elements is to never blindly trust user input. User input is a primary source of attack, but it can be mitigated through sanitization and validation.

A CGI program is often used to manage user queries sent from an interactive HTML page (Web page) with the CGI script functioning as the intermediary between the query and the database. CGI programs often accept user input from the browser to the Web server.

To help secure CGI, it's important to create and program CGI with security in mind, research known vulnerabilities with CGI programming, and incorporate security best practices in all programming efforts. Secondly, review the program periodically to verify and incorporate any updated vulnerability information, and apply security patches when necessary. Finally, as with other interactive elements, you must use user validation and sanitization.

JavaScripting

JavaScript is considered to be the scripting language of the Web. Programmers use JavaScript to add functionality and dynamic and interactive content to their Web sites. These interactive elements are almost limitless and may include e-commerce forms, setting and reading cookies, advertising, and various Web forms. Using JavaScript is quite easy, as the Web programmer can embed the JavaScript code easily into HTML pages, as shown:

```
<html>
<body>
<script type="text/javascript">
document.write ("Text goes here.");
</script>
</body>
</html>
```

Any programming language that can be used to execute content on Web pages can be used maliciously. Because loading a Web page can cause arbitrary code to be executed on your computer, stringent security precautions are required to prevent malicious code from damaging your data or your privacy. JavaScript provides some security in that it does not allow writing or deleting files or directories on the client computer. With no file object and no file access functions, a JavaScript program cannot delete a user's data or plant viruses on the user's system.

SQL Database Back-End

A back-end database is a database that is accessed by users indirectly through another application. The back-end database is fronted by a Web server, which in turn is accessed by client browsers. This is a common configuration for online e-commerce. For example, a shoe store houses all product details in the back end, which users browse through the Web server.

An SQL back-end database may be vulnerable to both physical and logical attacks. These may include physical threats, such as theft of the database server, and logical attacks such as injection attacks and brute-force password attacks. Securing any database requires a multilayered approach, including:

- Access controls
- Role-based authentication
- Encryption methods
- Integrity verification

One common attack against a SQL back-end database is a SQL injection.

> **NOTE**
>
> Although not directly related to security, one measure that must be considered is database backups. Backups are not a security measure, but a good backup may be necessary to restore a database that has been tampered with and compromised. Having up-to-date backups are a mandatory part of database administration.

As shown in this section, many elements must be considered to secure an entire site. Because of various security risks, a Web site requires vigilance and maintenance to ensure that the latest security mitigation strategies are incorporated into its design and that security patches are applied as necessary.

Your Development Process and the Software Development Life Cycle (SDLC)

Every day new software is developed and old software enhanced to meet a personal, production, or business need. In its development, all software passes through specific stages, referred to as the **software development life cycle (SDLC)**. Certain basic steps are followed in all software development projects. Although development models vary, all share some similarities. The oldest and the best-known model is the waterfall: a sequence of stages in which the output of each stage becomes the input for the next. Figure 7-1 shows the waterfall model for software development.

As shown in Figure 7-1, there are several stages in this SDLC model, as follows:

- **Systems analysis**—The analyzing stage seeks a clear definition of what the software is designed to do and what problem or issue it's intended to address. The analysis provides the direction for further development and refines project goals into clear functions and operation of the intended application.

- **Designing**—In the designing stage, the application's features and operational functions are clearly established. This includes documentation of application processes and screenshots. The design phase should give a clear idea of what the application will look like and what user needs it will address.

- **Implementation**—With a clear idea of the purpose of the software and a development plan, the code is written.

FIGURE 7-1

The waterfall model encompasses the software development life cycle.

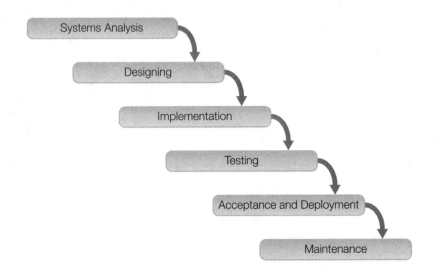

- **Testing**—This phase is sometimes overlooked in the rush to get a software application to market. The software is tested and examined for bugs, errors, interoperability failures, and more. A strong and comprehensive approach to testing will help ensure that the product works as expected.

- **Acceptance and deployment**—Once tested, the software product will either be accepted and shipped, or sent back to the design or implementation phase. Given the costs and competitive nature of software development, a testing phase failure can be a significant problem.

- **Maintenance**—Today's software packages are not stagnant; they are constantly improved, enhanced, and updated. This is done to address shortcomings in the application, to add new features, or to address end-user concerns. As long as the application is in use, maintenance continues.

The stages an application or piece of software passes through vary by developer and environment. However, each developer will follow a developmental process to ensure that the software is created as efficiently and error-free as possible.

Designing a Layered Security Strategy for Web Sites and Web Applications

It used to be that security administrators felt comfortable focusing their efforts on perimeter security. Firewalls were the name of the game and, for a time, networks were relatively safe behind them. Today's attacks—such as injection attacks, social engineering, and others—bypass many of a network's perimeter defenses, leaving it vulnerable.

Today, a network cannot be secure with a single security approach. A complete and layered approach to network security is required. There are any number of layers that a security administrator could use to protect a network, including perimeter security, **host-based security** mechanisms, authentication and access management, network and application access controls, and **vulnerability management**. The layers are defined as follows:

- **Perimeter security**—Perimeter defense strategies refer to those security measures that are on the edge of the network and protect the internal network from external attack. There are several types of perimeter defense mechanisms used, including antivirus/antispyware/antispam/anti-phishing software, intrusion detection systems (IDSs), intrusion prevention systems (IPSs), and firewalls.

- **Host-based security mechanisms**—Network-wide and centralized security is an important part of an overall security strategy but, increasingly, security is shifting towards host-based mechanisms. In network terms, this includes using host-based firewalls and IDS antivirus solutions. For Web applications and Web security, it involves placing increasing importance on host security, such as by increasing the security potential of browsers. This may include XSS filters for browsers, stronger error-handling mechanisms, and localized script sanitization filters.

- **End-user education**—A layered security strategy has to include end-user education. This includes information on the latest Web-based attacks, what they are designed to do, and how end users can help prevent them.

- **Authentication and access management**—Key to securing Web applications and Web sites is strong authentication. Access management controls dictate who can and cannot access a Web application or Web site.

- **Input validation**—Any layered security approach includes mechanisms to protect from malicious input, which can lead to a variety of injection attacks.

- **Vulnerability management**—Vulnerability management refers to the ongoing maintenance and management of existing Web sites and applications. It often involves updating, using patches, applying service packs, and using other techniques to ensure Web site and application security is up to date.

The exact layers of the security strategy often depend on the organization and developer involved.

Incorporating Security Requirements Within the SDLC

One of the biggest vulnerabilities in today's networks and online applications is poorly developed applications that have received little consideration as to confidentiality, integrity, and overall security. Many experts recommend that security be implemented during the design phase and throughout the maintenance of Web applications.

Listed previously in this chapter were several stages of software development. It's possible to incorporate security throughout the entire SDLC. The following sections highlight how security considerations can be incorporated into each stage of the SDLC.

Systems Analysis Stage

In the systems analysis stage, what the software is designed to do and what problem or issue it's intended to address must be clearly defined. In this stage, a qualified security person is brought into the development process. The security person's task is to understand the intent of the application and identify potential security threats. These may be injection attacks, buffer overflows, directory traversal, and more.

The security professional will ensure that the software's functions and operations are not exposed and cannot be exploited. The importance of incorporating security from the start cannot be understated; it guides the security process and ensures that security remains a concern throughout software development. Without incorporating security from the initial phase, security can become an afterthought.

Designing Stage

In the designing stage, the application's features and operational functions are clearly established. In this stage, incorporating security is a critical consideration because the security foundation for the software is established. This may include the following activities:

- **Information gathering**—The security professional may meet with potential clients and software users to determine their security needs. In this way, the security requirements are tailored to the software users' environment. Further information may include reviewing industry security standards and ensuring that the software meets these standards. These standards may include the ISO 27002 and the ISO 15408 standards, which provide an accepted code of practice for information security management.

- **Threat assessment**—While the design of the software is unfolding, the security professional can get a picture of threats and their potential impact on the software. With an understanding of the potential threats and exploitable areas, the security professional can begin to incorporate mitigation strategies into the design.

> **NOTE**
>
> During the SDLC, the security professional stresses the importance of security throughout the development phases. Security professionals should know the policies, standards, and guidelines of Web security to ensure they are met. Developers can then incorporate these security elements.

- **Threat mitigation**—With a clear understanding of the risks and threats, the security professional can develop strategies to mitigate those threats. Incorporating security in the initial steps of the SDLC allows developers to anticipate threats and build mitigation strategies into the software. This helps ensure that software out of the box is secure.

Implementation Stage

If the security professional has communicated the security concerns clearly, the developers can incorporate security into the coding. Several security guidelines and best practices that developers can follow when coding software include:

- **Input validation mechanisms**—Injection attacks are common. Creating input validation mechanisms in software helps mitigate the threat.

- **Strong encryption**—Developers need to use industry-accepted encryption and cryptography standards.

- **Securing data that's stored and in transit**—Developers should safeguard the security of data whether it's stored or is traveling through the network.

- **Authentication mechanisms**—Access controls should require proper authentication.

- **Error handling**—Software error messages should not reveal too much to malicious users.

There are several other coding practices that developers must keep in mind. Creating software without these considerations may lead to security holes.

Testing Stage

In the testing stage, the software is tested and retested to ensure that it's interoperable and functions as it should. Part of the testing involves a review of the software security structure. A security professional or an entire security team tests the software for least privilege, buffer overflows, injection attacks, error-handling risks, directory traversal risks, and more.

The final stage tests the software in a live production environment. Sometimes called penetration testing, it involves ethical hacking. With ethical hacking, professional hackers attempt to access and crash the software. The hacking occurs both by an outsider trying to access the software and by a malicious user within the network. The hacker's training and ability determine the value of ethical hacking.

Acceptance and Deployment Stage

Once security tests are complete and security requirements have been met, the software is ready for release. Although much security testing has been done, testing must continue throughout the lifespan of the software. In the deployment stage, the security professional monitors the deployment, searching for potential security threats and exploitable areas. As the software is deployed, the security professional may review the application's user manual, looking for security breaches or unforeseen threats. The deployment stage security plan may include:

* Creating document sources to review the status of the deployment
* Ensuring that user administration and access privileges are established
* Defining response process for handling security bugs

Maintenance

Live production software can be under constant attack from malicious users. Over time, the software may become exploited and need to be maintained with security measures that meet the new attacks and threats. Maintenance is a critical component for overall software security. Maintenance security procedures may include:

* Developing and deploying service packs and patches to manage security threats.
* Reviewing logs, audits, and other material to search for new threats and attacks that may have been found.
* Reviewing error report messages to see if they are accurate and not revealing information that an attacker could use.
* Monitoring feedback from software users.

Many developers may not fully appreciate the importance of incorporating security measures into each step of the development cycle. However, weaving security into the fabric of software development as a proactive measure will result in secure and robust software packages.

Using Secure and Unsecure Protocols

Transmission Control Protocol/Internet Protocol (TCP/IP) is the routable protocol on which Internet communication is based. Actually TCP/IP is a set or suite of protocols. Each of these protocols provides a different function. Collectively, the protocols provide TCP/IP functionality. The protocol suite gets its name from two of the main protocols in the suite, TCP and IP. Within the TCP/IP protocol suite are secure and unsecure protocols. The unsecure protocols are typically designed for speed, for use in a trusted environment, or when no sensitive data is involved. For example, HTTP is used for day-to-day Web access, but HTTP sends information in cleartext. That is, it's susceptible to man-in-the-middle attacks and can be read if intercepted. For sensitive Web communications, the **Hypertext Transfer Protocol Secure (HTTPS)** protocol is used for encryption.

HTTP and HTTPS are not the only protocols within TCP/IP that have a secure and unsecure option. If you are enabling traffic to and from a Web site, it may be necessary to know which ones are secure and which ones are not. Several protocols move data throughout the network and Internet. Table 7-1 shows some of the secure and unsecure protocols.

How Secure Sockets Layer Works

As mentioned, plain HTTP sends data in cleartext, which is too risky for bank sites or other data-sensitive transactions. HTTPS is used to ensure safe and secure communication between a client and a Web server. Secure Sockets Layer (SSL) is widely used to authenticate a service to a client and then to provide confidentiality (encryption) to the data being transmitted.

SSL works in a negotiation process—known as a handshake—between the client and the Web server. The handshake process is highlighted in Figure 7-2.

As shown in Figure 7-2, several steps are required in the SSL negotiation process:

1. The session begins by the client browser sending a basic "Hello" message to the server. This initial message includes a request for a secure communication channel, including various cryptographic algorithms supported by the client.

2. The server responds with its own "Hello" message, including its choice of algorithm to create the cryptography. If no mutual cryptography method can be agreed upon, the handshake fails. The server also sends its **digital certificate** and public key to the client. A digital certificate is a small electronic file that serves to validate or encrypt a message or browser session.

3. If the browser verifies the certificate, it sends a one-time session key encrypted with the server's public key.

4. Both the client and the server now have symmetric keys, and the communication between them is encrypted and decrypted at each end.

TABLE 7-1 Secure and unsecure protocols.		
PROTOCOL	**FULL NAME**	**DESCRIPTION**
FTP	File Transfer Protocol	Protocol for uploading and downloading files to and from a remote host. Also accommodates basic file management tasks.
SFTP	Secure File Transfer Protocol	Protocol for securely uploading and downloading files to and from a remote host. Based on Secure Shell (SSH) security.
HTTP	Hypertext Transfer Protocol	Protocol for retrieving files from a Web server. Data is sent in cleartext.
HTTPS	Hypertext Transfer Protocol Secure	Secure protocol for retrieving files from a Web server. HTTPS uses SSL for encrypting data between the client and the host.
Telnet	Telnet	Allows sessions to be opened on a remote host.
RSH	UNIX utility used to run a command on a remote machine	Replaced with SSH because RSH sends all data in cleartext.
SSH	Secure Shell	Secure alternative to Telnet that allows secure sessions to be opened on a remote host.
RCP	Remote Copy Protocol	Copies files between systems but transport is not secured.
SCP	Secure Copy Protocol	Allows files to be copied securely between two systems. Uses SSH technology to provide encryptio services.
SNMPv1/2	Simple Network Management Protocol v1/2	Network monitoring system used to monitor a network's condition. Neither SNMPv1 nor v2 is secure.
SNMPv3	Simple Network Management Protocol v3	Enhanced SNMP service offering both encryption and authentication services.

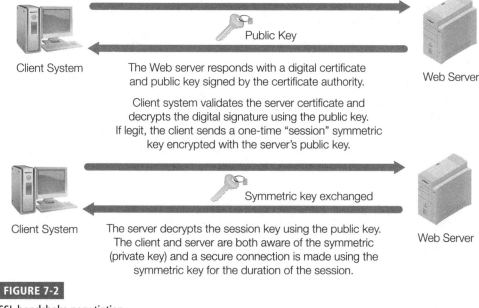

Client sends a "Hello" message to the server and requests a secure connection.

Public Key

Client System

The Web server responds with a digital certificate and public key signed by the certificate authority.

Web Server

Client system validates the server certificate and decrypts the digital signature using the public key. If legit, the client sends a one-time "session" symmetric key encrypted with the server's public key.

Symmetric key exchanged

Client System

The server decrypts the session key using the public key. The client and server are both aware of the symmetric (private key) and a secure connection is made using the symmetric key for the duration of the session.

Web Server

FIGURE 7-2

SSL handshake negotiation.

SSL Encryption and Hash Protocols

SSL uses various protocols for both encryption and hashing services. Hashing algorithms are used to verify the integrity of a data stream. They are not used for encryption. Hashing ensures that data has not been tampered with during transmission.

There are two hashing algorithm protocols to be aware of: Secure Hash Algorithm 1 (SHA1) and Message Digest 5 (MD5). MD5 offers a 128-bit hashing algorithm. SHA1 uses an algorithm with a 160-bit function. Although it provides more security than MD5, SHA1 can affect overall performance because it demands more system resources. Further, known vulnerabilities have been discovered with MD5.

As mentioned, SSL communication uses a symmetric key exchange to secure the communication channel. There are several key encryption protocols associated with symmetric key exchanges. These include the following:

> **NOTE**
>
> For integrity verification, hash algorithms are used to confirm that the information received is exactly the same as the information sent. A hash algorithm is essentially a cryptographic checksum used by both the sender and receiver to verify that the message has not been changed. If the message has changed in transit, the hash values are different and the packet is rejected.

- **Data Encryption Standard (DES) (40-bit)**—This encryption method provides the best performance but at a cost: the encryption security is lower. **Data Encryption Standard (DES)** can be used in environments where the need for data security is a little lower.

- **Data Encryption Standard (56-bit)**—Through your Internet Protocol Security (IPSec) policies, you can implement DES as the encryption method. The DES algorithm is a 56-bit encryption key. This algorithm was published in 1977 by the U.S. National Bureau of Standards and allows for the ability to frequently regenerate keys during a communication. This prevents the entire data set from being compromised if one DES key is broken. However, it's considered outdated for business use and should be used only for legacy application support. Specialized hardware has been able to crack the standard 56-bit key.

- **Triple DES (3DES)**—IPSec policies also allow the choice of a strong encryption algorithm, **Triple Data Encryption Standard (3DES)**, which provides stronger encryption than DES for higher security. 3DES uses a 56-bit encryption key as well, but, as the name implies, it uses three of them. There are three options for using 3DES, differing by whether any or all the encryption keys are unique to each other. If 3DES uses three unique keys, the result is considered 168-bit encryption. However, because of a discovered "meet in the middle" attack, the effective security is equivalent to 112-bit encryption. The "meet in the middle" attack involves guessing the algorithm's values between the three keys, hoping to reveal how it works. It's similar to a brute-force attack but with much better odds.

- **Advanced Encryption Standard (AES)**—Also known as Rijndael, **Advanced Encryption Standard (AES)** is a block cipher encryption standard. AES can create keys from 128 bits to 256 bits in length.

- **Rivest Cipher**—This is a family of secret key cryptographic algorithms from RSA Security, Inc. **Rivest Cipher** includes RC2, RC4, RC5, and RC6. Although RSA is widely known for its public key methods, its secret key algorithms are also widely used. The RCs were designed as a replacement for DES. RC2 uses a variable key and the block cipher method. RC4 uses a variable key and stream cipher method. Both RC5 and RC6 are block ciphers with variable keys up to 2,040 bits. RC6 uses integer multiplication for improved performance over R5.

FYI

The three items that access controls protect—confidentiality, integrity, and availability—are often referred to as the C-I-A triad. Some systems security professionals refer to the C-I-A triad as the "A-I-C" triad (availability, integrity, and confidentiality) to avoid confusion with the U.S. Central Intelligence Agency, which is commonly referred to as the CIA. Either abbreviation is acceptable. However, if you use CIA, make sure people understand you're referring to "confidentiality, integrity, and availability."

Selecting an Appropriate Access Control Solution

> **NOTE**
> The primary objective of access control is to preserve and protect the confidentiality, integrity, and availability of information, systems, and resources.

Access control is a cornerstone concept when designing a secure network and Web site environment. *Access control* refers to the mechanisms that identify and control who can and cannot access a network, a resource, an application, specific data, and more. To secure a network or computer and its resources, you must consider what access will be granted to other users and then design strategies to ensure that only required users actually have access. It's a fundamental concept and forms the basis of safe and secure Web applications.

It's possible to secure a Web application by granting users specific rights and privileges. These privileges dictate who can and who cannot access the application. Consider a Web server that shares applications. You can configure the server to allow only certain users or groups access to those shared resources. The Administrator account, for example, can access all aspects of the Web application while other users have limited access.

In the strictest terms, access control is a much more general way of talking about controlling access to a resource. Access can be granted or denied based on a wide variety of criteria, such as the network address of the client, time of day, the Web site visitor's browser, and other general restrictions. Access control involves controlling network access by an arbitrary condition that may or may not have anything to do with the attributes of a particular visitor.

You will most often see access control used to refer to any mechanism that restricts unwanted access to network resources and applications. This general definition would include the process of authentication and authorization. In practice, authentication, authorization, and access control are so closely related it's difficult to discuss them separately. In particular, authentication and authorization are, in most implementations, tightly linked.

A basic understanding of access control makes it possible to see why it plays such an important role in a security strategy. Several types of access control strategies are used, including mandatory access control, discretionary access control, rule-based access control, and role-based access control.

Authentication, Authorization, and Accountability

When talking about access control and resource security, it's important to understand the difference between authentication, authorization, and accountability. *Authentication* is any process by which you verify that users are who they claim to be. This usually involves a username and a password, but it can include other methods of demonstrating identity, such as a smart card and biometrics. *Authorization* is finding out if the person, once identified and authenticated, has trusted access to a particular resource. This is usually determined by finding out if the person is part of a group that provides the correct permissions or has a particular level of security clearance. *Accountability* refers to the tracking mechanisms used to keep a record of events on a system.

One method often used to determine accountability is auditing. *Auditing* is the process of monitoring occurrences and keeping a log of what has occurred on a system. It's largely up to the administrator to decide which types of events should be audited. The idea of tracking events on a system is to record and prevent attempts to access or otherwise compromise the system. The administrator can implement monitoring with an audit policy. An administrator decides what should be audited and configures the audit policy. In Windows 8, for example, the audit policy is configured through the Group Policy Management Console (GPMC). Although the GPMC facilitates high-level auditing configuration, the command-line tool auditpol.exe lets you get much more granular.

There are many different occurrences on a system that can be tracked. Table 7-2 lists some audit policies and their descriptions.

One of the core responsibilities of security administrators is to check the audit logs regularly. Even average users should be able to check audit logs, as they give great insight into what is has occurred on the system. It's a good idea to take the time to look through each of the audit options to see the types of tracking that are available.

TABLE 7-2 System audit policies.

AUDIT POLICY	AVAILABLE AUDIT OPTIONS	DESCRIPTION
Account logon	Audit credential validation; audit Kerberos authentication service; audit Kerberos service ticket operations; audit other logon/logoff events	Audits user activity related to logging into a system. Account logon settings can audit credentials, user authorizations, and logon attempts. These audits can be used to verify if an unwanted user is attempting to access the system.
Account management	Audit application group management; audit computer account management; audit distribution group management; audit other account management events; audit security group management; audit user account management	Audits account management, such as the creation or deletion of groups or users. It is a good way to see if a new account has been created with administrator privileges.
Detailed tracking	Audit data protection application programming interface (DPAPI) activity; audit process creation; audit process termination; audit RPC events	The detailed tracking audit policy is used to track system events such as the addition of new processes and deleted or stopped processes.
DS (Directory Services) access	Audit detailed directory service replication; audit directory service access; audit directory service changes; audit directory service replication	Tracks a user accessing an Active Directory object such as groups, users, or shares. Modifications to objects are tracked and stored on audit files on the domain controller.
Logon/logoff	Audit account lockout; audit IPSec extended mode; audit IPSec main mode; audit IPSec quick mode; audit logoff; audit logon; audit network policy server; audit other logon/logoff events; audit special logon	Tracks each instance of a user logging on or logging off, getting locked out, or making a network connection to this computer.

continued

7

Securing
Web Applications

TABLE 7-2   System audit policies, *continued.*

AUDIT POLICY	AVAILABLE AUDIT OPTIONS	DESCRIPTION
Object access	Audit application generated; audit certification services; audit detailed file share; audit file share; audit file system; audit filtering platform connection; audit filtering platform packet drop; audit handle manipulation; audit kernel object; audit other object access events; audit registry; audit security accounts manager objects	Tracks a user accessing an object, such as a file, folder, registry key, or printer, that has its own system access control list specified.
Policy Change	Audit policy change; audit authentication policy change; audit authorization policy change; audit filtering platform policy change; audit MPSSVC rule-level policy change; audit other policy change events	Enables tracking of changes to the audit policy.
Privilege Use	Audit non-sensitive privilege use; audit sensitive privilege use; audit other privilege use events	Records each instance of a user exercising a user right.
System	Audit IPSec driver; audit other system events; audit security state change; audit security system extension; audit system integrity	Tracks in the Event Viewer such audit system events as shutting down or restarting the system, and monitors changes to system security and the security log.

Discretionary Access Control

With **discretionary access control (DAC)**, information access is not forced from the administrator or the operating system. Rather, access is controlled by the information's owner. The level of access a user receives is based on the permissions associated with authentication credentials, such as a smart card or username and password combination.

DAC uses an access control list (ACL) to determine access. The ACL is a table that informs the operating system of the rights each user has to a particular system object, such as a file, directory, or application. Each object has a security attribute that identifies its ACL. The list has an entry for each system user with access privileges. The most common privileges include the ability to read a file (or all the files in a directory), to write to the file or files, and to execute the file (if it's an executable file or program).

Some of the characteristics of DAC include:

- Data owners control the level of access to information.
- Data owners can determine the type of access (read, write, copy, etc.) and can modify access privileges at any time.
- Access is determined by comparing the user against permissions held in an ACL.
- Authentication credentials are associated with the level of access.

Mandatory Access Control

With **mandatory access control (MAC)**, the creator of information does not govern who can access or modify data. Application administrators dictate who can access and modify data, systems, and resources.

MAC secures information and resources by assigning sensitivity labels to objects and comparing them to the user's assigned level of sensitivity. In the security world, a *label* is a feature applied to files, directories, and other resources in a system. A label can be thought of as a confidentiality stamp. When a label is placed on a file, it describes the level of security for that specific file and permits access by files, users, and other resources with a similar or lesser security setting.

In practice, MAC mechanisms assign a security level to all information and assign a security clearance to each user to ensure that all users have access only to that data for which they have clearance. For example, users are assigned a Top Secret or Confidential security label, and data and resources are classified accordingly. MAC restricts access to objects based on a comparable sensitivity between the user-assigned levels and the object-assigned levels.

In general terms, mandatory security policy represents any security policy that is defined strictly by a system security administrator along with associated policy attributes. The need for a MAC mechanism arises when the security policy of a system or network dictates that:

- Security decisions must not be decided or managed by the object owner.
- The system administrator and operating system must enforce the protection decisions.

Rule-Based Access Control

Rule-based access control governs access to objects according to established rules. A good example is the configuration and security settings on a router or a firewall.

As you probably know, if you tried to gain access through a firewall, your request would be reviewed to see if you meet the criteria for access through the firewall. For example, suppose you had a firewall that was configured to reject all addresses in the 192.166.x.x range of Internet Protocol (IP) addresses. If you had such an address and tried to get through the firewall, you would be denied.

In practice, rule-based access control is a type of MAC. An administrator typically configures the firewalls or other devices to allow or deny access. The owner or another user does not specify the conditions of acceptance, and safeguards are in place to ensure that an average user cannot change settings on such devices.

Rule-based access control uses ACLs to determine the level of access a user will have to a resource or application.

Role-Based Access Control

In a **role-based access control** configuration, access decisions are determined by the roles that individual users have as part of an organization. Organizations may have roles as marketers, sales people, managers, administrative assistants, and so on. Access to network objects is then determined by the role that has been assigned to a particular user. Role-based access requires a thorough understanding of how an organization operates, the number of users, and their functions.

Access rights are grouped by role name. The use of resources is restricted to individuals authorized to assume the associated role. For example, within a school system, the role of teacher can include access to data including test banks, research material, and memos. A school administrator role may have access to employee records, financial data, planning projects, and more.

The use of roles to control access can be an effective means for developing and enforcing enterprise-specific security policies and for streamlining the security management process.

When a user is associated with a role, the user should be assigned just the privilege level necessary to do the job. This is a general security principle known as *least privilege*. In practice, when someone is hired for an organization, the role is clearly defined. A network administrator creates a user account for the new employee and places that user account in a group with those who have the same role in the organization. Therefore, if a new teacher were hired, the new user account would be placed in the Teachers group. Once in the group, the new employee will gain the same level of access as all those who perform the same role.

> **NOTE**
> Role-based access is considered to be a type of MAC because access is dictated by an administrator, and the criteria for object access are not in the hands of the owner.

In the real world, this often is too restrictive to be practical. For instance, some teachers who have more experience or more responsibility may require more access to a particular network object than another teacher. It can be a time-consuming process to customize access to suit everyone's needs.

When roles overlap, responsibilities and privileges do as well. Access needs to reflect this. In such a case, you can establish role hierarchies to compensate for overlapping roles. A *role hierarchy* defines roles that have unique attributes and that may contain other roles; that is, one role may implicitly include the rights that are associated with another role. For example, if a user performs the roles of both a school administrator and a teacher, that user would be given access to areas permitted for each role.

Create Access Controls That Are Commensurate with the Level of Sensitivity of Data Access or Input

In many ways, establishing the need for access controls is the easy part; determining the right level and type of access control is not so easy. There often is a struggle between those in charge of securing Web applications and Web pages and end users who often want greater access than is necessary. Somewhere in the middle, the two must meet. For the security administrator the following are important:

- **Security**—Access control methods are great for ensuring that only those who should have access actually do. Allow only known and authorized users and devices onto your organization's network
- **Control**—Access controls enable administrators to restrict access to specific network resources based on identity of users and/or devices.
- **Organize access**—Access controls allow end-user access to appropriate resources based on their job or role of function.
- **Operational efficiency**—Controlled access to Web applications and Web sites often leads to a greater operational efficiency.

For their part, end users want sufficient access to perform their tasks unencumbered by restrictions. Security personnel need to apply access controls while at the same time not prevent end users from performing necessary tasks. Finding the right level of access control will often be accomplished by using multiple access methods simultaneously.

Best Practices for Securing Web Applications

Protecting Web applications from attack has become an important consideration for all organizations and developers. There are a number of general hints, tips, and tricks you can employ to help prevent Web attacks and the exploitation of vulnerabilities. This chapter has touched on many different methods that help mitigate the risks. Table 7-3 highlights some common vulnerabilities and threats, and mitigation strategies and best practices for securing Web applications.

TABLE 7-3 Common threats and vulnerabilities, and mitigation strategies and best practices.

ATTACK DESCRIPTION	MITIGATION STRATEGY AND BEST PRACTICES
Attacks performed by embedding malicious strings in query strings, form fields, cookies, and HTTP headers. These include command execution, XSS, SQL injection, and buffer overflow attacks.	Assume all input is harmful. Constrain, reject, and sanitize all input.
Data can be captured in transit, read, and used.	Use HTTPS to ensure data is encrypted during transit.
Log files and audit files may contain sensitive data that may be interpreted and used by a malicious user.	Use a principle of least privilege and access controls to ensure that only those needing access to log and audit files have it.
Malicious users may be able to authenticate using password cracking, elevation of privileges, and social engineering strategies.	Educate users on password security, use protocols to ensure passwords are not sent in cleartext, and develop password policies.
Malicious users may gain access to restricted and sensitive data or resources.	Ensure files, directories, and objects are explicitly unobtainable, not just out of sight. Validate authorization per object. Audit object access.
Malicious users are able to hijack a session and use valid credentials.	Manually log out of a session. Automatically log users out of sessions after a period of inactivity.
Hiding or ignoring file, folder, or resource locations.	Obscurity does not provide security by itself. Use access control mechanisms and security privileges to protect even hidden resources.

The Heartbleed Bug

Sometimes new threats are dealt with quietly by security professionals in the background, but others get a lot of well-deserved attention. One such threat is the Heartbleed bug. The Heartbleed bug takes advantage of a vulnerability in the OpenSSL encryption software library. OpenSSL is used to provide encryption services for Web users so that sensitive data such as credit card information or usernames and passwords cannot be read in transmission.

OpenSSL is an open source project; that is, it is not developed by a particular company but by a group of dedicated programmers. The version of OpenSSL released in 2012 had a bug that allowed malicious users to obtain information from a Web server's memory, leaving no trace of intrusion.

The malicious user takes advantage of a feature in OpenSSL known as **heartbeat**. The heartbeat refers to the transaction between the client and the Web server system, where a particular Web site responds to a user's system signifying that the server is active and awaiting requests. When the system receives requests, the Web server responds with a certain amount of data, as determined by the user request. The Heartbleed bug allows the malicious user to obtain more data beyond the initial requests and directly from the server's memory.

The problem is the access to this data that is stored in memory. Depending on what's in memory at the time the bug is exploited, the returned data could reveal credentials, personal information or, at the worst, the private encryption key. If a malicious user gained the private encryption key, all encrypted traffic would be readable.

No one knows for sure how many Web servers were vulnerable, but some put the number at 20 percent, while others estimate it was as high as 60 percent. The Heartbleed bug made the security world feel very vulnerable. It was a potentially significant security breach. The latest version of OpenSSL has repaired the vulnerability.

The Heartbleed bug was a great reminder to everyone of the importance of regularly changing passwords and using separate passwords for different functions.

CHAPTER SUMMARY

Any Web application with security holes may provide unwanted access to the network. Vulnerable Web applications allow malicious users to get around perimeter security measures and move straight to the network. Securing Web application security encompasses many elements, from end-user education to stronger programming and development. End-user education involves informing end users of the threats and the strategies to mitigate those threats.

On the developer's side, security measures need to be considered and implemented in each phase of the application software development life cycle. This creates a layered and well-designed approach to application security. In addition to implementing security in the development of applications, secure protocols and procedures must be adhered to when using any application. This includes the use of the HTTPS protocol and using access control methods.

KEY CONCEPTS AND TERMS

Advanced Encryption Standard (AES)
Canonicalization attack
Client-side validation
Data encryption standard (DES)
Digital certificate
Discretionary access control (DAC)

Heartbeat
Host-based security
Hypertext Transfer Protocol Secure (HTTPS)
Mandatory access control (MAC)
Rivest Cipher
Request for Comments (RFC)
Role-based access control

Rule-based access control
Software development life cycle (SDLC)
Triple Data Encryption Standard (3DES)
Vulnerability management

CHAPTER 7 ASSESSMENT

1. SFTP is a secure version of FTP.

  A. True
  B. False

2. You are the administrator of a large network. The network has several groups of users—including students, administrators, developers, and front-end staff. Each user on the network is assigned network access depending on his or her job in the organization. Which access control method is being used?

  A. Discretionary access control
  B. Role-based access control
  C. Rule-based access control
  D. Mandatory access control

3. Discretionary access control uses an access control list to determine access.

  A. True
  B. False

4. As a network administrator, you are concerned with the cleartext transmission of sensitive data on the network. Which of the following protocols are used to help secure communications? (Select two.)

  A. FTPv2
  B. SCP
  C. SSL
  D. SNMP

5. As part of the network's overall security strategy, you want to establish an access control method in which the owner decides who can and who cannot access the information. Which type of access control method is being described?

  A. Mandatory access control
  B. Role-based access control
  C. Discretionary access control
  D. Rule-based access control

6. _____ and HTTP are combined to secure online transactions.

7. Mandatory access control secures information and resources by assigning sensitivity labels on objects and comparing this to the level of sensitivity a user is assigned.

  A. True
  B. False

8. _____, also known as Rijndael, is a block cipher encryption standard. It can create keys from 128 bits to 256 bits in length.

9. As a network administrator, you have configured your company's firewall to allow remote users access to the network only between the hours of 1:00 p.m. and 4:00 p.m. Which type of access control method is being used?

  A. Discretionary access control
  B. Role-based access control
  C. Mandatory access control
  D. Rule-based access control

10. You are concerned about the integrity of messages sent over your HTTP connection. You use HTTPS to secure the communication. Which of the following are hashing protocols used with SSL to provide security? (Select two.)

  A. IPSec
  B. SHA1
  C. MD5
  D. SFTP

11. A malicious user can insert <form> tags into your Web pages, creating interactive content designed to steal information from your users.

  A. True
  B. False

12. Authorization is any process by which you verify that someone is who they claim they are.

  A. True
  B. False

© Rodolfo Clix/Dreamstime.com

CHAPTER

8

Mitigating Web Application Vulnerabilities

WEB APPLICATIONS ARE AN ESSENTIAL PART of the online experience. Every day, companies roll out Web applications to increase the appeal, functionality, and interactivity of their Web sites. These applications can take the form of portals, shopping carts, Web mail, online auctions, forms, discussion groups, and more. For all the good these Web applications introduce, they also bring a host of new vulnerabilities and security threats. Malicious users may invade a Web site through *backdoor access* of an unsecured Web application, completely circumventing perimeter security measures.

This chapter details the causes of these vulnerabilities and the largest targets for Web applications. In addition, this chapter contains information on secure coding best practices to help mitigate these risks from the beginning. To help understand changes that are made to any Web application source code, software development configuration management is essential; it tracks and controls any changes made. Revision-level tracking identifies what information was changed during any update, as well as when and by whom. The final section outlines how to mitigate Web application vulnerabilities and what the best practices are. It's important to keep these aspects in mind when designing any Web application because security of user data is essential to online components.

Chapter 8 Topics

This chapter covers the following topics:

- What the causes of Web application vulnerabilities are
- How policies mitigate vulnerabilities
- What secure coding best practices are
- How to incorporate Hypertext Markup Language (HTML) secure coding standards and techniques into your Web applications
- How to incorporate JavaScript secure coding standards and techniques into your Web applications
- How to incorporate Common Gateway Interface (CGI) form and Structured Query Language (SQL) database access secure coding standards and techniques into your Web applications
- How to implement software development configuration management and revision-level tracking
- What the best practices for mitigating Web application vulnerabilities are

Chapter 8 Goals

After you complete this chapter, you will be able to:

- Understand causes of vulnerabilities
- Understand policy developments that will mitigate vulnerabilities
- Understand how to implement secure coding best practices
- Understand how to incorporate HTML secure coding standards and techniques
- Understand how to incorporate JavaScript secure coding standards and techniques
- Understand how to incorporate CGI form and SQL database access secure coding standards and techniques
- Understand how to implement software configuration management and revision-level tracking
- Understand the best practices for mitigating Web application vulnerabilities

Causes of Web Application Vulnerabilities

The extensive use of the Internet for e-commerce enables companies to interact with customers from all over the world. Although the Internet allows a company to be available in the global market 24/7, Web applications on these sites can create security vulnerabilities that allow a malicious user to gain access to sensitive information, interrupt business activity, and commit fraud.

To better understand where vulnerabilities occur, it's important to understand what a Web application is. A **Web application** is a software program that generally contains computer scripts that interact with the end user. Some examples include Web mail, shopping carts, portals, games, forums, forms, online auctions, and other interactive Web page elements. A Web application consists of three main components: the Web server responsible for sending requested pages to the end user's browser, the application server responsible for processing data for the end user, and the database that stores all the required data.

With the growth of Web 2.0, Web applications are a common feature of Web site designs. The largest benefit of a Web application is that it enables thousands of users to interact with the site simultaneously. However, the benefit of incorporating Web applications to a Web site comes with a price. If applications are not coded and maintained correctly, they can open an unwanted doorway to an internal network. Therefore, before integrating a Web application, the designer must be aware of the associated risks as well as measures to mitigate those risks.

Over time, network administrators have established strong methods of securing the network perimeter. Firewalls, demilitarized zones (DMZs), intrusion detection systems (IDSs), secure protocols, and more have been combined to create strong perimeter security. To some extent, the security battle has shifted from almost a sole focus on perimeter security to internal security. That's because hackers look for different methods to gain access to sensitive information and attain their goals. It's estimated that about 70 percent of all hacking attempts against an organization's Web site come from the application layer. This indicates that hackers see Web applications as a prime target and that it's possible to take advantage of weak structure and coding to gain access to an organization's servers. Hackers often study the source code of a Web site to better understand its structure, and then target areas that appear weak. Three main areas targeted are:

- Authentication
- Input validation
- Session management

Authentication

A common security weakness of many Web applications is the failure to provide a strong authentication system to determine who the end user is. It's important to create a process in which end users must identify themselves with the appropriate credentials to gain access to the Web application. Without this precaution, a malicious user can gain access to another user's account, view sensitive information, and perform unauthorized tasks. The top concerns regarding authentication break down into four target areas:

- **Elevation of privilege**—When designing an authentication process, you must keep in mind that a hacker can try to gain access to an administrator's or local user's account and increase his or her privileges. In this process, a hacker overtakes all system processes and controls the Web application. Certain types of classic programming allow commands to run the application as the account with the highest amount of privilege, such as an administrator on the local machine. This grants the hacker all access to your Web application, data, and task management.

- **Disclosure of confidential data**—Confidential data disclosure occurs when users who are not authorized to view sensitive information gain access to it. Any data can be classified as confidential. In particular, customer credit card numbers, employee information, and financial records are at greatest risk when dealing with an insecure Web application. Restricting access by creating a strong authorization process is vital to ensuring all sensitive information is kept confidential and not accessed by a malicious user.

- **Data tampering**—Tampering with data is the process of an unauthorized modification to any information on a system. With a weak authorization process, any user can alter company or customer data, delete files, and alter the structure of a system. Authentication must be in place to mitigate the risk of data being tampered with.

- **Luring attacks**—In the method of luring, the malicious user tries to gain access by using an account with few privileges to coerce an entity with more privileges to perform an action on behalf of the malicious user. It's important to know who is logged on to the Web application to deter these attacks upon authorized users.

Input Validation

A hacker will attempt to compromise your Web application by analyzing every aspect of its design. One area of close examination is what type of input validation your Web application runs, if any. Unvalidated or poorly validated user input is a major threat to Web sites, databases, and Web applications. If malicious users discover that your Web application makes assumptions about the type, length, format, or range of input data, they will manipulate this weakness to achieve their own goals. When a secure Web application is designed, the only aspect that can be manipulated is public access areas. If your Web application is designed to blindly trust input, your application is weakened and at risk for the following:

- **Buffer overflows**—A buffer overflow is defined as a process in which data is stored in a buffer outside the designated memory that the programmer has set for the application. The extra data then overwrites the adjacent memory, which may contain program flow control data. The result: typically erratic program behavior, crashes, and program termination. If a buffer overflow occurs, the application is more susceptible to denial of service (DoS) attacks or code injection. If a DoS attack occurs within a Web application, the processes performed by the targeted application will crash. If a hacker injects code into the script of the Web application, the code alters the way the program executes and causes it to run the attacker's injected code instead.

- **Cross-site scripting (XSS)**—Cross-site scripting is defined as a computer security vulnerability that typically occurs in Web applications. This particular vulnerability allows a malicious user to inject client-side scripting into Web pages that are viewed by others. When attackers exploit cross-site scripting, they use it to bypass access controls of the Web application. In an XSS attack, a code created by the hacker runs in the user's Web browser while the browser is connected to your Web application. Essentially, a cross-site scripting attack uses your Web application as the vehicle to attack your end user, not the Web application itself.

  To initiate the cross-site scripting attack, the hacker presents a link that persuades the user to click on it and launch the vulnerable page within your Web application. The links typically arrive in e-mails, newsgroup postings, or by using the name of a trusted company or site that actually points to the vulnerable page. When the user activates the link, unvalidated code is sent to the Web application. In the event the Web application takes the query strings, fails to authenticate, and returns the code to the browser, the script is then executed. Typically a pop-up message is displayed, which allows the hacker to extract the user's authentication information. This allows hackers to gain authenticated user information, so they can log onto the Web application and gain privilege.

- **SQL injection**—An SQL injection attack is caused by exploiting the database layer of a Web application. A hacker using this technique can inject code and compromise the security of your Web application. The vulnerability is noticed when user input is incorrectly filtered in SQL statements, or when user input is not strongly limited or filtered and can be unexpectedly executed. SQL injection can occur when your Web application uses input to construct SQL statements to access the database layer. Another area where SQL injection may occur is if your Web application uses stored procedures that contain unfiltered user input. By taking advantage of this method of attack, the hacker can run commands arbitrarily in the database. This becomes a larger issue if the application uses an overprivileged account to connect to the database, further compromising any other connected system.

Session Management

Sessions allow a user to access a network or Web-based resource repeatedly, without having to reauthenticate every time. That is, once users have been authenticated and verified through an authentication method such as a username and password, they will not need to reauthenticate until they log off and end the session. Each authenticated user is assigned a session ID (SID). If a malicious user can gain the session ID, obtaining the authentication credentials is not necessary and the malicious user has access to the session. The session may be a network communication, online financial transaction, day trading, and more.

Session management is the term used to define how systems handle and manage user sessions. Session management security lies within the application layer of the database. To maintain an overall secure environment, it's critical to have session security. Top security threats to session management are:

- **Session hijacking**—This refers to the exploitation of a valid computer session to gain unauthorized access to information and services within a targeted computer system. Within a Web application, **session hijacking** occurs when the hacker uses network monitoring software to steal the authentication tokens (cookies) that are used to represent the authenticated user's session. With the stolen cookies, a malicious user spoofs the Internet browser and gains access to the application. This allows the hacker to acquire the same level of privileges as the legitimate user.

- **Session replay**—Can occur within a Web application when a user's authentication token is intercepted by attackers and used to bypass the application's authentication controls. If the token is visible through a cookie or a uniform resource locator (URL), the hacker can steal the information and post requests through a hijacked session.

- **Man-in-the-middle**—Refers to intercepting a message, altering its content, then sending it to its original recipient. This is a threat because the hacker can alter the content of the message as desired. In addition, the altered message appears to be legitimate and from someone like a coworker, upper management, or project manager. Therefore, the information is taken seriously and acted upon immediately. If the e-mail recipient responds, the hacker will intercept that message, alter it, and then send it back. Any network request involving client/server communication may be subject to man-in-the-middle attacks.

Vulnerabilities Are Caused by Non-Secure Code in Software Applications

Throughout software development, security must be a consideration. Too often, security measures are considered only after software is developed. A more proactive approach requires that security strategies be incorporated in each phase of application development. Secure coding is the highest priority and is a major component in the mitigation of many security risks. With a strong code, hackers cannot inject their own, take advantage of cookies, abuse user inputs, and gain access to your Web application. They cannot gain access to your databases, customer credit cards, employee information, and any other sensitive information.

Many coding errors can lead to vulnerabilities. Table 8-1 describes some common coding errors.

TABLE 8-1 Common coding errors.

TOP CODING ERRORS	DESCRIPTION
Failure to preserve Web page structure (aka cross-site scripting)	Cross-site scripting occurs when an attacker injects malicious code into your Web site. Other users visit your Web site expecting trustworthy content but instead code is executed against them.
Failure to preserve SQL query structure (aka SQL injection)	This mistake allows for SQL injection attacks. Failing to sanitize inputs used in a SQL command allows an attacker to obtain, modify, or delete data throughout the database.
Cross-site request forgery (CSRF)	Requests from attackers are sent to your site on behalf of a user, often without the user being aware. Fulfilled requests might return malware, masquerading as a response from you.
Unrestricted upload of file with dangerous type	Data is accepted without first confirming suitability.
Failure to preserve OS command structure (aka OS command injection)	This attack allows untrusted input to modify a command on your system. Without any validation or sanitization, that command may launch a program with the parameters of your attacker's choice.
Information exposure through an error message	Error messages intending to be helpful provide too much information.
URL redirection to untrusted site (aka open redirect)	Users are unknowingly redirected to a malicious and untrusted site.
Race condition	Poorly written code sends the processor into a panic, consuming all resources, ending as a denial of service.
Buffer copy without checking size of input (classic buffer overflow)	A buffer overflow occurs when a program attempts to put more data in a buffer than it can hold. The result is a downed or compromised application.
Improper control of file name for include/require statement in PHP program (aka PHP file inclusion)	Specific to the PHP language, PHP file inclusion occurs when a program does not adequately sanitize and filter input, allowing an attacker to potentially execute code on a remote system.
Improper limitation of a path name to a restricted directory (aka path traversal)	Path traversal occurs when external input is used to create a path name that is intended to identify a file or directory that is located underneath a restricted parent directory. Using common syntax elements such as .. and /, attackers are able to find directories not intended to be seen.

TABLE 8-1 Common coding errors, *continued.*

TOP CODING ERRORS	DESCRIPTION
Buffer access with incorrect length value	Sometimes occurring with languages such as C and C++, this is a buffer overflow attack in which input with an incorrect value length is written to a buffer that is outside regular memory space. As with other buffer flow attacks, the result may be crashes or the ability to run malicious code.
Improper check for unusual or exceptional conditions	The application does not account for unexpected or unusual conditions and is not written in a manner to manage them. This can occur in development if conditions that an application may encounter in live production are not considered.
Improper validation of array index cross-site request forgery (CSRF)	This is another form of input validation attack. In this case, when a program allows user input to control the array index, there is a chance of array index going out of bound. An array is a special type of variable that stores list-style data types.
Integer overflow or wraparound	The result of exceeding the integer boundary can lead to undefined and unpredictable outcomes such as crashes. Additionally, integer overflows can result in buffer overflows and can be used to execute malicious code.
Incorrect calculation of buffer size	Buffer size errors occur when the size of the buffer is not properly allocated. If the buffer size calculation is incorrect, a buffer overflow can occur.
Download of code without integrity check	This type of error occurs when an application fails to verify the legitimacy of code and accepts the code without proper validation. Allowing unverified code to execute could lead to confidentiality, integrity, and availability vulnerabilities.
Allocation of resources without limits or throttling)	Without placing limitations on resource usage, DoS attacks can occur if an attacker monopolizes resources to the exclusion of others.
Improper access control (authorization)	Access controls ensure that only those who should have access to resources or applications actually do. Failure to implement strong access controls may result in integrity, availability, and confidentiality vulnerabilities.
Reliance on untrusted inputs in a security decision	When authentication and authorization security decisions are based on potentially vulnerable areas such as cookies, environment variables, and forms, an attacker may be able to bypass security to gain access.

continued

8

Web Application
Vulnerabilities

TABLE 8-1 Common coding errors, *continued.*

TOP CODING ERRORS	DESCRIPTION
Missing encryption of sensitive data	All sensitive data, whether in storage or in transit, needs to be sufficiently secured using encryption protocols.
Use of hard-coded credentials	Sometimes credentials, such as passwords, are hard-coded into a configuration file or script to allow for inbound authentication or for outbound communication to external components. A vulnerability can occur if an attacker can gain access to the scripts and learn the hard-coded credentials.
Missing authentication for critical function	All access to critical functions should require authentication. Open access to critical functions may compromise the applications, data, and more.
Incorrect permission assignment for critical resource	Use the principle of least privilege to restrict those who have access to critical resources.
Use of a broken or risky crypto-graphic algorithm	When securing communications, the cryptography method used may be weak or has been compromised in the past. Ensure that the most current and trusted cryptography mechanisms and protocols are used.

Properly programmed applications can mitigate many of these coding errors. These attacks combined to breach millions of Web sites each year. With knowledge of these attacks, coders can prevent them and help ensure users' data remains safe.

More information on each of these coding errors can be found at *http://www.sans.org/top25-programming-errors/*.

Developing Policies to Mitigate Vulnerabilities

To help ensure that security strategies are part of the development and deployment of applications, policies provide a security framework for coders and administrators to follow. A policy is a documented plan outlining the goals, procedures, and objectives that guide decisions to a desired outcome. Many technical policies are used in business, including e-mail, Internet, backup, user, and remote access policies.

A business may have policies detailing acceptable use and compliance requirements. A security policy that all companies should have is one aimed at all aspects of security, including Web and mobile application vulnerabilities. The policy should include acceptable use, application development guidelines, and penalties for noncompliance.

Security policies are an organization's primary document for information security. A well-written and implemented security policy protects information and people in the organization and includes such elements as:

- Data security in storage and in transit
- Asset inventory and management
- End-user security
- Physical security
- Access control mechanisms
- Incident management and reporting
- Fault-tolerant measures
- Noncompliance consequences

There are many general guidelines for creating security policies, including well-documented ones at *http://www.sans.org/security-resources/policies/#primer.* Security policies vary by organization and are customized to the organization's security needs. When developing a security policy, a good approach is to answer a few questions:

- **What are the assets you are trying to protect?** Are you using a SQL back-end database? Do you have sensitive data communicated over the Internet? Before creating the security policy, it's important to identify exactly what needs protection.

- **What are the common vulnerabilities and threats?** Armed with research, you can discover known threats, such as XSS and SQL injection. Before developing the policy, it's essential to understand the types of threats you are up against.

- **What are the mitigation strategies?** Once you have identified the common threats, the security policy should include mitigation strategies for those threats. The policy often identifies not only how to apply the strategies but consequences for noncompliance.

- **When should the security policy be reviewed and updated?** A security policy is a dynamic document that is updated periodically to address new vulnerabilities and mitigation strategies.

A security policy often also includes:

- **Authentication policies**—The security policy highlights authentication methods to be used, reporting mechanisms if the authentication is compromised, and password policies. The security policy may outline how authentication is managed. For example, it could state that Hypertext Transfer Protocol Secure (HTTPS) is used for all Web communications to the database or that reauthentication is required at specific times.

- **Access privilege policies**—A common security practice is to use the least amount of authorization required for any task. Create user accounts that have no more privilege than is required for their duties. Don't create administrator accounts with complete access to the Web application's design and function. Create service access based upon the granted level of privilege. This includes not granting full service access to any one user account. Access policies may be documented in the security policy.

- **Disclosure of confidential data**—The security policy may set how data is handled both in storage and in transit. The worst case for a compromised system is to have confidential, sensitive data exposed. The best way to reduce the risk of your Web application becoming a target of data disclosure is to create policies that remove the risks. Countermeasures to keep data safe include performing role checks before allowing access to tasks that could potentially reveal or compromise sensitive information. Create a strong encryption key that can encode all confidential information that is stored in configuration files and databases.

- **Incident response**—The security policy often identifies procedures to be followed in case of a security breach.

Security policies are an integral part of an organization's overall security strategy. It's important to have a clear idea of what policies look like and what they are designed to do. The following short sample of an actual security policy provides a glimpse into how policies are designed.

Sample Data Confidentiality Policy

1.0 Purpose

The Data Confidentiality Policy is designed to help network users identify what constitutes sensitive data and the data that cannot be disclosed to non-employees or outside the organization without written authorization. The data referenced in this document applies to all information stored or in transit to and from the network.

All network users are required to familiarize themselves with the data access and handling guidelines presented in this policy. The intent is to protect the data integrity and confidentiality of <Organization Name> and to ensure policy compliance is in practice.

2.0 Scope

All <Organization Name> data is categorized into two main classifications:

- <Organization Name> Public
- <Organization Name> Confidential

Information that has been deemed public by <Organization Name> is general information that in no way compromises operations of <Organization Name>. Information classified as public may be shared outside of the organization. However, anyone who is unsure whether particular data is public must contact the manager before disclosing.

Information that is classified as confidential must be carefully managed by <Organization Name>. Confidential information in the property of <Organization Name> and disclosing of all sensitive data is strictly forbidden.

3.0 Policy

The Confidentiality Policy outlines the procedures for protecting information at various levels. For example, it identifies how the company expects both confidentially classified and publicly classified data to be handled.

3.1 Public data description—General business information, company newsletter data that contains no employee details.

>   **Allowed for viewing**—All internal employees and external contractors.
>
>   **Electronic communication**—No restrictions for e-mail or electronic communications.
>
>   **Storage methods**—All data regardless of sensitivity is electronically encrypted and stored. Data is not encrypted in electronic transmissions.
>
>   **Disposal/destruction**—Data is not sensitive therefore no special disposal techniques are required.
>
>   **Penalty for deliberate or inadvertent disclosure**—Misuse of public data may lead to disciplinary action including termination.

3.2 Confidential data description—Business secrets, financial documents, employee information, and so on.

>   **Allowed for viewing**—Restricted to those who need the data to complete job-related tasks. No unauthorized viewing or access of confidential data.
>
>   **Electronic communication**—All communication via e-mail or other electronic means require encryption both in transit and in the storage location.
>
>   **Storage methods**—Individual access controls are highly recommended for electronic information.
>
>   **Disposal/destruction**—In specially marked disposal bins on <Organization Name> premises; electronic data should be expunged or cleared. Reliably erase or physically destroy media.
>
>   **Penalty for deliberate or inadvertent disclosure**—Intentional disclosure of sensitive data will lead to immediate dismissal and possible criminal charges.

4.0 Enforcement

Any employee who intentionally sells or distributes company data may be subject to immediate dismissal and a criminal review. Employees who repeatedly disclose sensitive data unintentionally will be terminated unless end-user education can be implemented and proven effective.

This is just a quick overview of some elements in a security policy. In many organizations, the policy is several pages long, covering security aspects in great detail. In most cases, it's the employees' responsibility to familiarize themselves with security and other policies to ensure they are not in violation.

Implementing Secure Coding Best Practices

The best way to prevent software from attacks is to build security into the coding framework of your Web application. Many software tools help check, write, and ensure your Web application is secure. Software tools help inexperienced coders analyze the output and resolve security issues. Another advantage to using a software tool is the large database it comes with. Common software tools have knowledge of more than 100 common and uncommon security flaws in Web applications. This helps target issues the developer might be unaware of. No matter how great a software tool may be, however, its weakness can be its inability to follow the logic of your Web application and truly determine if an input value is, in fact, legitimate. Software tools also have many false positives, which the developer must sort through manually to determine if they are accurate. Most software tools are beneficial to prevent buffer overflow attacks.

Even with the help of third-party applications, the best way to implement secure code is to follow secure coding guidelines. These guidelines help to deter many of the malicious attacks and commonly exploited security vulnerabilities. The CERT program is a group of security experts who monitor public sources of vulnerability, inform technology experts of the threats, and develop mitigation strategies. CERT has published its top 10 tips for secure coding. These are:

- **Validate input**—Unvalidated user input is one of the greatest security risks. CERT contends that most vulnerabilities would be reduced if proper input validation mechanisms were used.

- **Heed compiler warnings**—When compiling code, use the compiler's most strict setting. Then take note of each warning provided and eliminate it. This practice ensures the most stable code.

- **Plan and design for security policies**—Application security should not be an afterthought. Rather, it should be considered at each phase of development. This allows for a layered approach to application security.

- **Keep the coding simple**—Often easier said than done, it's important to keep the coding streamlined and simple. Using complex and extra code can lead to difficulty not only in the application's functioning and troubleshooting but also with security. It may be easier for a malicious user to sneak code into a complex written code.

- **Deny access by default**—Often the best security measure is to deny access by default. This is a guilty-until-proven-innocent approach. In this way, everyone is denied access by default until adequate authentication is used. The authentication methods may be multilayered to ensure that only those who should have access actually do.

- **Use the principle of least privilege**—After authentication, security measures need to be employed that restrict authorization and access to resources. The principle of least privilege dictates that users are restricted to necessary permissions and access levels. User access is closely controlled and permissions tightly restricted.

- **Sanitize data sent to other systems**—When data transmissions are sanitized, the communication still occurs but the message is stripped of potentially harmful content. Sanitizing data helps prevent injection attacks.

- **Use layered security**—Software goes through many stages in the software development life cycle. In each phase of development, security strategies can be employed creating a strong, layered security approach.

- **Use effective quality assurance techniques**—There's pressure to get applications to market and release them as soon as possible. Quality assurance may suffer— and so, too, security. Adopting strong quality assurance helps ensure that applications are not released until all aspects, including code, are sufficiently tested.

> **NOTE**
>
> CERT® is a registered trademark, and it refers to the federally funded CERT Coordination Center (CERT/CC). CERT/CC is a part of Carnegie Mellon University (CMU). CERT/CC is different from the United States CERT (US-CERT), which coordinates defense and responses to cyber-attacks in the United States. You can learn more about CERT at *http://www.cert.org/*.

- **Adopt a secure coding standard**—Documented standards help regulate and standardize coding to ensure it meets security requirements.

The above list represents general security principles and guidelines for coding. The following sections explore specific coding recommendations.

Incorporating HTML Secure Coding Standards and Techniques

Hypertext Markup Language (HTML) is a widely used language for creating Web documents. As such, developing strategies and techniques to ensure HTML is secure is essential. Many general guidelines can be used to help ensure HTML is coded and deployed correctly. These include:

- **Encrypt HTML code**—The source code for HTML Web pages is, for the most part, transparent. Internet Explorer, Google Chrome, Firefox, and other browsers allow users to view the source code of the Web page. Some malicious users may use this feature to create identical pages for cross-site forgery attacks or to find areas to input their own malicious code into the HTML. For this reason, some Web page developers go the extra step, using third-party software to encrypt the HTML source code. Third-party software not only can encrypt source code but also can prevent theft of source code, prevent text selection, disable printing of source code, and prevent spam bots from harvesting e-mail addresses from your pages.

- **Keep the code clean**—When creating HTML pages, keep the coding clean and simple. When the coding is complex, there is a greater chance malicious coding can be inserted without your notice.

- **Monitor HTML code**—It sounds like a lot of work, but coders should periodically check their source code for changes. It's not necessary to verify each line of code but to track unexpected changes in the size of the code.

- **Use input validation with HTML forms**—Using HTML forms of any kind comes with a security risk. The key to proper coding and techniques when using HTML forms is, once again, to employ appropriate input validation mechanisms.

- **Validate URLs**—Directory traversal attacks leading to open directories may occur if scripts are placed in the URL. The recommendation is to secure the directories and ensure that malicious users are unable to get to sensitive directories.

Incorporating JavaScript Secure Coding Standards and Techniques

The **JavaScript** language has a unique set of security challenges. When designing or writing with JavaScript, it's important to remember to provide a secure environment for executing mobile code. The Java security architecture is designed to protect systems and users from hostile programs and downloads over a network, but it cannot defend against bugs in trusted codes. This means that if trusted JavaScript code is not implemented properly, it can open holes that the platform is designed to allow. In the worst case, computers can be turned into zombie machines where confidential and sensitive data can be exposed, along with many other malicious activities.

Secure coding standards have been created to assist Java developers in creating secure code while avoiding programmer errors. These guidelines are expected to be followed under all circumstances because they ensure that the Java platform is used and implemented accurately. When the guidelines are followed, Java developers create secure end-user applications and applets that can be trusted by users.

The following are fundamental aspects of the JavaScript secure coding standards:

- **Prefer to have obviously no flaws than no obvious flaws**—According to the standards, it's preferred to have obviously no flaws than no obvious flaws. This means that because of how large the JavaScript language is, flaws can easily slip past even the most advanced developer. Attempt to write code that does not require clever logic to understand that it is secure. Write code that is obviously safe. It's highly recommended to follow all the JavaScript secure coding guidelines unless there is a very specific, strong reason not to.

- **Avoid duplication**—The next fundamental guideline is to avoid duplications. This means to avoid duplicating code and data. Duplicating causes too many problems and can lead to unexpected errors within the application. Both code and data tend not to be treated consistently when they are duplicated.

- **Restrict privileges**—Even with well-reviewed code, flaws may exist. Code must be operated with reduced privileges, thus deterring the ability to exploit flaws. In extreme cases, the developer can implement the principle of least privilege. The developer restricts permissions through policy files, causing the application to run in *sandbox mode*, unable to execute any dangerous code. The application is then safe for the user.

- **Establish trust boundaries**—Trust boundaries are necessary to allow easy security auditing to be performed efficiently. This means that the Web browser is outside the system for the Web server. Additionally, a Web server should not be within the same system as the Web browser, so that the security behavior of one does not affect the other.

- **Contain sensitive data**—Due to obvious security issues, sensitive data must be contained in a secure manner and must be kept hidden to users who lack the privilege to view it. Certain information, such as Social Security numbers and passwords, are classified as highly sensitive data. This information should not be stored and not kept for any longer than required for application purposes. This information should not be seen even by administrators, should not be recorded in log files, and should not be detectable through searches.

- **Avoid dynamic SQL**—It's a well-known security vulnerability that dynamic SQL including untrusted input is subject to SQL injection.

- **XML and HTML generation require care**—Cross-site scripting is a common security vulnerability in many Web applications. The root cause is input and output that are accepted without the input being validated. Examples can be checking for illegal characters and escaping data properly. It's better to use a library that constructs XML or HTML than to try to insert escape codes for every field in the document.

- **Take care of interpreting untrusted code**—Code can be hidden in many places within JavaScript. If the source is classified as untrusted, a secure *sandbox* must be constructed to run it. Examples that can potentially run untrusted code are scripts within scripting and allowing of remote code, specified by the remote connection.

Sandbox Security

When reading about application security, you will no doubt encounter the term **sandbox.** In computer security terms, a sandbox is a strategy for separating programs and running them in their own virtual space. The sandbox, as the name suggests, is a bit of a play area where untested code, untrusted programs, and untrusted users can operate without posing a threat to the larger systems.

A sandbox is a tightly controlled area where malicious users have little or no chance of getting out of the sandbox and into the larger system. They can operate only within the safe confines of the sandbox.

Incorporating CGI Form and SQL Database Access Secure Coding Standards and Techniques

Anytime a Web site uses forms and databases, security is a major concern. **Common Gateway Interface (CGI)** is not a programming language. Instead, it's a standard that enables communication between Web forms and your program. A CGI script can be written in many different programming languages, including C, C++, Perl, Java, ASP, and others. CGI is commonly used on Web sites to create interactive forms, which may include:

- Order forms
- Contact forms
- Surveys
- Registration forms
- Signup forms
- Reservation forms
- Mail order forms

Forms such as these have become commonplace on today's Web sites. In most applications, these forms are secure; however, sometimes they are not. Securing Web forms is a critical security consideration for preventing various forms of injection attacks. Key to securing online forms is incorporating strong input validation strategies, using secure communication protocols such as Secure Sockets Layer (SSL) and HTTPS, using password-protected forms, and, if necessary, incorporating a second level of encryption with RSA military-strength encryption.

SQL Database Security

It can be argued that the databases and the network database servers are the most important elements of a network. Databases store client details, financial information, human resource details, medical data, and much more. Without access to this data, many organizations would cease to function. One such type of database is the SQL database.

Although there are many ways to access a database, the most popular is to use Structured Query Language (SQL). SQL was created by IBM in 1974 and popularized by Oracle in 1979. SQL is designed for database systems that are accessed by a number of users simultaneously. It works on the basis of commands that can be integrated within applications.

The database is normally accessed by a client using a variety of methods. Although the database can be interrogated directly using commands or programming languages, most databases are accessed through a client application, or *front end*. Databases themselves are basically systems for storing, retrieving, and managing data. It's up to the client application to access the data and to make it available in the necessary format to users. This approach allows the databases to maintain a level of simplicity that can make them more responsive to requests and queries.

Because of the importance of databases, strategies and techniques are used to protect those servers and back-end databases. Some of these strategies include:

- **Limiting user access to the database**—All user accounts with access to the database should be closely monitored with the principle of least privilege applied. Database access should be guarded and restricted.

- **Input validation**—Web applications use SQL statements that incorporate user-supplied data. If user-supplied data is unsafe and unfiltered, a Web application may be vulnerable to a SQL injection attack. A successful attack will allow the attacker to access, read, delete, and modify the information held within the database and even take control of the server on which the database is operating.

- **Limit error messages**—Error messages can be a form of information attack. Information leakage occurs when a Web site or Web application discloses sensitive information unknowingly. For example, error messages can reveal information about the server, an application, and the network topology that an attacker can use to exploit the system.

- **Logging and auditing**—To help track and monitor access, it's necessary to enable auditing and logging to track events related to the database and database access. Tracking mechanisms can help identify potential security risks.

- **Encryption protocols**—If the database contains highly sensitive data, as most do, it's important to ensure that any communications into and out of the database are secured. You apply this security using secure encryption protocols and strong cryptography procedures.

- **Physical security**—Logical security measures are one form of security strategy whereas physical security measures are another. Physical security measures restrict physical access to database servers, backups, and any other hardware related to the SQL database.

Implementing Software Development Configuration Management and Revision-Level Tracking

In the software development world, **software configuration management (SCM)** refers to the mechanisms used to track and control changes in software. This is important because applications in development are dynamic and change over time, and methods are required to control and document these changes. The ability to track and control such changes helps ensure that software development will be successful. Software configuration management tries to bridge this gap by defining a process for change control.

There are many advantages to implementing a SCM system, including:

- **Prevent unauthorized changes**—During development, applications may change significantly; the SCM ensures that these changes are authorized and that application development is unified in its approach.
- **Greater control**—Having a centralized framework for software development allows for greater control of the entire process. With the SCM, software development can follow a plan and developers have greater control over programming efforts.
- **Ease of management**—With centralized tracking efforts, it's easier to manage the development project to ensure all programming follows a specific format.
- **Quality control**—Using SCM, developers follow specific guidelines, ensuring the quality of the project. SCM helps ensure adherence to the organization's development process.

It's best to use a software development configuration management system along with a revision-level tracking process. This is essential in Web application design because it allows the developer to manage and view all changes that occur within the source code of the Web application. Software development configuration will track and control any change within the source code, and a revision-level tracking system will identify which areas have been modified, by whom, and at what time, along with other additional information. These two systems provide a systematic trail of a Web application's modifications.

Revision-Level Tracking

Revision control is the management of changes to a document, program, or other information stored as a computer file. This process is most commonly used in software development in which a team of people is altering the same file. Each revision is associated with a timestamp and is identified by the person making the change. In coding, revision tracking is any process that provides control over changes to the source code.

Best Practices for Mitigating Web Application Vulnerabilities

To deal with Web application vulnerabilities, it's best to determine and follow the best practices for mitigating risks. Many organizations follow these practices for maintaining Web application security. These are more than recommendations, given the ability of malicious users to circumvent traditional perimeter security measures and access networks and databases through application security holes. Many organizations help recognize and report known vulnerabilities. It's the security administrators' responsibility to be aware of these organizations and their security reports.

Best practices an administrator should adopt day to day to monitor Web application vulnerabilities include:

- **Incorporate security in development**—Web application vulnerabilities must be addressed in the development process. Consider security throughout the stages of application development, from concept to completion.

- **Train developers**—A key strategy to weave security into the development process is to train developers in security programming and concepts. If programmers know about security threats and mitigation strategies, they can incorporate them in all phases of application development.

- **Incorporate testing standards**—One way to mitigate Web vulnerabilities is to test and retest applications before they are released. This may slow down release dates but the end product will be more robust and more secure. Testing should involve attacking the application with known threats to see how it holds up. Additionally, testing should occur periodically after release as a proactive security measure.

- **Persistent monitoring**—One best practice for Web application security is to continually monitor current threats and review whether those threats can be applied to your application. It's essential that security administrators take a proactive, instead of a reactive, approach to Web application security.

- **Administrator controls**—It's important to restrict access to Web applications in whole or in part to prevent uncontrolled access. Key to this control is the restriction of access to administrator accounts. Administrator accounts in Active Directory and on the database level should be closely guarded. Further, administrator accounts can be segregated depending on role. In the world of enterprise resource planning (ERP), for instance, there is typically one administrator password for viewing the database, another for changing tables, another for running Web services, and so on. This is another safeguard against a single password potentially compromising an entire system.

- **Error messaging**—Another key way to secure Web applications is to prevent application error messages from falling into the wrong hands. Many error messages reveal too much information that can be used by malicious users to launch an attack.

- **System and application hardening**—Keep applications and systems up to date with the latest security patches and updates.

- **Configuration**—Part of the software hardening and testing procedures will likely include verifying application configuration. This involves turning off unused features and defaults, disabling default accounts, and removing unnecessary code that can be exploited. A configuration error can undermine the best and most secure coding.

- **Data validation**—Input data from the user and a Web form must be validated to prevent attacks such as SQL injection, denial of service, or buffer overflows. *Data validation*, essentially the same thing as input validation, is the verification of input data's integrity to ensure that it has not been tampered with, and that the input data uses expected and accepted characters and formats. This validation is essential to Web application security. Conversely, unvalidated data is a common Web application security weakness.

- **Cryptographic knowledge**—Communication to and from the Web server and applications must be secure. This is particularly true of sensitive data transactions that occur over the Web. The role of **cryptography**—the encoding of data so that it can be decoded only by certain persons—is to protect data integrity, confidentiality, nonrepudiation, and authentication. A small mistake in configuration or coding can negatively impact the role and effectiveness of cryptography.

As much as possible, security administrators need to be proactive, rather than reactive, in securing their applications. To be proactive, keep application patches up to date and keep track of current attacks and vulnerabilities and how to mitigate them.

CHAPTER SUMMARY

Unsecure Web applications can quickly undermine a network's security by completely circumventing perimeter security measures. The most secure firewall and perimeter defense systems will not protect users from security holes in applications. For this reason, focusing security efforts behind the firewall is an essential part of security.

Web application security is an involved process requiring both proactive and reactive measures. These measures include developer training, persistent monitoring, access controls, and system hardening. Developing policies and standards for programming is another important part of a security strategy. Policies regulate how programming is done and how programs are accessed and used within an organization.

Software development configuration management provides a way to track and monitor application development. SCM controls the direction of application development.

KEY CONCEPTS AND TERMS

Common Gateway Interface (CGI)
Cryptography
JavaScript

Sandbox
Session hijacking
Session management

Software configuration management (SCM)
Web application

CHAPTER 8 ASSESSMENT

1. Before integrating a Web application, a designer must be aware of the associated risks and measures to mitigate those risks.

A. True
B. False

2. Which of the following are primary components of a Web application? (Select three.)

A. Web server
B. Application server
C. Client browser
D. Database

3. When a secure Web application is designed, the only aspect that can be manipulated is private access areas.

A. True
B. False

4. A security policy may contain which of the following elements?

A. Secure coding procedures
B. Access control mechanisms
C. Noncompliance consequences
D. All of the above
E. B and C only

5. You are part of programming team developing a Web application. Your manager has implemented tracking mechanisms to ensure all developers work on the application within the same guidelines. What has your manager implemented?

A. Acceptable use policy
B. Application-based access control
C. SCM
D. Correct usage policy

6. A malicious user has gained access to the administrator's account and increased the user's account status. This is an example of _____.

7. Session management defines how systems handle and manage user sessions.

A. True
B. False

8. _____ can occur within a Web application when a user's authentication token is intercepted by the attackers and used to bypass the authentication controls of the application.

9. Which of the following are fundamental aspects of the JavaScript secure coding standard? (Select two.)

A. Duplicate code for redundancy
B. Restrict privileges
C. Establish trust boundaries
D. Use Dynamic SQL

10. You have decided to use several forms in your HTML Web site. Which of the following types of attacks may take advantage of poorly programmed HTML forms?

A. Social engineering
B. Injection
C. Man-in-the-middle
D. Elevation of privilege

11. Which of the following should you use to secure online forms?

A. Input validation
B. Secure communication protocols
C. Password protection
D. All of the above

12. Error messages can reveal information about a server that an attacker can use to exploit the system.

A. True
B. False

© Rodolfo Clix/Dreamstime.com

Maintaining PCI DSS Compliance for E-commerce Web Sites

CONSUMERS TODAY FREQUENTLY CHOOSE CREDIT CARDS over cash or debit cards to pay for goods and services. Credit cards offer the convenience of buy now, pay later, which many consumers have come to enjoy. In addition, credit cards have become an integral part of online shopping, which in recent years has exploded as a major competitor to traditional retail stores. Credit cards are at the forefront of payment methods for online auction sites and Internet stores. This technology usage requires security measures to protect cardholders' data, that, if misused, could lead to financial problems and personal stress.

Major payment brands formed the Payment Card Industry Security Standards Council to combat lack of security, as well as hackers and misuse of cardholder information. The council has created a list of standards called the Payment Card Industry Data Security Standard (PCI DSS) to help organizations achieve security. This list of requirements contains information to deter hackers from compromising any cardholder data.

This chapter explores how credit card transaction processing occurs and what PCI DSS is. The chapter will explain why PCI DSS compliance is important and how to design and build a Web site with PCI DSS compliance in mind. The chapter highlights what a PCI DSS security assessment entails and what the best practices are to mitigate risks for e-commerce Web sites with PCI DSS compliance.

Chapter 9 Topics

This chapter covers the following topics and concepts:

- What the most common types of credit card transaction processing are
- What the Payment Card Industry Data Security Standard (PCI DSS) is
- How to design and build a Web site with PCI DSS compliance in mind
- What a PCI DSS security assessment entails
- What best practices to mitigate risks for e-commerce Web sites with PCI DSS compliance are

Chapter 9 Goals

When you complete this chapter, you will be able to:

- Understand types of credit card transaction processing
- Define PCI DSS
- Understand why PCI DSS compliance is important
- Design and build a Web site with PCI DSS compliance in mind
- Understand what a PCI DSS Security Assessment entails
- Understand best practices to mitigate risks for e-commerce Web sites with PCI DSS compliance

Credit Card Transaction Processing

Credit card transaction processing has significantly increased the speed and efficiency of consumer spending; merchants can sell as fast as a customer can purchase. Almost every store, including Internet-based stores, now accepts credit cards.

Many different types of transaction processing occur and each can use different methods. The two most common types of transaction processing are batch processing and real-time processing.

> ▶ **NOTE**
> Transaction processing in e-commerce means the online store owner possesses a merchant account.

Batch Processing

Batch processing is the handling of several transactions at one time. The consumer is often not present for the processing of the transaction. In batch processing, receipts are often collected over a short time and then sent in as multiple *batches* or sets of information.

PayPal

In today's busy world, many companies have emerged that specialize in credit card transaction processing. These companies make the transaction process easier for merchants and offer additional security to the consumer. One of the largest companies is PayPal.

PayPal was founded in 1998 and acquired by eBay in 2002. PayPal acts as an alternative to credit card transaction processing. Customers using PayPal don't need to have a credit card. PayPal offers additional security for online consumers because a consumer does not share personal information with the other party in a transaction. PayPal has played an essential part in facilitating e-commerce. This company has become an intermediate step that performs the transaction processing for online merchants, auction sites, and other commercial users. In exchange for performing this function for a merchant, PayPal charges a processing fee. The fee depends on the currency, the location where the money is sent, the country of sender, the country of receiver, and other conditions.

Batch processing is used when an enterprise handles a large number of transactions but needs to save resources to handle the processing. Batch processing is much more common in brick-and-mortar stores than in online transactions.

Real-Time Processing

Real-time processing is the most common type of credit card transaction for e-commerce. A consumer's credit card is charged immediately when a purchase is made. In most cases, the product is shipped the day of purchase. Because the Internet runs in real time, real-time processing, which keeps accurate inventory and sales totals, appeals to merchants.

What Is the Payment Card Industry Data Security Standard?

Established in 2004, the **Payment Card Industry Data Security Standard (PCI DSS)** became a set of widely accepted requirements for enhancing payment account data security. The PCI Security Standards Council (PCI SSC) created the PCI DSS. These five payment companies were involved: American Express, Discover Financial Services, JCB International, MasterCard Worldwide, and Visa Inc. The standard has gone through major revisions. Most recent was version 3.0, which was released in 2014, although several individual requirements did not go into effect until summer 2015.

The PCI DSS was created to help organizations that process credit card payments prevent fraud by having increased control over data and its exposure. The PCI DSS requirements apply to all organizations that hold, process, or exchange cardholder information from any of the major payment brands that are members of the PCI Security Standards Council.

The requirements cover management, policy procedure, network architecture, software design, and other protective measures for handling transaction systems and cardholder data. The PCI Security Standards Council outlined the requirements and organized them under six major areas of concern. PCI SSC calls them the *six principles*. Within those principles exist 12 requirements, each with many details of what is required to maintain a secure cardholder data environment. The principles and requirements are listed in Table 9-1.

> **NOTE**
> Web applications represent only a small portion of the requirements to become PCI DSS compliant.

You will learn about the principles and requirements in detail in the "Best Practices to Mitigate Risk for E-commerce Web Sites with PCI DSS Compliance" section later in this chapter. In addition, the full set of standards is available to view at *https://www.pcisecuritystandards.org*.

TABLE 9-1   PCI DSS principles and requirements.

PRINCIPLE	REQUIREMENT
Build and maintain a secure network.	Requirement 1: Install and maintain a firewall configuration to protect cardholder data.
	Requirement 2: Don't use vendor-supplied defaults for system passwords and other security parameters.
Protect cardholder data.	Requirement 3: Protect stored cardholder data.
	Requirement 4: Encrypt transmission of cardholder data across open, public networks.
Maintain a vulnerability management program.	Requirement 5: Use and regularly update antivirus software or programs.
	Requirement 6: Develop and maintain secure systems and applications.
Implement strong access control measures.	Requirement 7: Restrict access to cardholder data by business need to know.
	Requirement 8: Assign a unique ID to each person with computer access.
	Requirement 9: Restrict physical access to cardholder data.
Regularly monitor and test networks.	Requirement 10: Track and monitor all access to network resources and cardholder data.
	Requirement 11: Regularly test security systems and processes.
Maintain an information security policy.	Requirement 12: Maintain a policy that addresses information security for employees and contractors.

If PCI DSS Is Not a Law, Why Do You Need to Be in Compliance?

Although the PCI DSS is not a government regulation, if a merchant is found not to be in compliance, hefty penalties can occur. If unable to meet requirements of PCI DSS specifications, a mid-sized merchant who deals with 1 million to 6 million credit card transactions annually could be fined thousands of dollars. From Visa, fines for a single month could accumulate to $25,000. If compliance still is not followed, payment brands that belong to the PCI Security Standards Council can remove the merchant's ability to make credit card transactions.

Security breaches have resulted in lawsuits directed at merchants and acquiring banks. Banks have initiated these lawsuits because they have issued credit cards to cardholders whose cardholder data was put in jeopardy. The lawsuits seek to recover costs of reissuing credit cards to their customers. In one example, seven merchants instigated a lawsuit against a software development company and one of its retailers over a security breach that resulted in thousands of dollars in expenses. Fines and lawsuits are just the start of fighting noncompliance with PCI DSS.

An example of the consequences of noncompliance with PCI DSS is CardSystems Solutions Inc. in Atlanta. CardSystems Solutions Inc. is a credit card transaction processing company that was hit by hackers, compromising 40 million card numbers. Visa and American Express cut ties with the company after an internal and forensic review revealed that CardSystems Solutions lacked the proper controls to protect sensitive cardholder information. CardSystems Solutions was stripped of the ability to process Visa and American Express transactions. MasterCard agreed to work with CardSystems Solutions in the short term to improve compliance. The company must prove that it's in full compliance with PCI DSS or risk losing the ability to process MasterCard credit card transactions as well.

Designing and Building Your E-commerce Web Site with PCI DSS in Mind

Designing and building an e-commerce Web site with PCI DSS seems like a daunting task. In reality, it's not as difficult as you might think. The first step is to determine what kind of merchant you will be. This determination assigns you a label in the form of a level number, from 1 to 4. The merchant level governs the types of audits and assessments your organization will participate in.

A level 4 merchant deals with fewer than 20,000 e-commerce transactions per year. A level 3 merchant processes 20,000 to 1 million e-commerce transactions per year. A level 2 merchant processes 1 million to 6 million transactions per year, and a level 1 merchant processes more than 6 million transactions per year. Level 2 through 4 merchants are required to participate in a self-assessment annually and a network scan quarterly; a level 1 merchant is required to undergo an annual onsite audit and network scans quarterly.

The PCI Security Standards Council provides a development framework for merchants to follow when designing and building an e-commerce Web site. The PCI Security Council refers to this framework as a prioritized approach, designed to mitigate the risks associated with storing, processing, and/or transmitting cardholder data.

The aim of the document is to lower the risks to cardholder data by providing details and recommendations for handling cardholder data. The framework provides general guidelines for organizations to follow to achieve PCI compliance. The six goals, or milestones, within this framework are:

- **Remove sensitive authentication and limit data retention**—Keep sensitive data no longer than necessary. This is an important security concept and a best practice, because if a system or application is successfully attacked, the damage is mitigated by not having too much sensitive data. Ensure also that data is disposed in a safe and secure fashion.

- **Protect the perimeter, as well as internal and wireless networks**—Use firewalls, demilitarized zones (DMZs), and other perimeter security mechanisms to protect the network on the perimeter. Additionally, use logical and physical security measures to protect the network hardware including access points.

- **Secure payment card applications**—Use secure protocols and procedures for the processing of cardholder applications and for communications involved in the processing.

- **Monitor and control access to systems**—Monitor, track, and control who can and cannot access servers and systems where cardholder data is stored. Role-based access control, secure protocols, and auditing are all part of controlling access to systems.

- **Protect stored cardholder data**—Take care that cardholder data is stored somewhere and that its location is secure from both internal and external sources. Internal protection may include physical security measures, role-based access controls, and data encryption. External control includes access controls and perimeter security measures.

- **Finalize remaining compliance efforts and ensure all controls are in place**—Ensure that policies, procedures, and processes designed to protect cardholder data are in place. This includes educating end users on policies and procedures and ensuring they are followed.

> **NOTE**
>
> More information and details regarding these recommendations can be found at *https://www.pcisecuritystandards.org/security_standards/documents.php.*

What Does a PCI DSS Security Assessment Entail?

An auditor conducts a PCI DSS security assessment to determine whether a merchant complies with the current Data Security Standard. A **Qualified Security Assessor (QSA)** is someone trained, licensed, and authorized by the PCI Security Standards Council to conduct a PCI DSS security assessment.

Scope of Assessment

It's helpful for a merchant to know what is examined during a PCI DSS security assessment. Armed with this knowledge, the merchant will know what is taken into account for each audit. The PCI DSS is divided into six major principles with one, two, or three subsections below each major principle. In all, the assessment covers 6 principles and 12 subsections.

According to the PCI Security Standards Council, security requirements apply to all system components. A *system component* is defined as any computer, network, server, or application connected to cardholder data. Network systems that the PCI SSC assesses include:

- Firewalls
- Switches
- Routers
- Wireless access points
- Network appliances
- Other security applications

In addition to auditing network systems, servers are included in the assessment. Common server types that have access to cardholder data include:

> **NOTE**
>
> **Network Time Protocol (NTP)** is one of the original protocols created for the Internet and remains very valuable today. NTP allows systems across various networks to synchronize their internal clocks.

- Web server
- Database server
- Authentication server
- Mail server
- Proxy server
- Network Time Protocol (NTP) server
- Domain Name Server (DNS) server

These are common server types generally used in business and are typical in a PCI DSS security assessment. Regarding applications, the PCI Security Standards Council refers to all purchased and custom applications, which include internal and external Internet applications. When a third-party provider manages firewalls, routers, databases, or any other computer application, the third-party provider may conduct its own PCI DSS audit or a PCI DSS auditor may do the assessment.

In addition to examining computer systems, several other categories must be assessed to determine if correct security is in operation. These categories include:

- **Wireless**—If wireless technology is used to store, process, or transmit cardholder information, the wireless network will be tested for required security features. The PCI Security Standards Council has agreed that because wireless technology is unable to be well secured, an organization should weigh the benefits and risks before implementing this technology. The PCI SSC advises that an organization should consider whether the technology is fully needed. If so, wireless use should be limited to non-sensitive information.

- **Outsourcing**—Companies that send their information to third-party service providers for storage, processing, or transmission are **outsourcing**. A Report on Compliance must detail the role of each additional third-party service provider. A key point here is that merchants must contractually require that third-party service providers adhere to the PCI DSS if they deal with sensitive cardholder information.

- **Sampling**—Sampling is the process of an auditor selecting representative elements of all the computer components in a merchant's network and testing them for PCI DSS compliance. The sample must be representative of the whole and reflect accurately the computer systems currently in place.

Instructions and Content for Report on Compliance

QSAs of the PCI DSS in a merchant's organization are required to complete a Report on Compliance (ROC) for that specific merchant. An assessor must follow each payment card brand's reporting format. Furthermore, the assessor must contact each payment card company and determine reporting instructions and requirements. The ROC includes:

- Contact information for the merchant being assessed
- Date report is being formulated
- Description of merchant's organization
- Third-party service providers with shared cardholder information
- Processor relationships
- Whether the merchant is directly connected to a payment card company
- Point-of-sale systems that the merchant uses
- Subsequent entities that require PCI DSS compliance
- Wireless technologies that are linked or connected to the cardholder environment
- Version of the PCI DSS used for the assessment
- Time frame of the assessment
- Focus of the assessment
- Areas excluded from examination
- Description and drawing of network topology and control mechanisms
- Individuals interviewed
- Documentation reviewed
- Hardware and software in use
- Scan of all externally accessible Internet Protocol (IP) addresses
- Template to report the findings of each requirement and sub-requirement

To create a ROC, the QSAs must complete many fields of information and thoroughly examine the merchant's system. At the end of an audit, the merchant receives a Quality Feedback Form to help ensure the QSA retains a high degree of professionalism and quality. The merchant sends the feedback form to the PCI Security Standards Council, where it's reviewed by the Council's Technical Working Group. If a QSA is deemed lacking, the Council will recommend ways the QSA can improve the auditing process.

If the QSA's audit methods do not improve, the PCI Security Standards Council will revoke the license of the QSA and remove his or her name from the QSA database available on the Web site.

Detailed PCI DSS Requirements and Security Assessment Procedures

The assessment process is a rigorous one in which every aspect of a merchant's security system is scrutinized and tested. In a security assessment, a merchant needs to know what is required to be PCI DSS compliant and how these aspects are measured.

Security Assessment Marking Procedure

In an audit on PCI DSS compliance, a QSA goes over the six major headings and grades the organization as either "in place" or "not in place." The QSA determines whether the requirement is in place by following assessment procedures outlined by the PCI Security Standards Council. If a requirement is deemed to be "not in place," the auditor determines a target date by which the organization must rectify the requirement. The auditor can also write additional suggestions or comments.

Best Practices to Mitigate Risk for E-commerce Web Sites with PCI DSS Compliance

The PCI DSS requirements may make the task of becoming compliant seem intimidating. Many organizations may be overwhelmed by the extent of the requirements and not fully understand where to start or how to make sure they stay compliant. Many organizations go about PCI DSS compliance as a one-time event of becoming "compliant." To become and stay compliant, organizations should know basic helpful tips:

- **Apply security measures properly**—Create a clean-up rule, enforce limited access, and enable encryption.
- **Simplify**—Reduce excessive firewall rules to make them as simple as possible. Complex firewalls and rules create environments that are difficult to manage, leading to security flaws that can be exploited.
- **Use firewalls**—Firewalls are easy to implement and help screen a lot of inbound and outbound traffic from the cardholder data environment.
- **Document**—Documentation for any policy or system in the organization helps create a rulebook to follow; it also allows a system administrator to see unnecessary rules that can be deleted for more simplicity.
- **Keep going**—PCI DSS is not a checklist. It's an ongoing process that needs to be monitored daily with full commitment, even when an auditor is not in the building. Stay on top of the requirements and tackle problems before they arise.

The SSC has set up the standards and requirements to help merchants create high-security environments. The best place to start is at the first requirement.

Build and Maintain a Secure Network

The first principle of PCI DSS is to build and maintain a secure network. It includes two requirements. To tackle this PCI DSS security requirement and lessen the risk of security compromise, it's easiest to break down the requirements and deal with them one at a time.

Requirement 1: Install and Maintain a Firewall Configuration to Protect Cardholder Data

A *firewall* is a hardware device or software that controls computer traffic in and out of a network. It examines all traffic, allowing friendly traffic and blocking intrusive traffic. A firewall also tracks, monitors, and controls traffic within sensitive areas of an organization's internal network. A firewall can also block users who don't have the correct security permissions. The PCI Security Standards Council deems firewalls an integral part of any computer security system because firewalls deny unknown interactions from entering the cardholder data environment.

The first requirement calls for a merchant to install and maintain a firewall to protect cardholder data. The following list highlights some of the key security requirements identified by the PCI DSS standard and suggested audit procedures for each one:

- **Use a DMZ**—The DMZ is part of perimeter network security in which servers that must be accessible by sources both outside and inside your network are placed outside the firewall. However, the DMZ is not connected directly to either network, and it must always be accessed through the firewall. This means that external users never gain access to the internal network.

- **Maintain network blueprints**—Maintain a current network diagram, including all connections involving transmission of cardholder data. Include any wireless networks the organization uses. This helps track where security holes might be.

- **Block unused ports**—Verify that the firewall configuration includes a documented list of services and ports needed for business operations. Ports and services falling outside this list can be blocked.

- **Streamline protocol use**—A network can use any number of protocols, many enabled by default. Ensure that all protocols in use have a legitimate purpose and are documented.

- **Review firewall configurations**—Network security requirements change. Verifying firewall configuration requires periodic review of the firewall and router rules to ensure they still apply and protect the network.

- **Restrict cardholder database access**—Examine the firewall to verify that there are indeed restrictions between publicly accessible servers and components storing cardholder data.

- **Verify wireless security**—Verify that perimeter firewalls are installed between wireless networks and cardholder data.

- **Hide IP addresses**—Implement IP masks. Hide IP addresses so they will not be translated and revealed on the Internet.
- **Use host-based firewalls**—Ensure that firewalls are installed and correctly configured on mobile systems such as laptops. Employees should not be able to alter the firewall.

Requirement 2: Don't Use Vendor-Supplied Defaults for System Passwords and Other Security Parameters

The second requirement is that merchants not use vendor-supplied defaults for system passwords and other security parameters. Hackers often use vendor-supplied passwords and default settings to gain access and compromise security systems. Vendor-supplied passwords are well known within the hacker community and can be determined easily.

This requirement is fairly simple to comply with. Change passwords and parameters to increase the security level. This list highlights recommendations for passwords and other security parameters:

- **Change passwords**—Change default vendor-supplied passwords on all equipment including routers and access points.
- **Change default wireless configuration**—Change the passwords and default security configurations on all wireless access points (APs). This includes changing the **service set identifier (SSID)** of each AP. An SSID is a unique client identifier sent over a wireless network as a simple password used for authentication between a wireless client and an access point.
- **Develop security standards**—Create configuration standards for all system components. Identify well-known security vulnerabilities and address them in configuration standards.
- **Streamline protocols and services**—Disable all unnecessary unsecure services and protocols.
- **Disable unused elements**—Remove all unnecessary functionality, for example, scripts, drivers, features, subsystems, file systems, and unnecessary Web servers.
- **Use encryption**—Ensure that all passwords are encrypted when stored and in transit. Sending passwords over a network in cleartext makes them vulnerable.

Protect Cardholder Data

The second principle of PCI DSS is to protect cardholder data. The best way for a merchant to comply with this PCI DSS security requirement is, once again, to break it down into smaller requirements.

Requirement 3: Protect Stored Cardholder Data

The third requirement of PCI DSS is to protect stored cardholder data. This is easily done by ensuring all cardholder information is unreadable no matter where it's stored—

in portable media, in backup logs, or even on wireless networks. Another simple tip is to ensure that your organization is not storing any more information that is necessary from the magnetic strip. Ensure that full magnetic strip data is never stored anywhere. Never store the card verification code or PIN verification elements. Store as little information as possible.

Some tips for protecting stored cardholder data include:

> **NOTE**
>
> According to the PCI DSS, encryption is an essential component of securing cardholder data. Encryption is essential because if a hacker gains access to sensitive information without the proper cryptographic key, the data is useless. With encryption, data will be unreadable and unusable by anyone without authority to read it.

- **Store only necessary cardholder data**—It's important to store only relevant and legally required cardholder data and destroy the rest. This approach limits the impact should cardholder data be compromised.

- **Develop a cardholder data retention policy**—All organizations with cardholder data should have a retention policy that states how long data is kept and how it will be stored.

- **Develop disposal policies**—Disposal policies highlight how data will be disposed of after it's no longer required. All data should be disposed of so that it cannot be recovered and stolen by a malicious user.

- **Don't store card validation codes**—Code validation numbers are used to verify non-present transactions such as those conducted over the Internet. These are typically three- to four-digit numbers on the back of credit cards. These numbers should not be stored but simply used as a means of authentication.

- **Don't store PINs**—If **personal identification numbers (PINs)** are obtained, they should not be stored or used in any way other than for authentication.

- **Use encryption**—All cardholder data should be encrypted both in transit and while stored.

- **Restrict access to cardholder data**—Some form of access control, such as role-based access control, should be used to restrict access to cardholder data.

Requirement 4: Encrypt Transmission of Cardholder Data Across Open, Public Networks

The fourth requirement under this principle is to encrypt the transmission of cardholder data across open, public networks. For this requirement, a strong, secure encryption strategy is needed. Ensure your organization's decryption software is stored separately. If a hacker does gain access to your data and then encrypts it with a strong encryption key, the data is then rendered useless.

> **NOTE**
>
> Confidential information that is part of the cardholder data environment must be encrypted when being transmitted across any public network. It must be encrypted because public networks are extremely easy for a hacker to access. A hacker can intercept, modify, and divert the transmission of data in progress.

To secure data in transmission, consider the following:

- **Use encryption protocols**—Use strong cryptography and security protocols to protect data when being transmitted over open, public networks. This includes using Hypertext Transfer Protocol Secure (HTTPS) to secure online transactions.

- **Secure wireless communications**—If transactions occur over a wireless link, use secure protocols to secure the transaction. For wireless, these may include **Wi-Fi Protected Access (WPA)** and WPA2. Don't use the Wired Equivalent Privacy (WEP) protocol to secure wireless connections—it's not considered secure.

- **Monitor communications and protocols**—Periodically verify that the most current and up-to-date protocols are being used to secure the communication. Also, ensure that the security protocols are configured correctly. For instance, use a minimum 104-bit encryption key and 24-bit initialization value.

Maintain a Vulnerability Management Program

The third principle under PCI DSS is to maintain a vulnerability management program, and it includes two requirements. Following the strategy used with the last two principles, start by breaking it down into its specific requirements.

Requirement 5: Use and Regularly Update Antivirus Software or Programs

The fifth requirement is to use and regularly update antivirus software. This requirement is quite clear. Whether the user is a typical consumer user, business user, or merchant, up-to-date antivirus software protects a system from malicious attacks, viruses, adware, and spyware.

Three main points to keep in mind about this requirement are:

1. Deploy antivirus software on all systems commonly affected by viruses. Include personal computers and servers.

2. Ensure that antivirus programs are capable of protecting against and, if necessary, detecting and removing other forms of malicious attacks, including spyware and adware.

3. Ensure that all antivirus mechanisms are current, actively running, and capable of generating audit logs.

FYI

Although e-mail offers many advantages in the workplace, the drawbacks include many vulnerabilities and malicious viruses that enter the network via employees' e-mail. Antivirus software must be used on all systems commonly affected by viruses to protect systems from malicious software. To be effective, anti-malware must be monitored and updated frequently to be sure it's able to respond to the latest threats.

Requirement 6: Develop and Maintain Secure Systems and Applications

The sixth requirement under PCI DSS is to develop and maintain secure systems and applications. Hackers often gain access to networks through security vulnerabilities. Often security vulnerabilities in programs and software are addressed by the vendor, and they provide security patches to correct these inconsistencies. Continuous updates and regular maintenance of systems and applications can stop hackers in their tracks. By applying the latest patches and updates immediately, an organization maintains the security of its system by fixing flaws within software programs. This prevents employees, hackers, and viruses from exploiting program and software flaws. Appropriate patches must be tested and evaluated to determine if they sufficiently fix security vulnerabilities.

> ⚠ **WARNING**
>
> Remember, attacks can come from other sources besides hackers. Employees and viruses can be the cause of internal malicious activity within your network. You should consider insufficient training, human error, and intentional circumvention of controls as possibly introducing vulnerabilities.

A few tips on maintaining application security include:

- **Keep patches up to date**—Ensure all system components have the most recently released vendor-supplied patches installed. Patches should be installed soon after the release date. In a business environment it is important to first test all patches and service packs in a test system before applying to a production system.

- **Develop patching and update policies**—Many organizations choose to develop firm update policies that administrators follow. Systems and applications that are patched and updated are far less likely to be vulnerable.

- **Monitor vigilantly**—Administrators must spend time reviewing and monitoring for the latest threats and vulnerabilities. The monitoring of logs and system errors is often audited in a corporate environment. IT managers who fail to perform and document this kind of monitoring may find themselves subject to discipline by their employers, and may even lose their jobs.

- **Configure automatic updates**—Many systems and applications can be configured to be updated automatically. This takes the human error out of the equation and helps ensure that applications are current.

- **Ensure development follows guidelines**—Develop all Web applications based upon secure coding guidelines. Review custom application code to reveal security threats. Cover prevention of common coding vulnerabilities.

Implement Strong Access Control Measures

The fourth principle of PCI DSS requires organizations to implement strong access control measures. The requirements include enforcing the principle of need to know and enforcing technological and physical access controls.

Requirement 7: Restrict Access to Cardholder Data by Business Need to Know

▶ **NOTE**

Requirement 7 ensures that sensitive cardholder data is restricted based upon a need-to-know basis. This means critical information can be accessed only by authorized personnel, creating another layer of security.

The seventh requirement of PCI DSS is to restrict cardholder data by the business' need to know. This is a requirement companies commonly overlook. Information often flows freely without much care taken to control who knows what within an organization. Many organizations allow employees who have no need to know to access sensitive cardholder data. This becomes a security vulnerability that PCI SSC takes very seriously.

The best way to adhere to this requirement is to initially limit cardholder data to employees whose job functions strictly require this information. All others are restricted. Create a "deny all" feature within the system. This allows the system to keep everyone without authorization from viewing cardholder data.

Some suggestions include:

- **Enforce role-based access control**—Limit access to cardholder information to those individuals whose job requires such access.
- **Create a "deny all" policy**—Create a method for systems with many users to restrict access based upon users' need to know. The method must be set to "deny all" unless specifically allowed.
- **Develop access policies**—Develop and publish guidelines outlining who can and cannot access specific information. Ensure these policies are reinforced with consequences if a breach occurs.

Requirement 8: Assign a Unique ID to Each Person with Computer Access

The eighth requirement instructs organizations to assign a unique ID to each person with computer access. This requirement seems trivial at first glance. Taking a further look, it's extremely important. If a security breach occurs, user activity must be tracked back to the authorized employee. To comply with this requirement, use passwords, tokens, or biometrics to maintain security. In addition, encrypt all passwords during transmission and storage on *all* system components.

Tips for this requirement include:

- **Develop a two-factor authentication scheme**—A two-factor authentication scheme typically involves combining multiple authentication methods. This may be an ATM card and something only the user knows, such as the card's PIN number. Create a two-factor authentication for remote access to the network for employees, administrators, and third parties. Authentication methods include passwords, biometrics, and access tokens.
- **Require individual access**—Some environments use group access to applications and systems, for example, administrators' groups or guest groups. It's more secure to identify all users with a unique username before allowing individuals access to system components or the cardholder data environment. To increase security, verify that a user has a unique username to access system components and cardholder data.

- **Encrypt passwords**—Encrypt passwords during transmission and storage on all system components.

- **Develop strong password policies**—Password policies may include such items as how often a password must be changed, what characters passwords must include, how long they must be, and how an account is to be locked out after a given number of failed logon attempts.

- **Disable unused accounts**—Accounts for terminated employees should be deactivated immediately and inactive accounts should be disabled after a set period of time.

- **Restrict access**—Ensure that all access to the cardholder data environment is authenticated, including applications, administrators, and other users.

Requirement 9: Restrict Physical Access to the Cardholder Data Environment

The ninth requirement of the PCI DSS states that an organization must restrict physical access to cardholder data. This is a commonly overlooked requirement of PCI DSS. The failure to restrict employees' proximity to cardholder data is a violation of PCI DSS. Organizations must enforce rules on physical access and proximity to the actual credit card data. The organization must also develop a procedure to identify employees and visitors.

> **NOTE**
>
> Any physical access to the cardholder data environment will compromise its security. If an individual gains access to the room that houses cardholder data, that individual can remove hard copies or devices. This presents a need for security measures to limit access to the cardholder data area.

Securing physical access is a significant consideration. Some physical security recommendations include:

- **Restrict physical access to sensitive areas**—Use facility access controls to monitor and limit physical access to systems that store, process, or transmit cardholder data. This may include verifying access control with badge readers, lock and key, or other devices.

- **Monitor the server room**—Use cameras to monitor data sensitive areas. Store camera recordings for at least three months, unless restricted by law.

- **Restrict access to networking hardware**—Restrict physical access to wireless access points, gateways, hard drives, and handheld devices.

- **Secure backups**—Secure access to backups that may control sensitive data. Many organizations use off-site backup measures as a precaution. Ensure offsite backups are secured during transit.

- **Create visitor policies**—Develop procedures to help personnel easily distinguish between employees and visitors. This is essential in areas where cardholder data is accessible. All visitors must be authorized before entering areas where cardholder data is processed or maintained. All visitors must be given a physical token that indicates they are not employees, and this physical token must expire.

- **Maintain a cardholder paper trail**—Physically secure all paper and electronic media that contain cardholder data. When no longer required, the paper should be disposed of in a secure fashion. This may include using a paper disposal company.

- **Maintain inventories and tracking mechanisms**—Maintain strict control over the storage and accessibility of media that contains cardholder data. Ensure it is known where all sensitive data is stored and how it moves throughout the network, from gathering to storage, backups, and disposal.

- **Dispose of electronic devices appropriately**—Destroy electronic media by purging, demagnetizing, or shredding to eliminate the possibility that the media could be reconstructed. This includes the destruction of hard disks and not just formatting the disk.

Regularly Monitor and Test Networks

The fifth principle of PCI DSS is to regularly monitor and test networks. The two requirements in this principle address network resources, cardholder data, security systems, and security processes.

> ▶ **NOTE**
>
> A log's presence in all environments allows tracking and analysis when something does go wrong. If a problem arises and a log is not available, it makes the problem difficult to track and analyze.

Requirement 10: Track and Monitor All Access to Network Resources and Cardholder Data

The tenth requirement of PCI DSS is to track and monitor access to network resources and cardholder data. Logging allows an organization to track all user activity within a system. This helps determine where a problem occurred. The main requirements are to establish a process for linking access to system components to each individual user. Implement automated audit trails for all system components. Secure audit trails so that they cannot be altered, and limit the viewing of audit trails to those with a need to perform a job function.

Some logging best practices include:

- **Develop logging policies**—Logging policies identify what should be logged, how long logs are retained, who has access to logs, and more.

- **Log access to cardholder data**—To track security breaches, it's important to log all individual access to cardholder data. All accounts viewing cardholder data can then be traced.

- **Log failed logon attempts**—To help identify if someone is trying to access cardholder data, log all invalid access attempts.

- **Restrict log access**—Clearly identify who has access to logs and what can be done with that access.

- **Develop retention procedures**—Determine how long logs should be kept and in what form.

Requirement 11: Regularly Test Security Systems and Processes

The eleventh requirement of PCI DSS is to regularly test security systems and processes. Without continual testing of the security systems, hackers can capitalize on systemwide vulnerabilities within processes and custom software. One key feature of this requirement is to conduct quarterly and annual testing of internal and external networks to identify any changes or any new wireless devices, and check for system upgrades.

Regularly testing the security system may include performing penetration testing at least once a year or after any major system infrastructure or application upgrade or modification, and running internal and external network vulnerability scans.

> **NOTE**
>
> Vulnerabilities are discovered every day by hackers and researchers alike. The vulnerabilities are introduced by new software. Therefore, all systems, processes, and custom software must be tested frequently. This ensures that security is maintained over time, even with any changes that occur within the software.

Maintain an Information Security Policy

The sixth section of the PCI DSS is to maintain an information security policy. This is important because it gives all employees, contractors, and visitors a written management-approved policy. It allows employees to have a guideline for what is the right and wrong use of information. This is considered one of the most basic tools to combat a security breach within an organization.

Requirement 12: Maintain a Policy That Addresses Information Security for Employees and Contractors

This requirement is to maintain a secure, strong policy that allows all employees to understand the security tone that the organization wants to set. It allows employees to know what is expected of them with regard to information security. All employees need to be aware of data sensitivity. It's important for employees to know that data security is everyone's responsibility. Security policy recommendations include:

- **Create and deploy policies**—Establish, publish, maintain, and disseminate a security policy.

- **Update policies**—Develop an annual process to identify new threats and vulnerabilities and include the results in a formal risk assessment. Incorporate this into the security policy.

- **Create usage policies**—Develop usage policies for employee-used technologies. Ensuring that employees are aware of the policy and consequences for not following it.

- **Develop an employee education program**—Implement a formal security awareness program to make all employees aware of the importance of cardholder data security. Educate new employees and current employees not once but as new security developments occur.

CHAPTER SUMMARY

Credit cards are a major part of today's lifestyle. E-commerce activity is a substantial source of revenue for many organizations. The Internet means any organization can become globally accessible. Credit cards enable consumers to purchase from the global market the Internet provides, and this global access brings the need for increased security. Major payment brands formed the Payment Card Industry Security Standards Council to combat lack of security, as well as hackers and misuse of cardholder information. The council has created a list of standards called the Payment Card Industry Data Security Standard (PCI DSS) to help organizations achieve security. This list of requirements contains information to deter hackers from compromising any cardholder data. With PCI DSS compliance, consumers, banks, and merchants can feel secure that their information, clients, and customers will be safe when making purchases.

KEY CONCEPTS AND TERMS

Batch processing

Network Time Protocol (NTP)

Outsourcing

Payment Card Industry Data
   Security Standard (PCI DSS)

Personal identification number
   (PIN)

Real-time processing

Service set identifier (SSID)

Qualified Security Assessor
   (QSA)

Wi-Fi Protected Access (WPA)

CHAPTER 9 ASSESSMENT

1. Because it's a perimeter defense strategy, a firewall is not a critical element of cardholder data security.

   A. True
   B. False

2. You are tasked with designing a security policy for cardholder data. Which of the following are recommended security strategies for cardholder data? (Select three.)

   A. Verify that data is retained for a limited period of time.
   B. Verify that user groups are used to access sensitive data areas.
   C. Verify that data is disposed of properly.
   D. Verify that passwords are encrypted during transmission.

3. Use WEP to secure communications sent over a wired network.

   A. True
   B. False

4. Which of the following elements are typically examined during a PCI DSS Security Assessment? (Select two.)

   A. Firewalls
   B. Network hardware
   C. Employee background
   D. Cached files

5. When credit card transactions are handled in _____, receipts are often collected over a day or week and then sent in as multiple sets of information.

6. PSS DSS is a set of standards designed to help organizations that process credit card payments prevent fraud by having increased control over data and its exposure.

   A. True
   B. False

7. When credit card transactions are handled in _____, a consumer's credit card is charged immediately to complete a purchase.

8. You are attempting to synchronize your Web server to online timekeeping. Which of the following protocols is responsible for managing system time?

   A. TTP
   B. TNP
   C. NTP
   D. CTP

9. Which of the following firewall considerations are recommended by the PCI Security Standards Council? (Select three.)

   A. Use open source firewall systems.
   B. Block unused ports.
   C. Use host-based firewall systems on mobile computers.
   D. Conduct periodic reviews of firewall and router set rules.

10. Merchants should develop a two-factor authentication scheme to protect access to cardholder data.

   A. True
   B. False

Testing and Quality Assurance for Production Web Sites

© Rodolfo Clix/Dreamstime.com

HIGH-QUALITY, SECURE, AND FUNCTIONAL applications and Web sites don't happen by accident. Rather, they are the result of many tests and retests. The end products are the applications and Web sites people use every day. To help ensure a successful deployment, an application must follow the software development life cycle, a framework that identifies stages from concept to deployment.

This chapter explores how applications are developed and thoroughly tested for vulnerabilities. The chapter also explores applications in production environments and they how are monitored and improved throughout their life cycle.

Chapter 10 Topics

This chapter covers the following topics and concepts:

- What production and development software environments are
- What policies, standards, procedures, and guidelines are
- How to build a test plan and functionality checklist for Web site deployments
- What testing strategies for new applications and features are
- How to detect security gaps and holes in Web site applications
- How to plug the gaps and holes that tests detect
- How Web sites are deployed in a production environment
- How Web site traffic, use, and access are monitored and analyzed
- What best practices for testing and assuring quality of production Web sites are

Chapter 10 Goals

When you complete this chapter, you will be able to:

- Understand the function of the software development life cycle (SDLC)
- Review the differences between development and production environments
- Identify types of documentation used to help secure Web sites and applications
- Understand the importance of pre-deployment checklists
- Identify security holes using testing features
- Manage Web applications in a production environment
- Use Web site monitoring tools
- Understand best practices for Web application release

Development and Production Software Environments

In the programming world, there are development and production environments. Both are important and both are part of the software development cycle. The purpose of the **development environment** is to develop, write, and upgrade software systems' applications. It's an area for programmers, coding, ideas, and application testing. It's where applications are conceived and created, separate from the real business environment. The use of development and test environments is not optional in the business and corporate world. During annual audits, network administrators must document that they have thoroughly tested updates and new developments outside the production environment. Failure to use test environments may result in failing to pass an audit.

A **production environment** refers to a real-world environment in which software runs the business. When an application reaches a production environment, it should be ready for public release. The application must be thoroughly tested and retested before it reaches the production environment. Bugs, however, are found in released applications, so support should be in place to resolve bugs. To address bugs and security holes found in applications within the production environment, organizations create and distribute patches and service packs.

Software development comprises several phases, or a life cycle. This cycle represents the stages software applications pass through from concept to development to a production environment.

What Can Go Wrong, Eventually Will

Recently a company faced a potential lawsuit after salary information was leaked on the company's intranet site. The intranet site had both a development and a production environment. However, a small change was requested on the intranet site and the programmer decided to make a live change to the production site instead of first testing the change on the development site. The change modifed an employee form and, in the process, salary information intended only for the eyes of the human resources (HR) department was exposed to everyone in the company. The fallout was swift and ugly.

Incidents such as this highlight the importance of policy, separate development environments, and rigorous testing before changes in code are posted to a production environment. One of the important security strategies a development environment offers is comprehensive configuration audits. Such audits are not performed by the programmer alone, but also by a selection of key users. Had the programmer taken the time to have someone in the HR department verify the changes, the problem would have been caught.

The moral: Working in production environments is fraught with risk. Without best practices in place, it is only matter of time before something goes wrong.

Software Development Life Cycle (SDLC)

Every application must pass through several phases on its way to release. This is to ensure quality in performance and security. Before any application is tested in a production environment, it progresses through the software development life cycle (SDLC). The SDLC uses different stages that describe the stability of a piece of software and the amount of development it requires before final release.

A life cycle provides the framework that guides a software development project in terms of prototypes, designs, implementations, tests, and release dates. The exact steps for the SDLC vary by development environment, but the following list provides the types of steps used in the SDLC:

- **Pre-alpha**—In the pre-alpha phase, the application is in its introductory state. Developers are unsure about which features to include in the application, and developers' roles may not be firmly established. The pre-alpha phase is the concept phase in which software functions and features are conceived, added, and rejected.

- **Alpha**—In the alpha stage of the SDLC, an application is coded and various features are added. The software is tested and initial bugs are found and repaired. Software testing occurs in the alpha stage to help isolate bugs. The alpha stage may also see a **feature freeze**, which means development continues but no additional features are added to the product.

- **Beta**—In the beta phase, the software is ready for limited release to conduct usability testing and test the application in a production environment. This is known as a beta release. Users are known as beta testers. Beta testing may reveal additional programming bugs, and developers fix them as needed.

- **Release candidate (RC)**—A successful beta release leads to an RC, which is a potential final version. The RC version of software has gone through several stages, and most of the bugs and usability shortcomings have been resolved. Often, an application goes through more than one RC version, such as RC1, RC2, and so on. If no major flaws or bugs are found, the last RC version is upgraded to the final release version, and the software can be deployed.

Policies, Standards, Procedures, and Guidelines

There are many elements to application development and network management. One of the more important tasks for administrators is documentation. Well-functioning and secure networks and well-developed applications have many policies, procedures, and documented configurations. Policies, procedures, and configurations are unique to every network and application environment, so every organization should have clear documentation for its network and security infrastructure. Similarly, applications need useful and thorough documentation for administrators and users. Creating the manuals can be tedious but it's a necessary task for developers.

Change management refers to a standardized approach to handling changes to the IT infrastructure and programming environment. Application development is a dynamic process, with changes occurring frequently to add new features and fix bugs. Key to change management is the documentation involved to ensure that standardized methods, processes, and procedures are used for all changes. Proper documentation facilitates efficient and prompt handling of changes, and maintains the proper balance between the need for change and the potential detrimental impact of changes. This is equally true for managing networks and for developing applications.

Network documentation comes in various forms, including policies, standards, procedures, and guidelines. Each of those documentation forms is discussed in detail below.

Policies

By definition, **policies** are an organization's documented rules about what is to be done or not done, and why. Policies set requirements at the highest level in an organization and are enforceable. Lower-level documentation may detail who can and cannot access particular coding systems, create consistent application outcomes, and access network resources. It may also detail how to respond to security vulnerabilities.

Although networks have different policies depending on their needs, some common policies include the following:

- **Application development policy**—Used to regulate software development and code management.
- **Cell phone policy**—Many employees have data plans and love to text and check social media at work. Cell phone usage policies are becoming increasingly common and often very restrictive.
- **Network usage policy**—This policy sets acceptable usage for network resources, such as PCs, printers, scanners, and remote connections. It outlines what can be done with network resources and what consequences for rule violations should be.
- **Internet usage policy**—This policy specifies how the Internet can be used on the job. Typically, usage should focus primarily on business-related tasks. The policy might state that incidental personal use is allowed during specified times.
- **E-mail usage policy**—This policy emphasizes that e-mail communication is subject to the same code of conduct as is followed in other forms of written or face-to-face communication. All e-mails are property of the company and the company can access them.
- **User account policy**—This policy typically states that each user is responsible for keeping password and account information secret. All staffers are required to log off their systems when they are finished using them. The policy may state what constitutes a violation, such as attempting to log on to the network with another user's account information.
- **Wireless security policy**—This policy dictates what can be done with a wireless connection and the protocols that will be used to secure both the access point and the wireless communication.
- **Standards security policy**—This policy identifies configuration and maintenance requirements of systems on the network, such as using strong passwords and applying patches in a timely manner.

FYI

This list is a snapshot of the policies that guide behavior for administrators and network users. Network policies should be clearly documented and available to network users and application developers. Often, these policies are reviewed with new staff members or new administrators. Policies are reviewed and updated regularly to ensure that they are current and consistently represent the rules and desired outcomes of the application development environment. As they are updated, policies are re-released to network users.

FYI

It isn't good enough just to have a policy—a policy must be reviewed and updated. Technology changes quickly, and policies must adapt to keep pace. As an example, a large manufacturing company with several hundred employees and a 24-hour operation noticed a significant decrease in overall workplace housekeeping. That is, basic work was being done, but cleanup and general cleanliness were falling behind. When a review was conducted, it was discovered that during the night shift, many employees were completing their tasks and then watching movies or playing games on their smartphones. The productivity hit was significant, but there was no policy against this practice.

In addition to application policies, a network may have security policies covering everything from e-mail to logical and physical measures. These policies help ensure the security of the application development network. Often, security policies are developed by first creating a risk analysis. A risk analysis should identify the risks to your network, network resources, and data. The foundation of a successful security policy rests upon a risk analysis. Table 10-1 shows an example of a company risk assessment.

> **NOTE**
>
> The terms *regulation* and *policy* are often used interchangeably; however, there is a difference. Policies are written by an organization for its employees. **Regulations** are actual legal restrictions with legal consequences. These regulations are created by government agencies, not by private organizations.

Table 10-1 shows how a risk assessment is created and the risks incorporated into a complete security policy. The risk assessment is a key component of the security policy and identifies who is responsible for what, and which security controls are applied to protect the network.

Similarly, the policy governing application development should require consideration of security. Securing code begins with involving security subject matter experts in the earliest discussions.

Standards

In general, a **standard** provides a means of ensuring quality. Standards in computer programming ensure a level of quality and a level of performance. Standards are often implied but many standards are also well documented and reviewed by all. Programming standards provide a foundation and a common ground when writing code and developing applications.

Developers learn how they must write their code from programming coding standards and related documents. Standards prevent programmers from writing code to their own preferences, styles, and substance. Standards ensure that applications are developed in a consistent style and allow programmers to flow between projects with relative ease.

TABLE 10-1 An example of a network risk assessment.

NETWORK DEVICE	DESCRIPTION	POTENTIAL RISK	USER ACCESS
Network switches	Centralized network devices can disrupt network functions if successfully attacked.	Medium	Physical access to switches is restricted to administrators. Administration control of switches is guarded using role-based access control.
Network routers and wireless access points	Routers are used to route network traffic. By using a compromised router, an attacker may be able to route network traffic to perform a man-in-the-middle attack.	High	Access is controlled and restricted to administrators and is guarded using role-based access controls.
Firewall	A firewall protects one network from another, typically a private network from a public network.	High	Access to firewall servers and configurations is tightly controlled and limited to a few.
E-mail servers	E-mail servers maintain corporate e-mail. A compromised e-mail server may reveal internal company information.	High	Administration of company servers is tightly controlled and restricted to qualified and trusted e-mail administrators.
SQL database	The SQL database holds sensitive information. A compromised database can result in intellectual property and/or revenue loss.	Extreme	Database access is tightly controlled using physical and logical access controls.

Programming standards are applied within an organization and follow industry programming standards. Good programming standards should do the following:

- Improve the compatibility of the code
- Create easier collaboration of projects
- Provide more manageable troubleshooting practices
- Provide a uniform approach to solving problems
- Make it easier to maintain source code
- Help to maintain secure coding

Procedures

A **procedure** differs from a policy in that it identifies the way in which tasks are performed. For example, ensuring that programming is backed up is a primary concern. Therefore, each administrator has backup procedures identifying the time of day backups are done, how often they are done, and where they are stored. The policy will dictate who performs the backups and who can access them. The procedure tells how the policy will be followed. An organization's internal application developers must follow a procedure when connecting a new application to a sensitive database. Procedures apply to networks and application development both for practical reasons and for security reasons. Perhaps the most important benefit of having documented procedures is consistency and standardization. You want little or no difference between how different individuals accomplish tasks. Procedures build confidence that systems will operate as planned and expected.

The number and type of procedures that administrators and developers must be aware of depend on the organization. The overall goal is to ensure uniformity and that tasks follow a framework. The overall goal of application development also is to ensure uniformity as well as consistency in the way security is considered. Without a procedural framework, different administrators and developers may approach tasks differently; this leads to confusion.

Some documented network procedures include:

- **Programming procedures**—These may determine such things as the programming languages used, type of code used, and testing procedures.

- **Security procedures**—Some of the most critical procedures involve security. These identify what the administrator must do in the event of a security breach; security monitoring and researching, and applying security updates.

- **Network monitoring procedures**—A network needs to be constantly monitored. Network monitoring procedures include reviewing bandwidth, applications errors, network operating system updates, and more.

- **Software updating procedures**—All software must be monitored and updated periodically. Documented procedures dictate when, how often, who, and why these updates are done.

- **Procedures for reporting violations**—Every network likely will have procedures for reporting violations. These may include physical theft, social engineering, authentication violations, and more.

Guidelines

Policies and standards are enforceable documents. Employees found in violation of policies and standards may face disciplinary action. **Guidelines**, however, are different; they typically are suggestions or tips that are usually not enforced. Guidelines provide suggestions for better systems and methods to complete tasks. In this respect, issuing guidelines is similar to offering best practices. Although guidelines don't require mandatory compliance, they form an important part of network security documentation and management. For application development, numerous guidelines or best practices are available to emphasize the importance of secure coding practices.

Building a Test Plan and Functionality Checklist for Web Site Deployments

Before any Web site goes live and is deployed in a production environment, it's essential to test its functionality and usability. Various guidelines and procedures provide a framework to ensure that when a Web site is released, it has been tested and is ready for full-scale operation. Web sites have to be tested in both the development stage and limited production environment to ensure operability and prevent end-user frustration.

Among the many elements to consider when deploying a Web site are those pertaining to overall functionality, usability, and security. Each of these areas must be verified before a Web site can be successfully deployed and launched for widespread distribution. To help ensure Web sites meet a standard of functionality, many organizations develop checklists that are reviewed and followed before Web sites are released. Web site deployment checklists vary, there are considerations common to most deployment plans:

- **Verify links**—Take the time to ensure that all links work and connect to the correct locations. Look for broken and failed links. Many link-check utilities are available online to automate the process, including the link-check utility located at *http://validator.w3.org/checklink*. However, for internal or intranet pages, you may require separate software. Checking links is not a one-time endeavor; rather, it must be done periodically to verify that all links are still current.

- **Test browser compatibility**—Web sites may display differently depending on which browser is used. For example, browsers used with mobile devices display differently than a browser on a desktop system. The bottom line is: Just because a Web site looks great in one browser doesn't mean it will in another. Some scripts and functions work fine in one browser and might not work at all in other browsers or devices. Minor tweaking can resolve many cross-browser, cross-platform functionality issues. Part of the deployment checklist should involve verifying the Web site in all commonly used browsers.

- **Test all downloads**—If your site offers downloadable files such as courses, event calendars and so on, verify that the download feature works and users are able to access the downloads.

- **Verify digital certificates and Secure Sockets Layer (SSL) URLs work correctly**—If the Web site has secure communication requirements, ensure that SSL uniform resource locators (URLs) and Hypertext Transfer Protocol Secure (HTTPS) are configured and working correctly.

- **Test forms and form controls**—Are the forms of the Web site secure? Verify that forms use input validation strategies to prevent injection attacks.

- **Verify path traversal**—Is the directory structure secure? Verify that path traversal is not possible; attackers should not get outside intended directories.

How Do I Know Which Browser to Test?

When it comes to knowing which browsers to test, nothing should be left to chance. Some of the most popular browsers today include Mozilla Firefox, Apple Safari, Google Chrome, and Microsoft Internet Explorer or its eventual replacement. If a Web site is not compatible with those browsers at a minimum, it runs a high risk of losing many visitors and potential customers.

Web administrators can monitor Web sites to determine who is coming to their site and characteristics of the visitors. One of these characteristics is to monitor and track which browsers visitors are commonly using to access the site. You can use a variety of Web tools to track visitor behavior; one of the more common tools is Google Analytics. Google Analytics is a tool that helps Web administrators track a wide array of visitor information. Analytic software is the Web administrator's go-to source for all Web visitor information. For more information on Google Analytics, refer to *http://www.google.com/analytics/*.

- **Review navigational structure**—The navigational structure should be tested both for active links and for usability. Navigational usability is often tested using beta testers to ensure navigation flows logically.

- **Verify shopping features**—If your Web site includes a shopping cart or similar functionality, thoroughly test back-end operations to ensure that all transactions are secure, and everything runs smoothly.

- **Web page load times**—Web sites that are slow to load due to heavy graphics or other features frustrate visitors. Web site checks should test and improve Web page load times.

The previous examples highlight security, usability, and overall function of Web site features that may be included in a test plan and functionality checklist. In addition to these criteria, functionality testing can verify that information is organized, available, and relevant to the visitor. This is particularly important on the first page of the Web site to catch the reader's attention. This information may include:

- **The headline**—The headline is the sentence at the top of your page that your visitor often sees first. Scanners have no choice but to see the headline, and it might be all they see. The purpose of the headline is to attract visitors' attention and entice them to keep reading. This is an integral element because almost everyone will read your headline.

- **A value or proposition statement**—The value or proposition statement is a concise, clear sentence stating what the visitor can expect from your site. It lets visitors know they are on the right site.

- **Benefit statements**—Benefit statements are not to be confused with your value statement or features of your product. Benefit statements show how your product or service solves an immediate problem. These statements go right to core of the matter by answering "What's in it for me?" Benefit statements often address base motivators like saving time, making money, increasing business, improving looks, and so on.

- **A call to action**—Just as it sounds, the call to action is a command that tells your visitors what to do. Be clear. Tell your visitors exactly what you want them to do.

- **Images**—People are attracted to images. When buying a product they cannot touch, they want to know what it will look like. Images can be very effective in demonstrating a product and helping visitors become more connected to it, such as when they see people in a picture using it.

- **Navigation**—Navigation is considered part of the information you offer because it provides links to important pages such as contacts, privacy statements, and guarantees. All play an important part in the decision to buy from your site. Landing pages typically have a different menu and header navigation format than the rest of a site; this keeps visitors on the page, reading, rather than enabling them to click away to another part of the Web site.

When developing a pre-deployment test plan and functionality checklist for a Web site, it's important to cover all key areas of the Web site, including security, functionality, usability and readability. When all of these areas are tested in a production environment, the Web site is ready for widespread deployment.

Testing Strategies for All New Applications and Features

As mentioned previously, all software passes through the software development life cycle on its way to being deployed in a production environment. In each of these phases, testing plays an important role. Testing and authenticating software applications to ensure conformity to approved standards is a key component of an application's success.

Different methods and testing strategies are used to achieve common goals—removing all the bugs and errors from the code and making the software error-free and capable of providing a reliable application. The different types of software testing techniques and methodologies include:

- **Black box testing**—A **black box testing** methodology looks at the available inputs for an application and what the expected outputs are from each input. Black box testing assumes no knowledge of the inner code or application processing.

- **White box testing**—A white box test examines the code of an application. **White box testing** is the most intensive, costly, and detailed of testing methods.

- **Gray box testing**—A **gray box testing** methodology is the middle ground between black box and white box testing. It looks at the input and output of applications and requires a knowledge of the inner workings of the application.

- **Unit testing**—With **unit testing**, a programmer verifies that individual units of source code are fit for use. A unit is the smallest testable part of an application.

- **Integration testing**—With **integration testing**, individual software modules are combined and tested as a group. Integration testing typically occurs after unit testing.

- **System testing**—**System testing** typically combines all the components that have successfully passed integration testing and assesses the system as a whole. It tests combined components to test their interoperability.

- **Regression testing**—**Regression testing** checks for additional errors that may have been introduced in the process of upgrading or patching to fix other problems.

- **Usability testing**—**Usability testing** is designed to check the actual usability of the application. This may be done in a limited production environment to get a sampling of potential application users. The usability test helps ensure that the application is user friendly and provides an intuitive interface.

- **Performance testing**—**Performance testing** provides an accurate view of how applications perform in a large-scale deployment in a variety of production environments. It tests responsiveness under various workloads to ensure that the application works well under normal operational circumstances.

- **Software stress testing**—In **software stress testing**, an application is pushed to its limits to see where the breaking points are. Stress tests go well beyond normal, real-world scenarios to find the limits of the application.

- **Recovery testing**—**Recovery testing** gauges the recovery capabilities of an application in the event of failure. It tests whether the application can recover from a crash or hardware failure.

- **Security testing**—**Security testing** checks the security of an application. This includes testing for injection attacks, path traversal attacks, and whether the software is vulnerable in other ways. These vulnerabilities need to be addressed before the software is released.

- **Compatibility testing**—Interoperability is a significant concern, and application testing must ensure compatibility with other popular software. **Compatibility testing** is designed to verify how well an application functions with other software, such as the operating system or other Web applications.

- **Regulatory compliance testing**—Coding must follow regulatory standards, and **regulatory compliance testing** ensures that the application meets and adheres to appropriate standards.

As shown in the preceding list, application testing is an involved process requiring a multi-layered approach to testing and problem discovery. It's all of these tests and procedures that help ensure quality, functionality, usability, and security of modern applications.

Detecting Security Gaps and Holes in Web Site Applications

A key component of the software development life cycle is verifying that the application is secure. Tests of an application's security can happen in any phase of the SDLC; however, in the alpha and beta phases, there should be constant security testing. It's hoped that security holes will be caught when the application is released in limited form as an RC, and certainly before it's deployed in final form. As you know, however, many applications are released with significant security flaws that are not discovered until the product is in use and a vulnerability has been exploited. This represents a failure in keeping security in mind throughout the SDLC.

Key areas that must be considered as part of overall security vulnerability testing include the application's design, default security measures, mass deployment security, and information and response abilities.

- **Design security**—Many security flaws can be traced directly back to the basic architectural design of the application. If detected early, these design flaws can be addressed in an early stage of development. Alpha testing is often critical in detecting design security holes. Ideally, security vulnerabilities would be eliminated in the code with a stringent review.

- **Default security**—Out-of-the-box secure applications are important. Default application security measures should include applying the principle of least privilege. Features should be off by default. In other words, restrict features using an "enable feature" option rather than a "disable feature" approach. This helps ensure that users will enable only the parts of the application they actually care to use while minimizing vulnerabilities from features users don't need.

Mitigating Any Identified Gaps and Holes and Retesting

In an ideal world, an application would be secure when deployed in its default configuration. This is rare. Rather, security holes continue to be found and demand mitigation and retesting. Once a complete security assessment has been performed and security holes found, developers must correct all problems that have been found. These problems range from usability issues to security holes.

Managing security holes and bugs found in applications is not an ad hoc process; rather, it follows a framework designed to address each issue by priority. To mitigate security holes, the following steps can be taken:

1. **Outline vulnerabilities**—The first step is to identify all known vulnerabilities. This information can come from error logs, auditing, or from end users.

2. **Classify vulnerabilities and establish a priority**—Security holes range from mild to extreme. Each security hole must be evaluated to determine its threat potential. All vulnerabilities must be mitigated, but a best practice approach is to manage those with the greatest threat potential first. Often, the highest risks are threats that may lead to compromised data.

3. **Develop a mitigation plan**—Once you know the vulnerabilities and have prioritized them, it's time to determine how long it will take to fix the problems and develop a mitigation plan. The plan includes timelines, establishing who is responsible for what, and documentation procedures. You'll need to document details of what was done to address a vulnerability, who did it, and why. This helps as a reference should the information be needed again.

4. **Retest**—It's hoped that the mitigation plan worked and that the security vulnerabilities have been adequately addressed. To confirm, it's necessary once again to put the application through a series of security-related tests. Known as regression testing, these checks look for additional errors that may have been introduced in the process of upgrading or patching to fix other problems.

Deploying Web Site Applications in a Production Environment

Once all the tests have been completed, the next step is to deploy the application to a production environment. The deployment can be limited to a small group or can be a wide-scale, unrestricted deployment. In either case, the application development process is still not complete. Once an application has been deployed, continued monitoring is required to verify how well it operates and what areas, if any, need to be improved upon. Some of the tasks that are performed while an application is in a production environment include:

- **Error messages**—Error messages sent from the application to the developer help isolate what problem has occurred and why. If an application crashes, the error code can be sent to the developer for study. The developer may find the error stems from resource limitations, compatibility issues, security holes, and more. Once an error message reveals a problem, the developer can fix it with a patch or other means. However, error messages should not reveal to an attacker any internal working knowledge of the coding.

- **Response time**—If problems are found in an application, it will not take long for developers to hear about them. Many organizations employ mechanisms to track feedback about a product, looking for both the good and the bad. Once a problem has been flagged in the production environment, response time is critical. If it's a major security breach, a press release may warn of the danger, to be followed as soon as possible by a patch. It is essential to respond swiftly to incidents when an application is deployed to a production environment.

- **Continued development**—By the time an application has been released, it's likely that changes in the IT landscape have occurred. While an application is in the production environment, developers once again may return to the drawing board to discuss new features and enhancements. This process may include having development teams use feedback from users who may have concerns about security vulnerabilities, product features, or usability, or may simply have some words of praise.

Monitoring and Analyzing Web Site Traffic, Use, and Access

Tracking and monitoring Web site traffic are critical for identifying trends and key visitor demographic statistics. There are many ways to track visitor behavior on a Web site, including directly from the source, such as surveys, forums, usability studies, and focus groups. All provide methods to identify areas on the site that need to be tuned, updated, or secured. In addition to these methods, another good strategy for gathering information is tracking or analytic software.

Analytic software reveals statistics that are invaluable for identifying Web page trouble spots. Among the statistics on your Web page that can be identified using software such as Google Analytics are:

- **Browser statistics**—Analytic software can identify the browsers visitors use, such as Firefox, Chrome, Internet Explorer, Safari, and so on. In addition, you can see if visitors are coming to your site directly by typing in URLs, perhaps due to offline marketing efforts.

- **Bounce rate**—The percentage of single-page visits to a Web site, or those visitors that "bounce away" to another site. The bounce rate is a standard measure of quality and relevance to the visitor. The lower the bounce rate, the better the site.

- **Network performance**—Use these statistics to understand Internet connection issues including load times. It's possible to track how fast your page is loading on various Internet connections. If your page is loading too slowly, visitors will bounce almost immediately.

- **Visitor paths**—The tracking software tells you where people visit on your page. This can help you identify navigation issues and the places where people go before they bounce off the site. If visitors are commonly bouncing from the same page, that page may need tuning.

- **Shopping cart abandonment**—Tracking software enables administrators to see if visitors are abandoning the site at the shopping cart. This often indicates a confusing checkout procedure.

- **Visitor location**—Your tracking efforts can also determine where the bulk of your visitors come from. You can track by broad area, such as country—Canada, United States, the United Kingdom, and so on—or by state or city. This helps you tune your page for location.

Analytic software can be configured to explore other statistics than those mentioned above. Which statistics used will depend upon the Web administrator's needs.

Best Practices for Testing and Assuring Quality of Production Web Sites

Web sites and Web applications are complex and require constant monitoring to discover and manage vulnerabilities. Assuring quality of production Web sites is an ongoing process encompassing many facets. Listed below are several best practices to consider when assuring the quality of a Web site.

- **Protect data**—Data is the most critical element of a Web site and must be secured. Strong Web sites incorporate standards, policies, and protocols designed to protect data. All data should be handled securely, using strong encryption protocols while data is in transit and while stored.

- **Minimize data collection**—Securing sensitive data is one thing but not having it in the first place is even better. Whenever possible, restrict the amount of personal data collected. This reduces your security risk.

- **Use tracking software**—Tracking and analytic software allows developers to have a good idea of the demographic coming to the site and the technologies they use. Analytic software allows developers to customize the site for the demographic and to have a better idea of who is coming to a site and what visitors are doing there.

- **Conduct usability tests**—Use online surveys, polls, questionnaires and other measures to obtain feedback from your demographic on Web site usability. Find out what they like and don't like; incorporate changes as needed.

- **Ongoing security testing**—Use ongoing security tests to ensure that vulnerabilities are found and fixed.

- **Develop standards, policies, and procedures**—Standards, policies, and procedures are designed to increase uniformity and in turn keep the quality of Web applications and Web sites high.

- **Use regression testing**—After a security vulnerability or another issue or feature has been added, use regression testing to ensure the changes have not introduced new problems.

- **Use a testing cycle**—Testing cycles ensure that the Web site or application is continually being monitored for vulnerabilities or other shortcomings.

This list represents a fraction of the guidelines for assuring a quality Web site. It's intended to show that many methods are available for securing production Web sites and ensuring that their quality remains high.

CHAPTER SUMMARY

In today's computing world, security is taking an increasingly predominant role for Web sites and Web applications. Key to this security is testing and retesting applications, searching for vulnerabilities within the development of an application. Applications go through specific stages in development-pre-alpha, alpha, beta, and release candidates. Testing occurs at each of these levels, and mitigation strategies are employed to reduce vulnerabilities.

Policies, standards, procedures, and guidelines are all forms of documentation designed to help ensure quality control over Web site and Web application development. Standards, procedures, and policies may be formal documents with consequences if not followed. Guidelines are more often suggestions, not mandatory to follow.

When testing applications, many methods are available, including black box testing, white box testing, gray box testing, regression testing, and compatibility testing. Each of these types of tests has a role within the testing cycle and each can be used to help ensure the usability and security of modern applications.

KEY CONCEPTS AND TERMS

Black box testing	Performance testing	Security testing
Change management	Policies	Software stress testing
Compatibility testing	Procedure	Standard
Development environment	Production environment	System testing
Feature freeze	Recovery testing	Unit testing
Gray box testing	Regression testing	Usability testing
Guidelines	Regulations	White box testing
Integration testing	Regulatory compliance testing	

CHAPTER 10 ASSESSMENT

1. The bounce rate identifies the percentage of people who leave your site from the page they initially visited.

  A. True
  B. False

2. You recently developed an application. In which SDLC stages would the application likely be in just prior to being released to the production environment? (Select two.)

  A. RC1
  B. Alpha
  C. Pre-alpha
  D. Beta

3. Recovery testing analyzes how an application manages in the aftermath of failures and crashes.

  A. True
  B. False

4. As a software developer, you have recently coded a security patch to a Web application. Which of the following might you do after finishing the patch?

  A. Perform a regression test
  B. Perform a compatibility test
  C. Perform a suitability test
  D. Perform a gray box test

5. You have completed an application and now wonder if it will work with both the Microsoft Internet Explorer and Mozilla Firefox Web browsers. Which of the following tests might you perform?

  A. Unit test
  B. Universal acceptance test
  C. Compatibility test
  D. System test

6. _____ incorporates features of black and white box testing.

7. Regulations are not set by organizations but by applicable laws.

  A. True
  B. False

8. You are using a testing mechanism that looks at the input and output of an application to determine potential problems. Which mechanisms may be in use? (Select three.)

  A. Black box testing
  B. White box testing
  C. Gray box testing
  D. Brown box testing

9. Which of the following is often developed by first creating a risk analysis?

  A. Web rules
  B. Test software
  C. Security policies
  D. SDLCs

10. Standards are typically non-enforceable while suggestions are used to guarantee a level of quality and performance.

  A. True
  B. False

Performing a Web Site Vulnerability and Security Assessment

© Rodolfo Clix/Dreamstime.com

S ECURITY TESTING is an absolute requirement for Web servers and Web applications. When you are performing Web application security assessments, there are multiple components to consider to adequately identify and remedy risks. There are also many tools, both freeware and commercial, available to perform security and vulnerability testing. The most accurate method will involve using multiple programs and manual techniques. In addition to selecting and using the right tools, it's equally important to plan the security assessment properly.

Some of the techniques and utilities mentioned in this chapter may be interpreted by systems administrators or security monitoring systems as intrusive or hostile. The techniques and utilities may also require administrator or root-level access to the system to successfully run or give the most accurate results. Be sure to have appropriate authority or permission, as well as the necessary access to the system, prior to performing any type of vulnerability or security assessment on a system.

Chapter 11 Topics

This chapter covers the following topics and concepts:

- What the difference is between software testing and Web site vulnerability security assessments
- How to perform an initial discovery on a targeted Web site
- How to perform a vulnerability and security assessment
- How to use planned attacks to identify vulnerabilities
- How to spot vulnerabilities in back-end systems and Structured Query Language (SQL) databases
- How to prepare a vulnerability and security assessment report
- What best practices for Web site vulnerability and security assessments are

Chapter 11 Goals

When you complete this chapter, you will be able to:

- Determine the difference between software testing versus Web site vulnerability and security assessments
- Perform initial discovery activities on a Web site
- Perform a vulnerability and security assessment on various Web site components
- Perform a planned attack to determine vulnerabilities of user input forms and screens on front-end systems
- Perform a planned attack on back-end systems and SQL databases
- Prepare a vulnerability and security assessment report
- Understand some of the best practices to use when performing Web site vulnerability and security assessments

Software Testing Versus Web Site Vulnerability and Security Assessments

Differentiating between software testing and security assessments can be difficult. Generally, software testing is a much broader set of procedures than Web site security assessments. In many cases, software testing includes an assessment of Web site security as a subset of the overall testing process.

Software testing often includes, at minimum, checks to ensure an application of any type:

- Meets the initial design requirements provided by the party requesting the application; referred to as verification and validation
- Operates as expected and without any errors
- Can be implemented so that it does not cause issues with other applications it may integrate with; referred to as compatibility

Depending on the software development life cycle methodology used, there can often be additional steps or phases in the testing process.

This chapter focuses on assessing the security of a specific type of application, a Web site, and its various parts and pieces. Web sites typically consist of four elements:

- Web server software, such as Microsoft's Internet Information Services or Apache HTTP Server
- A hardware server and operating system that the Web server runs on
- A software application that uses the Web server to collect or distribute information
- A database that stores the information being used by the application and/or Web server

A common implementation of these Web site elements involves three *tiers* or layers of hardware and software. These layers consist of a presentation tier with the Web server and its hardware, an application or logic tier with the software application and its hardware server, and a database tier which includes the database software and its hardware server. Although these three tiers are often implemented on physically separate hardware servers for optimal security, they represent logical parts of the overall Web site platform. In situations where software capability doesn't support three separate servers, or where budget might not allow for multiple servers, the tiers can be installed together on shared servers.

Performing an Initial Discovery on the Targeted Web Site

The first step in a Web site assessment is to identify the components that make up the Web site and that will be tested. In security terms, this discovery activity is also referred to as **fingerprinting** and **enumeration**—identifying and listing various components of a Web site platform that need to be tested or attacked. A variety of tools and techniques determine the following types of elements:

- Internet Protocol (IP) addresses associated with the Web site platform
- Services and/or applications that are running on the servers in the Web site platform, for example, Hypertext Transfer Protocol (HTTP), Domain Name System (DNS), File Transfer Protocol (FTP), Telnet, and Simple Mail Transfer Protocol (SMTP)
- The operating systems on all hardware servers supporting the Web site platform
- Any known (published) vulnerabilities with the services, applications, or operating systems

Both commercial and freeware programs are available to perform discovery activities. Commercial tools are generally more efficient and feature-rich than freeware tools. However, this chapter focuses on freeware tools that are sufficient for performing a vulnerability and security assessment.

Ping Sweep

Ping is a utility that was written for the IP protocol in 1983. Ping was designed to send a packet to an IP address to determine if it's active. If so, the utility measures the round-trip time of the packet that was sent and received. Because a ping serves much the same purpose as the sonar ships use, it was named after the characteristic "ping" noise that is made when sonar identifies an object in water. The ping command is typically executed against a single IP address; a **ping sweep** is the act of running the utility across a range of IP addresses.

> **NOTE**
>
> An active IP address is an address that's in use. An inactive IP address may mean the system is turned off or the IP address simply isn't assigned to a system.

Ping sweeps, sometimes called *host discovery*, are often the first step in a security assessment or attack because they can save time and effort by narrowing the number of IP addresses to assess/attack. Many other security testing tools are more intricate and exhaustive in the tests they run on each targeted IP address or system. To avoid wasting time trying to test or exploit an inactive IP address, ping sweeps are a valuable technique. The ping command is simple—it sends a packet to an IP address and waits a short time for a response. Scanning even an entire class C subnet, involving up to 254 hosts, can usually be done in less than 10 seconds depending on network speed.

> **⚠ WARNING**
>
> Almost any intrusion detection system (IDS) will immediately detect a ping sweep and warn administrators, depending on its configuration. IDSs may take active measures to stop your scanning or prevent results from being relayed back to the scanner. Consider this if returned results are different than expected. Scanning should be done with approval by an organization's security administrators.

Because the ping command was designed to communicate with a single IP address, it's necessary to use utilities specifically designed to ping sweep multiple IP addresses. Many freeware ping sweep utilities exist for nearly all major operating systems; here are some examples:

- **Windows**—Pinkie, IP Address Tracker by SolarWinds, SuperScan by McAfee, and Zenmap, a Windows version of Nmap with a graphical interface

- **UNIX/Linux**—Hping and Nmap

The utilities tend to offer easy-to-use, intuitive interfaces, such as the SuperScan interface shown in Figure 11-1.

Ping sweep capabilities are now included with many vulnerability scan and security assessment tools. Performing ping sweeps from within these utilities eliminates the need to reenter active IP addresses into the vulnerability programs.

The exact output received from a ping sweep utility depends on the version of the utility used. However, at a minimum, the output will include the IP address and an indication as to whether the IP address is considered "live." Most of the above-mentioned utilities allow you to print the output, or you can save it and then use Microsoft Word or Microsoft Excel to remove all non-responsive IP addresses.

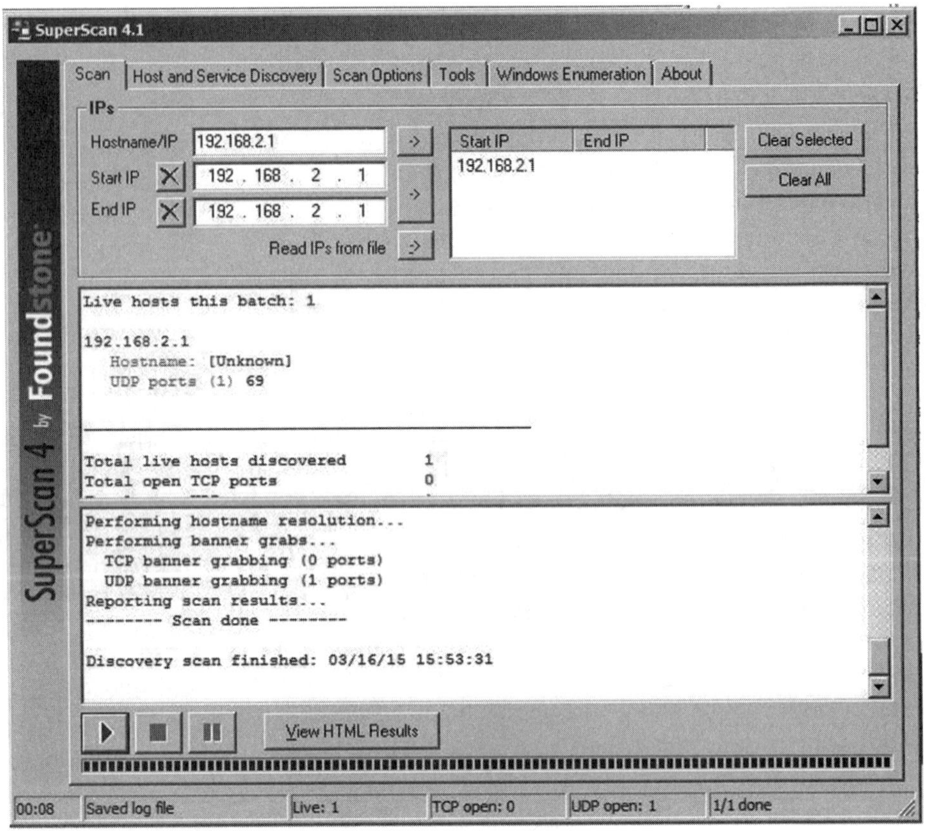

FIGURE 11-1

The SuperScan
ping sweep utility.

Nmap

Nmap, or Network Mapper, was developed in the late 1990s as a Linux port scanning tool to identify which IP ports, or services, were active on an IP address. Opinions are mixed as to whether the original intent of Nmap was to help systems administrators or hackers gain information about systems and networks. The result is that Nmap is one of the oldest and most widely used tools by security professionals and hackers alike. The tool identifies and assesses services and vulnerabilities on computer systems.

Nmap's core functionality consists of three features: ping sweeping, port scanning, and operating system (OS) detection. One of the most powerful and controversial features of Nmap, however, is its Nmap Scripting Engine. This scripting engine allows users to customize such things as how aggressively Nmap performs its scans and which IP port and services it probes. There are over 100 scripts included with the Nmap utility, and users familiar with the Lua programming language can create their own.

To use Nmap as a command-line utility, which is common for the UNIX and Linux versions, a user needs a strong fundamental knowledge of both Nmap's options as well as UNIX or Linux commands. For the more novice user, the Windows version of Nmap, known as Zenmap, has a graphical interface and is much easier to configure and execute. Although there are hundreds of scanning and probing options available in the utility, this section focuses on Nmap's abilities to discover and enumerate hosts. Additional Nmap capabilities will be discussed later in this chapter.

> **TIP**
>
> For the best results from Nmap, run the utility from a computer on the same network segment as the Web site server(s) being assessed. Nmap has a few options that either don't execute well or don't report properly if Nmap is run from the same machine it's trying to scan.

The "standard" Nmap scan performs non-intrusive activities—those unlikely to impact the server or appear to security systems as an attack, such as:

- Basic ping operations, such as whether the IP address is alive/up or down/non-responsive or total time for the ping packet to travel round-trip
- The Media Access Control (MAC) address of the network card using the IP address that was scanned
- Open/active or closed/inactive status of the 1,000 most commonly used Transmission Control Protocol (TCP) ports

Although Nmap was originally written for Linux, the Zenmap Windows version of Nmap is easy to use and has some advantages. For those who don't use Nmap frequently enough to memorize all the command-line options, Zenmap allows users to click on desired scanning options. However, it also has a field that displays the command line that corresponds to the options that have been selected, as shown in Figure 11-2. The command-line feature makes Zenmap useful for learning Nmap.

OS Fingerprint

Another important part of finding Web site vulnerabilities is identifying the operating system running on the hardware systems that support the Web server, application, and database components. This activity is known as *OS fingerprinting*. Operating systems are designed differently and have unique vulnerabilities. Identifying the underlying operating system of a Web site can help determine which tools will be needed to further assess the server, the skills required for manual assessment techniques, and even the types of attacks that should be anticipated. As with ping sweeps and basic discovery, numerous tools provide OS fingerprinting. Many of those tools perform other security assessment functions in addition to OS fingerprinting, such as ping sweeping, port scanning, and vulnerability testing. Two of the most popular OS fingerprinting tools are Nmap and Nessus.

FIGURE 11-2

The Zenmap interface.

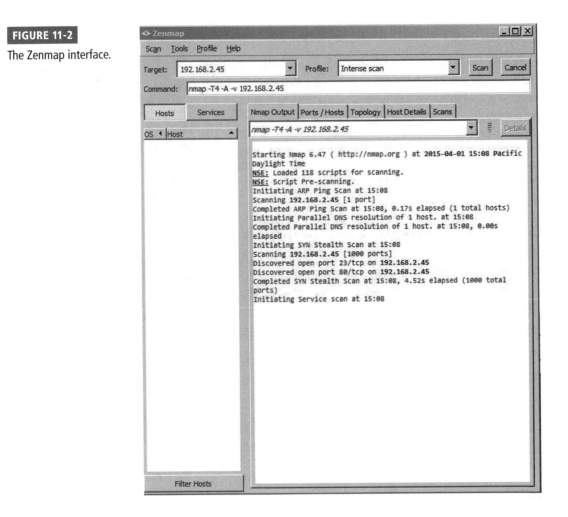

Nmap returns the OS fingerprint as part of a "regular scan" profile selected in Zenmap, or it can be specifically requested by executing the following command:

```
nmap -O ip address
```

The result will be a line in the output that resembles the following:

```
OS details: Linux 2.6.19 - 2.6.31
```

Nessus Vulnerability and Port Scan

Like Nmap, Nessus began as a free, open source application. Because it was created in the late 1990s, around the same time that network security was gaining in importance, it quickly became one of the most popular vulnerability scanning tools for security professionals. Although there are a few feature overlaps between Nessus and Nmap, they are largely considered complementary tools. Where Nmap's strengths lie in its ability to probe and identify systems and their services, Nessus is equally proficient at testing those systems and services for vulnerabilities. Nessus is now a commercial product for use in corporate environments, but it still is offered free to home users scanning personally owned systems.

Nessus is primarily comprised of two components: a scanning engine and thousands of plug-ins that associate vulnerabilities with items such as services, operating systems, applications, and so on. To scan a system, a user first creates a policy, which means choosing a set of options and plug-ins to use during the scan. After creating a policy, the user initiates the scan by entering information about the host system to be scanned and then choosing the policy against which to assess that host or hosts. Figure 11-3 shows the summary screen of a normal Nessus vulnerability scan.

> **NOTE**
>
> Some of the features that the commercial version of Nessus offers over the free home edition are customized scans for certain compliance acts like Payment Card Industry (PCI), "policy" testing such as password strength, and analysis of data for sensitive elements such as Social Security numbers.

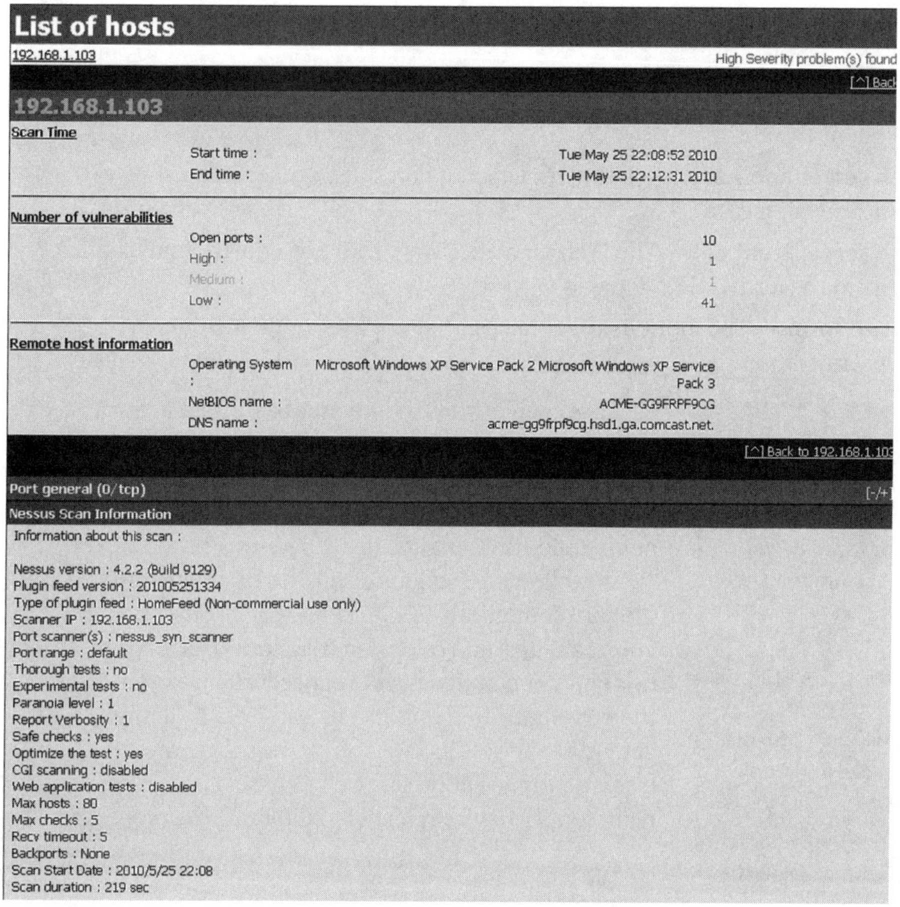

List of hosts

192.168.1.103   High Severity problem(s) found
                                                                        [^] Back

192.168.1.103

Scan Time

	Start time :	Tue May 25 22:08:52 2010
	End time :	Tue May 25 22:12:31 2010

Number of vulnerabilities

	Open ports :	10
	High :	1
	Medium :	1
	Low :	41

Remote host information

	Operating System :	Microsoft Windows XP Service Pack 2 Microsoft Windows XP Service Pack 3
	NetBIOS name :	ACME-GG9FRPF9CG
	DNS name :	acme-gg9frpf9cg.hsd1.ga.comcast.net.

[^] Back to 192.168.1.103

Port general (0/tcp)   [-/+]
Nessus Scan Information

Information about this scan :

Nessus version : 4.2.2 (Build 9129)
Plugin feed version : 201005251334
Type of plugin feed : HomeFeed (Non-commercial use only)
Scanner IP : 192.168.1.103
Port scanner(s) : nessus_syn_scanner
Port range : default
Thorough tests : no
Experimental tests : no
Paranoia level : 1
Report Verbosity : 1
Safe checks : yes
Optimize the test : yes
CGI scanning : disabled
Web application tests : disabled
Max hosts : 80
Max checks : 5
Recv timeout : 5
Backports : None
Scan Start Date : 2010/5/25 22:08
Scan duration : 219 sec

FIGURE 11-3

Summary page from a Nessus vulnerability scan.

Nessus also has the ability to perform both authenticated and unauthenticated scans; unauthenticated is the default. The difference between the two methods of scanning can be very important depending on how accurate the results need to be. Unauthenticated scanning means Nessus does not have permission to log onto the target system while scanning it. Nessus determines which vulnerabilities to report largely by first identifying the services present by the IP ports open and then searching the plug-ins to see which vulnerabilities are associated with those services and ports. In some cases, this leaves room for error because Nessus cannot confirm the exact configuration of the application or port and whether it already addresses its vulnerabilities. By configuring Nessus with the appropriate logon credentials, it can attempt to validate some of its findings by running additional tests that are only possible while being logged on.

Performing a Vulnerability and Security Assessment

To assess the vulnerabilities and security of a Web site application, you must first identify the components of the Web site environment. A typical single-server Web site consists of:

- **A Web server OS**—The operating system of the hardware server that the components reside on
- **A Web server application**—The actual application that is collecting, using, and/or providing data
- **A Web server front end**—The Web server software that presents the application to users in the form of HTTP pages
- **Web site forms**—The input fields, or forms, that are used to gather data from users

> ⚠️ **WARNING**
>
> It's worth mentioning again that the scan and assessment applications covered in this chapter, as well as many other security tools and commands, are very powerful and can harm systems, depending on how they are configured and used. Users should not attempt this type of testing without proper authorization and planning. If possible, testing should first be performed on mirrored, backup, or test systems to determine the likely impact.

Because each of these components is unusual in purpose and design, it's important to assess them separately, even if common tools or techniques are used. This is especially true for Web sites where the components reside on separate, dedicated servers.

The following sections discuss tools and techniques that are commonly used to assess each component for vulnerabilities and other security concerns. Because this chapter cannot cover every security program, or their configuration options, it describes the desired activities and results of a security assessment. The tools mentioned above, as well as other commands or techniques, may be referred to illustrate the process.

Web Server OS

Because the server operating system is like the foundation of a house, supporting all the other components, it's important to identify and assess the OS version and its running services accurately. At minimum, an assessment of the Web server OS should involve:

- Identifying the OS type and version
- Identifying major service packs and patches that have been installed
- Identifying the active services or ports being supported by the OS
- Identifying any known vulnerabilities associated with the components above

An unauthenticated scan is usually acceptable for OS assessment, but if privileged credentials are available, it's recommended that both an unauthenticated and an authenticated scan be performed.

A typical enumeration and assessment of the Web server OS might be as follows:

1. If the IP address of the Web server is unknown, or if multiple Web servers are suspected present on the network, run an Nmap scan with the "Quick" profile selected against the entire IP address range. Any IP addresses reported as having ports 80 and/or 443 open should indicate they are Web servers.

2. Once the Web server IP addresses are known, run a vulnerability scanner against those IP addresses. If using Nessus, a scan with the default plug-ins enabled would suffice. This will produce a report that includes information about the OS and any vulnerabilities associated with the OS and other running services.

3. If privileged credentials are available for the OS, such as a Windows administrator-equivalent logon or a UNIX root-equivalent ID, it's recommended to run an authenticated vulnerability scan. Depending on the scanner being used, this could help identify vulnerabilities with weak password policies, domain relationships, and so on.

4. Manually review the available services that are enabled at the Web server OS level and determine if they are necessary. Unnecessary services, even if found to have no vulnerabilities, can present a future risk to the system.

Arguably, the most valuable information gained from a Web server OS scan is whether the operating system is missing any critical security patches or running any insecure services. Patches are typically easy to address by applying patches that are missing and recommended by the scan program. Insecure services can be more difficult to remedy if they are truly insecure by design but are needed for business purposes. An example is Telnet services that allow users to remotely connect or logon to the Web server. Often, this is reserved for administrators who need Telnet services to manage the Web server's operating system. However, Telnet is insecure in that it does not require authentication and transmits data in plaintext. This includes transmitting logon IDs and passwords in plaintext even when Telnet is configured with authentication enabled. Some common remediations include limiting Telnet capabilities to certain workstations or implementing a more secure equivalent, Secure Shell (SSH).

Additional items to look for when scanning the Web server OS include:

- Insecure Simple Network Management Protocol (SNMP) configurations that use default names or strings and may allow an attacker to intercept server monitoring traffic.
- Weak passwords or password policies. Testing actual passwords typically requires using a separate password auditing/hacking utility.
- Services that allow remote connectivity to the Web server OS such as Telnet, SSH, rlogin, and so on. If present, use SANS Institute *(http://www.sans.org)* or the Carnegie Mellon University Computer Emergency Readiness Team *(http://www.cert.org)* Web sites to research vulnerabilities and attacks related to those services.

Web Server Application

Assessing Web server applications can be a complex task because applications are unique and offer a variety of services. A Web server application can be anything from a grouping of scripts to a fully custom-coded program. In many cases, assessing Web server applications consists of scanning the application for known vulnerabilities as well as performing more specific testing of the code itself.

Vulnerability scanning and security assessment of Web server applications are much like assessments of the Web server OS and front end. Depending on the type of Web application on the server, tools like Nessus or Metasploit may be useful in finding and testing vulnerabilities in the application. However, for traditional custom-coded applications, it's recommended that the code be reviewed by a commercial source code assessment tool such as WebInspect or IBM Rational Appscan. These source code tools examine various programming languages and find poorly designed or insecure coding techniques that could present risks, such as:

- The ability to circumvent the application's authentication process
- Code or command injection that forces the application to perform in a certain manner
- Manipulating uniform resource locators (URLs) and/or data input fields to traverse data directories or the application itself

As with the assessment of the Web server OS, it's recommended that both an authenticated and unauthenticated test of the Web server application be performed. This will identify potential risks that might be exploited by either an outside attacker or an authorized user. The following steps are typical of a basic Web application security assessment:

1. Identify the type of application that is running on the Web server, such as Microsoft SharePoint, an e-mail system, or a form-based front end for a database.
2. Research the application to determine the types of code or scripting languages being used, such as C++ or Java.
3. Select an appropriate utility to run against the Web application or scripts, such as N-Stalker. (See *http://www.nstalker.com.*)

Web Site Front End

Assessing Web site front-end software, the program that serves HTTP pages to users, is very similar to assessing OS software. Like an OS, Web site software typically consists of a core program combined with add-on services to support specific capabilities. In many cases, the vulnerability scan of the Web server OS will identify Web site front-end software and its vulnerabilities as part of its overall enumeration. However, depending on the scan tools used, there are typically some Web site-specific options that can help the scan application perform a more thorough assessment of Web site front-end vulnerabilities.

Because the Web site front-end software often integrates or supports the Web server application, many of the tools used to assess the application also can be used to assess the front end. Often, the Web site application consists of Web pages or forms that are designed in Java or PHP. Web site front-end software is often the platform for more popular but sometimes more exploitable technologies such as Flash, Shockwave, and others. These technologies are often targeted by exploits because they are used so heavily in Web sites and applications.

Some common activities performed when assessing Web site front-end software are:

1. Identify the type of Web site front-end software in use, such as Microsoft Internet Information Services (IIS) or Apache.

2. Determine the functions that the front-end software is supposed to provide—simple presentation of Hypertext Markup Language (HTML) pages, data input/output, access to sensitive files/data, and so on.

3. Run a Web server security utility such as Nessus, N-Stalker, or Acunetix Web Vulnerability Scanner. In addition to looking for basic vulnerabilities, the scanners should be configured to test for cross-site scripting.

4. Use a utility such as HTTrack Website Copier to crawl, or scan, the Web site's pages for hidden fields. Hidden fields are sometimes used to track the activities or actions of the Web site user.

5. HTTrack can also provide information about the Web site's directory structure. This can be useful in performing a directory traversal attack in which the user attempts to access hidden directories by simply changing the URL in the Web browser address bar.

6. Use resources such as Google's advanced search commands to search the Web site for potentially sensitive files or information. Some examples of useful Google search commands that can be entered directly into the Google search field include:

   - **ssn site:acme.com**—Searches the site Acme.com for any Web pages that include the text "ssn"

   - **acme.com -filetype:doc**—Searches the Acme.com site and returns all files with .doc extensions stored on the Web site

Web Site Forms and User Inputs

Web site forms allow Web site users to input data either into the Web site front end or the Web site application. Although data input forms and fields are useful, they present a significant security risk to a Web site if not implemented properly. When a user enters data into a Web site field or form, there are usually scripts and programs that process that data. Depending on how well the Web site front end or applications have been configured, or are designed, they may have problems if a user enters bad or improperly formatted text.

There are a few ways that input can be incorrectly entered, causing Web site problems. The most common involves entering a very large number of characters into a field that might expect only a few. For example, an attacker tries to enter 100 characters into a phone number field. A properly configured, or well-written, Web site application would either require the correct number of characters before processing the data or check for incorrect data and not process it.

Another form of improperly formatted data involves entering special commands into fields. This is often known as code injection or cross-site scripting (XSS). Cross-site scripting has long been one of the most widely exploited vulnerabilities. It's popular because it takes advantage of two common features of Web sites: JavaScript and data input fields/forms. The term stems from the nature of the technique: An attacker accesses a Web site and provides data in the site's fields that cause issues with how JavaScript interprets the data and/or executes it. This produces results ranging from wrong characters or data being displayed to compromising the security of Web browser sessions that interact with the Web site.

Most vulnerability scanners, commercial or free, can perform at least a basic scan for cross-site scripting and code injection vulnerabilities. Because there are so many types of cross-site scripting and code injection vulnerabilities, it's recommended that multiple scan programs be run against a Web site.

Incorporate PCI DSS for E-commerce Web Sites

One of the most common uses for Web sites is e-commerce. Web sites that store, transmit, or process credit card numbers must comply with security standards that have been set by the payment brands—Visa, MasterCard, American Express, Discover, and JCB. These standards are known as the Payment Card Industry Data Security Standards (PCI DSS). Although this chapter won't cover PCI DSS in detail, it's worth noting the sections within PCI DSS that apply to Web site security testing. Failure to comply with PCI DSS can lead to a Web site's losing the right to process credit card transactions as well as to fines for the Web site's owner by the payment brands.

PCI DSS consists of 12 major security requirement sections, each with numerous specific controls. These major requirement sections are:

1. Install and maintain a firewall configuration to protect cardholder data.
2. Don't use vendor-supplied defaults for system passwords and other security parameters.
3. Protect stored cardholder data.
4. Encrypt transmission of cardholder data across open, public networks.
5. Use and regularly update antivirus software.
6. Develop and maintain secure systems and applications.
7. Restrict access to cardholder data by business need-to-know.
8. Assign a unique ID to each person with computer access.
9. Restrict physical access to cardholder data.
10. Track and monitor all access to network resources and cardholder data.
11. Regularly test security systems and processes.
12. Maintain an information security policy for employees and contractors.

For Web sites that handle credit cards, all 12 requirements will apply. The requirements most related to this section are:

- **Requirement 2, vendor-supplied defaults**—Although changing vendor-supplied default passwords and account names is largely a manual process, some advanced vulnerability scan tools can check for well-known vendor default values. If a Web site must be PCI compliant, then it's recommended that a security assessment tool be used that can check for vendor default accounts and passwords.

- **Requirement 6, secure systems and applications**—Some controls in this requirement are most relevant to this chapter in that they require tests for specific types of issues, such as input validation, cross-site scripting, data injection flaws, malicious code execution, and error handling.

- **Requirement 11, testing systems and processes**—This requirement contains the mandate that Web applications and systems be regularly scanned for vulnerabilities, from both inside the network where the server sits and from the Internet. Internet-based scans must be performed by an approved third-party scanning vendor whose scanning product tests for specific vulnerabilities determined by the payment brands. For a Web system to be eligible for PCI compliance, both the internal and third party/external scans must be performed and successfully passed quarterly, meaning no vulnerabilities are found. To be deemed compliant, the system and environment also must be assessed and meet all the other controls in the PCI DSS standard.

Using Planned Attacks to Identify Vulnerabilities

One of the most effective ways to complement vulnerability scanning and comprehensively assess the security of a Web system or application is to perform a planned attack. Many security professionals refer to this as **penetration testing**, or *pen testing* for short.

The specific activities performed during planned attacks vary depending on the skill of the tester, the type of system, and the desired outcome. However, the commonly used process consists of three steps:

1. Developing a plan of attack
2. Identifying the security gaps and holes
3. Attempting to escalate privilege

A good site to reference when planning attacks on applications and Web technologies is the Open Web Application Security Project (OWASP) at *http://www.owasp.org*. OWASP has been helping set application security standards and practices for years. Similar to SANS and CERT, OWASP tracks data on evolving attack methods, common security coding issues, and so on. By researching how application security should work, per OWASP, an assessor can develop ideas and techniques for how to pen test a specific application or system.

Develop an Attack Plan

The attack plan for Web front-end systems often centers on the application's user interface and how a Web site visitor, legitimate or not, could gain unauthorized access to data through the Web server or application. If system availability is an important issue or if the Web server is part of a larger group of systems, then the tester might also incorporate attacks such as denial of service (DoS) and/or deeper reconnaissance attacks. To keep the planned attack efficient and focused, it's important to establish the exact strategies that will be attempted as well as possible outcomes. A basic planned attack on a Web site front end might include:

- Strategy: Attacking input fields and forms in an attempt to gain unauthorized access
- Systems: Web site Acme.com
- Techniques: Input invalid data into fields, attack authentication form, and attempt buffer overflow

Identify Gaps and Holes

Earlier scans with vulnerability programs should have produced information on the OS version, type of Web software running, patch levels, and perhaps even configuration settings. Those pieces of information provide insight into possible security gaps.

technical TIP

While you are viewing a Web page, you can see the source code by selecting View, Page Source, or just Source, from the browser's menu bar. Performing a search on the text "type=hidden" should identify whether any hidden fields exist on the Web page. Depending on the nature of the field, it may be possible to modify files or gain access to resources by manipulating the hidden field values.

Another technique to identify Web front-end security gaps is to review the HTML source code for hidden fields. A Web developer might want to calculate or store data on a Web page that the application needs but users shouldn't see. For example, an online sales order form might use hidden fields that contain price and quantity information about products being purchased. Upon checkout, the Web site might use those hidden fields to calculate the final order total and number of items purchased. If the Web site and application are not properly secured, an attacker could discover the hidden fields, manipulate the values, and place a fraudulent order with lower prices.

Escalate the Privilege Level

Privilege escalation involves exploiting a vulnerability or flaw in a system to gain access to resources not otherwise available to the attacker or tester. Privilege escalation applies not only to gaining a higher role in the system, known as *vertical privilege escalation*, but also to gaining access to files or data that normally are restricted to peer users. The latter scenario, known as *horizontal privilege escalation*, may be much easier for an attacker to accomplish than vertical privilege escalation yet provide a comparable benefit.

One scenario used to test for horizontally escalated privilege levels involves visiting Web server pages where documents, files, or other pieces of information are requested, perhaps a secure area where user-specific documents are stored. A sign of potential vulnerability can be a URL that looks like:

```
http://www.acme.com/showmydocuments.asp?DocID=13
```

A valid test would be simply to change the "13" in the URL to other numbers and see if documents are accessible that normally shouldn't be—perhaps documents belonging to other users. This test actually uses two pen testing techniques—URL manipulation and directory traversal.

Another, perhaps more popular, form of attempted privilege escalation is buffer overflow attempts. By sending improperly formed information to the Web site or application, it's sometimes possible to overflow the computer's memory and cause the application to crash. Most buffer overflow attacks result in the Web application and system simply shutting down or rebooting. However, with improperly secured Web systems, it's sometimes possible that the server will close the Web application but keep the applications logon session, and rights, active. This has led to occasions where the Web system, upon closing the application, returned to a command prompt that had full administrative rights still active. This meant that if attackers could crash the application simply by flooding the computer's memory, their level of privilege could be escalated once they were at the console prompt.

Spotting Vulnerabilities in Back-End Systems and SQL Databases

Back-end systems are also subject to risk if not properly secured. Because the back-end databases of a Web application solution typically don't offer the same variety of services that a front-end system does, planned attacks may be easier. The strategy for attempting to compromise back-end systems is relatively the same, though. The intention is to gain access to data, either through compromising a database or escalating a privilege level.

Develop an Attack Plan

Developing an attack plan for a back-end system or database is very similar to developing one for a Web front-end system. Many attack methods can be performed through the same Web application or forms.

The most likely difference in planning an attack on a database is that additional discovery tools need to be used to identify the database type. Most scanning tools identify database types based on open ports or services running on the system. However, if the database type cannot be determined by scan tools, then another method that sometimes works is field manipulation and forcing error messages. Inputting a wrong value in a field the database processes may cause an error. The resulting error message displayed on the screen may give information about the database.

Once the database type is identified, the general plan of attack on a database might attempt to:

1. Access or retrieve data by injecting data into fields or forms
2. Access or retrieve data by gaining privileged access
3. Crash the database to gain privileged access to other portions of the system

Identify Gaps and Holes

Probing database applications for gaps and holes is a common feature of the penetration testing software on the market. Metasploit, a freeware tool, is adept at exploit testing, as its name implies. Metasploit has modules, or preconfigured test scripts, for numerous database types and their vulnerabilities, but it isn't as user-friendly as some other tools mentioned in this chapter. Even the Windows version runs as a command-line utility.

Many of the Web application scanners also have scripts and tests for back-end databases. Acunetix is one of those programs and will attempt to connect to the database as well as run Structured Query Language (SQL) commands.

Escalate the Privilege Level

Attempting to escalate privileges for back-end databases is very similar to the strategy used for Web server applications. Once again, Metasploit is a good utility for attempting various strategies for escalating privileges. One item to be cautious about, however, is that many of the scripts and techniques used to gain escalated privilege level involve strategies to crash either the application or the database itself. If the database is crashed, then accessing data may be considerably more difficult, even if privileged access is gained.

Perform an SQL Injection for Data Extraction

Most scanning and pen test utilities now have built-in SQL injection testing capabilities. However, SQL injection is a fairly simple activity that an attacker can attempt manually by manipulating URLs in a browser.

SQL injection is the act of inserting various SQL commands into a URL, or sometimes into a form field, so that the command will be run against the back-end database. The steps below contain a basic SQL injection attempt:

1. Look for Web pages that contain data entry fields, for entering data, such as a username or password. Web pages for that purpose are typically not static HTML but written using a language like ASP or PHP. These Web pages will contain extensions such as .asp, .php, or .jsp somewhere in the string of characters. For example, `http://mydatabase.com/index.asp?user=` might correspond to a text box asking for a logon ID.

2. Upon typing the name Sam into the logon ID field on the Web page, the string would look like: `http://mydatabase.com/index.asp?user=Sam`. The database might then start a query to look for the name Sam in its tables, and the actual database query might look like: `SELECT*FROM customers WHERE User='Sam'`

3. By either manipulating the URL or entering data into the field, you can now try some characters that have special meaning in SQL queries such as a single quote `'`, or two dashes `--`. The single quote, for example, tells SQL to escape from the search criteria and back to the SQL statement. Knowing this, you can enter data to the Web page's field to be injected as part of the SQL statement. For example, entering the characters `' OR 1=1` tells the statement to return data if statement processes are true. Because 1 always equals 1, the statement is true and all data is returned.

4. From here, more advanced knowledge of SQL query formatting and/or SQL server commands are necessary to get creative with SQL injection. Basically, though, any type of SQL command can now be inserted into the text box or URL and, if properly formatted, cause the SQL server to execute the command as if the attacker was sitting at the SQL console. For example, the following text would cause SQL to stop its normal query and execute anything after the semicolon, such as a privileged SQL server exec command: `'; exec....`

With some quick Google searching, an attacker could find information on the exec command and its options allowing for some very powerful capabilities. Exec can then be used to perform actions such as:

- `EXEC xp_cmdshell 'dir *.exe'` which returns a list of all .exe files on the server
- `EXEC @retstat...`, which runs a script, or collection of commands, from a remote server

Preparing a Vulnerability and Security Assessment Report

Reporting can be the most difficult part of performing a vulnerability or security assessment. Often, there are numerous audiences—with varying levels of technical knowledge—that need the results of the assessment. In some cases, there may be a need to present the data from different perspectives, such as a report focused on risk versus one focused on compliance. The general structure for an assessment report includes:

- Executive summary
- Summary of findings
- Details of the vulnerability assessment
- Details of the security assessment
- Recommended remediations

Many of the vulnerability and security assessment tools on the market, particularly the commercial programs, have the ability to generate data and graphs, if not an entire assessment report. However, it's often necessary to take the data from those tools and manually build an assessment report that will best suit the audience. The next few sections will discuss best practices for manually creating an assessment report.

Executive Summary

An executive summary is typically designed to do what its name says—provide executives, or other levels of management, the ability to understand the assessment's major points. Usually the first section or chapter of an assessment report, an executive summary should be relatively short and focus on the findings of most interest. This typically includes "critical" or "high" vulnerabilities and security gaps as well as any that might affect the system's compliance status—such as being PCI compliant/certified.

A good executive summary will include information that is specific and clear so it can be quickly consumed and understood. It should also include points management needs to know to make business decisions about risk, budgeting, resource planning, and so on. It's perfectly acceptable for an executive summary to include detailed information, or even advanced topics and terms, as long as it reads quickly and gets its points across clearly. Many executive summaries are no longer than a single page and contain graphs and charts to consolidate information and help focus the reader's attention.

In today's world of security and compliance, there is a big push for performing due diligence or due care—or asking external parties for proof of security assessments and remediation efforts. It's very common for companies to ask to see, or even insist on seeing, each other's security assessment and/or audit reports to ensure good security is in place. Keep this in mind when designing an assessment report and, specifically, the executive summary. Try to write the executive summary so that it can be used as a standalone report and is safe to distribute to external parties.

Some points an executive summary should cover include:

- A description of the systems or applications that were assessed.
- A brief explanation of why the systems or applications needed to be assessed, for example, for an annual compliance assessment or a post-incident assessment.
- A description of who performed the assessment and the general strategy or techniques used, for example: "Third-party forensics firm ScanCo performed the assessment and used a combination of automated discovery and vulnerability scans as well as manual penetration techniques."
- A high-level description of the most critical findings and the risks they present or how they affect compliance.
- A brief summary of any remedies committed to or underway.

Remember to keep the executive summary fairly high level. Avoid mentioning potentially sensitive information such as IP addresses, version numbers, and names of programs used that could be used by another party to compromise systems and applications. This keeps the executive summary clean of technical details and usable as a standalone document to show customers or other outside parties that an assessment was performed.

Summary of Findings

The summary of findings section should go a step farther than the executive summary and outline most or all the findings rather than just the most critical findings that are included in the executive summary. Many scan tools can generate summary graphs or tables straight from the collected data. The summary of findings is a good place to use graphs to show analysis or trends, such as:

- Percentage or quantity of vulnerabilities found by vulnerability type/category
- Percentage or quantity of vulnerabilities found by Web site component, for example, Web application versus Web front end versus OS and/or by IP address
- Percentage or quantity comparison of vulnerabilities by criticality, for example, high versus medium versus low
- Table or list of security gaps confirmed to be present on each Web site component or system

▶ **NOTE**

A very useful but time-consuming feature to add to a summary of findings is summary data from any previous assessments. Historical assessment data can show trends which, in turn, can lead to identifying issues such as breakdowns in technology processes, poor security awareness, training, and so on.

The summary of findings can also include text descriptions or observations about the percentages/quantities that are shown. For instance, if the vulnerability scans were performed only in a non-authenticated manner and did not log onto the systems being assessed, the assessor might want to mention that fact. The assessor might also want to explain briefly how that might generate false positives, or "suspected but not necessarily confirmed," vulnerabilities that could make the results look worse than they really are.

Vulnerability Assessment

The vulnerability assessment section of the report is typically one of the easiest to generate, but it also contains the largest amount of data. Many vulnerability scanning tools are adept at generating detailed reports. The better tools can even export that data in various formats so that it can be easily imported and manipulated into a manual assessment report or presentation. Depending on the purpose for the vulnerability scan and report, it may be required to use the report provided by the scan tool, so that the findings cannot be manipulated or deleted. When selecting a vulnerability scan application, be sure to take into consideration its ability to report or export data in a convenient format.

The type, or complexity, of vulnerability scan usually determines the amount of data or findings that will be generated. It's not unusual for a single system or IP address to generate 50 to 100 findings. Considering that most vulnerability scan tools devote up to a half-page description for each vulnerability found, this can create a long report. Each write-up for a vulnerability finding typically includes the following information:

- The vulnerability name and description
- A Common Vulnerabilities and Exposures (CVE) number that uniquely identifies it across various security vendors and applications
- A Common Vulnerability Scoring System (CVSS) number that is often used to determine its criticality or importance
- Some type of criticality rating or designation, such as red, yellow, or green; high, medium, or low
- Information regarding any patches or configuration procedures to remedy the vulnerability

If the native report from the vulnerability scanning utility proves to be too long, try exporting the data into a format that allows for the fields to be manipulated, such as Excel. This will work, however, only in situations that don't require a certified, or non-modifiable, report. In the case of PCI, where it's required that authorized third parties perform the scans, the reports must be generated and delivered in PDF format so that the results cannot be altered.

Security Assessment

The security assessment, or penetration test, section of the report is likely to be the least structured due to the subjective nature of security assessment testing and tools. Depending on the approach used, there are a few ways that security assessment information can be reported.

One effective way of organizing security assessment information is to group the findings by system or component and then sub-group the findings within each system by the type of attack performed or the functionality that was being tested. The following is an outline of a method for reporting security or penetration test results:

   I. Web site front end
      a. Authentication attack findings
         i. Tools/techniques used
        ii. Result
      b. Field manipulation attack findings
         i. Tools/techniques used
        ii. Result
      c. Code/field injection attack findings
      d. Scripting attack findings

  II. Web site database
      a. Authentication attack findings
      b. Field manipulation attack findings
      c. Code/field injection attack findings

Recommendations

The recommendations section, also referred to as the remediation section, of the report is arguably the most important section. Because vulnerability remediation will likely have been mentioned as part of the data from vulnerability scan tools, this section is primarily a summary of fixes. There may be a large number of findings to fix and complexity involved from one fix to another. Therefore, you should consider categorizing the recommendations by short term and long term.

Short Term

Short-term recommendations should include fixes for the most critical findings, or those that are most likely to have a significant impact on the system in the near future. Because short-term fixes are likely to get the most visibility and attention, it's a good idea to streamline and group these recommendations. If some of the remediations involve the same personnel, processes, or systems, consolidate the recommendation into a single statement or item, if possible. This will help organize the effort to fix the issue and ensure that fixes are consistent across systems or technologies.

▶ NOTE

One effective technique is to display recommendations in a table with information that helps readers understand how best to implement the fix. That can include security information, such as the potential impact if the recommendation isn't followed or alternative solutions if the fix isn't possible now. It may also contain non-security information such as an estimate of resources that will be needed.

It's also necessary to define what's meant by short term. This may have to be defined per recommendation. Some vulnerabilities and security gaps that are considered extremely critical and easily exploited may need to be addressed in hours or days. Other highly critical findings that are harder to exploit might be considered short term but can be addressed in weeks. This difference may also have to do with the time needed to test the recommended fix. It's best to define the short term in a range of time, say 0 to 30 days, and then associate a number of days or weeks with each recommendation. This also will allow IT and business personnel to prioritize the recommendations, if needed.

In addition to simply using the vulnerability criticality ratings, it's also highly recommended that the assessor refer to other sources of attack trend information, such as *http://www.sans.org* or *http://www.cert.org*, to determine if any recent attacks or trends should escalate findings into the higher-risk, short-term recommendation category.

Long Term

Long-term recommendations, perhaps better stated as longer-term recommendations, should include all the remediations that don't fall into the short-term category. As with short-term recommendations, it will be necessary to define the long term. This will help IT and business personnel keep fixes on schedule.

Long-term recommendations may also include non-technical suggestions, such as procedural improvements or technology evaluations. For example, if a large number of vulnerabilities or findings were associated with an aging operating system, the short-term recommendation could be to patch or secure the operating system and a long-term recommendation would be to evaluate an alternative OS or a more expedient patch process.

Best Practices for Web Site Vulnerability and Security Assessments

Web site security testing can involve a number of tools and techniques. However, some best practices may prove helpful when choosing or using the method for assessing a Web site application.

Choose the Right Tools

Although there are very few bad tools for performing security assessments and vulnerability scans, some are certainly better than others. Rarely will one tool find every vulnerability or security hole. Don't be afraid to evaluate different tools and use multiple tools, even for the same function, when performing security assessments. That certainly results in more effort and data to review, but the end goal isn't necessarily speed and convenience when testing application security. In most cases, attackers use a wide variety of tools—often the same tool run from different operating systems. Not only does that give the attackers a better chance of compromising a system or application, but it also helps them learn the various operating systems and application languages. A thorough assessor will follow the same practice. Some additional items to remember when selecting tools:

- Keep data export capabilities in mind for when it's time to manipulate and report the findings.

- Know the capabilities of the utilities being used and how they may affect production systems or data.

- Try to use both commercial and freeware programs. Commercial security tools are typically updated more frequently with the latest vulnerability and attack data.

Test Inside and Out

As mentioned earlier in this chapter, there often are differences in the results of non-authenticated scans and tests versus authenticated ones. It can be difficult or even impossible to get the credentials needed to perform authenticated tests—so many times authenticated testing is simply passed over. However, authenticated scans need to be performed in order to accurately evaluate an application's true security risks. If authenticated testing of production systems is simply too controversial or risky, then perform authenticated scans on a test system—which can help justify getting a test system in place if one isn't already present.

Think Outside the Box

Attackers are as familiar with security testing tools as security professionals are—probably more so. Although the standard tools and techniques are still necessary, be on the lookout for new techniques. Using Google advanced search techniques is one way of performing non-standard testing. Be on the lookout for new crawlers and other utilities or services that are designed to help advertise or improve search results for Web content. Many of these engines will find ways, albeit usually well-intentioned, to get to data within the Web server or Web application quicker than some attackers or security tools can.

Research, Research, Research

There are plenty of Web sites available that monitor attack trends, offer unique testing tools, and even support forums that attract assessors and attackers alike. It's not enough to simply run tools or perform a few manual techniques and consider an application tested. The tools and techniques are a start—but knowing things like the technology behind the attacks, how attacks are evolving, which industries the attacks are happening in, and so on will prove invaluable in truly securing an application or Web site. Perform a Web search for the server's name occasionally to see if any attackers or online tools are targeting the system or application.

CHAPTER SUMMARY

The chapter has covered in detail how important it is to test Web applications. Testing Web applications involves not just the underlying database, but also the Web server front-end software and Web server operating system, because all are interconnected. Testing may require the use of testing tools.

Many of the tools available are so feature-rich that using them without a plan can be time-consuming and possibly even dangerous to the system. Spend the extra time needed to run non-invasive discovery and enumeration tools. This will help determine which tools, or options within tools, are worth running and could save scan time and data. It will also help identify the technologies involved and the techniques, both automated and manual, that would be most effective in performing deeper penetration tests on the system or application.

Finally, a security assessment cannot be considered a success unless the resulting data, or findings, are clearly documented and communicated. Resolving security issues likely will involve various parties, and the data from the security assessment often must be fashioned so that it's relevant to each audience. A good executive summary is important for getting traction with higher-level management and can also be a valuable means of satisfying external parties who need to see evidence of security testing. A clear set of recommendations is also important for remediation.

In summary, an effective Web site vulnerability and security assessment relies on a combination of fundamental technical know-how, thoughtful planning, a variety of tools, and effective communication.

KEY CONCEPTS AND TERMS

Enumeration	Penetration testing
Fingerprinting	Ping sweep

CHAPTER 11 ASSESSMENT

1. The "percentage of vulnerabilities not found" metric is a useful way of reporting assessment data.
   A. True
   B. False

2. How many tiers are commonly used for Web sites?
   A. 2
   B. 1
   C. 3
   D. 4

3. The act of fixing vulnerabilities or findings resulting from an assessment is known as _____.

4. Which of the following activities are considered parts of a Web server OS assessment? (Select two.)
   A. Identifying the source code author
   B. Identifying the patches and updates that have been installed
   C. Identifying the services and ports that are active
   D. Identifying the databases that are running

5. Ping sweeps are a part of what process?
   A. Code review
   B. Discovery
   C. Attack vectors
   D. Remediation

6. Web site forms and user input fields are often attacked using cross-site scripting.
   A. True
   B. False

7. Which section of the assessment report is intended to be a high-level briefing of the findings?
   A. Summary of findings
   B. Vulnerability findings
   C. Recommendations
   D. Executive summary

8. An in-depth security assessment of a Web server application includes performing which of the following?
   A. Error-based code compiling
   B. OS patching
   C. A source code review
   D. TCP/IP routing

9. SQL _____ is an attempt to manipulate a database by inserting commands into a field or URL.

10. Nmap's primary features include which of the following? (Select three.)
   A. Password cracking
   B. OS fingerprinting
   C. Port scanning
   D. Code analysis
   E. Ping sweeps

11. What is the purpose of exploiting a vulnerability or flaw in a system to gain access to resources not otherwise available to the attacker or tester?
   A. Acceleration
   B. Enumeration
   C. Privilege escalation
   D. Field injection

12. OWASP is the organization known for developing secure application development standards and practices.
   A. True
   B. False

13. Nessus uses thousands of _____ to identify vulnerabilities associated with services, applications, and operating systems.

14. Which attack involves exploring the files and folders of a Web server by manipulating URLs?
   A. Man-in-the-middle
   B. Buffer underflow
   C. Brute force password attacks
   D. Directory traversal attacks

15. Unauthenticated scanning requires the scanner logging onto the systems being assessed.
   A. True
   B. False

© Rodolfo Clix/Dreamstime.com

PART THREE

Web Applications and Social Networking Gone Mobile

© Rodolfo Clix/Dreamstime.com

Securing Mobile Communications

WITH THE CONVERGENCE OF COMPUTERS and mobile communications devices, the need to secure endpoint devices is growing. The demand for smartphones and personal digital assistants (PDAs) is as great as ever because of functionality that was previously reserved for home or office computer systems, such as e-mail, Internet-based banking, and file storage. The popularity of real-time mobile communications, such as texting, tweeting, and sharing of photos, also underscores the need for greater security. As the boundaries of personal and business computing blur, and users demand more functionality from mobile devices, the importance of securing endpoint devices will garner more attention.

This chapter covers some of the more popular endpoint devices and communications as well as some of the security risks to those devices and how best to address them.

Chapter 12 Topics

This chapter covers the following topics and concepts:

- What endpoint devices are
- What wireless networks are and how they work
- What forms of communications are frequently used on endpoint devices
- What some of the common risks, threats, and vulnerabilities for endpoint device communications are
- What the Open Web Application Security Project (OWASP) Top 10 Mobile Risks are
- What some best practices for securing endpoint device communications are

Chapter 12 Goals

When you complete this chapter, you will be able to:

- Define endpoint devices and discuss some of the common forms of those devices
- Understand the definition and function of 3G and 4G networks
- Identify common forms of communications used on endpoint devices
- Identify risks, threats, and vulnerabilities associated with endpoint devices
- Understand the OWASP top 10 mobile risks
- Identify some of the tools and techniques used to secure endpoint devices and their communication applications

Endpoint Devices

Loosely defined, an **endpoint device** is any system or application at the periphery, or user end, of a data network. In more traditional computing terms, endpoint devices once consisted primarily of personal computers, laptops, and terminals. In today's computing environment, however, the number and types of endpoint devices have significantly grown. Devices like cell phones, smartphones, tablet PCs, and gadgets such as Apple iPad tablets and e-readers are all considered endpoint devices. They qualify as endpoints because most are *data-enabled* and attach to a public or private data network.

In many cases, these devices no longer can be classified as "just" a cell phone or computing device. In fact, the trend toward the convenience of one device for all computing and personal communications needs has led many of these devices to look and operate similarly. This is particularly important to note because the convergence of these devices combines their strengths and weaknesses in terms of security threats and vulnerabilities. For simplicity, this chapter will discuss the technology and security issues behind some of the common endpoint devices including smartphones and tablets.

> **NOTE**
>
> The term **convergence** describes the merging of various types of devices and technologies into a common or single form.

Tablet and Smartphone Devices

Cell phones are arguably the most pervasive form of mobile communication device today with billions of mobile subscribers worldwide.

Cell phones were developed from two-way radio technology and were designed as a more mobile form of voice communication. The term *cellular* came from the idea of arranging towers so that they created *cells* of coverage. The primary intention of cellular phones was to extend the capabilities of two-way radio in a more user-friendly manner. Two-way radios were extremely valuable during their time but suffered limitations. One major limitation was that only one person could "key the microphone" and speak at a time. Another was that the radio user typically had to select a channel to speak or listen on. Cellular phone systems were designed, at least in part, to eliminate these challenges while also providing greater mobility and range.

Fast-forwarding to modern-day cell phones, now commonly referred to as *smartphones*, it's somewhat amazing to see the advancements that have been made in only a little more than 50 years. Smartphones have dramatically decreased in size, weight, and power consumption. They have incorporated additional communications features such as text messaging/Short Message Service (SMS), global positioning system (GPS), and cameras. Even the most basic cell phones typically have a light-weight browser, some form of organizer, a calendar, and the ability to use data services for ringtones and music downloads. Although not considered a true "computing" platform, cell phones qualify as an endpoint device capable of supporting numerous methods of communication.

Tablets are endpoint devices designed to make information readily available to the mobile user with a larger navigation surface than a smartphone has. Although slightly different from one another in terms of features and purpose, various types of tablets have found a strong foothold both in personal use and in corporate environments. Tablets have not yet pushed laptops into obsolescence, however, although that was suggested at one point.

Tablets today come in a range of shapes, sizes, and features. Manufacturers such as Microsoft (Nexus), Apple (iPad, iPad mini), Samsung (Galaxy), and others are each releasing tablets with more capacity, faster speeds, and a large array of business and productivity applications. Tablets provide both 4G and Wi-Fi access, giving users access to the Internet virtually anytime, anywhere. This mobility brings with it not only convenience but also a new range of security considerations.

If tablets didn't increase security issues enough, smartphones certainly did. Today many households have multiple smartphone devices, and corporations arm their employees with smartphones to give them access to work anytime, anywhere. With billions of smartphones worldwide, they are an attractive target for attackers.

Every endpoint device, whether at home or in the corporate network, presents significant security risks. Later this chapter will review the top 10 mobile device risks. Each one has the potential to lead to a breach of the confidentiality and integrity of sensitive data.

Wireless Networks and How They Work

Since the introduction of the cell phone in the late 1970s and early 1980s, there have been continuous efforts to expand and improve cellular networks and services. Cellular service is available in nearly all parts of the globe, and most countries have multiple carriers. As with any classic supply versus demand model, cellular providers must drive innovation to attract and maintain their customer base. The industry categorizes that innovation into four major "generations" of cellular networks and technology. Each generation typically maps to detailed technology standards set by international standards bodies. To help provide perspective, this section will give a brief overview of all four generations. The focus, however, will be on the two most recent generations, 3G and 4G, as they pertain more to digital communications and data services.

1G/2G Networks

First generation, or 1G, cellular networks emerged in the late 1970s in Japan and Denmark. Ameritech started the first U.S. 1G network in 1983. 1G networks supported analog service, much like preceding radio service, and relied on a narrow band of frequencies for transmission. The narrow frequency band resulted in the network supporting a very limited number of simultaneous callers. Transmissions were also susceptible to interference and eavesdropping. However, the defining feature of 1G networks was the use of multiple cell sites and the ability to hand off calls from one cell to another. Unfortunately, there were relatively few cell towers, so phones needed to produce more transmitting power, resulting in larger phones and shorter battery life. Some may remember the large DynaTac "brick" phones of this period. Nevertheless, cell-to-cell handoff was a huge advancement in mobility and played an important role in the growth of the cellular industry.

Second generation, or 2G, came about in the 1990s and was arguably one of the most revolutionary periods for cellular communications. One of the most notable features of 2G was the introduction of digital transmissions, which provided the foundation for data services and greater security features. 2G also supported wider frequency bands for transmission, enabling more users to place calls simultaneously.

SMS messaging and downloadable content such as ringtones also made their debut with 2G's data capabilities. Somewhat separate from, but equally important to, the development of 2G service was the proliferation of cell towers. This brought greater mobility to cell phone use, and led to greater popularity. It also played a major role in cell phones becoming smaller and having longer battery life. With more towers, cell phones required less transmitting power and, thus, smaller batteries. Chip design also evolved to allow greater functionality from smaller cell phone circuitry. These features all played a part in the cell phone becoming the communication device of choice, over pagers and radios, as well as challenging the traditional Personal Digital Assistant (PDA) for data functionality.

3G Networks

Like the two generations before it, third generation (or 3G) is actually a set of international cellular technology standards. The 3G standards cover all the usual items from previous generations including bandwidth specifications, security features, and transmission types. It also introduced new capabilities such as global roaming. Arguably the most noticeable improvement made by the standard, however, is data transmission speeds. Data download speeds on 2G networks and phones had a theoretical maximum speed of 14.4 kilobits per second (Kbps). Actual download speeds were typically much slower. That is roughly equivalent to the speed of the first modems back in the 1990s. The 3G technology standards, however, increased transfer speeds ranging from 144 Kbps for fast-moving devices to a theoretical 2 megabits per second (Mbps) for stationary devices. The exact data transmission speed depends on the "flavor" of 3G that a carrier implements.

With that type of speed, mobile phones can download data, such as e-mail, Web pages, and music files, at nearly the same speed as a broadband cable modem or digital subscriber line (DSL) Internet connection. Thus, 3G technology coined a new term in the cellular industry—**mobile broadband**. Because 3G establishes such a wide variety of standards, it even covers such new, non-cellular technologies as Digital Enhanced Cordless Telecommunications (DECT) for home cordless phones and Worldwide Interoperability for Microwave Access (WiMAX), a microwave-based successor to Wi-Fi for desktops and laptops.

Considering the significant increase in data transfer speeds, 3G opened the door to a whole new level of features for mobile devices. Enhanced audio and video streaming, video conferencing, faster Web browsing, IPTV (TV via Internet), instant messaging, and cellular VoIP are some of these capabilities. To handle these new services yet avoid affecting voice communications, 3G networks added a separate signal channel specifically to transmit data packets. Figure 12-1 shows how a basic 3G network operates to transmit and route both voice and data communications.

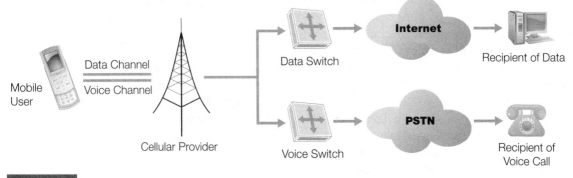

FIGURE 12-1

Basic 3G routing diagram.

4G Networks

Fourth generation, or 4G, has emerged as the next major evolution of communications. The two most significant advancements for 4G networks are use of an entirely Internet Protocol (IP)-based system, which resembles computer networks, and significantly higher theoretical data transmission rates. In practice, 4G is proving that it can provide DSL/cable modem data speeds at its maximum distance of 31 miles (between endpoint device and tower.) At shorter distances, speeds will likely reach the 30 Mbps level, which would exceed DSL and cable modem services with a range significantly greater than Wi-Fi. The move to an all-IP system, much like that of current computer networks, could also have significant effects. Many of the services and security features used with IP-based computer networks likely will be available to cellular devices and systems.

Figure 12-2 shows how a 4G network combines voice and data over a single IP-based data channel.

Considering the speed increases and the benefits of an all-IP infrastructure, 4G is positioned to rival 2G as the most influential advancement in mobile communications. Applications for such fast and long-range data communications likely will include full digital TV services over IP, full VoIP services, and use of 4G devices as both an endpoint device and an Internet gateway. As 4G networks proliferate, a user will be able to carry the functionality of a cell phone, DSL/cable modem, and digital TV receiver in one device. Business travelers will have high-speed Internet access for their laptops anytime and anywhere. As more phones are equipped with front-facing webcams, live video conferencing might completely replace voice-only cellular calls. 4G may result in the ultimate convergence of cell phones, PDAs, laptops, camcorders, digital cameras, and high-speed Internet access into a single device.

Table 12-1 summarizes key 3G and 4G network characteristics, as well as some pros and cons of 3G and 4G networks.

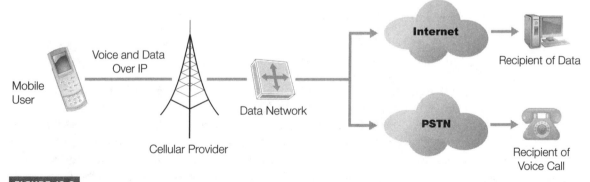

Basic 4G routing diagram.

TABLE 12-1 A brief comparison of 3G and 4G networks.

	TRAFFIC ROUTING METHOD	TYPICAL DATA TRANSFER SPEEDS	ROAMING	PROS AND CONS
3G	Circuit-switching for voice calls Packet-switching for data transfers	144 Kbps (while user is on the move) to 2 Mbps (stationary user/device)	Global roaming available but compatibility and/ or speed issues may exist between providers	Pro: Well-established technology Con: Relatively slow data rates for today's needs
4G	Packet-switching for both voice and data; entirely IPv6-based network	3 Mbps (30 miles from tower) to 30 Mbps (less than 1 mile from tower)	Greater roaming compatibility between providers	Pro: Extremely fast data rates Con: New technology; relatively few devices and services offered

FYI

Circuit-switching is typically slower but more reliable than packet-switching. Because voice transmissions prefer reliability to speed, to avoid broken or inaudible playback, circuit-switching has traditionally been better suited for voice transmissions than data transfers. Packet-switching is a faster routing method but can sometimes lose or drop packets. This makes packet-switching better for data transfers, because Web sites and video require high-speed transmission rates for optimal viewing.

Security Features of 3G and 4G Networks

While 2G services introduced some security features to the cellular industry, such as digital encryption of conversations, 3G made significant security improvements and 4G likely will follow suit.

3G improved on encryption capabilities by allowing stronger ciphers to be used. Kusami, or A5/3, is a 128-bit cipher widely used in 3G Global System for Mobile communication (GSM) networks. This is a significant upgrade from the A5/1 64-bit cipher that was used with 2G. 3G also introduced the capability for enhanced authentication so that two-way authentication could occur between a phone and a network. 2G had only one-way authentication from the cellular device to the network. This left open the possibility of someone's setting up a rogue receiver and intercepting transmissions from phones trying to attach to a network.

The exact type of security improvements with 4G are still emerging because one of the two competing versions of 4G—the Long Term Evolution (LTE) system, backed by Verizon, T-Mobile, and AT&T—has limited implementation as of this writing. However, it's expected that 4G will improve upon some existing 3G network security measures as well as introduce new features related to the all IP-based nature of 4G.

4G will definitely improve upon 3G by supporting higher strength encryption for communications. Current specifications for 4G include support for either 168-bit Triple DES or 128-bit AES—both of which improve 3G's Kusami encryption. WiMAX, the second of the two competing 4G versions (backed by Sprint), has committed to supporting the AES algorithm as well as an authentication system based on X.509 certificates to protect over-the-air transmissions. This is an improvement over previous authentications that used less formal certificates or challenge/response methods. For complete, end-to-end encryption of data, WiMAX 4G will also support options such as user-provided virtual private network (VPN) tunneling, carrier-provided VPN tunneling, and static IP addressing.

> **NOTE**
> DES stands for Data Encryption Standard, and AES stands for Advanced Encryption Standard. Triple DES is often written as 3DES.

Table 12-2 summarizes a comparison of key 3G and 4G security features.

TABLE 12-2 A brief comparison of 3G and 4G security features.

	ENCRYPTION	AUTHENTICATION	OTHER BENEFITS	RISKS
3G	Kusami (or A5/3) 128-bit (developed by Mitsubishi) on voice channel Packets are not encrypted on data channel.	AKA (authentication and key agreement) using info from SIM card; phone and network authenticate each other for added protection	IPSec is supported but not required on data channel.	Denial of service (DoS) attacks are considered possible; so is compromise of data packets if data channel is not encrypted.
4G	168-bit Triple DES (3DES) or 128-bit AES Both are standard algorithms in the security industry.	3 Mbps (30 miles from tower) to 30 Mbps (less than 1 mile from tower)	Increased data transfer speeds will support many of the security solutions designed for wired computer networks such as VPNs.	Use of an entirely IP-based network could subject callers to viruses, malware, and attacks already designed for IP-based systems.

Endpoint Device Communications

As this chapter has shown, communication drives the evolution of endpoint devices. Communication, in this sense, means more than just the data transfer rates or network types. This section will discuss communications in terms of the messaging services and applications that live on endpoint devices.

Voice

Voice communication was the force behind the increase in cellular phones during the 1990s and early 2000s. Looking at the trials and successes of cellular technology, one can see that both actually helped drive improvements for voice and data convergence. The popularity of cellular voice communications helped phone companies establish robust networks that support one of the key desires of consumers—mobility. Troubles with interference and dropped calls pushed carriers towards better and more reliable signaling.

Even though voice communication is almost taken for granted in today's market, it still factors heavily into the features of endpoint devices. With advancements in video conferencing, voice communication is once again coming to the forefront of people's interest as well as their concerns about security. It's also continuing to help drive the need for faster transmission speeds, higher quality video and voice, and better processing power.

Services like Skype have renewed people's interest in voice communications. Once a fad, the video conferencing application Skype has grown into nearly a household word. For those with a high-speed Internet connection, it remains a free alternative to traditional public switched telephone network (PSTN) phone lines and a popular method of video-conferencing for family and friends. Skype is also giving a renewed focus to voice by challenging the very way that voice calls are conducted over mobile devices. As mobile broadband speeds continue to increase, applications like Skype conduct voice conversations over digital mobile channels. This is common for callers who frequently make long distance or international calls. Because services like Skype traverse the digital portion of a carrier's network, they often avoid the tolls and fees charged for traditional long-distance calls. As providers continue the move toward all-digital networks like 4G, the trend of using "soft phone" applications like Skype likely will grow.

Security Risks with Voice

Security concerns surrounding voice communications are somewhat different today than they were in the past. In the 1G era, cellular voice communications were significantly easier to intercept. Signaling was strictly analog, and in some cases rudimentary devices like frequency scanners or handheld radios could pick up local cellular conversations. The advent of 2G and 3G significantly decreased the ability to eavesdrop easily because encryption was in use. Even after methods were discovered to crack the weaker encryption schemes used in 2G and 3G, the effort, time, and equipment required to eavesdrop made it an infrequent risk.

As voice communications make the transition to all-digital, all-IP networks such as 4G, there will be a slight increase in risk due to all the vulnerabilities, malware, and hacks that exist for PC-based systems and applications. That increase should be slight, though, because of improved security features that accompany 4G, as mentioned in an earlier section. Considering that IP-based networks and applications have been around— and attacked—for many years now, it's reasonable to believe that 4G devices likely will benefit from security controls and measures developed for computer networks. The added data speed capabilities of 4G should allow it to support more efficiently security solutions like VPN tunnels, strong authentication mechanisms, and even filtering/blocking measures like intrusion prevention systems (IPSs) and software firewalls.

Internet Browsing

Given the importance of Internet access, it was only a matter of time before users would demand, and possibly need, every endpoint device to be equipped with Internet browsing capabilities. Despite the fact that early data-enabled cell phones and smartphones made browsing somewhat challenging, the sheer range of services on the Internet made browsing capabilities important no matter what the device. Now that most endpoint devices sport screens large enough for Internet navigation (2.5-inch or larger), users can take advantage of most Internet Web sites normally designed for display on desktop monitors.

Advancements in Web offerings, such as online banking and map services, have also helped drive the importance of mobile browsing. As users find themselves banking online at home and using navigation systems while driving, they naturally grow accustomed to having access to such data anytime they need it. They expect to be able to check bank balances, pay bills, transfer funds, view and place stock trades, and so on while at the playground, at a sporting event, in a store, or on a day trip. Finding an address or phone number, or using the mobile device as a GPS receiver during travel is also convenient and commonplace.

Two of the most popular uses of Internet browsing on mobile endpoint devices, however, are social networking and multimedia (video and music) downloads. The public's addiction to social networking has resulted in users needing anytime access to read and post information on such sites as Facebook, Twitter, and MySpace. The very nature of these sites—allowing "in-the-moment" communication of thoughts and opinions—makes them almost tailored specifically for mobile users.

Security Risks with Internet Browsing

Internet browsing on cell phones, particularly newer and larger 3G/4G smartphones, is very similar to browsing from a PC. Depending on the type of device and its operating system, some or all of these risks may apply to browsing from an endpoint device:

- Interception of sensitive data if browser doesn't support SSL/Hypertext Transfer Protocol Secure (HTTPS)
- Infection by virus or other malware upon visiting a Web site

- Unsolicited or rogue IP connection requests from malicious systems on the Internet (for example, DoS attacks on the endpoint device); attempts to attach/log on to the endpoint device; or unauthorized port scans of the endpoint device

- Automatic execution of malicious Java scripts embedded in Web pages

Again, depending on the operating system and browser in use, there may be security vulnerabilities within the browser that make it susceptible to being controlled, manipulated, or subject to the risks mentioned above. For this reason, a manual or automated procedure should be used for applying security patches and updates to the endpoint device.

E-mail

E-mail isn't quite as glamorous as some of the other messaging formats used on mobile devices. However, it's considered by many to be the de facto standard for business communication and is a common requirement for personal use devices. Today, anyone owning an endpoint device of any type has complete remote access to all e-mail.

Considering that e-mail is typically considered the lifeblood of most corporations, it's understandable that companies consider "anytime, anywhere" access to their e-mail system a must. As mobile devices have proliferated, the business world has quickly incorporated them into more of the work culture than ever before. Mobile endpoints are now considered critical components of many corporate telecommuting programs. Business continuity plans often rely on employees being able to manage corporate e-mail from mobile devices should a disaster occur. Even the idea of a workday has changed somewhat with employees routinely checking company e-mail after work hours and throughout weekends.

Security Risks with Mobile E-mail

E-mail on mobile devices faces many of the same security risks as e-mail on wired stations such as laptops and desktops. Unsolicited e-mail containing attachments can pose a risk of virus or malware infection on the endpoint device.

One of the biggest risks to e-mail on mobile endpoints, though, is the increased potential for physical theft of the device. Since so many people store the passwords to their e-mail accounts on their phones, it's often easy for a thief to gain access to those accounts on a stolen device. When you combine the facts that corporate e-mail is more readily accessible and sensitive information is often transmitted by e-mail, the risk of theft is even more significant. To help protect e-mail communications on a stolen phone, IT departments can remotely wipe a phone to remove access and data. By the time they do this, however, it may already be too late.

Instant Messaging (IM) Chat

Instant messaging is a popular messaging format on mobile devices because it tends to fill the niche between e-mailing and texting. Like text messaging, it provides the satisfaction of "real-time" communications and its short messaging-like format lends itself well to smaller mobile device screens. Like e-mail, it has the ability to exchange files (although MMS messaging can also partially address this need) and usually has more features than texting, such as emoticons. The only real challenge to IM becoming more prevalent is that it isn't as universally compatible as e-mail and texting are. Each IM service usually has a proprietary client that is required to talk to its users, and even though some "multiservice" IM clients exist, none supports every IM service.

Security Risks with IM Chat

Even though many instant messaging services support the ability to encrypt a conversation as well as provide other controls like disabling file transfers, there are still some inherent risks associated with IM. First is that relatively few antivirus programs integrate with IM clients—leaving open the possibility that viruses could propagate easily through IM networks. This is an even greater risk when file transfer capabilities are used.

Second, many IM services rely on advertisements (adware) displayed within the client to subsidize the free use of the IM service. Considering the lack of antivirus protection discussed above, this is a significant risk because adware is becoming a widely used format for distributing malicious code.

SMS/Text Messaging

Text messaging, or **Short Message Service (SMS)**, is easily the most popular form of data communications on mobile devices today and, according to a number of reporting agencies, is also the most widely used form of any type on cell phone, including voice calls. The likely reason for this popularity is that texting is easy and is compatible across all cell phones and networks. There's no real evidence at this time that texting/SMS capabilities are driving any form of advancement in mobile device or cellular technology. Messages are extremely small in footprint and don't consume many network resources nor do they require advanced software or capabilities. If texting contributes any advancement at all, it likely will be higher sales of cell phones for the sole purpose of texting and revenue generated by subscriptions to texting/SMS plans through the cellular provider.

Security Risks with SMS/Text Messaging

From a security perspective, texting is subject to fewer risks than other communications methods. The primary issue to date has been physical security concerns around texting while driving—which many states have now made illegal. A second risk, typically posed by business phone use and corporations, is that very few monitoring solutions exist to prevent users from texting sensitive information, in plaintext, outside the company.

Because text messages are very simple and lightweight, there is very little chance that they will be conduits for viruses, hackers, and the like. One of the few findings, published in Apple Support article HT3754, is the theoretical chance that a denial of service (DoS) attack would be used to interrupt SMS services within a particular cell range. In real-world terms, that could translate to the inability of some types of emergency services to receive text alerts. With the very small chance that such an attack would be a success and performed at exactly the right time of an emergency, the security industry considers the risk fairly low. A second finding by IBM Internet Security Systems determined that a properly crafted SMS message might allow an attacker to take control of an iPhone or Google Android phone. Both providers issued patches for their phones.

MMS Messaging

Multimedia Messaging Service (MMS) messaging is very similar to texting. It's an extension of SMS, except that MMS is designed to allow the sharing of multimedia data, such as pictures, rather than just text. In addition to photos, it also supports the delivery of video, text pages, and ringtones. Consumers use MMS mostly to send and receive photos taken by camera-enabled phones. However, commercial uses include services such as companies who send news alerts (text plus graphics) and security systems that send text plus graphics alarm messages to offsite monitoring companies.

Security Risks of MMS Messaging

Because MMS is very similar to SMS in being a point-to-point short messaging method, it shares many risks with SMS, such as DoS or interception of plaintext messages. Commercial products are available to enhance MMS with encryption (especially for use when sending MMS messages into a more sensitive environment such as an e-mail system), but these products are rarely used by consumers, who make up the majority of the MMS user base. Like SMS, MMS resides within a cellular network and has limited functionality, so it too has relatively few security threats or vulnerabilities that would result in compromised sensitive data. The exception is when users are in roaming areas away from their home network. In this case, SMS and MMS messaging may traverse the Internet.

Endpoint Device Communication Risks, Threats, and Vulnerabilities

Some of the risks, threats, and vulnerabilities associated with the various communications methods have already been mentioned in their specific sections earlier in this chapter. However, as a result of combining one or more of those communications methods in one device, there can be cumulative or shared risks to the endpoint device.

Table 12-3 recaps some of the security shortcomings of endpoint device communications that were defined in earlier sections.

TABLE 12-3 Summary of endpoint communication risks, threats, and vulnerabilities.

TYPE OF COMMUNICATION	POSSIBLE DENIAL OF SERVICE	POSSIBLE DATA COMPROMISE	POSSIBLE VIRUS OR MALWARE INFECTION	OTHER THREATS AND VULNERABILITIES
Voice	3G—Not likely 4G—Yes	No	No	Eavesdropping
Internet browsing	Yes	Yes	Yes	Embedded Java scripts; phishing
E-mail	Not likely	Yes	Yes	Phishing
IM chat	Not likely	Yes	Yes	Control of system via file-sharing and so on
SMS/text Messaging	Yes	Possible but not likely	No	Interception/viewing of plaintext message
MMS messaging	Yes	Possible but not likely	Yes	Interception/viewing of plaintext message

An example of "combined" risk is a device that has both e-mail (with encryption capabilities) and MMS messaging. The e-mail would normally be safe due to the encryption, but if the device is infected by malware or a virus through MMS, then the e-mail, as well as any other applications on the device, could possibly be compromised. Even if each communication method uses its own separate connection or client to reach other people, the device and its operating system are a common link among all those methods. Securing four communication methods but leaving one unsecured raises the possibility that the unsecured communication method could be compromised, putting the entire device, its data, and other communication applications at risk.

Securing an endpoint device should be done in a fashion that adequately protects it from any and all risks. Users should determine where the most sensitive type of data or communication is within the device and secure it accordingly. Next, secure the remaining applications or communications methods to the same level as the most sensitive one. If a particular application or communication method is not needed, disable it. If an application or communication method is needed but can't be secured properly to ensure the safety of the other applications and the device, then look for as many alternative or compensating security measures as available. Security is most effective when implemented in layers. Therefore, adding a single security measure might seem insignificant, but it will play a part with all the other controls, acting together to protect the endpoint device.

A similar approach can be taken with the underlying networks and services that support endpoints and communications. For existing services like 3G and Wi-Fi, pay attention to the specific implementation or version that is being offered and the security strengths and shortcomings that exist. Often providers market the version or "flavor" of the service with the best features and lead the consumer to believe those features exist in all versions of the product. Considering that there are many versions within each major generation of cellular service, it's particularly important to know what type of 3G or 4G service your carrier provides. For instance, 3G supports formats such as GSM, Enhanced Data Rates for GSM Evolution (EDGE), and Code Division Multiple Access (CDMA). 4G will support Long Term Evolution (LTE), Ultra Mobile Broadband (UMB), and WiMAX, as well as offshoot Digital Enhanced Cordless Telecommunications (DECT).

The Open Web Application Security Project Top 10 Mobile Risks

The use of mobile devices carries with it many potential risks. These risks are as important for corporate IT managers to understand as for everyday mobile users. The loss of data and privacy associated with a mobile breach is a significant concern, and given the billions of mobile users worldwide, malicious users find the opportunity too great to pass up.

To help understand these risks, the Open Web Application Security Project (OWASP) has published its top 10 list of risks associated with mobile devices and remote computing. These risks are summarized below.

1. Weak Server-Side Controls

Weak server-side controls are not directly related to a mobile device vulnerability but rather to a server-side vulnerability that can be exploited through a mobile device. An incorrectly configured or inaccurately secured server—Web server, file server, authentication server, or other type—may allow a mobile device to launch an attack. The server-side vulnerabilities correspond to the list of threats identified by OWASP as known vulnerabilities. A list of known and potentially harmful vulnerabilities is shown in Table 12-4.

2. Unsecure Data Storage

Many mobile users store very sensitive data on portable devices. Some of this data they are aware of, such as files and images. As for other items, such as cookies or log files, most users are unaware that they even exist and so have no idea what they may contain. Information such as usernames, passwords, account numbers, codes, and messages, as well as pictures, appointments, and much more, is commonly held on portable devices. In the event of a stolen device, a thief may be able to gain access to some or all of this data. This is known as **unsecure data storage**. It is a significant concern and can lead to identify theft and financial loss.

TABLE 12-4 Server-side vulnerabilities.

THREAT	THREAT DESCRIPTION	MITIGATING STRATEGY
Injection	Injection flaws enable the attacker to bypass applications' access controls and create, change, delete, or read any data the application can access.	Require input validation, verifying all data that is received. This helps prevent malicious data from entering an application.
Broken authentication and session management	Compromised authentication strategies lead to data loss.	Develop strong password policies and secure session ID management.
Cross-site scripting (XSS)	Malicious scripts are applied to the Web server but run on the client browser. With XSS, attempts are made to execute malicious code by injecting it and running it on the client browser.	Educate users in how to identify questionable links; restrict access to high-risk sites.
Insecure direct object references	Attacker can access and abuse object references, or unprotected files or folders.	Ensure that the ability to traverse folders and files is locked down.
Security misconfiguration	Applications or hardware may have settings and configurations that create security risks.	Harden applications by removing or controlling access to non-essential functions and features.
Sensitive data exposure	Sensitive data such as credit card numbers, research secrets, student records, personal information, banking data, and employee records may be accidentally released or captured.	Understand what data is sensitive, where it is stored, and who has access to it.
Missing function level access control	Security issues may arise when a user is authenticated to a network, system, or application, but individual function access is not controlled.	Test systems to ensure that the right levels of permissions are set to each system and application.
Cross-site request forgery	CSRF attacks exploit a Web site's "trust" of the user's browser.	Log out of Web sites when finished and effectively store usernames and passwords.

continued

TABLE 12-4 Server-side vulnerabilities, *continued.*

THREAT	THREAT DESCRIPTION	MITIGATING STRATEGY
Unvalidated redirects and forwards	A trusted URL domain may be modified with unvalidated URL data by someone using links to redirect a user to a malicious site. Once the redirect has occurred, the attacker may steal user credentials or have users download a malicious application.	Limit the use of redirects, especially 302 temporary redirects. Use a whitelist to control where redirects can go.
Malicious file execution	Applications can be executed on the Web server or remote system.	Ensure appropriate input validation.
Information leakage and improper error message handling	Attackers gain information from error logs and messages.	Secure error messages and develop policies restricting access to error reports.
Insecure cryptographic storage	Sensitive data are stored in plaintext.	Use encryption protocols to ensure that no captured data can be read.
Insecure communications	Network communications are sent in cleartext. All captured data can be read.	Use security protocols to secure transmissions in transit.
Failure to restrict URL access	This is similar to unsecure direct object reference: An attacker may browse unprotected areas and data.	Lock down files, folders, and directories to ensure unwanted viewers cannot access them.

When protecting data on a mobile device, try assuming that at some point your mobile device will be either lost or stolen. This mindset will help ensure you follow strong security practices. The following are some things you should routinely do:

- Use encryption on the device to ensure that stored data is unavailable and not stored in cleartext.
- Use authentication for logging onto all mobile devices.
- Do not store passwords or other sensitive data in cleartext.
- Lock the mobile device and set applications to log you out after a period of time.
- Research and use mobile security software to protect against malware and intrusion.

- Ensure that the mobile device operating system and applications are up to date.

- Ensure that encryption methods are used when synchronizing data to the cloud or other storage media.

- Wipe all data and storage when disposing of the mobile device.

- Ensure that if all else fails and the device is lost or stolen, you are able to wipe it remotely.

> ⚠ **WARNING**
>
> Many people use the auto-fill option on their smartphones. This allows the phone to remember usernames and passwords so they do not need to be typed in each time. If auto-fill is set and the phone is stolen, however, this gives easy access to banking sites or other sites with a stored password. It is a best practice to avoid convenience and retype the username and password in each time you access a site.

3. Insufficient Transport Layer Protection

Some years ago, an incident occurred in which several users were connecting wirelessly to an unsecured wireless access point from their rooms in a well-known hotel. While the wireless access point was open, many users were using this connection instead of the one offered by the hotel. The transmissions sent and received using this connection were being captured and monitored by malicious users. Over several months, a large amount of personal and business data was stolen.

The example above highlights the dangers of **insufficient Transport Layer protection**— the lack of security when data is in transit. Today, any mobile device may be busy inputting and outputting data using either a carrier network or a Wi-Fi connection. The type of connection can greatly affect your mobile security. As a best practice, don't check banking information or other data-sensitive sites from public Wi-Fi connections, such as those in coffee shops or airports. These public connections are for convenience and not security. If you must check your bank balance remotely, turn off your Wi-Fi and use your telephone connection, which is much more difficult to intercept.

Further, you can check personal accounts more securely from a mobile device by using the institution's specifically designed app rather than open surfing or other methods such as e-mail. Official applications for investment sites, banks, and retailers are designed with security in mind. Owners of such sites go to great lengths to help secure communications. It is a good idea to go directly to the institution's Web site to ensure you are downloading the latest and recommended app for your mobile device.

There are also various mobile applications that can be used to help secure communications. One such app available for both Apple mobile devices and Android devices is wickr. Wickr is designed as a tool to secure and encrypt messages from end to end, and as an added feature, a self-destruct time can be set for messages and content, including images and attachments. A message can be configured for deletion at any point from 3 seconds to 6 days away. Each message sent from a mobile device is encrypted with a unique key stored directly on the mobile device itself. Other encryption systems store information on the Web server. This is part of wickr's zero-knowledge system designed to protect user messages even if wickr's servers are compromised.

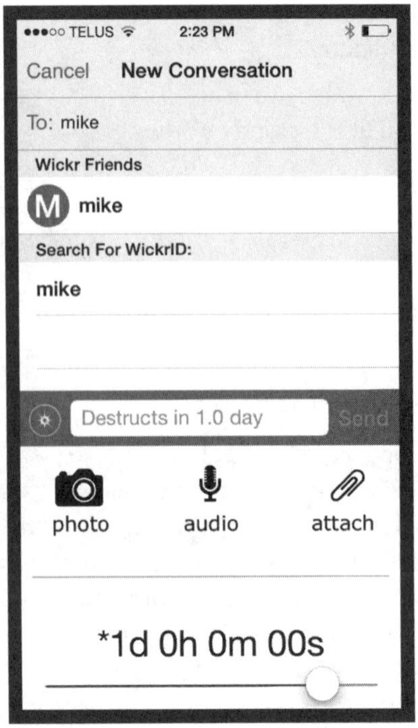

FIGURE 12-3

Using message and self-destruct options with wickr.

It's necessary to research Apps such wickr carefully; however, using such a system can go a long way in protecting cleartext messaging. Figure 12-3 shows configuration screens from the wickr application.

⚠ **WARNING**

A network user in a manufacturing environment was in the habit of cutting and pasting his passwords between form fields on his computer. This included the password for his banking site. A colleague using his computer one day found that he had unintentionally pasted the computer owner's banking password into a Microsoft Word document. Fortunately, there was no malicious intent in this case. But it shows how easily unintended data leakage can occur.

4. Unintended Data Leakage

Unintended data leakage can occur when sensitive data is stored on a device and accessed by a malicious user using malware or other means. Many people try to keep their sensitive data to a minimum, but it is very possible to overlook some potential leakage sources.

From time to time, an application or processes may store sensitive data in an unsecure location on a mobile device. Leakage occurs when this unsecure location is accessed by a malicious user either using an application or by stealing the device. Examples of common data leakage sources include:

- URL caching
- Copy/paste caching
- Application logs
- Cookies

FYI

Data leakage is a serious concern with children using apps on mobile devices or social networking sites. Testing the level of personal information leaving a home, and ensuring that everyone using family computers understands what is and isn't acceptable to share, are good practices for all households.

Another form of data leakage occurs when you sign up for applications without knowing which types of data they have access to and remaining signed up long after you are no longer using them. There are many applications that can test vulnerability in this area. One such application available for Apple and Android is MyPermissions.

MyPermissions enables a user to query social networks such as Facebook, Google, flickr, Yahoo, or Twitter. Once you log on to one of these services, you will be shown a list of Apps that can access your personal information. Figure 12-4 shows the screenshot of the review of a Facebook account.

Once you identify the various apps, you can review the types of personal data to which they have access. Figure 12-5 shows the personal information access for the Xbox Live Social Experience.

Once you've reviewed the app, you can revoke its access to personal information, trust the app, or report the app as shown in Figure 12-6.

FIGURE 12-4

Review of Facebook apps using MyPermissions.

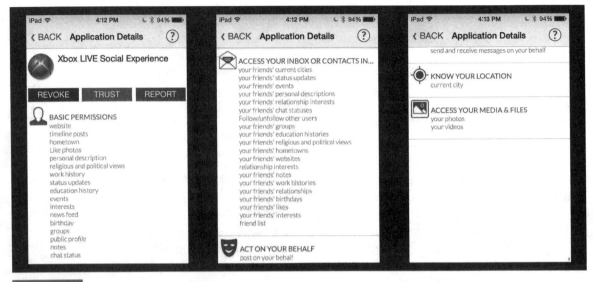

FIGURE 12-5

Reviewing personal data in Facebook apps.

FIGURE 12-6

Reviewing personal
data access.

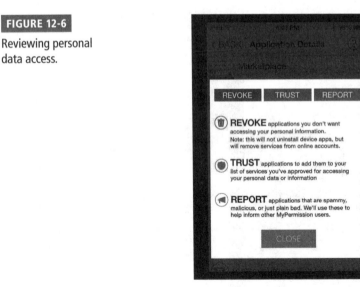

5. Poor Authorization and Authentication

Poor authorization and authentication is a very common threat. Where this condition exists, an adversary can anonymously execute functionality within the mobile app or back end server the mobile app uses. *Authentication* refers to the methods used to verify that a person should have access to a particular application, device, or service. Authentication is often a username and password combination, biometrics, or a visual pattern, such as with certain applications and Android devices. *Authorization* is the access and permissions a user has once he or she is authenticated.

Authentication for mobile devices can occur when you log on to a device, when you access an application on a device, and—on the server side—when you access a service on a Web server. Poor authentication on the client side occurs when you don't use usernames and passwords or use weak ones. Various forms of attacks are used to capture client-side authentications. You can protect against by using password polices and a series of best practices for business and home users.

On the server or service side, it's important to ensure that appropriate levels of authentication and authorization are in place. Developers manage this, not the end user. If a developer creates a mobile app or ports one over from a traditional Web app, the developer must ensure that authentication and authorization methods must be in place. Often, developers use mobile device hardware identifiers as a form of authentication. For example, the Unique Device Identifier (UUID) on Apple devices is used as to identify and authenticate a device. The number can also be used to blacklist devices. However, this is weak authentication, as the UUID can be easily spoofed so the device will not display its actual UUID.

In another example, the International Mobile Station Equipment Identity (IMEI) is a number assigned to mobile devices as an identifier. The IMEI number has two primary purposes: to identify the mobile device and to prevent the use of a device if it's stolen. Devices are trackable because IMEI numbers are hard-coded into device hardware, making it difficult to change a device's IMEI. However, if this unique number is used in an authentication or authorization scheme and the number is compromised, not only would access be gained but changing the identifier, even with a factory reset, would not be an option.

> **NOTE**
> Want to see your IMEI number? On an iPhone, click Settings>General>About or (for some carriers) dial *#06#.

6. Broken Cryptography

Many applications may be vulnerable to **broken cryptography**, which occurs when the data on a mobile device is not encrypted properly. According to OWASP, the mobile app may use a process behind the encryption/decryption that is fundamentally flawed and very weak. This refers to how encryption keys are used, stored and maintained.

FIGURE 12-7

Listing recent MD5 cracks.

A second cause of broken cryptography results from using encryption methods with known vulnerabilities. The result is that the encryption/decryption is vulnerable to cracking software. For example, if MD5 is used as a security encryption solution there may be vulnerability. MD5 can be exploited using readily available tools. The Web site *http://www.hashkiller.co.uk/* lists and maintains a database of cracked MD5 hashes. The site also offers utilities for SHA1, WPA, and NTLM. Figure 12-7 shows the homepage of the hashkiller website.

7. Client-Side Injection

As the name suggests, a **client-side injection attack** looks for vulnerabilities on mobile devices, often by executing malicious code from within a mobile application. Like any other computer, the mobile device stores the data needed for application retrieval. This information may include user credentials, financial information, contact information, invoices, and more. Because of the sensitive nature of this information, it's a prime target for attackers.

Like Web applications, mobile devices have back-end databases for storage of data. Database options such as Realm, Core Data, and SQLite may be used in the back end on mobile devices. These databases may be susceptible to injection attacks similar to Web applications and services. In the case of SQLite, a SQL injection attack "injects" or manipulates SQL code within the mobile device. There are many forms of injection-flaw attacks that enable the attacker to bypass access controls and create, change, delete, or read any data the application can access.

8. Security Decisions Via Untrusted Inputs

The **security decisions via untrusted inputs** vulnerability refers to making security decisions on potentially untrusted sources. In most cases, this risk refers to a communications mechanism known as the **interprocess communications (IPC)**. IPC is a tool designed for developers to allow communication and sharing of data between applications. Some of the devices you use on a daily basis—Web servers, for example—use IPC to share Web-based documents and media with users through a Web browser.

Many key processes using IPC to share information between applications may be running in the background. For example, pipes and named pipes provide a service to exchange messages between processes over a network. The message queue is a list of memory segments where processes a can store and retrieve data. It's also possible for applications with the same back end to share authentication and security tokens.

The ability to share communications between processes is valuable and efficient, but weak implementation of an IPC mechanism can lead to untrusted inputs. For example, someone might launch a denial of service (DoS) attack taking advantage of IPC communication between processes.

Most end users both at home and in the corporate environment are likely not aware of back-end vulnerabilities in their favorite mobile apps. This is why in a corporate and business environment, companies typically tightly control the applications that can be installed on company-issued phones.

9. Improper Session Handling

A *session* is the tracking of requests and communications between the Web server and, in this case, a mobile app. **Improper session handling** refers to an application that leaves a session open or unsecured, creating a vulnerability. Common protocols used to establish a session include HTML and **Simple Object Access Protocol (SOAP)**, which are stateless by design. A stateless protocol does not require the server to retain information or status about each user for the duration of multiple requests. However, this may be required by any app that requires features such as customized content and user specific information. This may include a calendar app, fitness app, or any other program that uses specific user data. So Web and mobile applications must create and manage the session themselves. Two popular ways that Web sites arrange a session are by creating cookies and by creating a random string of characters in the URL or Web address. Both methods create a unique identifier for you that can be passed on as you browse and use the Web site.

In this process, applications use a session token. The session token is a unique identifier generated and sent from a server to a client to identify the current interaction session. The client usually stores and sends the token as an HTTP cookie or browser cookie. If the session tokens are not properly protected, an attacker can hijack an active session and assume the identity of a user. Also, unless all authentication credentials and session identifiers are protected with Secure Sockets Layer or other encryption methods, an attacker can hijack a user's session and identity.

To help protect against tokens being stolen during a session, mobile app developers create timeouts that limit the session time. For example, if a banking app sits idle for 10 minutes, the session will close and the user will need to reauthenticate. Session timeouts vary depending on the sensitive nature of the application. This helps prevent an unauthorized user from gaining access to an existing session and assuming the role of the authorized user. If you use an app that does not time out, it's a best practice to ensure that you log out when you're not using the app.

10. Lack of Binary Protections

The **lack of binary protections vulnerability** refers to an attacker's ability to gain access to the underlying code of an application, analyze it, reverse-engineer it, and then modify the program. Once the app has been rewritten with the new malicious code, the attacker has access to the personal information within the app. Unfortunately, maintaining integrity of apps is not an easy task, and while secure coding plays a huge role, coding alone cannot secure against this type of attack. Tools are readily available online that allow users to read underlying code and attempt to reverse-engineer a program.

Best Practices for Securing Endpoint Device Communications

Based on the risks, threats, and vulnerabilities discussed earlier, this section covers some best practices for securing mobile endpoint devices using technological and physical controls. Many of these security measures are based on components common to most cellular endpoint devices and carriers. If an endpoint device has more features than those mentioned in this chapter, then more comprehensive controls may be necessary. Check with the endpoint manufacturer for the features available for the specific device and any additional recommended security features.

Technological Security of Devices

Because there are different types of controls that can help secure devices and communications, this section is divided into three sections: Applications and Systems, Configuration Changes, and Actions and Practices.

Applications and Systems That Provide Security

- Ensure the browser supports SSL for entering or transmitting sensitive information to/from a Web site.

- Ensure an antivirus client is installed and configured to automatically scan all incoming files.

- Ensure antimalware/anti-spyware capabilities are installed and configured to monitor as many communication methods as they are capable of integrating with.

- Install a personal firewall or similar packet-filtering measure on the endpoint device to protect against unsolicited inbound connections or communications, for example, DoS attacks, incoming probes/scans of services, and so on.

- Use services or software that provides encrypted transmissions:

  - **Voice**—Most cellular voice services are now encrypted. Be sure any VoIP or voice-over-data applications can encrypt their transmissions.

  - **Internet browsing**—When logging onto or viewing sensitive information on Web sites, be sure the site is enabled for SSL/HTTPS. Look for the "lock" icon on your browser's menu or status bars; check that the Web site address starts with "https."

  - **E-mail**—Install message or file encryption software on the device for sending sensitive information in an e-mail. Freeware encryption software is available for most e-mail clients.

  - **IM chat**—Use IM services or programs that offer encrypted, or "private," connections to recipients.

  - **SMS texting/MMS**—If using a traditional cell phone, check that the carrier encrypts SMS and MMS transmissions. For PDA and smartphones, install and use an SMS or MMS application that supports encrypted messaging.

Configuration Changes That Provide Security

- Disable unnecessary browser functions such as Java script support to prevent the browser from automatically executing malicious scripts embedded in Web sites.

- Use proxy servers or services when possible. Proxy servers sit between the endpoint device and other systems, receiving and resending all incoming and outgoing traffic. This can add an additional layer of protection against viruses and malicious code as well as provide extra logging capabilities for troubleshooting or investigations.

- If the device's user is unfamiliar with identifying phishing uniform resource locators (URLs), implement any anti-phishing capabilities the browser or anti-malware/virus client may offer.

Actions and Practices That Provide Security

- Don't respond to communications that are unfamiliar or unsolicited. Phishing attacks and spam or unsolicited e-mail messages are often used to attract users to malicious Web sites or disclose sensitive information.
- Be cautious about sending e-mail, SMS, and MMS to multiple recipients. Sending "bulk" messages increases the likelihood of error, such as sending the message to a wrong person.

As 4G networks emerge and compete, some providers may offer built-in or add-on Internet security features similar to those some Internet providers offer to home users. These "value-added" Internet services might provide proxied Internet access through a security gateway device. Similar to what some corporate networks provide, the gateway/proxy might perform all the services mentioned above without having to install a client on the device itself.

Physical Security of Devices

In addition to the more technology-related security risks mentioned above, another area of risk is equally important for endpoint devices and communications—physical security. With the number of endpoint devices in use today, the variety of places where they are used, and their value/popularity, it's no surprise that the risk of lost or stolen systems is increasing. Fortunately, solid solutions and practices can significantly reduce physical security risks as well as protect the device's data in case of theft or lost equipment.

Lock the Device

The first line of defense for protecting an endpoint device should be enabling and using the password/PIN locking feature. Nearly all phones support some form of screen and keypad locking with a password or personal identification number (PIN) required to unlock the device. Many devices now support the use of longer and more complex passwords. In some countries outside the United States, cell phones are even being equipped with fingerprint readers for biometric authentication.

Ideally, passwords on endpoint devices should be constructed according to the same recommendations for systems like laptops, desktops, and servers. Passwords should not contain complete words or be predictable but should instead contain a random combination of eight or more lower and upper case characters, numbers, and special symbols.

Quite often, though, it's more difficult to enter such complex, or strong, passwords on mobile endpoint devices because accessing those characters on smaller keypads can be a challenge. Short of using a complex password as mentioned above, the following practices should be followed at a minimum for mobile endpoint devices:

- Don't use plain English words in the password.

- Don't use passwords with predictable groups of characters (like "qwerty," the top row of keys on a keyboard starting from left to right).

- Create a password or PIN with at least six characters.

- Choose a sentence with at least eight words and use the first letter from each word in the sentence. Example, for the sentence "The quick brown fox jumped over the lazy dog," the first letter of each word would result in a password of "tqbfjotld."

Device Encryption

Whole-drive, or whole-device, encryption is a popular method for mitigating the effects of a lost or stolen endpoint device. Once considered too costly and difficult to implement, encryption technology has become so affordable and efficient that it likely soon will be standard on devices. Device encryption is designed to encrypt the entire device (or at least its storage mechanism) so that the device is rendered inaccessible when away from its owner. Even though device encryption is a very useful measure, it does not completely replace the need for "data" encryption, which is mentioned elsewhere in this chapter. Data encryption techniques (such as VPNs, SSL, 3G/4G cellular encryption, and software applications to encrypt e-mail/SMS/MMS messages) are still necessary to protect the device and its communications while in use by the device's owner.

The increase in laptop use, and the subsequent rise in laptop theft/loss, over the past few years have prompted major advancements in the encryption product industry. While there is no absolute way to protect mobile devices from theft, encryption affords a user or company comfort in knowing that data on a stolen or lost device will be inaccessible to unauthorized parties. Most encryption software can now protect an entire drive or system with extremely strong key strengths yet have minimal impact on the performance of the device. Vendors like GuardianEdge, SecuBox, and Check Point produce encryption products specifically for endpoint devices like smartphones and PDAs.

Some desirable features to look for in endpoint encryption software include:

- The ability to centrally manage encryption keys, which are needed to access the device should the encryption software have a malfunction, the device is transferred to a different user, and so on. In addition to issuing and storing keys, a good encryption solution should also allow for easy revoking and/or replacing of encryption keys. Keys are like passwords and should be changed periodically to prevent the possibility of the key becoming compromised and rendering the encryption useless.

- Use of strong encryption keys, a minimum 256-bit or higher. If the device can support it without a significant impact to performance, it's best to use 1,024-bit encryption or higher because the 256-bit minimum eventually will be insufficient.

- The ability to encrypt not only the device itself but also other storage options, that is, SD chips and thumb drives.

Remote Erasure/Reset

In addition to encryption, many organizations also implement software that allows a central administrator to erase or hard-reset an endpoint device remotely. Even though encryption is a very strong protective measure for endpoints, there is always the possibility that a malicious user, with enough time and computing power, could crack an encryption routine and access the device. Although encryption provides very good protection immediately after a device is lost or stolen, erasing or resetting the device is the only guaranteed method of ensuring that the device's data will never be accessible again. As an added benefit, remote resetting of a device can also be used as an IT support tool for fixing devices that can't be brought back in for servicing.

Disabling Integrated Cameras

In corporate environments, especially sensitive ones like data centers, it's often necessary to disable cameras or webcams that may be integrated into the endpoint device. This minimizes the risk that the device will be used to view or transmit sensitive information. On occasion, IT support teams will use devices with webcams to capture and send pictures of error messages or configuration screens to an offsite vendor support person. This is a legitimate use of endpoint communications, but the same technology can be maliciously used in the wrong hands. Disabling cameras doesn't completely eliminate the risk of distributing sensitive data, but it can reduce the risk by making malicious activity more difficult. For example, disclosing the contents of a configuration screen would take significantly longer to type and send by e-mail, IM, or SMS than it would with a photo of the screen.

Inventory and Backup of the Device

If a device is lost or stolen, it's important to have the serial number, make and model, and other information available. Recovering the device will obviously depend heavily upon such information. However, even if the device is not recovered, authorities can use the information to identify trends and determine if other users of the same model in the same area, should be notified. Vendors sometimes use trending data to determine if additional protections are needed.

Backing up the device is also an important security measure—not only for the ability to regain access to data but also to have a copy of important data such as configuration files and logs. The lost or stolen device, or its applications may have had special access to other systems or data. Having a full backup may provide information necessary to help protect other systems or data from being compromised, especially if the lost or stolen device wasn't encrypted. An example might be: A stolen smartphone had a VoIP software package installed. Upon restoring the backup to a new device, the owner is able to contact the VoIP service provider and change account information such as login passwords, preventing the thief from using the victim's VoIP service.

CHAPTER SUMMARY

The definition of an endpoint device is constantly changing to include advancements in technology. The technology boom of the 1990s and 2000s produced numerous special-purpose devices such as PDAs, pagers, cell phones, and computers. As data and voice communications have matured, consumers are demanding that these devices be connected, yet remain mobile. Users want the capability of a desktop and mobility of a cell phone to fit in the space of a wallet or purse. The desire for such functionality and flexibility brings great innovation.

In the not-so-long-ago era of dial-up modems and five-pound cell phones, it was almost unthinkable that computers might wirelessly access the Internet at LAN speeds. However, the telecommunications industry provided us in 2001 with global wireless speeds comparable to modems (3G) and now is using technology and networks (4G) to combine LAN speeds with cellular mobility. All forms of communication (voice, texting, chatting, e-mail) are quickly becoming "always on" and "always available." It's to be expected that with such robust communications every new device now strives to be "connected." With convenience driving advancements in communications, it's only logical that users would want devices influenced by the trend toward convenience. Tablets, cell phones, and laptops now provide nearly the same features to their respective audiences: wireless voice calling, live video streaming, text and e-mail communications, and Internet browsing, to name just a few.

Innovation breeds capability. In the technological world, that translates into a need for improved security. The ability to move packets faster, exchange more messages, store more data, and do all of these activities for longer time periods presents new risks. Because of new Web services and software applications, people store and process more sensitive information on endpoint mobile devices now than ever before. Fortunately, security is now a much more familiar topic and is attempting to keep pace equally with computers and communications. Security controls such as VPNs, encryption techniques, firewalls, and anti-malware applications have often affected functionality due to their need for high data transfer speeds or computing power. 3G and 4G networks are certainly starting to address the need for faster data transfers as well as to allow for more network-based security measures. For example, cellular networks are encrypting traffic rather than forcing devices to support processor-intensive software. Computing power in endpoint devices has also increased so that they can now leverage many of the existing security applications and products that desktop computers do—lowering the cost and effort to better secure endpoint devices.

KEY CONCEPTS AND TERMS

Broken cryptography
Client-side injection attack
Convergence
Endpoint device
Improper session handling
Insufficient Transport Layer
    protection
Interprocess communications
    (IPC)

Lack of binary protections
    vulnerability
Mobile broadband
Multimedia Messaging Service
    (MMS)
Poor authorization and
    authentication
Security decisions via untrusted
    inputs vulnerability

Short Message Service (SMS)
Simple Object Access Protocol
    (SOAP)
Unintended data leakage
Unsecure data storage
Weak server-side controls

CHAPTER 12 ASSESSMENT

1. Which two security risks apply to IM chatting?
   (Select two.)

   A. Theft of device
   B. Possible data compromise
   C. Viruses and malware
   D. Denial of service (DoS)

2. 3G networks use packet-switching to route
   voice calls.

   A. True
   B. False

3. _____ is a form of messaging used to share
   pictures, text pages, and ringtones.

4. 4G network speeds are comparable to DSL
   and cable modem Internet services.

   A. True
   B. False

5. Which of the following risks does not apply
   to Internet browsing?

   A. Viruses and malware
   B. Physical theft
   C. Phishing
   D. Java script execution

6. _____ is the threat related to voice
   communications and involves an unauthorized
   party listening in on conversations.

7. The term *endpoint* is typically used to describe
   what type of device?

   A. A device with large storage capacity
   B. A device with server capabilities
   C. A device that is no longer being manufactured
   D. A device that is connected to a public
      or private network

8. What is the minimum strength recommended
   for whole-device encryption?

   A. 144 Kbps
   B. 256-bit
   C. 248-bit
   D. There is no minimum.

9. The term _____ describes the merging of
   various types of devices and technologies into
   a common or single form.

10. Which two controls provide physical security
   for devices? (Select two.)

   A. VPN
   B. Locking the device
   C. Remote erasure
   D. Proxy servers

11. A handoff, or the transfer of communications from one cell to another, was a significant factor regarding the mobility and popularity of cellular phones.

    A. True
    B. False

12. Which form of communication is compatible across nearly all cellular networks and is widely considered to be the most often used communication method, by quantity, on today's phones?

    A. SMS Texting
    B. Voice over IP
    C. Text-to-speech
    D. File transfer

13. Which of these mobile risks are included among the OWASP Top 10? (Choose three.)

    A. Weak Server-Side Controls
    B. Poor Authorization and Authentication
    C. Locked Binary Protections
    D. Client-Side Injection

14. The OWASP mobile risk "Security Decisions Via Untrusted Inputs" refers to what unsecure practice?

    A. Storing sensitive data on a device which may be accessed by a malicious user using malware or other means
    B. Making security decisions on potentially untrusted sources
    C. Fundamentally flawed use, storage, and maintenance of encryption keys
    D. Tracking requests and communications between a Web server and a mobile application

15. What are two popular ways that Web sites arrange a session?

    A. By creating cookies
    B. By utilizing stateless protocols such as HTML and SOAP
    C. By storing a session identifier on the server
    D. By creating a random string of characters in the URL or Web address

12

Securing Mobile
Communications

Securing Personal and Business Communications

© Rodolfo Clix/Dreamstime.com

COMMUNICATION TODAY uses a wide variety of devices and technology, such as e-mail, SMS, and voicemail. People communicate with these devices to discuss both personal and business affairs. Security is necessary to maintain the availability, integrity, and confidentiality of these communications. Many people are somewhat overconfident that their information is secure, but that confidence may not be well founded.

Different people have different expectations of how secure their communication needs to be, but security is often lower than many people realize. This chapter will differentiate between two types of communication: store-and-forward and real-time. You will learn how devices and methods of popular communication fit into these two types. You also will gain a better appreciation of various communications threats and how to mitigate them.

Chapter 13 Topics

This chapter covers the following topics and concepts:

- What store-and-forward communication is
- What theats are associated with voicemail
- What e-mail and social networking threats exist
- What real-time communication is
- What best practices for securing telephone or private branch exchange communications are
- What best practices for securing Voice over IP communications are
- What best practices for securing unified communications are

Chapter 13 Goals

When you complete this chapter, you will be able to:

- Differentiate between store-and-forward communication and real-time communication
- Describe advantages and disadvantages of real-time and store-and-forward communications
- List best practices for securing telephone, VoIP, and Session Initiation Protocol (SIP) applications
- Highlight the threats involved in the communication methods
- Provide risk mitigation strategies across various devices

Store-and-Forward Communication

Have you ever stopped by a coworker's cubicle and started talking, but realized she is on the phone? You both note your need to talk, but she is simply not available. You have two choices at this point:

1. You can head back to your desk and then try again later when you're both free.
2. Assuming it's a question with a quick answer, you can write it on a piece of paper and give it to your coworker's assistant. Your coworker later picks up the note from the assistant and either writes the answer and has the assistant contact you, or contacts you directly. Either way, the communication is complete.

The first option is a failed attempt at communication. The second option is an example of **store-and-forward communication**.

Communication is a two-way street. There are generally two parties involved, the speaker and the listener. Unfortunately, just because one party is willing to speak doesn't mean the other party is able to listen. Store-and-forward communication is one way to handle that issue. This isn't a new phenomenon. Store-and-forward communication is any exchange in which information is temporarily kept or stored at an intermediate point. The information continues or is forwarded when the next intermediate point or the final destination is available.

This section covers many examples of how the store-and-forward technique is used for different communication methods. Some technologies such as voicemail and faxing have been around for many years, whereas others, such as messaging on social networking sites, are more recent.

Threats Associated with Voicemail

Nearly everyone in the world has enjoyed telephone conversations. Telephones are commonplace in the home, office, and, with mobile phones, basically anywhere. Telephones provide direct communication between two people. The only challenge to that communication is both parties have to be available. When that isn't possible, there's still a need for communication. What you need then is voicemail.

Years ago, it was typical that only offices would have a voicemail system. That system was central to the organization or outsourced to the telephony provider. At home, it was more common for a household to have an answering machine. Today, voicemail is routine and accessible anywhere anytime though mobile services.

Voicemail systems today are typically centralized on a voicemail server rather than on a dedicated device per phone number. Centralization creates a voicemail system capable of several new features. For example, a centralized server can handle several connections at once and provide functions that were unavailable with the old-fashioned answering machine. Centralized voicemail services are available to both business and personal users, and they offer many advanced features.

Calling voicemail directly allows you to communicate a personal message even though the recipient is away or busy. For example, the recipient may be across several time zones. Voicemail provides the benefits of a direct, personal telephone conversation without the need for both parties' synchronized availability. Being centralized, voicemail systems provide additional advanced features for distributing, transferring, and personalizing messages.

One voicemail-related service in particular is growing in popularity. This service converts received voice messages into text. The text is then sent via Short Message Service (SMS) to a designated phone number of your choosing. Many services that allow you to make voice calls over the Internet, such as Skype, provide the SMS option. The service can convert voice messages to SMS text messages that are also sent over the Internet.

> **NOTE**
>
> Many services also save voice messages to audio files, and then forward them to your e-mail address and/or make them available on a password-protected Web site.

This is especially convenient for international callers. The SMS messages can originate from one of several different countries, keeping the SMS sending fee to a minimum, if not free. For example, a person who moved from the United States to Europe uses Skype with a U.S.-based number. SMSs are sent to a primary phone number in Europe. This allows inexpensive local calling for U.S. callers to leave voice messages. Meanwhile, the message is converted to an SMS text message at little or no cost to the person in Europe. Other providers of this service are YouMail and SpinVox, and the service is also available through some home cable and telephone service packages. You'll learn more about SMS later in this chapter.

Voicemail Risks

Voicemail can be intercepted, listened to, forwarded, or deleted—all without your knowledge. With store-and-forward communication, the information is stored out of your control and is available to anyone who gains access. Listed below are a few of the potential threats associated with voicemail systems.

- **Automatic attendants**—Many companies have automatic attendants that direct calls to specific people after hours. This system will allow people to leave messages for individuals and allow employees to access their voicemail remotely. It may be possible to get the direct extension numbers of employees, dial back, and, by pressing a key (usually "#" or "*"), get to the credential system of the automatic attendant. More often than not, the password is easy to guess. Often it is 1234 or the actual last four digits of the employee's work phone number. Once in, the malicious user can check voicemail or, depending on how the system is set up, make calls from the company's phone number.

- **E-mail notifications**—In a business environment it is commonplace to get an e-mail alert or a voice message left in an e-mail. The message will be an audio file format such as a .wav file. However, it does happen that the e-mail is a spoof attack designed to have you click on the attached file, which is actually not a sound file but an executable malware file.

- **Remote checking of voicemail**—Many people call into their offices to see if they have voicemail messages. When calling in to the office, someone needs a password to access messages. If this password is compromised, it is possible to use the credentials to access potentially confidential voice messages.

- **Imposters**—Sometimes imposters leave realistic-sounding voicemails threatening consequences if a call is not returned. In the US, for example, the Federal Trade Commission listed imposter IRS calls in its list of Top 10 Consumer Complaints. In this attack, someone posing as an IRS agent leaves an urgent voicemail message threatening the subject with arrest or other grave consequences if an alleged tax violation is not remedied immediately. If the subject phones back, the scam continues, because the caller believes he or she is actually talking with the IRS.

Mitigating Voicemail Risks

Voicemail systems can provide a security risk to an organization or individual, and in many companies, e-mail scams and threats are often overlooked. There are a few commonsense steps that can help protect against voicemail threats. These include:

- Creating policies requiring passwords that are difficult to guess
- Educating users on potential e-mail scams involving voicemail sent to e-mail accounts
- Deleting or disabling unused voicemail accounts
- Restricting long-distance or 900-number calls from office phones

FYI

As an IT administrator managing mobile devices, you must be concerned about security. Often, if a device is lost, it is possible to locate it by tracking, and if not, once the device is activated, it can be wiped clean. All e-mails, voice-mail, and data are removed. Further, most companies will have usage policies governing what can and cannot be done with devices, such as password enforcement, and what programs can be installed. Overall, managing mobile devices and security is a very challenging task for IT administrators.

- Enforcing a password change policy so that passwords are changed periodically
- Reviewing telephone records to identify unusual activity

The security considerations don't end with the voicemail system at work; they extend to voicemails on mobile devices. Whether it is a work phone or a personal phone, many people use no PIN, or they use one that is easy to guess, to access voicemail on their mobile devices. In the case of a lost phone, this could be a significant problem.

E-mail and Social Networking Threats

E-mail Threats

E-mail is widely used and depended upon by both personal and business users. In addition, sending an e-mail to millions of people costs very little. Both of these factors make e-mail a prime vehicle for malicious behavior.

For users of e-mail there are many ways an incoming e-mail can fool, subvert, or attack the recipient and his or her computer. Some attacks rely on the user to click on a link; other attacks need only be rendered as a Hypertext Markup Language (HTML) e-mail. Still others just need to be read and believed. The following are some of the most insidious and prevalent attacks on your e-mail inbox today:

- **Pictures embedded with scripts**—A picture file is attached or inserted in the message. This attack has become especially popular. A malicious script is embedded in the picture file; when rendered, the system executes the script with elevated privileges. In the notorious case of Microsoft vulnerability "integer overflow in GDI," the script could execute arbitrary code. This code might install new programs, create new users, or delete data.

- **Phishing**—This involves an illegitimate message disguised as one from a legitimate organization, such as a bank or university. Especially common at the time of this writing are phishing attempts from social networking sites. The intent is to trick the user, perhaps to give the user's credentials or personally identifiable information.

- **419 scam**—This is a message preying on the reader's trust and greed. This attack relies only on the user's gullibility to follow instructions, such as "Send your banking details to receive 20% of a 6 MILLION DOLLAR inheritance, signed Yours sincerely, recently deceased Prince Farquah of Lagos, Nigeria." (The name comes from the number of the section of the Nigerian Criminal Code dealing with fraud.)

- **Social engineering**—This is a message taking advantage of the reader's desire to help or respond to authority. Phishing is a form of social engineering when a message seemingly from the IT department prompts users for their e-mail account password.

- **Referenced links from search engine results**—This is a relatively new method to outsmart spam filters. The provided link doesn't go direct to the malicious domain, but instead presents a well-known search engine's link. The search engine link presents results that lead the reader to the spamming pages.

- **Phony patches**—These are messages carrying phony patches or linking to Web sites with patches. The patches are not genuine but are instead malware. The deceived user installs the malware, destroying local files or installing a backdoor Trojan to allow the attacker easy remote access and control.

- **Eavesdropping**—E-mail, when sent without encryption, is subject to eavesdropping or unauthorized reading. Often this is not much more than an invasion of privacy, since the subject matter is hardly valuable to anyone besides the sender and recipient. Eavesdropping becomes a more significant threat, however, if the information is actively used. This leads to the last threat, spoofing.

- **Spoofing or forging**—When an e-mail is sent under the guise of being from someone else, this is an invasion of privacy and integrity. If the recipient believes the message is from someone trustworthy or in authority, the impact is more damaging.

The preceding list describes e-mail threats that exist regardless of e-mail client, spam filter software, or other layered defenses. Most of the listed e-mail attacks are successful whether the message is in plaintext or HTML. However, the attractive presentation of e-mail has become more appealing to users. Rendering e-mail in HTML may look good, but the e-mail client uses the same code to display HTML-based messages as a Web browser uses to display Web pages. Those HTML-based messages are prone to the same attacks that take advantage of Web pages. Viewing messages in plaintext reduces your chances of becoming a victim of some e-mail attacks. For example, an attack relying on pictures embedded with a script is ineffective if the recipient uses only plaintext e-mail. Although e-mail has matured over the years, the threats remain remarkably simple and effective.

E-mail Mitigation Techniques

A valuable defense against e-mail threats is user awareness. Still, other defensive measures are most effective when targeting a certain kind of attack or threat. Table 13-1 associates threats with effective mitigation techniques.

13

Securing Personal and
Business Communications

TABLE 13-1 Threats and mitigation techniques.

THREAT	MITIGATION TECHNIQUE
Phishing and social engineering, e.g., 419 scams	Increase user awareness of these threats
Eavesdropping	Implement encryption
Spoofing or forging	Add nonrepudiation with digital signatures
Pictures with embedded scripts	Use plaintext e-mail or ensure antivirus is up-to-date
Referenced links to malicious sites and phony patches	Use plaintext e-mail, increase user awareness, and use modern spam filtering

Messaging on Social Networking Sites

A social networking site exists to create and maintain connections with people. This is like networking in the real world, for example at a conference or cocktail party.

Connecting with new people and the people connected to them offers new opportunities personally and professionally. Examples range from finding a new job, new relationship partner, or new friendship to reuniting with lost friends. The added value of a social networking site is being able to socialize without being physically close.

A popular feature of social networking Web sites is the ability they offer users to leave messages for friends to read later. A user can create and send a message, even though the other user is not readily available to read it. This is a classic example of store-and-forward communication as the message is centrally stored for retrieval at a later time.

If you're on Facebook, perhaps the most popular social networking site, you're already aware of the Web site's use of store-and-forward communication. All the messages left on a user's Facebook "timeline" are created, transmitted, and stored centrally on Facebook's servers. Once the recipient or anyone with access to the recipient's "timeline" logs on, the message is forwarded for viewing.

Typically, a social networking Web site offers ways to secure site messages. Some, however, have more convoluted ways to maintain privacy than others. The temptation for such Web sites is to keep your information open and freely accessible to everyone for the benefit of more-targeted marketing. While this may be understandable for personal likes and dislikes, even private site messages can fall victim to poor security.

Threats and Mitigation Techniques for Site Messaging

Users should be wary of how much private information they divulge on social networking sites, regardless of what privacy settings seem to protect. As social networking sites become more complex, their ability to adequately protect users' information becomes more difficult.

The safest way to avoid the threats mentioned above is not to use site messages at all. For many, that's not a reasonable option. The next best defense is to strictly monitor what is said. For personal use, you should write only what you would not mind sharing with a much wider audience, be it friends, family, or strangers.

For business use, the need to restrict content becomes more important. Never divulge intellectual property or any information that would be harmful if exposed outside the organization. The business user should complete user-awareness training and understand that transmitted messages are out of organizational control. In fact, the terms and conditions statements of popular social networking sites state explicitly that all user-submitted content becomes the property of that Web site.

Business use of social networking sites has become quite common. Social media have significantly changed the way companies and organizations interact with customers and clients. Companies use social media to release news, post jobs, reinforce branding, and announce new product releases. However, maintaining a social network presence for businesses or other groups, such as schools and nonprofit agencies, can be tricky. A social media strategy that is poorly planned and implemented can leave an organization's reputation exposed to significant security vulnerabilities and threats.

> **NOTE**
>
> Given the potential risk to employees and the threat of unintentional data leakage, some companies now offer workshops to inform employees of social media security vulnerabilities. Parents, meanwhile, should discuss safe social networking strategies with their children.

One best practice to help secure social networking and your data is to understand the rules. All social media sites list terms of use, identifying what can be done with your data and identifying the best ways to secure your social media presence. The following lists the security sites for popular social networking sites.

- **Facebook**—A Facebook management console can be used to review password strategies, privacy basics, and online safety resources. You can find it at *https://www.facebook.com/help/*.
- **Instagram**— Many children and youths have Instagram accounts to share pictures among friends and follow others. To help understand how an Instagram account works, refer to *https://help.instagram.com/*.
- **Linkedin**—A LinkedIn site may maintain significant sensitive data about work, employers' contact information, and more. Before you put information online, it would be best to review LinkedIn security guides and the information at *https://help.linkedin.com/app/safety/home*.
- **Twitter**— Links from the Twitter support center explain recommended best practices at *https://support.twitter.com/*.

This is a sample of the documentation available for understanding social media security. Google, Tumblr, and others will each have their own security documentation. Part of your use of these sites should include periodically reviewing this documentation.

FYI

Most social network sites require children to be 13 years old before they can sign up for accounts. LinkedIn requires users to be 14, WhatsApp requires people to be 16, and Vine and Tinder have minimum signup ages of 17. Path requires users to be 18. Another group of social networking sites (Flick, Foursquare, Keek, Kik, WeChat, and YouTube) requires participants to be 18 to sign up, unless they have parental permission, in which case the minimum is age 13.

Another common approach to mitigating unwanted data leaks is to use two-step verification. As the name suggests, this strategy requires duplicate authentication verification. That way, if your credentials are stolen and someone tries to use them from another device, another level of authentication is required. For example, if an attempt is made to log on to a Linkedin account from an unrecognized device, an SMS message can be sent to a smartphone for verification. Two-step verification details for various social network sites are listed below.

- **Facebook**— *https://www.facebook.com/help/148233965247823*
- **YouTube**— *https://www.google.com/landing/2step/*
- **Linkedin**—*http://blog.linkedin.com/2013/05/31/protecting-your-linkedin-account -with-two-step-verification/*
- **Twitter**— *https://blog.twitter.com/2013/getting-started-with-login-verification*

Real-Time Communication

Real-time communication is communicating "live." When you're talking with your friend or coworker who is standing in front of you, that's live. Talking face-to-face is the most personal, immediate method of exchanging information. Of course, not everyone is available for face-to-face discussion.

Often when you need to communicate in real time with someone, having a face-to-face chat is not feasible. The primary reason is likely the distance between you and the other person. Another is that you or that person is occupied with another activity.

Does this mean you can't communicate in real time with that person? No. Being busy with another task doesn't preclude communication for the short term. Any distance between two people can be conquered by technologies available today.

Real-time discussion can be enjoyed provided the technology allows you and your conversation partner to exchange dialogue within a reasonable latency. **Latency** is the term for the lag or delay in response in certain kinds of communications. Many of those technologies are discussed in the following sections.

Telephone

The telephone is the most popular method of real-time communication discussed in this section. Aside from face-to-face conversation, this is the oldest tool. You don't need to think twice about having a real-time discussion with your friend just because your friend happens to be elsewhere. When your manager needs to speak with you, does she wait until you're within sight? No, she calls you right away. Lastly, among business partners and stakeholders, the telephone offers the opportunity for direct and immediate dialogue. All this happens without arranging cross-country flights and scheduling meeting times. A conference call can bring people all over the globe together in the same real-time discussion.

Telephone isn't limited to real-time audio exchange. Today, many organizations also have the capability to have video conferencing phone calls. An organization that offers video conferencing might have a dedicated meeting room set up with a screen and mounted projector, which is integrated with video phone conferencing equipment.

Telephone Threats

The main threat to a telephone is physical access by a malicious user. Unlike an organization's business-critical servers, the telephone is highly accessible as one likely exists on every desk. All an attacker has to do is be there, pick up a phone, and dial. This can result in several threats, demonstrated in Table 13-2.

An ill-natured person can abuse telephone access by making unauthorized calls and incurring long-distance charges. This isn't as high a concern today now that telephone rates are much lower than they once were.

Telephone Mitigation Techniques

The primary way to mitigate most risks above is to require employees to log on to their phones. If a phone will be unattended for an extended period of time, for example, by an employee going on holiday, then the phone must be logged out. A residual risk would be wiretapping.

TABLE 13-2 Attacks possible for someone who has physical access to a telephone.

ATTACKS	AFFECTING
Denial of service	Availability
Spoofing	Integrity
Eavesdropping	Confidentiality
Wiretapping	Confidentiality

Presence/Availability

Information about your presence and availability is as real-time as it gets. The two terms can easily be confused as synonyms, but there are important differences. Presence speaks to accessibility, while availability speaks more to the willingness to communicate.

Recall in the beginning of the store-and-forward section a reference to your coworker. You stopped by her cubicle but she was occupied on the phone. Therefore, you immediately knew she was present but not available.

This is obvious when the coworker is near, but not so if the coworker is in the adjacent building or halfway around the world. Providing, tracking, and reporting on presence and availability solve this problem. **Presence and availability** is the term for the ability and willingness of an end user (typically an employee) to engage in communication, as signaled by some technological channel, such as by setting instant message status to "available" or "in office."

For the most part, the typical level of reporting presence is limited to status updates on an application. Whether that application is Microsoft Office Communicator reporting "Away" or your status on Facebook being reported as "Offline," your status is governed by that application alone. When your status reports to an online peer that you're away, does it mean that you are inaccessible? Probably not. You probably have your phone on, or you might be logged on to a different computer.

Today it is becoming possible for managers, for instance, to gather presence information about their employees from multiple devices. This allows them to track what are known as **multiple points of presence (MPOP)**.

Benefits of Presence and Availability

The benefits are immediate to both you and people who have access to the information. If a project manager has a quick question, she might note a project team member's availability. Rather than draft an e-mail and wait for a response, she can immediately contact the person for a one-minute conversation. Some managers are reluctant to allow their direct reports to telecommute, given the "out of sight, out of mind" mentality. When an employee's presence and availability are immediately viewable, the manager's doubt is removed.

FYI

Presence and availability information can be gathered by both pull and push techniques. An example of a pull method of collecting someone's presence is a cellular provider actively polling for certain customers. In an organization, a centralized application might actively observe activity at the end user's desktop. An example of a push method is a flag or trigger. That trigger might be set off as the user is moving. For example, a mobile device switches cellular towers or the user's laptop switches network ports, connected to a certain switch port. In any case, the trigger assists software to continually monitor and report a user's presence and availability.

Without availability monitoring, coworkers cannot be certain they will be successful if they start an impromptu conversation. The uncertainty comes from not knowing if a coworker is free, in a meeting, on the phone, away from the desk, or otherwise unavailable. When availability is always monitored, peers can be more certain. Availability information can save coworkers time and increase their productivity.

Issues with Presence and Availability

However, you might already see a few potential issues with tracking presence and availability. First is general privacy. Perhaps someone does not want to alert others constantly that he or she is available. For example, a coworker might casually ask you why you were available at 2:30 in the morning. That could be annoying.

Perhaps the information is suitable only for some people some of the time. For example, you likely don't want to alert your manager that you are available on the network at 11 p.m. on Friday. Having your manager call you after 11 p.m. on a Friday could definitely be annoying.

Therefore, one issue with applications presenting your presence is being able to segregate the audience. Whether you are available may depend on the topic of the discussion. Similarly, you may not want your neighbor to contact you at work. However, segregating the need to know by the audience is not a feature of presence and availability applications. The issue of segregating audiences is largely determined by the social network presenting your availability. For example, your manager likely will not monitor your availability on Facebook.

In general, alerting others to your immediate availability helps increase productivity. Fellow workers know you are immediately accessible to answer a question or to help resolve a problem. You also may benefit personally and professionally.

Instant Messaging Chat

Instant messaging is another real-time method of communicating. Unlike the audio dialogue of a telephone conversation, instant messaging is text-based dialogue. The exchange is similar to talking on the telephone, but the conversation is not as quick.

Although the communication method is considered real-time, there is some lag or latency with instant messaging. It's not uncommon for users to perceive a delay during the exchange of one or two seconds. The user perceives the lag during sending the message, transmission, and receiving a response.

The amount of latency varies, depending on a few factors. For example, latency differs by the instant messaging client used and the different networks the message traverses. This might be especially so in the corporate environment as instant messages (IMs) are relayed across application gateways in the LAN-to-WAN Domain. Latency also occurs when one of the users is busy with other tasks or is juggling several instant message conversations at once.

13

Securing Personal and
Business Communications

Instant Messaging Threats

Instant messaging carries multiple serious risks that go beyond similar risks in e-mail or voice communications. Unlike several commercial e-mail clients, few, if any, instant messaging clients offer secure IM communication. Threats instead must be mitigated by using layered defenses external to the client.

Threats to IM span risk to availability, integrity, and confidentiality. Availability-related threats are similar to others discussed throughout this chapter, chiefly denial of service (DoS) by flooding a user's IM client with messages. The messages could originate from one or several sources, making it difficult for the recipient to block the unwanted traffic.

Integrity comes into question when the flood of messages seems to originate from a user's known contacts. This is possible since IM messages can be spoofed as easily as any other communication technology. IM clients lack any strong mechanism for authentication, since your "buddy list" or "friends" are automatically trusted from the initial connection.

Confidentiality is also a problem because IM traffic is not normally encrypted unless specifically done so by a special IM client. The Trillian IM client, for example, offers encryption in both the free and paid versions.

Perhaps the foremost threat inherent to IM is the immediate delivery of uniform resource locators (URLs). This includes sharing of URLs to malicious Web sites. Instant messaging permits sharing of URLs easily, without any automated filtering.

Instant Messaging Mitigation Techniques

Strengthening user awareness is the first and foremost way to address weaknesses in integrity and confidentiality. The more a user understands the dangers of clicking on URLs sent by IM, the fewer instances of instant delivery of malware.

SMS Text Messaging

Short Message Service (SMS) gives users the ability to send and receive short text messages often via smartphones or tablets. The qualifier "short" is based on the limited length of a message. An SMS message is limited to 160 characters when using seven-bit characters or 140 eight-bit characters.

One primary vulnerability with the security of SMS messages is the vulnerability of the user's mobile phone or other mobile device. Mobile phones are easily lost or stolen. Loss of the phone means loss of the messages. Compounding the risk is the fact that users rarely take the time to purge their message inbox of old messages.

Another vulnerability related to SMS messaging involves sending a specially crafted SMS message. As written about and demonstrated at prominent conferences, this vulnerability might provide an attacker with the ability to corrupt or even control a phone. The attacker, using presently available tools, can send a maliciously formed SMS text message to the target's phone. Once in control of the phone, the attacker may wish to send an SMS that, by virtue of the sending phone, grants authority and authenticity to the message. The possibilities are covered in the next section.

SMS Threats

The primary vulnerabilities concerning SMS messaging are in transmission and delivery. The risks of the most common attacks are with confidentiality and integrity. Although SMS delivery is not guaranteed service delivery, availability is not so much a concern.

Confidentiality is a problem with SMS messaging because encryption during transmission is optional. With encryption, messages are difficult to intercept and read while being delivered over the cellular network. Without encryption, an attacker can more easily eavesdrop on messages. The risk of insecure transmission is worse while the user is roaming. When a user is roaming, delivery of SMS messages are likely to involve the Internet for part of the way. SMS messages along the Internet are subject to far greater risk of interception.

The worst threat known to date involving SMS is SMS spoofing. Spoofing means someone is impersonating the legitimate user and sending SMS messages. The result depends upon the message and the original user. Considering the way people trust that an SMS message is coming from whom it says it's from, the impact is significant. The attack, although relatively new, is remarkably easy to carry out. Tools and services to do this exist online. For example, one service makes caller ID spoofing available for low-cost purchase of "spoofing minutes" you can use to spoof SMS texts, phone calls, and e-mail messages.

MMS Messaging

Multimedia Messaging Service (MMS) is an extension of SMS. While SMS allows you only to send text messages, MMS allows you to attach audio, images, or video. Extending simple text messages to include multimedia lets you make a much richer message. However, with richer features come greater security risks including, but not limited to, multimedia embedded with a virus or other malware.

Differences Between MMS and SMS

The names Short Message Service and Multimedia Messaging Service suggest the two are closely related. Technically, however, the two are very different in how service providers deliver them.

Recall that SMS text messages are limited to 160 characters. For the most part, service providers send these 160-character messages effortlessly, and the service provider's cost is null. Method of delivery for SMS and MMS messages is also different. SMS messages are delivered purely by the cellular network, as described noted above, with one exception: When users roam outside their domestic network, SMS messages might be delivered using the Internet between SMS relays.

On the other hand, MMS messages likely use the Internet for delivery. This depends largely on whether the MMS message stays within the user's cellular service provider's network or hops between cellular networks. Messages with multimedia first convert the attached multimedia in a format not unlike MIME or e-mail messages. Encoding formats are available in great detail in the **Multimedia Messaging Service Encapsulation Protocol**, which is a specification available from the Open Mobile Alliance.

Content Adaptation

The MMS specification details the many conditions and restrictions on how multimedia messages are handled. However, the specification does not restrict much of how phones produce the content. Given the rather limited processing power and screen size of mobile phones, their content must be adapted. To handle this issue, mobile phone vendors and mobile phone operating systems have created a variety of methods for content adaptation. **Content adaptation** is the term for the way mobile phones handle Web and multimedia content intended for more powerful systems with larger screens.

The real challenge, however, isn't how the different vendors handle this task but whether their techniques are compatible with each other. As a result, the content produced by one vendor's mobile phone and adapted by that user's cellular service provider might not be rendered correctly on another user's mobile phone on a different service provider.

> **TIP**
>
> If you would like to know ahead of time if your SMS text was delivered, you can precede your message with *0# or *N#. Then you will get a delivery report that will confirm whether your message reached the recipient.

Delivery

Guarantee of MMS messages also differs from SMS. SMS or text messages are delivered as "best effort" and are not guaranteed. It's a rare case that a message doesn't actually make it. However, if an SMS is lost in delivery and fails to reach the recipient, the sender will not be aware of the failure unless it's specifically requested. On the other hand, if a MMS message fails to be delivered, the sender will be notified of the failed attempt.

MMS Threats

Endpoint devices that can deliver and receive messages are exposed to threats. Being able to handle multimedia-laden messages compounds the risk involved.

The most popular and easiest threats involve exhausting resources, such as a mobile phone's memory or bandwidth. Because of the inherent insecurities in how MMS messages are handled, there exists one kind of attack that forces a mobile phone to exhaust its battery power as well. In fact, significantly decreased performance or battery life can be a symptom that your phone is infected by malware.

Another attack, demonstrated by Collin Mulliner and Giovanni Vigna, two researchers from the University of California, shows that code can be injected remotely by an MMS message. The attack is confirmed by proof-of-concept code. That attack demonstrates two noteworthy threats:

1. MMS messages can successfully carry remote code to be run at the end user's device.
2. End-user devices will receive unsolicited MMS messages, by design, and properly execute injected code within the MMS multimedia.

It's uncertain now how to mitigate these threats, but mitigation will involve cooperative efforts between service providers and mobile phone vendors.

VoIP Threats

Voice over IP (VoIP) is a real-time service that allows voice telephone communications over an Internet Protocol (IP) network such as the Internet. VoIP has become a popular low-cost or free alternative to traditional telephone use.

Threats to VoIP are a combination of two sets of threats: threats to any telecommunications service and threats to any system requiring general availability. In the former, attacks against VoIP systems are aimed at profiting or defrauding the service owner, depending on your perspective. For example, an attacker may make toll calls using the VoIP service, but the toll is to be paid for by the VoIP owner, not the caller. To facilitate this, an attacker may connect an unauthorized phone to the VoIP network. If access is granted without challenge, the attacker can freely dial anywhere any authorized caller can. Only with sufficient authentication can an organization mitigate this risk.

In the second set of threats, those against availability, a VoIP system in a large organization may be vulnerable to DoS attacks. Two reasons for this are the wide range of services offered and the wide range of protocols involved in delivering those services.

Regarding the range of services, consider how many different services a VoIP system offers. The VoIP equipment is composed of several specific subsystems, each offering a particular feature. When an attacker performs a DoS attack against even one or a few of those subsystems, the entire functionality of the VoIP equipment might likely fail.

Regarding the complexity of protocols, the range of services requires a complex set of protocols. Some of those protocols include Session Initiation Protocol (SIP), H.323, Media Gateway Control Protocol (MGCP), IP, and Real-time Transport Protocol (RTP). Each protocol introduces its own set of vulnerabilities and risks. If any of those protocols, or services behind it utilizing the protocol, is not kept up to date and secured, the respective service can be denied. Again, as with the range of services, if one key service is rendered unavailable, the VoIP service as a whole might be made unavailable.

> **NOTE**
>
> As VoIP is a function of the network, a VoIP system is only as secure as the underlying network management and infrastructure. So network security audits must include the VoIP servers and VoIP policies and update practices.

Best Practices for Securing Telephone and Private Branch Exchange Communications

Private Branch Exchange (PBX) administrators must take the necessary precautions and exercise due diligence like administrators of any other system. PBX or private branch exchanges are not new technology. PBXs are the central routers or switching devices for handling telephone traffic. That includes voice telephone, fax, and modems. Some of the more modern PBX systems might also handle VoIP and other SIP traffic.

PBXs are as prone to malicious behavior as any other equipment and, given the wide range of valuable data crossing through them, PBXs make an attractive target. However, if you do your due diligence, you can secure a PBX with relatively high confidence. Further securing the PBX might require vendor-specific configuration changes. Some of the best practices for securing a PBX are:

- **Physical security**—The PBX should be physically isolated and protected from unauthorized users.

- **Attention to remote management capabilities**—Virtually any PBX allows the administrator to manage the device remotely. Disable these capabilities if not used. If used, protect them by changing the default password, if any. In addition, any local physical ports are a security risk if they are not routinely used.

- **Security for remote management**—Remote management is done via the Internet, likely via Telnet or File Transfer Protocol (FTP). Those protocols are insecure, sending your authentication "in the clear" or using no encryption. To ensure confidentiality, instead use secure alternative protocols, if the option exists. You may also tunnel them through a VPN. Consider using an isolated virtual local area network (VLAN) specific for device management.

- **Training and administration**—Maintaining the PBX doesn't happen frequently. Likewise, many systems administrators are unfamiliar with PBX administration. Therefore, poor configuration and inadequate training are commonplace. The person most familiar with administering the PBX should take the time to document lessons learned with that PBX. For example, documenting the most frequent problems and common configuration changes can save a lot of time for junior PBX administrators.

- **Document control**—Documents for the PBX, such as operational procedures, policies, and configuration settings, are too valuable to leave lying around. Keep them securely protected when they're not needed.

- **Defense against denial of service (DoS)**—Many attacks don't take control of a PBX system but consume all its resources. This robs legitimate users of availability of the PBX or at least limits its functionality. You must mitigate the risk of DoS attacks by filtering service requests to trusted networks, keeping device software up to date, and enabling only necessary features and services.

In summary, the PBX is a central, necessary piece of equipment for any organization. Because more and more services are available through the common PBX, the device is a strong target for attacks. While many attacks exist, security can be achieved with defense in depth, due diligence, and awareness.

Best Practices for Securing VoIP Communications

Threats concerning voice over IP (VoIP) technology were discussed earlier in the chapter, in the real-time communication section. As popular as VoIP has become, it's important to implement best practices with VoIP. The primary reason for having VoIP capability is for the user. To have a successful VoIP capability, the user must perceive the expected level of quality—few or no dropped calls, and little to no latency, for example. Security best practices must be implemented to preserve that quality.

> ### Demand for New Availability Can Cause Unavailability
>
> When introducing VoIP equipment, be mindful of the impending impact it will have on the network. There is a big variety of VoIP equipment available today, and it may be tempting to implement, for example, an IP telephone per employee, a software IP phone client at each workstation, and cameras for video conferencing for each desk. Much of this equipment extends the same reach and employee availability through different ways. While the primary focus of introducing VoIP into an organization is for more availability, the outcome can be very different.
>
> Introducing additional hardware and software demands planning and consideration of the impact. However, introducing added equipment as the project continues might be difficult to avoid. Going further, the demand for VoIP might be driven harder by senior managers who are looking forward to the new capability. End-user devices such as software phones on the workstation and IP phones on the desk can introduce a flood of both real-time and store-and-forward traffic, overwhelming the network.
>
> The flood of traffic can cause unforeseen strain on the network. This will affect both related and unrelated services. Congested networks can hurt VoIP call quality. If the network is seriously congested, internal business services such as e-mail might slow down or become unavailable. If services like e-mail suffer because of VoIP, senior management may demand immediate improvements. Depending on your options, you might find yourself compromising a security control for the sake of immediately improved bandwidth.

VoIP Planning Best Practices

Some top best practices related to introducing and implementing VoIP phones are:

- **Weigh the network impact**—Assess the organization's ability to handle the additional load.
- **Train users**—Develop and distribute adequate training for users to adapt to and make use of the new technology.

Before an organization decides to implement VoIP, all costs must be considered. The network impact, user training, and security risk mitigation techniques discussed in the next section all factor into the total costs.

VoIP Implementation Best Practices

Some best practices relevant to maintaining VoIP phones in the organization are:

- **Monitor capacity and usage**—Capacity should not pushed to limits by VoIP but only moderately affected.
- **Employ VPNs**—Use encrypted traffic for VoIP traffic to avoid potential eavesdropping.

- **Segregate traffic from the data network**—Use VLANs or dedicated networking equipment to isolate VoIP traffic from data network attacks.
- **Protect traffic**—Use VLANs to protect and prioritize VoIP traffic.
- **Isolate traffic**—Use application-layer gateways or proxies in the LAN-to-WAN Domain.
- **Patching and antivirus**—Always maintain a sound patching program and keep antivirus software and signature files up to date.
- **Detect and prevent** — Install, tune, and staff intrusion detection and intrusion prevention systems.

Introducing VoIP devices to an organization's network means introducing a new attack vector. Prior to the new devices, the threat of VoIP attack posed no real risk. With VoIP devices on the network, so are a myriad of vulnerabilities that come with each new device. Mitigating the risk beforehand can save a lot of time and headache for administrators and potential downtime for users.

Best Practices for Securing Unified Communications

Session Initiation Protocol (SIP) is the protocol used for managing communication sessions, particularly those involving multimedia, over the Internet. Some examples already covered in the chapter are instant messaging, presence information, and VoIP. Other examples of multimedia sessions are online gaming and streaming multimedia.

SIP allows the management of more than one simultaneous multimedia channel at once, for example, a file transfer over the instant messaging client. SIP also controls sessions that are unicast, or client to client, as well as multicast, or single client to multiple clients at once.

SIP Features and Essentials

It's important to understand that SIP is only a signaling protocol, not an all-purpose communications protocol. Using the telephone as an analogy, SIP would govern how a telephone rings, connects, and hangs up. SIP would not provide, for example, what the telephone physically looks like, which features are included, or how users should communicate. Text-based SIP packets can be inspected directly by administrators using a protocol analyzer for troubleshooting.

According to Request for Comments (RFC) 3261, which fully describes SIP, the protocol provides five aspects in helping initiate or end a multimedia connection:

- **User location**—Discovering and detecting the user to be reached
- **User availability**—Finding out if both ends are available to hold the session
- **User capabilities**—Finding out the type of media and parameters involved
- **Session setup**—Notifying the end device or user agent, also known as *ringing*, and setting up the parameters between both ends
- **Session management**—Including session transfer and termination, altering parameters, and initiating related services.

FYI

RFC 3261 was developed by the Internet Engineering Task Force (IETF). The IETF is an organized community made possible by the Internet Society (ISOC), a nonprofit group of thousands of organizations and individuals. The IETF strives to keep the quality level of documented standards, policies, and guidelines as high as possible. It achieves this through peer review and a formalized approval process.

SIP User Agents and Communication Between Them

A session of two SIP user agent clients (UACs) is controlled by SIP. A **SIP user agent (UA)** is a network endpoint that is enabled to function as a either a SIP user agent client or user agent server. A **SIP user agent client (UAC)** is a SIP user agent that makes requests and receives responses. Figure 13-1 shows how this works. In the figure, the two user agents are telephones starting and managing a peer-to-peer session.

Figure 13-2 shows how a session of three SIP user agents is controlled by SIP. The difference between this and Figure 13-1 is the additional SIP UA acting as a **SIP user agent server (UAS).** The UAS acts as a proxy between the two user agent clients. Although SIP is a peer-to-peer protocol, it's more likely to have a proxy between two clients in real-world application. There might be several proxies between SIP user agent clients. In addition, a SIP session relies on the **Real-time Transport Protocol (RTP)**, which streams audio or video in packets over an IP network. The **Real-time Transport Control Protocol (RTCP)** manages and maintains the quality of RTP.

13

Securing Personal and
Business Communications

TABLE 13-3 SIP response numbers and message examples.

SIP RESPONSE NUMBER	TYPE OF MESSAGE AND EXAMPLES
1xx	Information Message 100 = trying 180 = ringing
2xx	Successful Request Completed 200 = OK
3xx	Call Forwarding 302 = temporarily moved 305 = use proxy
4xx	Error 403 = forbidden
5xx	Server Error 503 = server internal error
6xx	Global Failure 606 = not acceptable

SIP Messages

SIP User Agent Client

Invite

100 Trying

180 Ringing

200 OK

ACK

RTP Data

BYE

200 OK

SIP User Agent Client

FIGURE 13-1

SIP controlling a SIP call session between two user agent clients.

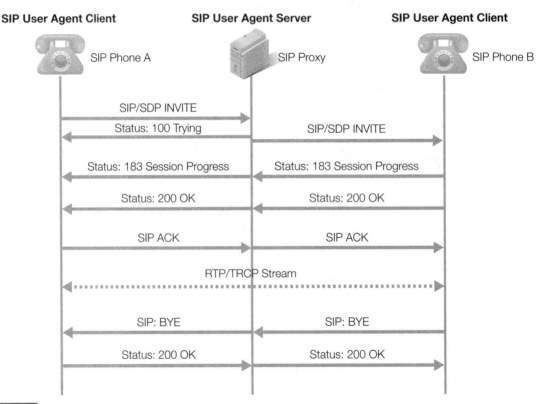

SIP User Agent Client   **SIP User Agent Server**   **SIP User Agent Client**

SIP Phone A   SIP Proxy   SIP Phone B

SIP/SDP INVITE

Status: 100 Trying   SIP/SDP INVITE

Status: 183 Session Progress   Status: 183 Session Progress

Status: 200 OK   Status: 200 OK

SIP ACK   SIP ACK

RTP/TRCP Stream

SIP: BYE   SIP: BYE

Status: 200 OK   Status: 200 OK

FIGURE 13-2

SIP controlling a session with three SIP user agents.

SIP was created for use with other protocols to provide a complete multimedia delivery architecture, such as for streaming media. SIP is text-based and is similar to Hypertext Transfer Protocol (HTTP) and Simple Mail Transfer Protocol (SMTP).

Response messages are formed similarly to HTTP with a three-digit code. Table 13-3 shows various SIP response numbers and their meaning.

Implementation Best Practices

With all its elegance, SIP is a vulnerable protocol and must be implemented with that understanding. After some due diligence, the SIP environment can be considered as secure as any part of the organization's network. The following is a list of best practices to follow before putting SIP into practical use.

- Ensure the SIP infrastructure is included in the organization's patch program.
- All SIP hardware should be running antivirus with consistently up-to-date definitions.
- Employ application-level gateways in the LAN-to-WAN domain.
- Enforce strong physical security to protect access to areas with SIP infrastructure.
- Utilize VLANs to separate SIP traffic network from data network.

This list is not exhaustive. Other special conditions in any organization may warrant additional controls.

Having SIP devices and applications carries the same responsibility as having any other network asset. SIP infrastructures must be regularly tested and monitored to ensure no malicious traffic is in play. Further, devices dependent on SIP, such as VoIP phones, may suddenly experience dropped calls or extreme latency. The cause might be a DoS attack on SIP hardware.

> ⚠ **WARNING**
>
> SIP is vulnerable to DoS attacks by a simple flood of INVITE requests to a user agent.

13

🔒 CHAPTER SUMMARY

This chapter covered two types of communication: store-and-forward and real-time. For both types, the chapter provided several example technologies, along with their benefits and disadvantages. The types of threats and vulnerabilities are covered per technology as are some mitigation steps, where applicable.

The typical threat to real-time communication affects availability, while threats to store-and-forward communication center on confidentiality. These are the prevailing types of threats, but different threats affect either communication form in various ways.

KEY CONCEPTS AND TERMS

Content adaptation

Latency

Multimedia Messaging Service Encapsulation Protocol

Multiple points of presence (MPOP)

Presence and availability

Real-time Transport Control Protocol (RTCP)

Real-time Transport Protocol (RTP)

Session Initiation Protocol (SIP)

SIP user agent (UA)

SIP user agent client (UAC)

SIP user agent server (UAS)

Store-and-forward communication

CHAPTER 13 ASSESSMENT

1. When information is temporarily kept at one or more middle points during transmission, that technique is called _____ communication.

2. Which of the following describes multiple points of presence (MPOP)?

   A. Aggregating multiple e-mail accounts to your current logged on account

   B. Aggregating presence information from multiple applications or devices

   C. Dividing voicemail to lessen the risk of eavesdropping

   D. Dividing MMS messages to separate text and graphics or video pieces

3. Phishing, social engineering, and 419 scams are some of the threats encountered when using
_____.

4. Messaging or chatting on social networking sites can be considered very private and secure.

   A. True

   B. False

5. Why are PBXs an attractive target to attackers?

   A. Several services depend on the PBX's operation.

   B. Numerous protocols are involved.

   C. The device is usually left out in the open.

   D. All of the above

   E. A and B only

6. Store-and-forward communication is preferred over real-time communication in which environments? (Select two.)

   A. When delivery is unreliable

   B. When the destination is not always available

   C. When source and destination are not in the same country

   D. When low latency is critical

7. Which areas of concern are associated with SMS vulnerabilities? (Select two.)

   A. Availability

   B. Integrity

   C. Confidentiality

   D. All of the above

8. SMS and MMS are primarily the same service apart from the addition of multimedia with MMS.

   A. True

   B. False

9. Protocols such as SIP, H.323, MGCP, IP, and RTP are encountered when discussing which of the following?

   A. E-mail

   B. Voicemail

   C. VoIP

   D. Fax

   E. SMS

10. This chapter discussed which issues brought on by adding VoIP devices to an organization? (Select two.)

A. Performance issues: significantly more network traffic

B. Security issues: new attack vectors and more vulnerabilities to deal with

C. User-related issues: users require additional training and might be less productive

D. Facility issues: finding the space to put the phones

11. A networking method of segregating VoIP traffic from data traffic is _____.

12. Select one way SIP does not assist with establishing a multimedia connection.

A. User availability

B. User location

C. User capabilities

D. User distance

13. SIP manages multimedia sessions with features similar to how the telephone system dials, rings, and manages responses from phones.

A. True

B. False

14. The SIP session request and response messages are formed similarly to _____ messages.

A. DHCP

B. DNS

C. HTTP

D. SNMP

Security Training, Education, and Certification

© Rodolfo Clix/Dreamstime.com

AN AWARENESS OF WHAT YOU WANT AND NEED from a job and a work environment is essential when you're deciding on a career in IT. IT jobs offer many types of different working conditions. Some require working long hours alone, some require working exclusively with clients, and others are very social, requiring ongoing collaboration with coworkers. The number and diversity of these work environments within IT allow those entering the industry the opportunity to choose an area that best suits their personality and skill set.

One thing most or all of these IT jobs have in common is a need for security training and an awareness of the role they play in overall Web and network security. For example, database administrators are responsible for information security in the database, programmers for secure coding, network administrators for communication and hardware security, and IT managers for policies. Regardless of the area within IT, it will have a role in the overall security strategy.

When selecting the area you think is right for you, you must consider such factors as your ability to deal with stress and the variety of work you want to do. You must also consider other factors, such as whether you crave interaction with others and whether your communications skills or other skills needed are suited for that position. Of course the only way to really know whether a job is right for you is to do it. But by looking at what kind of things you can expect from a certain job, and considering the experiences and observations of others, you can narrow the possible fields in terms of which job you believe suits you best.

This chapter looks at four areas of IT: computer programming, networking, Internet technologies and Web design, and database design and administration. The technical areas introduced in this chapter are by no means inclusive of all areas within IT. However, these areas represent the current "hot spots" of the IT industry. This chapter gives an idea of the role each plays in creating a secure IT environment.

This chapter covers the following topics and concepts:

- What the different roles of a database designer and database administrator are and what certifications are available for each
- What the roles of a programmer and an application developer are and what certifications are available for each
- What is involved in secure network management and what certifications are available
- What the responsibilities of a Web designer and a Web administrator are and what training is available for each

Chapter 14 Goals

When you complete this chapter, you will be able to:

- Identify the tasks and security responsibilities for those managing databases
- Review common certification paths for database administration
- Describe the day-to-day tasks and security requirements for programmers and app developers
- Identify the role security plays in network management
- Review common network management certifications
- Identify the security considerations for a job as a Web administrator
- Describe common industry security certifications

14

Security Training, Education, and Certification

Security and Careers—Database Design and Administration

Companies must keep track of information, whether it's customer records, production statistics, financial results, demographic data, or something else. In this information age, a lot of data is accumulated, and someone or something has to manage it in a way that allows it to be useful. For example, if you had a lot of money, you'd want an accountant to keep track of it and be able to tell you, when you ask, where it is and how much there is. You wouldn't necessarily want him or her to point to a pile and say, "it's everything in there." You would want more precision.

FYI

In the IT world, the terms *information* and *data* are sometimes used interchangeably. There is, however, a distinction between the two. Data typically refers to raw unorganized facts. In a production environment data comes from multiple sources, which may include machinery, asset management systems, and tracking systems. Once this raw data is organized and structured, it can be presented in meaningful ways. This is information. One of the challenges for IT managers working in manufacturing environments and other large companies is to isolate all data sources and correlate this data into meaningful information on which to base decisions. In today's world, this is often referred to as **business intelligence (BI)**.

In a sense, putting data into a database does the same thing a good accountant would do—organizing a collection of data into information that is useful to those who care about it. E-commerce sites use databases to track their orders and inventory. The phone company uses databases to track the physical location attached to phone number 253-555-5504. Just about every large collection of information in a company is stored in a database—meaning there are many professional opportunities for those who create and maintain those databases.

The classic definition of a database says that a database has three pieces: files, records, and fields. A file can be thought of as a grouped collection of information. The set of your city's White Pages and Yellow Pages telephone books could be considered a database, consisting of at least two primary collections of information. Your city's White Pages would be considered a file in this analogy. An example of a record would be the entry with your name, address, and phone number. Each other person's telephone book entry would be considered a record in the "telephone book" file as well. So, as you can see, a file can contain many hundreds of thousands of records—far more than can be organized and sorted easily by hand. Continuing with this example, there would be three individual fields where the various types of information are entered. In this case, the names of the fields would be name, address, and phone number. However, a database is not limited to these specific three fields. In virtually any modern database, fields may be added or subtracted at will, depending on what data the organization needs (or wants) to store. In the case of older databases, it's sometimes necessary to create a new database and import the information into it, because the structure of some older databases cannot be changed once created.

There are different types of databases, and each major database system software product is based on a specific type. Today you are likely to find the database world has emphasized a particular type of database known as a *relational database management system (RDBMS)*. A **relational database** is one in which the required information is organized into tables that are related to each other by specific rules established during the database design.

Most databases in use today, such as Microsoft SQL Server and Oracle, are relational, so it's important for those in the database field to be familiar with relational database terminology and concepts. In an RDBMS, data is organized as a table, and a database is considered to be a collection of these tables. An entry of data in a table is called a *record* or a *tuple*, and is organized in rows in a table. Attributes about those records are organized in columns.

This more closely describes the concept of a database to most people, because if you picture any sort of written table, such as a transit schedule, you can easily see the table's actual rows and columns. The way in which that table would be implemented in a relational database is sometimes as simple as making the table's column headings into the names of fields in the table, and then adding each row of the written table to the database table, as data. A spreadsheet is a simple example of a table, with rows and columns; however, the records and attributes in an RDBMS table can hold much larger data than commonly found in a spreadsheet.

What's a database good for? In addition to providing a single, secure location for storing an organization's valuable data, it also provides useful ways to access that data. For example, you can ask a database that contains a list of tens of thousands of customers to display the names of customers whose accounts receivable balance is more than $1,000, and it can provide the list in seconds. A database request of this sort is referred to as a *query*, and the process of asking the database for this information is referred to as *querying the database*. When you ask a database for information like this, you can also ask it to list the results in a particular order, such as in alphabetical order by name, or in order by balance, from highest to lowest. In this way, databases can efficiently keep track of even very large quantities of information.

Another benefit of using a database is that most modern databases typically provide support for *transactions*. Transactions are logical groupings of related activities involving a database's data. For example, if you are entering a product order with 10 line items, you want to make sure that the overall order information, such as customer number, date, and sales rep, is correctly added to the Order table, and that each of the 10 line items of information, such as product number and quantity, is added correctly to the Order Item table. The order is not considered "complete" until all 10 items have been added, because (for example) you wouldn't want the warehouse shipping out the first seven items to the customer at 11 a.m. and marking the order as filled, because someone looked at the order database just a minute before the data entry clerk finished entering the last three items into the order. Transaction support makes it possible for database designers and programmers to ensure that such confusion is less likely to occur.

Comparing Database Administrator and Designer

Many career paths in IT have two sides or descriptions to them. This is true of database management as well. You will find that the difference between a database *designer* and a database *administrator* is actually a fine line because in the database world you can wear many "hats" at one time. One week you might be doing management on one database and another you might be helping with design as well as the management of the database.

In knowledge and ability, there's a clear difference between the roles of a designer and an administrator. Additionally, the larger an organization is, the more specialized your responsibilities will be, and the more likely it is that you'll need to choose whether to emphasize database design or database administration in your career. Regardless of which you choose, you'll need to understand specific security strategies and best practices.

Knowing the daily tasks involved in such a career is important and can help identify the job-specific security considerations. Not every task typically done by a database designer is performed daily by a specific person. This is partly because larger organizations typically have a team of database designers or administrators, and on any given day one of several qualified people may perform a particular task. Similarly, not every important database task (such as creating a new database from scratch) is done every day—but it's still a vital task that both database administrators and designers must know how to perform. Because tasks may be shared, all database administrators must understand and adhere to security policies and best practices.

Database Administrator

A **database administrator** is responsible for databases used in the business environment, much as a network administrator is responsible for an organization's file and print servers. A database administrator's duties might include the following:

* Performing database updates required by the development staff on test and live systems
* Tuning database performance on the basis of statistics accumulated during use of the live system
* Coordinating with IT staff regarding server hardware and OS issues
* Defining backup and restore strategies
* Importing third-party data into the database,
* Resolving errors reported by the database software, such as full log files

The database administrator also maintains security for the database, determining which groups of users can have access to which data stored in the database. He or she also sets policies for how that data can be accessed—for instance, certain data can be viewed over the Internet; other, more sensitive data is available only on the company's intranet. The database administrator may provide input to the database designer on such questions as how frequently certain database contents are used and which parts of the application might benefit from performance improvement. Organizationally, the database administrator may report to the director of technical support, and his or her workgroup peers may include system administrators and network administrators.

Database Designer

A **database designer** is a business analyst or software developer rather than a production-support technician. A database administrator can likely speak knowledgeably on the fastest way to organize the indexes on a specific large, complex table. A database designer, on the other hand, will know how to efficiently organize an application's required data into related tables, specifying the most appropriate characteristics for each data item being stored. A database designer is concerned with creating a database whose architecture meets the user community's current and future needs, to the degree they can be foreseen, for data storage and reporting. The designer also must create a database that can be used effectively by project development staff that creates the programs to store data in, and retrieve data from, the database.

In doing this, designers interact with the user community and development staff, maintain the database model (usually a combination of diagrams and written documentation), and create the development database used by project staff. The database designer sets standards for data access. The designer may specify, for example, that a particular procedure always be used to move an order from "data entry" to "fulfillment" status, to maintain system efficiency and data consistency. The database designer also serves as a resource for the database administrator in resolving production issues. Organizationally, the database designer may report to the director of systems development, and his or her workgroup peers may include business systems analysts, application programmers, and application project leaders.

The database administrator is the person whose primary responsibility tends to be the "production" version of the database, whereas the database designer is the person whose primary responsibility tends to be the "development" version of the database. In general, the database designer will be more skilled in the precise considerations involved in database design (such as deciding whether a particular piece of data belongs in one table or another) and programming. The database administrator will be more skilled at trouble-shooting random problems that occur day to day (such as what to do when the database runs out of disk space) and choosing the best way to perform administrative tasks such as database backups. However, each normally has some familiarity with the other's duties, because on any given day, he or she may have to perform those tasks.

Database Management Tasks

Database projects go through stages, and designers in particular will find their daily job tasks evolving as the project progresses and the database itself evolves. Similarly, an administrator's daily tasks will depend on whether there are urgent system problems to resolve that day or whether the day can be dedicated to improving the database or system performance. The daily tasks for this job are important, because the database is often the center of a business application project. A well-designed, well-maintained database can make a project successful. A less carefully designed or poorly maintained database can cause a project to fail. The daily tasks listed below are not a complete list of all the tasks you might encounter when working in this field. But they are common in jobs concerned with a database's upkeep and design.

- Meet with the application project team and end users to discuss the data required in the database, its characteristics, and the activities the end users want to perform with this data.

- Administer database security, such as by monitoring the list of users who have access to all or part of the database, and the security rights they have. (For example, some users are allowed only to view inventory information, and others are allowed to change it.)

- Keep the database software current (with patches and service packs) to protect against new forms of attacks.

- Ensure that appropriate security measures are followed during development.

- Monitor user access and maintain system security.

- Develop and test implementation of conceptual models, using specific database software such as Microsoft SQL Server or Oracle, on the development server. Update related project documentation.

- Develop database-specific secure program code to access and update database objects, and ensure that proper relationships among database objects are maintained.

- Recommend to programmers efficient ways to access specific sets of data stored in the database.

- Implement secure strategies for backup and recovery of database information.

- Install database system software (and perhaps operating system software) on the database server, according to project requirements and organizational policies.

- Restore a test database that was accidentally written over due to an error in a new program.

- Work with application project staff to move application upgrades from the development server to test servers and production servers as required.

- Test new versions of the third-party database software being used to implement projects.

- Keep up to date on database technology, and research new threats to database security.

Database Security Training and Certification

Because databases hold sensitive information, it's critical to implement and manage them securely. Professional management of databases requires hands-on practice as well as formal training. Many colleges and private education organizations offer diplomas and certificates in database management. While they may approach the curriculum in different manners, upon completion their students will be expected to know:

- Industry standards for data modeling and database design and maintenance
- Development and design of database management systems (DBMS)
- Relational database theory, data modeling, industry standards, SQL programming, and day-to-day administration, including security configurations
- How to set polices for users and ensure that the entire information system is protected from any loss, compromise, or failure
- How to implement administrative policies and security measures, and develop plans for disaster recovery
- Techniques used by malicious users to exploit database flaws and vulnerabilities

This is just a sample of the types of database and security information that well-designed postsecondary programs provide. In addition to postsecondary training options, vendor-specific certification training offers opportunities to learn product-specific management strategies.

Microsoft SQL Training

Microsoft has a virtual academy online offering SQL training and various certifications for creating reliable, secure, and robust database systems. The following are some of the Microsoft certifications that include SQL training:

- **Microsoft Technology Associate (MTA)**—This is an entry-level Microsoft certification with three education tracks: Developer, IT Infrastructure, and Database. Students who complete the Database exam will earn the MTA certification.
- **Microsoft Certified Solutions Associate (MCSA)**—Completion of this certification requires the student to pass three exams: Querying Microsoft SQL Server 2012, Administering Microsoft SQL Server 2012 Databases, and Implementing a Data Warehouse with Microsoft SQL Server 2012. According to Microsoft, earning the MCSA will qualify the student for a position as a database developer or database analyst.
- **Microsoft Certified Solutions Expert (MCSE): Data Platform**—The MCSE certification requires the successful passing of five exams and will prepare the student for jobs such as database analyst and database designer. This certification requires you to show continued ability to perform in your chosen solution area by completing a recertification exam every three years.

Refer to *https://www.microsoft.com/learning/default.aspx* for more information on Microsoft certifications.

Oracle University

Oracle offers extensive training and certifications for Oracle database management and other applications. They are four categories of certification paths for Oracle certifications. These include:

FYI

For a general overview of security concepts and approaches, CompTIA offers its Security+ course. It introduces students to a wide range of security basics. Refer to the certification site at *http://certification.comptia.org/getCertified/certifications/security.aspx*.

- **Applications**—Oracle applications are a broad collection of business solutions, from asset management to customer relationship management (CRM), Web commerce, and more.

- **Database**—There are three streams of certifications for Oracle database management: Database Application Development, MySQL, and Oracle Database. Each of these will prepare candidates for day-to-day management of a database, including security considerations.

- **Enterprise Management**—Studying Oracle's Enterprise Management will prepare students to test and manage large-scale enterprise solutions, as well as cloud and Web applications.

- **Foundation**—This entry-level Oracle certification provides an overview of Oracle solutions and products, including an introduction to database management.

For more information about Oracle and the database management certification, refer to Oracle's online certification portal at *http://education.oracle.com/*.

Security and Careers—Programming and Application Development

Essentially, a program is a set of instructions or directions understood by the computer, allowing it to perform predetermined functions. These instructions are given to the computer with the use of specific programming languages. A computer language is basically a form of communication understood by both programmers and machines.

Deciding to become a programmer is just the first step. Identifying and choosing a programming language or languages to learn is the next step. Like most technologies, computer languages are developed through a transitional process. New programming languages are created, and old ones enhanced, by examining the shortcomings of previous languages and making the necessary improvements.

Larger and more complex computer programs demand the continued development and evolution of programming languages able to take full advantage of current technology. If these languages aren't continually modified and developed, programs may be unable to meet user's current and future. For this reason, the future for programmers looks very good. The IT industry relies on skilled programmers able to securely create, modify, and expand programming languages and the programs that they create.

The development of a simple program may take a skilled programmer just a few hours to complete. Other programs—such as operating systems that require complex detailed instructions—can take a group of programmers more than a year of work. Even though programmers often work behind the scenes, far removed from the eyes of the end user, their influence on daily computer use is keenly felt.

Today it isn't enough to just know how to program; it's essential to know how to program securely. Secure programming, sometimes referred to as **defensive programming**, is really just a mindset whereby programmers work with a clear understanding of current threats and how they may affect the program today and in the future. For example, this means that programmer is fully aware of the potential vulnerabilities and prepares for injection attacks to validate input. It's difficult to imagine that programmers today would not familiarize themselves with current vulnerabilities, such as those presented by OWASP in their Top 10 lists, and adjust their programming accordingly.

Common Programming Tasks

Programmers will mostly find themselves working in highly creative and technical environments. Often programmers must work independently, while at the same time maintaining a strong sense of teamwork and a collaborative spirit. It's essential that programmers be reliable, dependable, and self-motivated and be able to cope with the stress of inflexible deadlines. Once these conditions are met, the programmer will be called upon to perform a variety of jobs and responsibilities. These different duties may include the following:

- **Developing, testing, and debugging client/server applications**—Debugging applications is critical for ongoing security, as program bugs may be exploited as vulnerabilities.

- **Converting designs and specifications into secure computer code**—This means working with a specification or design that someone else has produced. Your task is to turn the concept into a programmed reality. If the design is very detailed, you may not have any room for creative flourishes, but security design must be a priority.

- **Analyzing program code to discover the causes of errors and revising as necessary**— Programmers of any language must be able to do this. The process of running down errors in a program, known as *debugging*, is an essential programmer skill. This means that you must have a thorough knowledge of your chosen programming language.

- **Delivering high-quality, usable code in a timely fashion, without sacrificing appropriate testing**—Programmers are often faced with inflexible timelines, so they must be able to work quickly and flexibly.

- **Developing code in order to implement well-structured and reusable design**— Code must follow technology standards and take into account known vulnerabilities.

- **Analyzing, installing, and testing upgrades of externally developed application programs**

- **Monitoring programs' performance after implementation to keep up to date with users' needs and software bugs**—A programmer's work does not finish when the program is passed to the user. Even if there are no errors in the program, continued monitoring and updating may be required.
- **Writing or reviewing documentation that describes installation and operating procedures**—This may be dull, but it's absolutely essential.
- **Designing and coding screen layouts, graphical user interfaces, printed outputs, and interfaces with other systems**—Sometimes the a program's appearance can be like an electronic signature that a programmer leaves behind. Creating a usable and effective user interface can heavily influence the user's opinion of a program's usability.
- **Compiling programs and correcting errors detected in the compilation process**—Programmers must be able to do this. Looking for your own mistakes is perhaps not the most encouraging of pastimes, but it's essential nevertheless. This is part of the defensive programming mindset.
- **Providing technical assistance by responding to inquiries regarding errors, problems, or questions with a program**—Sometimes what's needed will be as simple as helping a user to install the program. At other times it will involve troubleshooting a major problem with an application.

Overall, the programmer is typically responsible for software design, coding, compiling, debugging, program testing, and revision. Programmers generally work in an office setting and may have to work evenings or weekends to meet deadlines or debug programs. With advancing technology, however, programmers can now work outside the office. In fact, it's completely possible and often required for programmers to write and troubleshoot programs and perform daily tasks in their off hours and away from the office.

Programming Training and Certification

It's not difficult to search the Internet and find an employer looking to hire skilled programmers. In these advertised jobs, there seems to be little variation on the tasks and responsibilities employers require from their programmers. There is, however, a confusing level of variation of job qualifications and educational requirements.

Interestingly, some employers demand an overwhelming, and seemingly impossible, amount of education and experience from potential candidates. These employers require extensive knowledge in numerous operating systems, languages, and a bachelor's degree or higher. Other employers are far less concerned with formal education and focus their requirements on a programmer's level of experience. Some companies so desperately need programmers that they actively try to recruit them away from other companies.

This range of qualifications an employer will accept from candidates can leave those interested in programming as a career confused as to what level of knowledge and training is required to get a job. It's no secret that the IT industry as a whole is experiencing a shortage of skilled professionals, and programming is no exception. It's because of this shortage that employers will take a programmer with no formal education and hire solely on experience and a proven ability to program.

Companies requiring that candidates have bachelor's degrees specify that degrees should ideally be in computer science, mathematics, or information systems. Computer science degrees are preferred, as they give training in a number of specific computer areas, including best practices for programming security.

But degrees and diplomas are not the only form of training in the IT world. Students widely seek and employers widely recognize IT certifications. Certifications have the following key advantages over degree or diploma programs:

- Certification programs take less time, meaning that students are typically ready to enter the job market faster.

- Certification courseware and training materials are focused and directed, whereas degree programs often require elective courses that are not always related to the specific area of IT.

- Hardware and software change at a very rapid pace. Shorter, more-focused certification programs are better able to accommodate retraining for changing technology.

Training and Certification

Like many other areas of the IT industry, training options and opportunities for those interested in becoming programmers are varied and diverse. This diversity allows you to choose which training method best suits your learning style and provides you with the necessary training to be competitive in the labor market.

It's important to keep in mind that regardless of which training method you choose, employers will have their own preferences with regard to training. Today, employers will look more favorably upon someone who has completed training in a college or university. Degrees and diplomas obtained from a respected post-secondary institutions are a definite asset and do attest to quality instruction. This instruction, however, does not come cheaply. Certifications are also widely sought, but these certifications are more valuable when obtained from a recognized source.

A number of options are available for specific computer language and product training. Microsoft, for example, offers its Microsoft Certified Solutions Developer (MCSD) certification system. The following are four popular certifications:

- **Windows Store Apps**—For this certification, users learn Programming in HTML5 with JavaScript and CSS3, Essentials of Developing Windows Store Apps Using HTML5 and JavaScript, Advanced Windows Store App Development Using HTML5 and JavaScript, Programming in C#, Essentials Developing Windows Store Apps Using C#, and Advanced Windows Store App Development Using C#.

- **Web Applications**—Completion of the Web applications certification requires three courses—Programming in HTML5 with JavaScript and CSS3, Developing ASP.NET MVC Web Applications, and Developing Microsoft Azure and Web Services.

- **SharePoint Applications**—To be certified as a SharePoint administrator or programmer, you need the following courses: Programming in HTML5 with JavaScript and CSS3, Developing ASP.NET MVC Web Applications, Developing Microsoft SharePoint Server 2013 Core Solutions, and Developing Microsoft SharePoint Server 2013 Advanced Solutions.

- **Application Lifecycle Management Solutions Developer**—The courses for this certification are Administering Microsoft Visual Studio Team Foundation Server, Software Testing with Visual Studio, and Delivering Continuous Value with Visual Studio Application Lifecycle Management.

Microsoft isn't the only large vendor to offer programming certification. The following is a list of other online programming opportunities.

- **C++ Institute**—The C++ Institute focuses on the computer languages of C and C++. Training certifications include Associate (entry level), Professional (advanced level of programming understanding), and Senior (master-level understanding). (*http://www.cppinstitute.org/?p=5*)

- **Oracle Certified Professional Java SE 7 Programmer**—Oracle offers a certification for Java SE 7, a widely used object-oriented development platform. (*http://education .oracle.com/*)

- **Certified Secure Software Lifecycle Professional (CSSLP)**—Application vulnerabilities are a significant concern for organizational security. The CSSLP certification from (ISC)^2 prepares students to understand application security from a software development life cycle perspective. (*https://www.isc2.org/csslp/default.aspx*)

Reviewing Security Documentation

There are many computer languages from which to choose to develop a particular application. A programmer may need to know several to meet different programming requirements. No matter what language is used, it's important to review the latest documentation to see which new vulnerabilities have been detected. As an example, a programmer using Ruby would likely search the Web site *https://www.ruby-lang.org/en/security/* for known and new vulnerabilities. In the case of Ruby, the newly listed security considerations include the following:

- Ruby OpenSSL Hostname Verification (2015-04-13)
- Another Denial of Service XML Expansion (2014-11-13)
- Denial of Service XML Expansion (2014-10-27)
- Changed default settings of ext/openssl (2014-10-27)
- Dispute of Vulnerability CVE-2014-2734 (2014-05-09)
- OpenSSL Severe Vulnerability in TLS Heartbeat Extension (2014-04-10)

It's a best practice to review the latest news and documentation and consider any security vulnerabilities in program development.

Security and Careers—Network Management

Of all the IT career fields currently available, few can offer the diversity that computer networking provides. First, the networking industry is huge, encompassing hundreds of companies and a massive range of technologies. Second, the sheer demand for skilled individuals means that opportunities with companies of all sorts and sizes abound.

The reason for this high level of demand is simple. Practically every company has a network, and almost all have the need for a skilled individual to manage it. Even if companies cannot justify the cost of having a full-time administrator of their own, they are likely to have an arrangement with a computer company that does. For the past few years, computer networking has been one of the primary growth areas of the IT industry and is forecast to remain so in years to come.

In the early days of networking, the two main uses of a computer network were the sharing of data and the shared use of expensive peripherals, such as printers. Today, these two tasks still form the basis of most networks. But networks are now used in many other ways as well. Without a doubt, the defining point in the history of networking was the creation and explosive growth of the Internet. Although it's difficult to convey in just a few lines, the Internet is basically a massive network. In fact, the term *Internet* is derived from the term *internetwork*, meaning a group of connected networks. Although it's obvious that the scale of the Internet makes for differences in the technology used, the basis for the Internet is the same as that of many of the networks used in businesses around the world. All these networks must create and maintain a secure environment.

Essentially, networking is a concept or principle that requires a few core components including hardware (routers, servers, cabling etc.), software (applications, server operating systems), and protocols (TCP, UDP, IP etc.). These are the core components that make up the network and the components that network administrators must know inside and out in order to secure them adequately.

There is a great need for individuals to work on and secure the hardware aspect of networking (sometimes called the *infrastructure*). Equally, there is a demand for those that are skilled in securing the software and protocols that networks require. An in-depth understanding of how a network operates and communicates is critical for designing security strategies.

One of the most attractive features that a career in networking offers is sheer diversity—there are so many different aspects to the networking field. As a network administrator, you must have an understanding of the network operating systems that are in use, the products that provide backup capabilities, and (at least to some extent) the products that run on the servers you are supporting. You must have an understanding of network infrastructure issues, cabling, machine locating, and so on. In addition to these skills, there are a number of other areas in which you must have experience, such as business objectives, project planning, governance and much more.

Common Network Administration Tasks

Networking is a truly diverse field. Network administrators will find themselves in a variety of situations during a working day, which is part of the job's attraction. Much of their time will be spent working with systems, including securing those systems. The following list contains some of their most common tasks:

- **Performing general system maintenance**—Even the most basic computer network is a complicated device. The primary task of a network administrator is to ensure the overall health of the network. For this to be the case, continuous attention to all systems is necessary, although many companies use a management system to make the monitoring easier. Even so, the data supplied by the monitoring systems must be interpreted, and if necessary, acted upon. All of this can keep the network administrator busy.

- **Dealing with system failures**—The words a network administrator never likes to hear are "the system's down." Unfortunately, even the most diligently maintained network is likely to experience occasional problems. In many cases, the problems will be minor and isolated, but every so often a major problem will come along that will test not only your troubleshooting skills, but also your patience and ability to deal with stress. These are the times when network administrators really earn their salary. Every minute that the system is unavailable can potentially cost a company money. When the systems are down, the meter is running, and everyone's eyes are on the person who can make everything work again.

- **Applying software updates and fixes**—The complexity of software packages, coupled with the need for them to work securely, requires manufacturers to release updates to their software. The installation of these updates is essential to ensure that systems run smoothly and consistently. In addition, certain software programs, particularly programs such as virus checkers, require frequent updating. Though most updates are easily applied, network administrators must always consider what effect the updates may have on other software products. If suitable equipment is available, they must test the products before implementation.

- **Evaluating new solutions**—Just because an administrator has the network up and running smoothly does not mean that the job is done. The versatility of computer networks means that there will always be some other enhancement to add to the network or a new security vulnerability to address. This extra functionality often involves products that will change the layout of the network, could potentially affect the other components, and present new security implications. For this reason, any solution must be tested fully, and the results of those tests documented. Many larger companies provide a dummy test network for these purposes, although not all do. Because implementation of new solutions can require the network to be taken offline, a great deal of this kind of work takes place in the evenings or on weekends, so users are not disrupted. Network administrators must be flexible in this respect.

- **Documenting systems**—One of the most overlooked and neglected of all network administration tasks is that of documentation. Documentation provides a reference point for configuring the network. It's an invaluable resource when troubleshooting problems or investigating network-related issues. It also is very useful when planning upgrades to the system or when deciding to introduce new products. Unfortunately, the ever-changing nature of the network means that the process of updating the system documentation can be endless. The good news is that no one is awarding prizes for creativity, either. An easy-to-read, concise, and above all, accurate rundown on the specifics of the system is more than sufficient.

- **Performing and securing backups**—Sometimes referred to as a *disaster recovery measure*, backing up system data is probably one of the most important tasks performed each day. Most modern backup systems are highly automated, but the maintenance and checking of the system is very important. In addition, network administrators will periodically restore data from a backup to test that the system is working as it should, and that the data being restored can be used in the event of a failure. All backup data should be encrypted and stored in a physically secure location.

- **Maintaining hardware**—Much of a network administrator's work is software related, but because the software runs on hardware, a good knowledge of computer hardware is also required. Tasks that a network administrator may perform will range from upgrading or replacing individual components to replacing entire network segments. Maintaining hardware also includes firmware updates to ensure equipment is operating optimally and securely.

- **Maintaining cabling and network devices**—Cabling is the medium that makes computer networking happen. Even though a cabling contractor may install the main cabling system, there will always be computers needing relocation, new systems to be added, and equipment faults needing diagnosis and correction. In addition, many modern networks use hardware devices to connect systems together. Although novice network administrators may be excused from knowing all about these devices, those with even a few months' experience will almost certainly have to deal with them, even if infrequently.

- **Preparing for audits**—In corporate and other business environments, the entire IT infrastructure may be audited by a third party. If deficiencies in the management or security of the network are found, they may be reported to the board of directors and shareholders. Audits are annual events that are sure to cause network administrators much stress. Adherence to internal policies and general security best practices is the best way to complete a successful audit.

14

Security Training, Education, and Certification

Network Administration Training and Certification

Some argue that networking cannot be learned from a book or in a classroom and must be learned through real-world, on-the-job experience. The problem is, as elsewhere, getting the experience before you can get a job invokes the old chicken-and-egg situation: You need a job to get experience, but if you don't have experience, you sometimes can't find a job. Given the importance of network security, companies are naturally reluctant to allow those without significant real-world experience to manage their systems.

From an academic perspective, any college or university degree in a computer-related field is likely to be a valuable tool. For many graduates, the path to a given company will be via a graduate intake program, where the company recruits graduates, and then grooms them for certain positions. Without a graduate intake program, many graduates will find it necessary to display some specific knowledge in their chosen area of technology.

So how do employers choose the people for their vacant positions? Often, they use vendor certification programs, of which there are many. Currently, some of the most popular certification programs are the Microsoft Certified Solutions Expert (MCSE) program, the VMWare virtualization certification, Citrix and CompTIA. The relative popularity of these programs is no mystery—they closely reflect demand (and reward) in the marketplace.

From a personal perspective, those in the networking field must possess a wide range of skills: an ability to deal with stress, excellent communication skills, and the ability to remember (and at the appropriate moment retrieve) a wide range of facts on an even wider range of products.

Popular Network Management and Security Certifications

The number of networking related certifications can be overwhelming to those looking for a credential. Many vendor and vendor-neutral options are available. This section reviews some of the certifications, with a brief description of each.

- **Microsoft Certified Solutions Expert (MCSE)**—The MCSE program is recognized throughout the world as a measurement of an individual's knowledge of Windows operating systems and applications. There are nine MCSE specializations from which a student can choose. These include Server Infrastructure, Desktop Infrastructure, Private Cloud, Enterprise Devices and Apps, Data Platform, Business Intelligence, Messaging, Communication, and SharePoint. To become an MCSE, candidates must pass a series of Microsoft Certified Professional (MCP) exams. However, how an individual prepares for each exam is up to him or her. Once the required exams are successfully completed, Microsoft grants the designation of MCSE, allowing the holder to use the credentials and accompanying logo on résumés and business cards. For more information on the MCSE program, visit the Microsoft training Web site at *https://www.microsoft.com/learning/en-us/mcse-certification.aspx*.

- **CompTIA Security+**—The Security+ certification is a vendor-neutral security designation offered by CompTIA. The Security+ objectives cover a broad range of foundational security concepts without focusing on any specific vendor's technology. For more information and detailed exam objectives refer to CompTIA's Web site at *http://certification.comptia.org/getCertified/certifications/security.aspx*.

- **Certified Computer Examiner (CCE)**—The CCE certification is from the International Society of Forensic Computer Examiners (ISFCE). It's a vendor-neutral certification providing training around network infrastructure and network communications. For more information on the CEE refer to *https://www.isfce.com/certification.htm*.

- **EC-Council Certified Security Analyst (ECSA)**—Managing security is a complicated requirement for network administrators and IT security managers. The EC-Council Certified Security Analyst provides an intense training program focusing in three areas: Ethical Hacking (discovering vulnerabilities), Security Analysis (methodology of penetration testing), and Penetration Testing (security report and document control). More information on these certifications can be found at *http://www .eccouncil.org/about-ec-council-certified-security-analyst*.

- **Certified in the Governance of Enterprise IT (CGEIT)**—IT governance refers to the systems and processes used to ensure technology helps meet an organization's goals. Someone with this certification has the training to align technology with business goals. For more information on CGEIT certification refer to *http://www.isaca.org/ certification/*.

- **Cisco Certified Design Associate (CCDA)**—This certification indicates detailed training in network design and efficient network implementation. It's primarily for network design engineers, technicians, and support engineers, who enable efficient network environments with an understanding of network design fundamentals. A CCDA professional demonstrates the skills required to design basic campus, data center, security, voice, and wireless networks. The CCDA training covers many elements of networking including design, data centers, and security. More information can be found at *http://www.cisco.com/web/learning/certifications/associate/ccda/index.html*.

- **Citrix Virtualization Certification**—Citrix Education offers two tracks for virtualization training: Citrix Certified Enterprise Engineer (CCEE) for Virtualization, and Citrix Certified Integration Architect (CCIA) for Virtualization. Both provide detailed information on the implementation and management of a network-wide virtualization infrastructure. More information can be found at *http://training.citrix.com/cms/ education/certification-links/ccee-and-ccia-for-virtualization/*.

- **VMWare Certified Design Expert**—Virtualization is common in both large and small networks. VMware is commonly used for both desktop virtualization and in server rooms. Given the popularity of virtualization, there is a huge need for IT professionals able to securely implement and manage virtual infrastructure. VMWare offers a number of courses, which can be viewed at *http://mylearn.vmware.com/ portals/certification/*.

These certifications and courses represent just a small sample of the courses that are available online. Finding training is really not difficult, but finding the right course for your needs and work environment can take a little time.

Security and Careers—Web Design and Administration

Of all the career paths available in IT today, working with Internet-related technologies is the broadest in scope and the most significant in demand. Corporations and businesses of all sizes require an integrated online strategy. External-facing Web sites collecting customer data, fulfilling orders, and marketing are commonplace. Internal-facing Internet and intranet sites are equally important. In order to understand how the Internet came to be what it's today, a bit of history may be helpful.

The focus of this section is on three specific job roles in Internet technology, which are closely related and often filled by the same person: Web developer, site designer, and webmaster.

The terms Web developer and Web designer are sometimes used interchangeably. They are similar roles with some differences. A Web developer is perhaps more of a specialist concentrating on the back-end development of a Web site. A developer will incorporate appropriate security measures from initial concept to completion. Web developers will often be part of writing the actual code that makes Web pages work. Site designers, on the other hand, formulate how the site is structured. This includes the organizational flow, navigational design, and usability features.

Finally, webmasters perform many of the administrative duties of maintaining the site, including upgrading the Web server hardware, adding newly created Web pages, performing security audits, managing permissions, updating documentation, and troubleshooting hardware challenges. Quite often, usually in smaller companies, these three job roles are combined into one. Although such a multifaceted position can offer you varied experiences, the division of focus and attention that you might encounter on a daily basis may be difficult to manage and may cause other challenges at times. Regardless, these three job roles come with their own individual set of responsibilities.

People in these three positions are no longer responsible for traditional Web sites only. The increasing popularity of touchscreen phones and tablet devices has forced a new knowledge and implementation requirement. Web developers need the ability, not only to develop sites for mobile devices, but to do it securely. Client-side input and client-side authentication on mobile devices are more complex to manage and control. Essentially today's Web developers, designers, and webmasters must ensure that Web sites are accessible and securely meets the needs of business. Perhaps now more than ever, testing, patching, and updating Web sites is mandatory. Data integrity and the public's privacy are in the hands of these Internet technologies.

The Deep Web

Have you ever wondered where all those Web sites are that are not indexed in Google or other search engines? In fact, only a small percentage of Web sites are actually indexed and therefore searchable. The large majority of Web sites are hidden from Google in what is known as the **Deep Web** or Dark Web. The Web familiar to you is what is known as the surface Web. It includes millions of sites, such as Amazon, Facebook, CNN, and others you commonly use. Beneath the surface, however are sites not found by the search-engine crawlers. These sites don't want or need search engines. In fact, it's estimated that like the tip of an iceberg, the surface Web represents only a small percentage of Internet content. The majority of Internet content is below the surface in the Deep Web.

The Deep Web is a place of anonymity and beyond the reach of regular search engines. Perhaps the best-known way of accessing the Deep Web is known as The Onion Router (TOR). The *onion* refers to the way encryption layers are stripped of Deep Web communications as they pass through Deep Web relays. This makes accessing the Deep Web much slower than the regular Web. In general, the Deep Web is not a place for Web developers to spend a lot of time, as it's full of threats and of all manner of illegal activity. While there are many legitimate uses for the Deep Web, the anonymity it provides creates a perfect environment for criminals of all sorts. The Silk Road black-market drug site was a well-known Deep Web site recently shut down—but not before creating a massive Deep Web drug portal. Also, it's suggested that the 2014 hack of Sony servers used a virus readily available on the Deep Web. Security professionals, programmers and developers need to have an idea of the threats that lie underneath the surface.

Securing Programming Languages for Web Developers

As stated earlier, the field of Web development consists of many technologies and skill sets that depend on a company's or a client's specific needs. These skills can include HTML authoring, programming Web applications, creating artwork optimized for the Internet, performing usability testing, and so on. In general, most Web developers are responsible for coding Web site content into HTML. Often this involves creating custom scripts in JavaScript or Active Server Pages (ASP) to enhance the functionality of the Web site.

Today, it isn't enough that Web developers and designers know various computer languages and platforms. They must know them well enough to ensure that coding and Web implementations are secure. In addition, each of the languages used requires maintenance and updates to ensure there are no vulnerabilities in the Web development process. Many of these languages come from large vendors who provide documentation and downloads, and their Web sites provide strong vendor support. Other Web development languages are available through GNU Public License, offering no paid support but a significant amount of online community help and support. The following is a short list of some of the programming languages Web developers use:

- **Adobe ColdFusion**—ColdFusion is a scripting language based on standard HTML. It's commonly used to create both standard Web sites and mobile applications. As with any other application, there are security updates and service packs to address potential development vulnerabilities. Security information and updates for ColdFusion can be found at *https://www.adobe.com/support/coldfusion/downloads_updates.html.*

- **Hypertext Preprocessor (PHP)**—PHP is a common open-source Web-development language commonly used within HTML to create Web forms, surveys, picture galleries, sign-in pages, and more. PHP is used to enhance HTML with additional features and interactivity. Because of the interactivity PHP provides, secure programming is essential. Updates for PHP can be downloaded at *http://php.net.* To ensure PHP programming is secure and follows best practices, refer to OWASP's PHP programming cheat sheet at *https://www.owasp.org/index.php/PHP_Security_Cheat_Sheet.*

- **Java**—Java is a widely used programming language used to create objects within standard and mobile Web sites. Java is used within Web sites to create integrated Web programs such as games, calculators and more. Details on Java security can be found at *https://www.java.com/en/security/.*

- **Perl**—Perl is an open source programming language used, among other things, to make dynamic Web pages and interactive Web elements. Updates and security information for Perl can be found at *https://www.perl.org/docs.html.*

- **Active Server Pages (ASP)**—ASP.NET represents Microsoft's training option for **Active Server Pages (ASP)**. ASP is a programming language used for creating Web sites. It's great for building standards-based Web sites with HTML5, CSS3, and JavaScript. Details and security information can be found at *http://www.asp.net/.*

Many other programming languages are used in the creation of Web ad mobile apps. Regardless of which one you choose, the best practice is to make sure that you apply security updates and periodically review vendor Web sites and community pages for security developments.

Daily Tasks for Web Developers

If an organization's primary revenue stream is from online sales transactions, quite often there is an extensive team of developers, content writers, graphic artists, and programmers collaborating on creating the various parts and pieces that make up a large e-commerce Web site.

In such situations, a Web developer might specialize in one or more of the areas that make up Web development. For example, you may be required to code ASP to integrate a database into the Web site. You could then find yourself working with database architects to create your code, and then handing the code off to another Web developer to write the HTML code around it for presentation to the end user over the Internet.

However, to truly master an area such as creating ASPs, you must also be somewhat proficient at HTML coding and database technologies. You should also know a programming language, such as Visual Basic. Because these technologies are so interrelated, you must familiarize yourself with the various areas that relate to your specialty in order to truly master it.

If you work for a smaller organization or one that uses a Web site as a sales tool to bring customers to a retail location, you will quickly find yourself handling many of these tasks or working with a group of developers having similar skills. The reason for this is that the Web site may not necessarily be generating a high volume of income for the company and therefore not have the budget to hire staff who specialize in one area or another. The upside is that the site itself will not be required to perform very sophisticated tasks that require experienced specialists.

Regardless of the employment environment, most of a Web developer's day is spent in front of a computer generating the code for Web pages on the site. A more challenging aspect of being a Web developer is working with all the other individuals who create the Web site's content and. Generally, you will find yourself taking content from a copy editor and artwork from the art director, and combining it into the design that the site designer has specified. The challenge arises when each department has a specific idea of how its elements should be implemented into the final design. It's easy to find yourself being an ambassador of sorts to all of the departments. However, many Web developers feel this is the most fulfilling part of their job. The following list contains some of the more common day-to-day tasks of a Web developer:

- **Develop secure end user interfaces**—This task involves working with a site designer who has determined how the Web site will look and function. It's the developer's responsibility to write the secure code that makes the design happen. An additional challenge is keeping the code compatible with both traditional Web sites and mobile applications.

- **Write supporting client- or server-side code**—In addition to writing HTML or any other code, many Web developers find themselves writing scripting code that enhances user interactivity, for example using JavaScript (client-side) and ASP (server-side). Secure interactive coding requires strict validation of user input.

- **Integrate supporting applications**—On many e-commerce sites, the programs that check inventory, process orders, and complete credit card transactions are written in compiled languages, such as Java or C++. It's the duty of the Web developer to securely integrate these applications into the HTML code used on the Web site.

- **Integrate supporting databases**—Many sophisticated Web sites use databases for collecting and storing customer and inventory information, as well as user authentication. As with applications, it's up to the Web developer to securely integrate a database into the Web site. This usually involves writing scripts to parse the data and formatting it into HTML.

- **Write or update content**—The most common task of a Web developer is to write content in HTML, the Web's standard programming language. Furthermore, that content must be kept fresh and up-to-date with the latest security developments in mind. Therefore, updating current pages with new content becomes routine for a Web developer.

Training and Certification

To be truly qualified in Web development, you need not only proficiency in languages such as HTML, JavaScript, PHP, and ASP, but also some extensive skills in graphic design and page layout. These skills are not limited to image manipulation only, with a program like Photoshop. They also include the ability to combine images and content in such a way that is useful and engaging to the site's visitors. The best Web developers have backgrounds in communication media, graphic arts, and computer science.

With the increased demand for Web developers, many continuing education schools and universities are offering courses in Web development. You should look for a training program that teaches you not only about HTML and Internet technologies, but also more intermediate- and advanced-level topics, such as JavaScript, ASP, database integration, and of course, security. Additionally, some basic programming skills would be beneficial as well. Many of these programs offer graduate recruitment and internship offerings. Thereafter, the particular company that hires you will most likely provide you with any additional training in areas that are valuable to its business model.

If you don't have the benefit of a job-placement program, you should create a personal Web site that showcases your abilities. Many Internet service providers (ISPs) give their members personal Web site space as part of their service agreement. This Web site space provides you with the capability to create an online portfolio of sorts that will give a potential employer a good idea of your skills as a developer.

There are not nearly as many certification programs available to a potential Web developer as there are for network administration. Individuals seeking to break into the Web development field will find a handful of vendor-neutral certifications available online that test for entry-level knowledge, but don't go into detailed or specific areas of development, such as ASP or Perl.

That's not to say these certifications are not valuable, however. They will provide you with the ability to prove to a potential employer that you know the basic skills required of a Web developer. This will greatly aid you in getting your foot in the door and working in a development environment. It's then up to you to train yourself to specialize in a particular skill that interests you.

More and more certifications for Web development are beginning to appear regularly. The following are two of the more widely recognized and accepted certifications available today, in addition to the Microsoft Certified Solutions Developer Web Applications track touched on earlier in this chapter:

- **Zend PHP Certification**—Zend provides an industrywide certification demonstrating competence in PHP programming. More information can be found at *http://www .zend.com/en/services/certification.*

- **W3Schools Online Certification**—W3Schools offers a number of certifications for Web developers. These include certification for HTML, HTML5, CSS, Javascript, JQuery, PHP and XML. More information on these certifications can be located at *http://www.w3schools.com/cert/.*

CHAPTER SUMMARY

Securing Web applications is not just the responsibility of Web developers, designers, and security specialists. Creating a secure Web infrastructure involves all the professions within IT. This includes a database administrator securing the backend databases; a network administrator securing hardware, software, and network communications; the programmer keeping programming tools up-to-date; or the IT manager and CIO creating robust security policies. When it comes to security, everyone has a role to play.

There are many programming languages; some of them are supported by large vendors, while others are open source, supported by active online communities and passionate developers. Regardless of the language chosen, you must examine each language, policy, and procedure keep abreast of updates and maintenance. This is the only way to ensure IT security and to minimalize vulnerability wherever possible.

KEY CONCEPTS AND TERMS

Active Server Pages (ASP)	Database designer	Relational database
Business intelligence (BI)	Deep Web	
Database administrator	Defensive programming	

CHAPTER 14 ASSESSMENT

1. Data typically refers to raw unorganized facts.

A. True
B. False

2. A SQL server database is an example of a relational database.

A. False
B. True

3. The TOR browser is used to access which of the following?

A. SQL databases
B. Relational databases
C. Deep Web
D. Oracle databases

4. Which of the following represents a mindset whereby programming is done with a clear understanding of current threats and how these threats potentially impact overall security?

A. PHP secure
B. ASP.Net
C. Defensive programming
D. CSSLP

5. Which of the following professions are concerned with the back-end development of a Web site and will incorporate appropriate security measures from initial concept to completion?

A. Network architect
B. Web developer
C. Webmaster
D. Database designer
E. None of the above

6. A(n) _____ is a set of instructions understood by the computer allowing it to perform predetermined functions.

A. Program
B. Web site
C. Database
D. RDMS

7. Which of the following professions are open-source programming languages?

A. ASP
B. Perl
C. PHP
D. ColdFusion

8. _____ refers to the systems and processes used to ensure technology helps meet and organizations goals.

A. Policy
B. Scripting
C. Governance
D. Tracking

9. Certification courseware and training materials are focused and directed, but degree programs often require elective courses that are not always related to the specific area of IT.

A. True
B. False

10. Which of the following professions are concerned with managing database security, such as the list of users who have access to all or part of the database?

A. Network architect
B. Web developer
C. Webmaster
D. Database administrator
E. Both A and D

© Rodolfo Clix/Dreamstime.com

Web Application Security Organizations

THERE IS NO SINGLE NATIONAL OR INTERNATIONAL governing body for information security. A large number of national security interests exists—private and government sectors and academic and commercial interests, among others.

In addition, a wealth of information security qualifications and education programs is available, ranging from academic and professional to independent and vendor certifications. In short, it's no easy task to understand all the details and match them with your particular requirements. This chapter discusses the key qualifications in information security and sheds light on the purpose of each one.

Chapter 15 Topics

This chapter covers the following topics and concepts:

- What the Department of Homeland Security (DHS) is
- What the National Cyber Security Division (NCSD) is
- What the United States Computer Emergency Response Team Coordination Center (CERT®/CC) is
- What the MITRE Corporation and the CVE list are
- What the National Institute of Standards and Technology (NIST) is
- What the International Information Systems Security Certification Consortium, Inc. (ISC)^2 is
- What the Web Application Security Consortium (WASC) is
- What the Open Web Application Security Project (OWASP) is

Chapter 15 Goals

When you complete this chapter, you will be able to:

- Understand the responsibilities and interests of various national and international security organizations
- Understand some of the non-vendor certificates and programs available
- Determine which qualifications are applicable to your areas of interest

Department of Homeland Security (DHS)

The DHS is responsible for a wide area of the federal coordination of security issues and the specification and implementation of security controls. Within the information security arena, DHS has specific management responsibility for the National Cyber Security Division, the National Infrastructure Advisory Council, and the Critical Infrastructure Partnership Advisory Council.

The DHS also manages the U.S. Secret Service, which used to be part of the Department of the Treasury. Other DHS components that have significant information security responsibilities include Customs and Border Protection and the Transportation Security Administration (TSA).

Advisory Bodies

The National Infrastructure Advisory Council is a presidential advisory panel of up to 30 appointed members. Its role is to provide advice on securing key sectors of the economy and government. This covers many areas, including finance, utilities, telecommunications, transportation, and health care. The focus is on public-private cooperation.

The Critical Infrastructure Protection Panel is a much wider membership organization that promotes cooperation between the government and sector councils in support of the National Infrastructure Protection Plan. More information about DHS cybersecurity initiatives can be found at *http://www.dhs.gov/topic/cybersecurity*.

The U.S. Secret Service (USSS)

The U.S. Secret Service (USSS) has a historic role in protecting the stability of the national financial system. It initially started with an anti-counterfeiting role in 1865. Its official mission is "to safeguard the nation's financial infrastructure and payment systems to preserve the integrity of the economy."

The 2001 U.S.A. PATRIOT Act approved the creation of a network of electronic crimes task forces (ECTFs), and over 20 have been established in the United States. Any crime or investigation involving electronics/technology—including the Internet— can fall within the task forces' range of operation. Additionally, since 1994, the Secret Service has provided technical and computer forensic support to law enforcement in the investigation of missing and exploited children. More information on the USSS electronic crimes task force is available at *http://www.secretservice.gov/ectf_about.shtml*.

The Federal Law Enforcement Training Center (FLETC)

FLETC runs a range of technology and security training programs in its Technical Operations Division. Some programs of interest are:

- **Computer Network Investigations Training Program (CNITP)**—This program is designed to allow participants to conduct digital forensic seizures and investigations on networked systems.

- **Seized Computer Evidence Recovery Specialist (SCERS)**—This is an introductory program to computer forensic principles. It introduces students to leading forensic software products. It's used as a preliminary requirement for many other training programs.

- **Digital Evidence Acquisition Specialist Training Program (DEASTP)**— This is a fast-paced introduction to evidence recognition and seizure. It's a prerequisite for SCERS training.

- **First Responder to Digital Evidence Program (FRDE)**—A short program for first-response personnel, covering recognition and seizure principles.

Mutual Legal Assistance Treaties

Mutual legal assistance treaties (MLATs) define, in many cases, how law enforcement agencies in different countries should cooperate. For the United States, these agreements are generally managed through the legal attaché offices in embassies and consulates, which often are staffed by FBI Special Agents who pass requests to relevant national or local FBI teams.

MLAT activities are often inaccessible to the private citizen or corporate investigator. Processing requests generally takes considerable time both for authorization—necessary at the requesting and providing nations—and the communication of requests through diplomatic channels.

Many law enforcement organizations don't accept direct reporting from outside their local jurisdictions. This is known to significantly discourage victims from reporting Internet-related crime. However, both the ECTFs and the FBI Internet Crime Complaint Center (IC3) will accept notifications of Internet-related crimes if either the victim or the alleged criminal is in the United States.

- **Macintosh Forensics Training Program (MFTP)**—Specific training in forensic issues and activities for Apple systems running Mac OS.
- **Mobile Device Investigations Program (MDIP)**—Training focused on forensic recovery and interpretation from cellular telephones and fusion devices.

You can learn more about these training programs by visiting *https://www.fletc.gov/.*

National Cyber Security Division (NCSD)

Established by presidential decree, the NCSD is part of DHS and has responsibility for protecting the security of cyberspace and U.S. cyberassets. It works with federal, state, commercial, and international organizations. NCSD runs the National Cyberspace Response System and a range of cyber-risk management programs.

The National Cyberspace Response System is a comprehensive program that covers:

- **Computer vulnerabilities**—Under the Cybersecurity Preparedness and the National Cyber Alert System and the vulnerability investigation capabilities of US-CERT
- **Computer incident response**—Under US-CERT and the National Cyber Response Coordination Group
- **Information sharing**—Among attack investigators via the Cyber Cop Portal

United States Computer Emergency Response Team (US-CERT)

Founded in 2003, US-CERT is the operational arm of the NCSD, responding to incidents for the federal government. It cooperates with other national and commercial **computer incident response teams (CIRTs)** and law enforcement agencies to investigate and stop online attacks and restore services. It also provides a public threat and vulnerability alert service.

National Cyber Alert System

US-CERT takes Really Simple Syndication (RSS) feeds from several government agencies to make available several e-mail lists and associated feeds. Presently, five RSS feeds can keep you up to date on security tips, bulletins, and alerts, as well as the most recent security activities with leading vendors. The feeds range from detailed technical alerts for system administrators to a "tips" feed aimed at the home or non-technical user.

Cyber-Risk Management Programs

Currently, the NCSD offers three main public risk management programs:

- **Cyber Exercises: Cyber Storm**—A biennial event for federal and state agencies, international partners, and businesses, this exercise covers different industry sectors to provide practice and improve coordination and information-sharing in case of a massive cyberattack.

- **National Cybersecurity Awareness Month**—Every October since 2004, this event has provided the general public and smaller businesses with education and tools on basic Internet security techniques.

- **Software Assurance Program**—Through initiatives such as "Build Security In" and the Community Resources and Information Clearinghouse, this program enables software developers and vendors to deliver more secure and reliable products.

Additionally, the National Cybersecurity Awareness Campaign Challenge was set up to crowdsource new ways of communicating information security advice and techniques to the American public.

Computer Emergency Response Team Coordination Center (CERT®/CC)

CERT/CC was founded in 1988 under contract from DARPA, after the Morris Worm attack used various UNIX vulnerabilities and weaknesses (and a basic programming error) to bring a significant percentage of the fledgling Internet to a halt. CERT/CC is part of the Software Engineering Institute at Carnegie Mellon University. Although it no longer plays an active role in the investigation of computer incidents, CERT/CC conducts research and training for the wider **computer security incident response team (CSIRT)** community. (A CSIRT is an all-hours or on-call group for an organization, a corporation, or even a country designed to respond to online attacks or similar events.) CERT/CC also is a major sponsor of the international **Forum of Incident Response and Security Teams (FIRST)**. FIRST is a worldwide voluntary and collaborative body bringing together incident response teams and related organizations.

CERT/CC has a wide role in software assurance, secure systems engineering, risk management, and governance. It provides development support for countries and organizations wishing to implement CSIRTs and conducts significant research into new attack methods and forensic analyses of attacks.

Its education program, which is open to the public, includes:

- **The Certified Computer Security Incident Handler qualification**—A range of courses and an online examination to support a DoD 8750.1M-compliant certification in incident handling.

- **CSIRTs**—Courses are available for organizations in the creation and management of CSIRTs.

- **OCTAVE (Operationally Critical Threat, Asset, and Vulnerability Exposure)**—This is the risk management methodology developed at CERT/CC.

- **Malware**—Training in the analysis of malicious code is provided. This course is currently open only to employees of the U.S. government or its contractors.

Training is also provided in the application of various metrics and models developed by CERT/CC and in secure coding.

The MITRE Corporation and the CVE List

The MITRE Corporation is a major government and defense contractor, albeit one set up and operating as a not-for-profit corporation. MITRE runs four Federally Funded Research and Development Centers (FFRDCs) and provides technical consulting to federal agencies and other bodies. The MITRE Corporation also maintains the **Common Vulnerabilities and Exposures (CVE) list**. The National Cyber Security Division of the Department of Homeland Security sponsors the CVE.

> **NOTE**
>
> SecurityFocus is now part of Symantec Corporation.

Why CVE?

In the 1990s, there was no commonly accepted reference system for computer and software vulnerabilities. The famous Bugtraq and Vulnerability Development (Vuln Dev) mailing lists were run by the private SecurityFocus organization. In addition, many Web sites, conferences, and other private, public, and academic mailing lists announced new vulnerabilities.

These lists allow researchers to release a brief description of a problem, a full academic paper, or a proof-of-concept exploit. Individual software authors and vendors published details about problems and patches. Keeping track of whether a particular problem was relevant to your systems and whether a patch was available was not a trivial issue, especially across large organizations with heterogeneous IT architectures.

Many security testing tools used their own reference system. This helped IT managers determine whether a detected problem was common between different parts of an organization or even different architectures within the same business area. This required a detailed knowledge of the security vulnerability publication process. However, systems administrators—then and now—are generally responsible for maintenance and update, not security. However, the lack of a commonly accepted system existed until the Common Vulnerabilities and Exposures (CVE) list was created.

Common Vulnerabilities and Exposures (CVE) List

MITRE established the CVE list in 1999 in collaboration with a number of software and security vendors. The CVE list was rapidly accepted by the general industry as a basic reference. In 2003, "CVE-Compatible" accreditation for testing products was launched. To date, nearly 100 products from more than 50 companies have been formally certified, with over 150 more declared compatible.

CVE does have its problems. For example, when an entry is initially added to the CVE list, the entry has a status of "candidate." After the entry has been reviewed and accepted, its status is changed to "entry." There can be a long delay between a candidate appearing on the list and finally being accepted as an entry. However, its enormous success has been its near-universal acceptance as a single reference for vulnerability reports, allowing effective cross-reference between detection engines, vendor bulletins, patch management software, and other utilities.

What Is a CVE Identifier?

CVE is intended to be a basic list, neither a database nor the repository of all information about a particular vulnerability. A single entry on the list is known as a "CVE identifier" and is composed of the following information about a vulnerability:

- **CVE number**—This is in the form of CVE-YYYY-nnnn, for example, CVE-2010-1868.

- **Identifier status**—Either "candidate" or "entry." Before 2005, candidates were identified with a "CAN" label rather than a "CVE" prefix.

- **Description**—This is a brief, standardized description of the vulnerability. In the case of 2010-1868, the description is "The (1) sqlite_single_query and (2) sqlite_array_query functions in ext/sqlite/sqlite.c in PHP 5.2 through 5.2.13 and 5.3 through 5.3.2 allow context-dependent attackers to execute arbitrary code by calling these functions with an empty SQL query, which triggers access of uninitialized memory."

- **References**—These may be to the discoverer's announcement, the vendor's security bulletin, or third-party reports such as the Open Source Vulnerability Database at *http://osvdb.org.*

- **Additional**—Candidates may also have information on the stages of the CVE process, and any votes from the CVE Editorial Board. This also includes a comment field.

Quite deliberately, there is a lack of data within each CVE identifier. More information is available through other tools such as the National Vulnerability Database.

Generating New List Entries

Anyone who discovers a potential vulnerability can report the basic details directly to MITRE or to one of the CVE Numbering Authorities. MITRE also scours public vulnerability lists for new vulnerabilities.

A "candidate number" will be assigned and the basic information can be recorded. Before a candidate can become an entry, it must be reviewed by the members of the CVE Editorial Board, who then vote for it to be rejected, modified, or accepted. Once sufficient votes are cast for acceptance, the vulnerability will be published as an entry. Entries may continue to be modified after publication, normally to add additional references.

Sincere Flattery

The success of the CVE model has led to the creation of a number of similar ones. These include Common Configuration Enumeration (CCE) and Common Attack Pattern Enumeration and Classification (CAPEC), which are also run by MITRE. The requirement for categorization has led to the creation of a number of formalized language schemes such as MAEC (for malware), CWE (for weaknesses), and OVAL (for vulnerabilities).

An exception is in the world of malicious code. Although the Computer Antivirus Researcher Organization (CARO) has been in existence since 1991, antivirus products continue to use naming schemes particular to each vendor. This can make it difficult, if not impossible, to determine common cause between infections in different organizations or even different parts of the same organization.

National Institute of Standards and Technology (NIST)

Founded at the turn of the 20th century as the National Bureau of Standards, NIST has both a historic and a continuing role in information security, largely through its Computer Security Division. As the name implies, it's the U.S. federal authority on standards. NIST publishes essential information such as the Federal Information Processing Standards (FIPS) series, the Special Publications 800 series of guides and recommendations, and the Federal Desktop Core Configuration. The United States Government Configuration Baseline (USGCB) initiative provides security configuration baselines for information technology products widely deployed within the federal government—primarily Microsoft products, including operating systems and firewalls.

However, NIST does not play a significant role in U.S. representation to the International Standards Organization, responsible for the ISO 27000 series. That is coordinated by American National Standards Institute (ANSI). ANSI is also the U.S. national representative body for the International Electrotechnical Commission (IEC).

Technical Security Standards

The FIPS series sets specifications for essential security components. For example, FIPS 197 covers the Advanced Encryption Standard (AES) algorithm. FIPS 180-3 details the Secure Hash Standard, including SHA-1. FIPS 140 covers security requirements for encryption modules across four levels. Standards also exist for security areas as wide as personnel vetting and automated password generators. Although these standards are generally binding only on the U.S. federal government, many are widely used commercially and internationally.

technical TIP

When you are looking for an evaluated encryption product and the salesperson claims FIPS 140 certification, your first question should be "To what level?" If you require multifactor authentication for crypto administration—a common control within Payment Card Industry Data Security Standard (PCI DSS) encryption management schemes—this is not mandated until the highest level, which is 4. In comparison, solutions at level 1 don't require any form of user authentication.

NIST also runs the processes for replacement standards, such as the competition for an AES algorithm to replace DES between 1997 and 2000, won by the Rijndael algorithm. In October 2012, NIST announced that Keccak (pronounced "catch-ack") would become NIST's SHA-3 hash algorithm. It was created by Guido Bertoni, Joan Daemen, and Gilles Van Assche of STMicroelectronics and Michaël Peeters of NXP Semiconductors. Their entry beat out 63 other submissions that NIST received after its open call for candidate algorithms in 2007.

> **NOTE**
> Data Encryption Standard (DES) FIPS 46 was based on the IBM Lucifer cipher. The cipher was developed by Horst Feistel, a German and naturalized American citizen. Joan Daemen and Vincent Rijmen, who developed AES, the replacement for DES, are both Belgian citizens.

Publications that don't meet the requirements for issue of a FIPS are often issued under the "Special Projects" report system. Titled "Guide to" or "Recommendation for," these publications don't have the legal force of FIPS and cover wider areas of general interest to the information security community. Recent reports have included guides to protecting personally identifiable information, the use of encryption algorithms and appropriate key lengths, and the secure deployment of Internet Protocol version 6 (IPv6) addressing technologies.

Computer Security Resource Center (CSRC)

Within NIST, the Computer Security Division was established as part of the Information Technology Laboratory in response to Section 303 of the Federal Information Security Management Act of 2002. The act requires NIST among other things, to "develop standards and guidelines, including minimum requirements, for providing adequate information security for all agency operations and assets."

Within the Computer Security Division, the CSRC provides public access to NIST final and draft reports, the Federal Computer Security Program Managers' Forum, and the work of the three operational groups. It also hosts the National Vulnerability Database.

The National Vulnerability Database

To allow for rapid and open dissemination of new vulnerability data, CVE identifiers contain minimal information about the actual vulnerability.

The National Vulnerability Database (NVD) is intended to allow automation of vulnerability management activities and the production of compliance metrics, as part of the Federal Information Security Automation Program. The NVD provides a standards-based repository, using the Security Content Automation Protocol and standard dictionaries such as the Common Platform Enumeration (CPE) standard. Although it's funded and hosted by the U.S. government, the database is freely accessible and incorporated into many security testing and management tools.

In fact, PCI DSS documentation requires the incorporation of NVD reference data into vulnerability reports.

International Information Systems Security Certification Consortium, Inc. (ISC)^2

The **International Information Systems Security Certification Consortium (ISC)^2** is a nonprofit professional and certification body that focuses on programs for information security professionals. (ISC)^2 is one of the largest and oldest information security qualification organizations in the world.

(ISC)^2 runs a variety of widely accepted security certifications. Launched in 1989 in the United States, it now claims over 70,000 qualified members in 135 countries. As well as providing certification examinations and training, it hosts monthly e-symposia and coordinates the "Safe and Secure Online" education program for children between 11 and 14.

Since 2004, the organization has been gaining accreditation for its certifications, as well as expanding the range and depth of certifications available. Gradually, the examinations are being moved to an online format through the Pearson VUE network of test centers.

Each (ISC)^2 qualification requires:

- A set amount of professional experience, from one to five years, requiring endorsement by a current (ISC)^2 member
- Adherence to the (ISC)^2 code of ethics
- Self-certification regarding the applicant's criminal record and background
- Completion of a multiple-choice examination

Once qualified, an (ISC)^2 certification is valid for three years. Certificate holders must pay an annual maintenance fee. They must also complete annual, continuing professional education (CPE) credits.

Certified Information Systems Security Professional (CISSP)

The Certified Information Systems Security Professional (CISSP) is the first (ISC)^2 certification, launched in 1994. With over 67,000 qualified professionals, this is the must-have qualification in the eyes of many recruiters and human resources (HR) departments.

U.S. DoD Directive 8570

The trend in the information security community is toward increased, verifiable professionalism. A strong driver for the rapid growth in formal security certifications has been the December 2005 introduction of DoD Directive 8750.

In the recently revised and reissued Directive 8750.01M, the U.S. Department of Defense (DoD) requires that anyone with privileged access to departmental information systems obtain and maintain a commercial information security qualification accredited to ISO 17024. This applies to military personnel (regular or reserve) and civilian and contract employees, and is being extended to DoD contractors. Overall, the directive affects an estimated 110,000 people—about the same number as the total certified membership of the two largest certification bodies—(ISC)^2 and ISACA.

There are 22 qualifications on the basic approval list, which you can find in Appendix 3 of the directive. The approved suppliers are (ISC)^2, CERT-CC, SANS GIAC, CompTIA, ISACA, and SecurityCertified. The precise qualifications depend on the role(s) you might fill: technical, manager, engineering, or computer network defense. As many as five qualifications or as few as one are currently approved depending on role or level: for the System Architect and Engineer specialization, only CISSP and its concentrations are currently acceptable.

Like the rest of the (ISC)^2 programs, the CISSP is based on a published Common Body of Knowledge (CBK). The CBK includes several domains, or topic areas. The CISSP examines the following domains, requiring you to have five years of practical experience covering at least two of the domains:

- Access Control
- Application Development Security
- Business Continuity and Disaster Recovery Planning
- Cryptography
- Information Security Governance and Risk Management
- Legal, Regulations, Investigations, and Compliance
- Operations Security
- Physical (Environmental) Security
- Security Architecture and Design
- Telecommunications and Network Security

Criticized in the early 2000s for its focus on U.S. law and jargon, (ISC)^2 began a comprehensive internationalization program and now offers the exam in multiple languages based on a comprehensive, internationally relevant question bank.

The exam has 250 questions; candidates have six hours to complete it. This exam format differs from similar certification tests elsewhere in the world, such as in Europe. Nevertheless, at least 138 countries accept the certification. There are, in fact, more than 36 countries with at least 100 qualified CISSPs.

CISSP Concentrations

Although promoted as the gold standard information security certification, the CISSP is a generalist qualification, lacking the depth to assess more detailed areas of knowledge. As a result of industry demand, three concentrations were introduced in 2004:

- CISSP Information Systems Security Architecture Professional (CISSP-ISSAP)
- CISSP Information Systems Security Engineering Professional (CISSP-ISSEP)
- CISSP Information Systems Security Management Professional (CISSP-ISSMP)

Each of these credentials requires the holder to have the CISSP qualification and two years' experience in the relevant discipline. The candidate must also pass an additional three-hour, 125-question exam.

The Architecture and Management concentrations are fully international, with residents of over 40 countries holding each qualification. The Engineer concentration was developed with assistance from the U.S. National Security Agency. Although it's available internationally, it focuses on U.S. laws, regulations, policies, guidelines, and standards. It also addresses U.S. federal government information assurance governance. Accordingly, over 95 percent of ISSEP holders work in the United States, with Canada the only other country to have more than 10 qualified people. Table 15-1 lists the three CISSP concentrations and the CBK domains they cover.

With over 600 holders of each concentration, and especially considering the higher attainment requirements, these qualifications seem to be a moderate industry success. All three concentrations have been ISO 17024 accredited since October 2008. (**ISO 17024** is the international standard for accrediting schemes that certify personal competences.)

Systems Security Certified Practitioner (SSCP)

Introduced in 2001 as a more focused technical certification, the SSCP requires only one year of professional experience and is significantly narrower in scope than the CISSP. The SSCP covers the following seven domains in the CBK:

- Access Controls
- Cryptography
- Malicious Code and Activity
- Monitoring and Analysis
- Networks and Communications
- Risk, Response, and Recovery
- Security Operations and Administration

TABLE 15-1 CISSP concentrations and associated CBK domains.

CISSP CONCENTRATION	CBK DOMAINS COVERED
CISSP-ISSAP	Access Control Systems and Methodology
	Communications & Network Security
	Cryptography
	Security Architecture Analysis
	Technology-Related Business Continuity Planning (BCP) & Disaster Recovery Planning (DRP)
	Physical Security Considerations
CISSP-ISSEP	Systems Security Engineering
	Certification and Accreditation (C&A)
	Technical Management
	U.S. Government Information Assurance Governance
CISSP-ISSMP	Security Management Practices
Note: The CISSP-ISSMP credential is intended as a higher-level management qualification than the ISACA CISM.	Systems Development Security
	Security Compliance Management
	Contingency Management
	Law, Investigation, Forensics and Ethics

The SSCP exam has 125 questions for candidates to complete in three hours. It's pitched as a lower-level qualification. As such, it competes against a wide range of vendor technical security certifications, some SANS qualifications, and entry-level certifications such as CompTIA Security+. There are just over 1,000 SSCP certification holders in 50 countries.

The SSCP received ISO 17024 accreditation in 2006.

(ISC)² Associate

In November 2001, a 16-year-old Indian boy, Namit Merchant, passed the CISSP exam. A thorough investigation was conducted, and, to general incredulity, Merchant proved he had the then-necessary three years of relevant industry experience. He had started at 13 implementing security controls in financial software for the Bombay-based company Compuware. At the time of the exam, he was still attending high school and working for Network Intelligence India.

Since then, many people have wanted to take the exam while still in school or shortly after completing their education and before gaining the professional experience needed. (ISC)² introduced the Associate program in 2003.

Associates pay reduced fees and can take either the CISSP or the SSCP exam; they have time after passing to gain the necessary professional experience. Associate status is considered ISO 17024 accredited, provided that the candidate has passed either of the allowed exams and is working in the relevant area.

Certification and Accreditation Professional (CAP)

This qualification was introduced in 2006 and is aimed at people involved in risk management and accreditation of systems. Although this level of formalization is rare in private companies, it's common in the government and government suppliers sectors internationally. There is now a four-domain CBK, the first two of the initial five having been combined:

- **Initiate the Preparation Phase**—Formerly known as "Certification and Accreditation Process" and "Certification Phase"
- **Perform Execution Phase**—Formerly known as "Accreditation Process"
- **Perform Maintenance Phase**—Formerly known as "Continuous Monitoring"
- **Understand the Purpose of Security Authorization**

The CAP examination comprises 125 questions, and candidates have up to three hours for the exam.

Given the niche nature of this qualification and competing mandatory government qualifications in some countries, the certificate has been relatively successful, with approximately 700 issued. CAP was ISO 17024 accredited in October 2009.

Certified Secure Software Lifecycle Professional (CSSLP)

The most recent (ISC)² credential, CSSLP is aimed at a wide sector of the information technology profession, which rarely receives security training or testing. Since September 2008, about 900 project managers, quality assurance testers, technical architects, analysts, developers, and programmers have earned certification. The seven CBK areas are:

- **Secure Software Concepts**—Security implications in software development
- **Secure Software Requirements**—Capturing security requirements in the requirements phase
- **Secure Software Design**—Translating security requirements into application design elements
- **Secure Software Implementation/Coding**—Unit testing for security functionality, resilience after attack, and developing secure code and exploit mitigation
- **Secure Software Testing**—Integrated quality assurance testing for security functionality and resiliency to attack
- **Software Acceptance**—Security implications of the software acceptance phase
- **Software Deployment, Operations, Maintenance, and Disposal**—Security issues around steady state operations and software management

The examination is the standard multiple-choice format, with 175 questions in four hours. This is the pilot qualification for the new online examination and has been available through Pearson VUE centers since April 2010.

Web Application Security Consortium (WASC)

The Web Application Security Consortium (WASC) was founded in January 2004 to compile best practices in securing Web applications, then a relatively new area. The consortium brings together industry and academic experts and major corporations concerned with tools' development and performance. WASC contributes to the open availability of information and methods of attack research. It also contributes significantly to the effort in evaluating and ensuring consistency in the commercially available security automation tools.

WASC Projects

WASC runs a number of projects aimed at improving the distribution of information about Web vulnerabilities. The results of these projects are distributed openly, mostly under the Creative Commons Attribution license, and are available for use in commercial products:

- **The Web-Hacking Incident Database**—A regularly updated database, containing nearly 1,000 records at the time of this writing. This is a Web-accessible, searchable 15-field database describing publicly exploited Web security issues. It's an excellent resource for researchers and security operations teams seeking to justify additional testing or controls.

- **Distributed open proxy honeypots**—A **honeypot** is a carefully monitored system set up by security professionals to be attacked, so that attack sources and methods can be analyzed. The concept of using honeypots to distract hackers became popular in 1999. Open proxies are computers that anonymously accept and forward requests for network services, and they are often used to shield attackers from tracking. Maintaining a suitably attackable Web site honeypot is a difficult and time-consuming exercise. To get around that problem, this project combines the two ideas—running a series of open proxies and allowing their use, while carefully recording and analyzing the traffic for malicious content.

FYI

Open source refers to a copyright or licensing system that, compared with conventional commercial licensing schemes, allows wide use and modification of the material. But not all open source licenses are equal. You need to take considerable care when using open source components in or as a resource for non-commercial and commercial work. Some licenses provide significant flexibility, requiring mere attribution. Others impose onerous conditions, such as requiring that derivative or inclusive work be licensed under identical terms.

- **(Web) Threat Classification**—This provides a detailed and comprehensive dictionary for both Web attack types and target system weaknesses, allowing specific vulnerabilities or incidents to be reliably categorized.

- **Evaluation criteria**—WASC supports two evaluation criteria projects, one aimed at Web application security scanning tools, the other concerned with Web application layer firewalls. Both projects produce detailed lists of expected functionality. Developers can use these criteria to ensure that functionality is comprehensive. Analysts and reviewers regularly use the lists to evaluate the capabilities of competing products.

- **Security statistics**—An annual project collates and publishes sanitized Web site vulnerability data. The latest report (2008) analyzes results from more than 10,000 site reviews, varying from simple Internet scans to white box penetration tests and nearly 100,000 specific detected vulnerabilities. Cross-site scripting issues and information leakage form the bulk of the detected issues—together comprising nearly three quarters of all issues.

- **Additional projects**—The Web Security Glossary attempts to provide a comprehensive dictionary. The Script Mapping Project tackles the complex interactions between various Web browser versions and implementations and Hypertext Markup Language (HTML) specified "intrinsic events" that can cause script execution.

Open Web Application Security Project (OWASP)

OWASP, like WASC, is an open source community project. Unlike WASC's concentration on automation of testing, OWASP's focus is on educating application developers on security risks. It produces the OWASP Top 10 List, a number of security testing tools and security application programming interfaces (APIs), a range of guidebooks, and the Open Software Maturity Model. You'll learn about these OWASP offerings in this section.

OWASP content and tools can be distributed under any Open Source Initiative approved license. You need to ensure that the license for any tool you wish to use or modify is appropriate for your organization.

OWASP Top 10 List

OWASP maintains a Top 10 list of Web application vulnerability types. These are not specific coding errors but rather more generic groupings of potential flaws. Testing for the OWASP list is mandatory within PCI DSS and has been accepted by the Federal Trade Commission, the DoD, and a large number of government and business organizations in the United States and internationally.

You can read more about OWASP security initiatives on its Web site at *https://www .owasp.org/index.php/Main_Page*.

WebScarab

WebScarab is an application analysis tool for Hypertext Transfer Protocol (HTTP) and Hypertext Transfer Protocol Secure (HTTPS) communications. It's written in Java and therefore is relatively platform independent. It's normally used as a recording proxy server, allowing the capture and analysis of Web application data. It will intercept and re-encrypt HTTPS communications, allowing plain language analysis of secure sessions to help to identify weaknesses that would normally be hidden by the encryption.

A large number of plug-in components are available for WebScarab. They allow, for example, automated or manual modification of requests, submitting random data values, and crawling of Web content.

AntiSamy

AntiSamy was inspired by the Samy worm attack against MySpace and its users. It's a downloadable API, available in both Java and .NET, that allows you to automatically filter user-supplied HTML code. Called from your application, the API will strip out potentially malicious content, allowing that code to be incorporated into your Web site.

Four basic configurations are supplied—one based on the filtering policies of the Slashdot Web site, one on eBay, one on MySpace, and one referred to as "anything goes" or "Not even MySpace is _this_ crazy." Any of the configurations can be further tailored to meet your needs. The Java version also implements a range of directives that can further enhance security or improve the appearance of the filtered code.

No PHP version is available because the non-OWASP HTML Purifier tool fulfills an equivalent function.

Enterprise Security API (ESAPI)

Available for a wide range of programming languages, including .NET, PHP, and Java, ESAPI is designed to enable programmers to write more secure code. Specifically, ESAPI enables security to be added to or improved in existing applications. It provides both a set of security control interfaces and a reference implementation for each security control.

WebGoat

WebGoat is a training aid for application developers and testers. Written in Java (J2EE), it guides users through a series of deliberately engineered vulnerabilities that can actually be exploited. Containing over 40 lessons at this writing, it demonstrates HTML comment weaknesses, SQL injection attacks, and cross-site scripting, among other exploits.

Additionally, one of the project members has produced several online training videos showing practical solutions to a number of the tests.

Open Software Assurance Maturity Model (OpenSAMM)

Originally a separate project, OpenSAMM is derived from the basic structure of the Carnegie Mellon University Software Engineering Institute's Capability Maturity Model.

OpenSAMM uses a 0 to 3 grading structure across four critical business functions, each containing three security practices to rate software development activities. You can learn more about OpenSAMM at *http://www.opensamm.org*.

OWASP Guides

As well as producing documentation for its projects and tools, OWASP produces three core guides:

- *The OWASP Guide to Building Secure Web Applications and Web Services*
- *The OWASP Testing Guide*
- *The OWASP Code Review Guide*

Building Secure Web Applications and Web Services

This guide is aimed at the wide range of the developer community—from architects to auditors. It covers the principles of secure coding and a long list of security objectives and development techniques. It contains specific code examples for PHP, .NET, and Java, although the principles are applicable to any high-level coding language.

Testing Guide

This book covers a wide range of security testing—from manual inspection to penetration testing. It describes a comprehensive testing framework, based around the industry standard Software Development Life Cycle Model. Most of the book is a detailed guide to Web application penetration testing, covering test objectives, methods, and tools for more than 60 different controls groups.

Code Review Guide

Earlier versions of the Testing Guide included information on manual review of code for security flaws. This has been extracted in a separate guide, which covers 16 key testing areas and advice on reviewing standard programming languages and components.

CHAPTER SUMMARY

Large numbers of government, private, and volunteer organizations contribute to the field of information security. National and international organizations set standards. Victims of online attacks and fraud are encouraged to communicate and cooperate by law enforcement, national and industry CSIRTs. Many academic, nonprofit, and commercial organizations provide training and educational materials. Certification and examinations are available in both broad information security disciplines and narrow specializations.

The relationships among these many organizations and security professionals are complex and fluid, but the strength of the international security community is its willingness to share information, best practices, and assistance.

KEY CONCEPTS AND TERMS

Computer incident response teams (CIRTs)

Computer security incident response team (CSIRT)

Common Vulnerabilities and Exposures (CVE) list

Forum of Incident Response and Security Teams (FIRST)

Honeypot

International Information Systems Security Certification Consortium (ISC)^2

ISO 17024

Open source

CHAPTER 15 ASSESSMENT

1. Which organization provides incident response support for the federal government?

   A. OWASP
   B. The Secret Service
   C. US-CERT
   D. FIRST

2. Which organizations investigate Internet crime? (Select two.)

   A. MLATs
   B. IC3
   C. ECTFs
   D. OWASP

3. Which of the following standards are governed by NIST? (Select two.)

   A. Advanced Encryption Standard (AES)
   B. ISO 27001
   C. The United States Government Configuration Baseline
   D. CISSP

4. Which of the following are (ISC)^2 qualifications? (Select three.)

   A. CISM
   B. CISSP
   C. CISSP-ISSEP
   D. Security+
   E. CSSLP

5. You must pass an exam to become an (ISC)^2 Associate.

   A. True
   B. False

6. Which certification organization is not approved under DoD Directive 8750?

   A. CERT/CC
   B. ISACA
   C. SANS GIAC
   D. FLETC

7. What is the purpose of open proxy honeypots in relation to Internet-based Web attacks?

   A. Silently record for later analysis
   B. Act as deliberate weakened targets for
   C. Obscure the source of
   D. Detect and terminate

8. Roughly how many site reviews were used to generate the most recent WASC Web Security Report?

   A. 5,000
   B. 10,000
   C. 20,000
   D. 100,000

9. ISO 17024 is the international standard for which of the following?

   A. Information security management systems
   B. Web application penetration testing
   C. Evaluation criteria for IT security
   D. Certification programs for personal competence

10. The National Institute of Standards and Technology (NIST) represents the United States in the International Standards Organization.

    A. True
    B. False

Answer Key

CHAPTER 1 From Mainframe to Client/Server to World Wide Web

1. Authentication   2. TK   3. B and C   4. B   5. D   6. Blind patching
7. Data integrity   8. B   9. B   10. C

CHAPTER 2 Security Considerations for Small Businesses

1. A   2. A, B, and D   3. A, B, and D   4. A and D   5. B   6. A, B, and D
7. A   8. C   9. B   10. A

CHAPTER 3 Security Considerations for Home and Personal Online Use

1. B   2. A   3. C   4. B   5. A, B, and D   6. A and C   7. B   8. B   9. C   10. B

CHAPTER 4 Mitigating Risk When Connecting to the Internet

1. A   2. A and B   3. B   4. C   5. A   6. Intrusion detection system or IDS
7. A   8. 80   9. Proxy server   10. B   11. A

CHAPTER 5 Mitigating Web Site Risks, Threats, and Vulnerabilities

1. A   2. A   3. B   4. A, C, and D   5. C   6. Encapsulating Security Payload
or ESP   7. A   8. Authentication   9. A   10. B   11. B

CHAPTER 6 Introducing the Web Application Security Consortium (WASC)

1. A   2. E   3. XSS attacks exploit the trust that a user has in a site, while CSRF
attacks exploit the trust a Web site has in the user's browser.   4. C and D
5. A   6. A, B, and C   7. SQL injection   8. A and D   9. B, C, and E   10. A
11. B, C, and D   12. C

CHAPTER 7 Securing Web Applications

1. A   2. B   3. A   4. B and C   5. C   6. Secure Sockets Layer or SSL   7. A
8. Advanced Encryption Standard (AES)   9. D   10. B and C   11. A   12. B

CHAPTER 8 Mitigating Web Application Vulnerabilities

1. A   2. A, B, and D   3. B   4. E   5. C   6. Elevation of privilege   7. A
8. Session replay   9. B and C   10. B   11. D   12. A

CHAPTER 9 Maintaining PCI DSS Compliance for E-commerce Web Sites

1. B   2. A, C, and D   3. B   4. A and B   5. Batch processing   6. A
7. Real-time processing   8. C   9. B, C, and D   10. A

© Rodolfo Clix/Dreamstime.com

CHAPTER 10 Testing and Quality Assurance for Production Web Sites

1. A   2. A and D   3. A   4. A   5. C   6. Gray box testing   7. A
8. A, B, and C   9. C   10. B

CHAPTER 11 Performing a Web Site Vulnerability and Security Assessment

1. B   2. C   3. Remediation   4. B and C   5. B   6. A   7. D   8. C
9. Injection   10. B, C, and E   11. C   12. A   13. Plug-ins   14. D   15. B

CHAPTER 12 Securing Mobile Communications

1. B and C   2. B   3. Multimedia Messaging Service or MMS   4. A   5. B
6. Eavesdropping   7. D   8. B   9. Convergence   10. B and C   11. A
12. A   13. A, B, and D   14. B   15. A and D

CHAPTER 13 Securing Personal and Business Communications

1. Store-and-forward   2. B   3. E-mail   4. B   5. E   6. A and B   7. B and C
8. B   9. C   10. A and B   11. Virtual local area networks or VLANs   12. D
13. A   14. C

CHAPTER 14 Security Training, Education, and Certification

1. A   2. B   3. C   4. C   5. B   6. A   7. B and C   8. C   9. A   10. A

CHAPTER 15 Web Application Security Organizations

1. C   2. B and C   3. A and C   4. B, C, and E   5. A   6. D   7. A   8. B
9. D   10. B

Standard Acronyms

ACD	automatic call distributor	**CCC**	CERT Coordination Center
AES	Advanced Encryption Standard	**CCNA**	Cisco Certified Network Associate
ALE	annual loss expectancy	**CDR**	call-detail recording
ANSI	American National Standards Institute	**CERT**	Computer Emergency Response Team
AO	authorizing official	**CFE**	Certified Fraud Examiner
AP	access point	**C-I-A**	confidentiality, integrity, availability
API	application programming interface	**CIPA**	Children's Internet Protection Act
APT	advanced persistent threat	**CIR**	committed information rate
ARO	annual rate of occurrence	**CIRT**	computer incident response team
ATM	asynchronous transfer mode	**CISA**	Certified Information Systems Auditor
AUP	acceptable use policy	**CISM**	Certified Information Security Manager
AV	antivirus	**CISSP**	Certified Information System Security Professional
B2B	business to business		
B2C	business to consumer	**CMIP**	Common Management Information Protocol
BBB	Better Business Bureau		
BC	business continuity	**CMMI**	Capability Maturity Model Integration
BCP	business continuity plan	**CNA**	computer network attack
BGP4	Border Gateway Protocol 4 for IPv4	**CND**	computer network defense
BIA	business impact analysis	**CNE**	computer network exploitation
BYOD	Bring Your Own Device	**COPPA**	Children's Online Privacy Protection Act
C2C	consumer to consumer	**COS**	class of service
CA	certificate authority	**CRC**	cyclic redundancy check
CAC	Common Access Card	**CSA**	Cloud Security Alliance
CAN-SPAM	Controlling the Assault of Non-Solicited Pornography and Marketing Act	**CSF**	critical success factor
		CSI	Computer Security Institute
		CSP	cloud service provider
CAP	Certification and Accreditation Professional	**CTI**	Computer Telephony Integration
		CVE	Common Vulnerabilities and Exposures
CAUCE	Coalition Against Unsolicited Commercial Email	**DAC**	discretionary access control
		DBMS	database management system
CBA	cost-benefit analysis	**DCS**	distributed control system
CBF	critical business function	**DDoS**	distributed denial of service
CBK	common body of knowledge	**DEP**	data execution prevention

DES	Data Encryption Standard
DHCPv6	Dynamic Host Configuration Protocol v6 for IPv6
DHS	Department of Homeland Security
DIA	Defense Intelligence Agency
DISA	direct inward system access
DMZ	demilitarized zone
DNS	Domain Name Service OR Domain Name System
DoD	Department of Defense
DoS	denial of service
DPI	deep packet inspection
DR	disaster recovery
DRP	disaster recovery plan
DSL	digital subscriber line
DSS	Digital Signature Standard
DSU	data service unit
EDI	Electronic Data Interchange
EIDE	Enhanced IDE
ELINT	electronic intelligence
EPHI	electronic protected health information
EULA	End-User License Agreement
FACTA	Fair and Accurate Credit Transactions Act
FAR	false acceptance rate
FCC	Federal Communications Commission
FDIC	Federal Deposit Insurance Corporation
FEP	front-end processor
FERPA	Family Educational Rights and Privacy Act
FIPS	Federal Information Processing Standard
FISMA	Federal Information Security Management Act
FRCP	Federal Rules of Civil Procedure
FRR	false rejection rate
FTC	Federal Trade Commission
FTP	File Transfer Protocol
GAAP	generally accepted accounting principles
GIAC	Global Information Assurance Certification
GigE	Gigibit Ethernet LAN
GLBA	Gramm-Leach-Bliley Act
HIDS	host-based intrusion detection system
HIPAA	Health Insurance Portability and Accountability Act
HIPS	host-based intrusion prevention system
HTML	Hypertext Markup Language
HTTP	Hypertext Transfer Protocol
HTTPS	Hypertext Transfer Protocol Secure
HUMINT	human intelligence
IaaS	Infrastructure as a Service
IAB	Internet Activities Board
ICMP	Internet Control Message Protocol
IDEA	International Data Encryption Algorithm
IDPS	intrusion detection and prevention
IDS	intrusion detection system
IEEE	Institute of Electrical and Electronics Engineers
IETF	Internet Engineering Task Force
IGP	Interior Gateway Protocol
IMINT	imagery intelligence
InfoSec	information security
IP	intellectual property OR Internet Protocol
IPS	intrusion prevention system
IPSec	Internet Protocol Security
IPv4	Internet Protocol version 4
IPv6	Internet Protocol version 6
IS-IS	intermediate system-to-intermediate system
(ISC)²	International Information System Security Certification Consortium
ISO	International Organization for Standardization
ISP	Internet service provider
ISS	Internet security systems
ITIL	Information Technology Infrastructure Library
ITRC	Identity Theft Resource Center
IVR	interactive voice response
L2TP	Layer 2 Tunneling Protocol
LAN	local area network

MAC	mandatory access control		PoE	power over Ethernet
MAN	metropolitan area network		POS	point-of-sale
MAO	maximum acceptable outage		PPTP	Point-to-Point Tunneling Protocol
MASINT	measurement and signals intelligence		PSYOPs	psychological operations
MD5	Message Digest 5		RA	registration authority OR risk assessment
modem	modulator demodulator		RAID	redundant array of independent disks
MP-BGP	Multiprotocol Border Gateway Protocol for IPv6		RAT	remote access Trojan OR remote access tool
MPLS	multiprotocol label switching		RFC	Request for Comments
MSTI	Multiple spanning tree instance		RIPng	Routing Information Protocol next generation for IPv6
MSTP	Multiple Spanning Tree Protocol		RIPv2	Routing Information Protocol v2 for IPv4
NAC	network access control		ROI	return on investment
NAT	network address translation		RPO	recovery point objective
NFIC	National Fraud Information Center		RSA	Rivest, Shamir, and Adleman (algorithm)
NIC	network interface card		RSTP	Rapid Spanning Tree Protocol
NIDS	network intrusion detection system		RTO	recovery time objective
NIPS	network intrusion prevention system		SA	security association
NIST	National Institute of Standards and Technology		SaaS	Software as a Service
NMS	network management system		SAN	storage area network
NOC	network operations center		SANCP	Security Analyst Network Connection Profiler
NSA	National Security Agency		SANS	SysAdmin, Audit, Network, Security
NVD	national vulnerability database		SAP	service access point
OPSEC	operations security		SCADA	supervisory control and data acquisition
OS	operating system		SCSI	small computer system interface
OSI	Open Systems Interconnection		SDSL	symmetric digital subscriber line
OSINT	open source intelligence		SET	secure electronic transaction
OSPFv2	Open Shortest Path First v2 for IPv4		SGC	server-gated cryptography
OSPFv3	Open Shortest Path First v3 for IPv6		SHA	secure hash algorithm
PaaS	Platform as a Service		S-HTTP	secure HTTP
PBX	private branch exchange		SIEM	Security Information and Event Management system
PCI	Payment Card Industry		SIGINT	signals intelligence
PCI DSS	Payment Card Industry Data Security Standard		SIP	Session Initiation Protocol
PGP	Pretty Good Privacy		SLA	service level agreement
PII	personally identifiable information		SLE	single loss expectancy
PIN	personal identification number		SMFA	specific management functional area
PKI	public key infrastructure		SNMP	Simple Network Management Protocol
PLC	programmable logic controller		SOX	Sarbanes-Oxley Act of 2002 (also Sarbox)
POAM	plan of action and milestones			

B

Standard Acronyms

SPOF	single point of failure		**UC**	unified communications
SQL	Structured Query Language		**UDP**	User Datagram Protocol
SSA	Social Security Administration		**UPS**	uninterruptible power supply
SSCP	Systems Security Certified Practitioner		**USB**	universal serial bus
SSID	service set identifier (name assigned to a Wi-Fi network)		**UTP**	unshielded twisted pair
			VA	vulnerability assessment
SSL	Secure Sockets Layer		**VBAC**	view-based access control
SSL-VPN	Secure Sockets Layer virtual private network		**VLAN**	virtual local area network
			VoIP	Voice over Internet Protocol
SSO	single system sign-on		**VPN**	virtual private network
STP	shielded twisted pair OR Spanning Tree Protocol		**W3C**	World Wide Web Consortium
			WAN	wide area network
TCP/IP	Transmission Control Protocol/ Internet Protocol		**WAP**	wireless access point
			WEP	Wired Equivalent Privacy
TCSEC	Trusted Computer System Evaluation Criteria		**Wi-Fi**	Wireless Fidelity
			WLAN	wireless local area network
TFA	two-factor authentication		**WNIC**	wireless network interface card
TFTP	Trivial File Transfer Protocol		**WPA**	Wi-Fi Protected Access
TGAR	trunk group access restriction		**WPA2**	Wi-Fi Protected Access 2
TNI	Trusted Network Interpretation		**XML**	Extensible Markup Language
TPM	technology protection measure OR trusted platform module		**XSS**	cross-site scripting

Glossary of Key Terms

© Rodolfo Clix/Dreamstime.com

301 (permanent) redirect | A way to tell Web browsers and search engines that a Web page or site has been permanently moved to a new location.

302 (temporary) redirect | A way to tell Web browsers and search engines that a Web page or site has been temporarily moved to a new location.

A

Active Server Pages (ASP) | A programming language used for creating Web sites. It's good for building standards-based Web sites with HTML5, CSS3, and JavaScript.

Advanced Encryption Standard (AES) | Also known as Rijndael, a block cipher encryption standard that creates keys from 128 bits to 256 bits in length.

Adware | Adware is any software application in which advertising banners are displayed while the program is running.

Application hardening | The process of securing applications in use on a network.

Archie | The early search tool of Gopher.

ARPANET | The first computer network based on the packet-switching principle.

Auditing | Keeping records of operations and transactions to assess the accuracy of processes.

Authentication | The process of establishing the validity of a person's identity.

Authentication Header (AH) | A protocol primarily responsible for the authentication and integrity verification of data packets. AH does not provide any form of encryption.

Authorization | The process of giving an individual access to information after authentication.

Automatic directory listing | Identifies all of the files within a given directory on a Web server if the base file is not found. The base files refer to such files as *index.html, default.htm, index.php*, and so on.

Availability | The degree to which a system is operable and committable at a start of a process or function.

B

Batch processing | A processing strategy in which transactions are not handled immediately; rather, receipts are collected and processed as a batch.

Black box testing | A software testing methodology that looks at available inputs for an application and the expected outputs from each input.

Blacklist | A practice to define what is unacceptable, excluding all other input as acceptable.

Broken authentication | The result when an attacker compromises authentication credentials, gaining access to all resources associated with those credentials. Social engineering is a common method of obtaining user IDs and passwords.

Broken cryptography | Occurs when the data on a mobile device is not encrypted properly.

Brute-force attack | Involves programs designed to guess at every possible combination until the password or key is cracked.

Buffer overflow | Occurs in an application when more information is stored in the buffer than the space reserved for it.

Bulletin Board System (BBS) | A centralized system through which users can exchange messages; a message board.

Business intelligence (BI) | Raw data derived from manufacturing and other business processes that has been organized and structured into meaningful information on which decisions can be based.

C

Calendaring software | Software used to maintain personal or group schedules.

Canonicalization attack | An attack involving backtracking up a directory path using "../" or dot, dot, slash to access areas not intended to be accessible.

CAPTCHA (Completely Automated Public Turing Test to Tell Computers and Humans Apart) | Mechanisms used to protect against automated attacks. The function of CAPTCHA is to provide a challenge/response mechanism to help ensure that a Web form is being filled out by a human and not an automated process.

Centralized processing | Processing is offloaded from the client onto a centralized server. Cloud computing is an example of centralized processing.

Change management | A standardized approach to handling changes to the IT infrastructure.

Circuit switching | A dedicated, physical, point-to-point connection between the sending and receiving devices.

Clickjacking | Inserting into a legitimate Web page links that lead to fake forms or downloads for malware.

Client privacy agreement | An agreement that outlines what can and cannot be done with the personal data of visitors to a Web site.

Client/server | A computing environment in which one machine (the client) makes requests while another machine (the server) fulfills the requests.

Client-side injection attack | A kind of attack that involves looking for vulnerabilities on mobile devices, often by the execution of malicious code from within a mobile application.

Client-side validation | Input validation mechanisms on the client side using the client browser.

Cloud computing | Delivering hosted services over the Internet, which includes providing infrastructures, platforms, and software as services.

Collection of data not required for the primary purpose | One of the OWASP Top 10 Privacy Risks, this refers to the risk of data provided for one purpose being collected and used for another, typically to target advertising.

Common Gateway Interface (CGI) | A standard that enables communication between Web forms and your program.

Common Vulnerabilities and Exposures (CVE) list | Run for the Department of Homeland Security by the MITRE Corporation, a basic description of computer application and operating system vulnerabilities.

Compatibility testing | A software testing method designed to verify how well an application functions with other software, such as the operating system or other Web applications. Interoperability is a significant concern, and application testing must ensure compatibility with other popular software.

Computer incident response teams (CIRTs) | CIRTs are now normally higher-level coordination bodies with wider responsibilities for vulnerability and attack research and issuing warning and vulnerability notices. CIRT was the original term for what is now commonly called a CSIRT.

Computer security incident response team (CSIRT) | An all-hours or on-call group for an organization, corporation, or country designed to respond to online attacks or similar events. May also be called an information system incident response team (ISIRT).

Confidentiality | Ensuring that information is accessible only to authorized users.

Content adaptation | How mobile phones handle Web and multimedia content intended for more powerful systems with larger screens.

Content spoofing | Creating a fake Web site or Web application and fooling victims into thinking it is a legitimate one. An attacker lures victims to an authentic-looking but illegitimate Web site. The attacker then steals logon credentials, credit card information, or other forms of personal data.

Convergence | The evolution of different types of devices into a more common form that has a combination of features.

Cookie | A very small data file that a Web site may write to a hard drive. It contains information such as when a user visited certain Web pages, what he or she clicked on, as well as possibly even the person's username and password are.

Cracker | A cybercriminal intending harm to systems and networks.

Cross-site request forgery (CSRF) attack | Exploits the trust a Web site has for a user's browser. This can occur because once a visitor is authenticated and logged onto a particular Web site, that site trusts all requests that come from the browser.

Cross-site scripting (XSS) | A well-known Web application vulnerability in which attempts are made to execute malicious code by injecting it and running it in the client browser. If the script code can be executed, the attacker may have access to your data, financial information, and more. *See also* XSS attack.

Cryptographic key | The confidential component of a cryptographic system. The key defines how the cryptographic algorithm converts plaintext to encrypted text and back.

Cryptography | The encoding of data so that it can be decoded only by certain persons. The role of cryptography is to protect data integrity, confidentiality, nonrepudiation, and authentication.

Cyberstalking | Constant and unwelcome electronic tracking of another person.

D

Database administrator | One who is responsible for databases used in the business environment; duties might include performing database updates, tuning database performance, coordinating on server hardware and OS issues, defining backup and restore strategies, and of course, security.

Database designer | More of a business analyst/software developer than a production support technician, someone who can efficiently and appropriately organize an application's required data into related tables.

Data Encryption Standard (DES) | An encryption standard using a 56-bit key encryption method.

Deep Web | The place where the large majority of Web sites exist, beneath the surface of the Web and out of the reach of search engine crawlers.

Defensive programming | Also known as secure programming, this is really just a mindset whereby programming is done with a clear understanding of current threats and how they may impact software today and in the future.

Denial of service (DoS) attack | An attack that can result in decreased availability of the targeted system.

Development environment | The environment in which programmers develop, test, and upgrade software systems applications. Compare with a production environment.

Digital certificate | A small electronic file that serves to validate or encrypt a message or browser session. Digital certificates are often used to create a digital signature which offers non-repudiation of a user or a Web site.

Discretionary access control (DAC) | An access control method in which access is not forced from the administrator or the operating system; rather, access is controlled by the information's owner.

Distributed application | An application whose processing is divided across multiple computers over a network. Typically, the divisions, or tiers, are presentation, business logic, and data store layers.

DNS namespace | An organized, hierarchical division of DNS names.

Domain Name System (DNS) | A hierarchical system for naming resources on a network as well as providing translation between the resource's IP address and its domain name.

E

E-commerce | The buying and selling of goods and services over electronic systems such as the Internet.

Electronic cash | Currency that you purchase with a credit, charge, or debit card, and then download to your computer or smart card.

Electronic wallet | An electronic storage device for electronic currency and information about the owner of the wallet.

E-mail filtering | The process of identifying potentially risky e-mail and stopping it from reaching the end user.

Encapsulating Security Payload (ESP) | A protocol that provides encryption services to network data. Can also be used for authentication and integrity services. Differs from AH authentication in that ESP includes only the ESP header, trailer, and payload portions of a data packet. The IP header is not protected, unlike with AH, which protects the entire data packet.

Encryption | The process of encoding information. The act of making text or data unreadable without possession of a translation key.

Endpoint device | A device or system that connects users to a communications or data network.

Enumeration | Identifying the types of services components that are running on a system.

Extensible Markup Language (XML) | A set of rules for encoding documents electronically. XML was chosen as the standard message format because of its widespread use and open source development efforts.

F

Failure to restrict URL access attack | Occurs when an attacker browses unprotected areas and data on a Web server. This attack is enabled by Web applications that fail to restrict vulnerabilities.

Fax server | A computer-based fax machine.

Feature freeze | A software state in which development continues but no additional features are added to the product.

File Transfer Protocol (FTP) | A protocol used for file exchange.

Fingerprinting | Identifying the type and version of operating system that is running on a system.

Forum of Incident Response and Security Teams (FIRST) | A worldwide voluntary and collaborative body bringing together incident response teams and related organizations. It encourages rapid and secure communications between affected communities and allows in-confidence information sharing. It also supports an annual conference and hosts special interest groups and regular training events.

G

Google Docs | Google's proprietary Web-based office application software that offers word processing, spreadsheets, and presentations.

Gopher | An early computer network that featured searches through a file tree.

Graphical user interface (GUI) | An interface based on graphical elements as opposed to text only.

Gray box testing | A software testing methodology that provides the middle ground between black box and white box testing. It looks at the input and output of applications and the inner workings of the application.

Groupware | A system of tools that facilitates group collaboration. Groupware may include calendar software and instant messaging applications.

Guidelines | Non-enforced suggestions for increasing functioning and performance.

H

Hacker | Generally known as a cybercriminal. However, hackers are actually well-intentioned or "good" infiltrators who edit and modify applications. Crackers are those with malicious intent. Most people today use the term "hacker" to mean "cracker."

Heartbeat | A term for the transaction between the client and Web server system where a particular Web site responds to a user's system signifying that the server is active and awaiting requests.

Honeypot | A carefully monitored system set up by security professionals to be attacked, so that attack sources and methods can be analyzed.

Host-based security | Security measures such as firewalls, IDSs, and antivirus solutions installed directly on a client system.

Hypertext | Text as non-sequential links to other text or documents.

Hypertext Markup Language (HTML) | A set of tags, or rules, primarily used to specify formatting of Web documents.

Hypertext Transfer Protocol (HTTP) | A transfer protocol for exchanging hypertext documents over the Internet or an intranet.

Hypertext Transfer Protocol Secure (HTTPS) | Combines the HTTP protocol with the SSL protocol to provide secure online transactions.

I

Identify theft | Assuming someone else's identity by obtaining personal information.

Impersonation | From a Web site or Web application perspective, an attacker's attempt to use the session credentials of a valid user.

Improper session handling | Refers to an application that leaves a session open or unsecured, creating a vulnerability.

Indexing | An automatic process in which software programs known as spiders or bots examine Web sites collecting data and analyzing the Web sites' keywords. The results are stored and indexed in the search engine's database.

Information leakage | The exploitation by an attacker of information found or gathered which was intended only for authorized users.

Infrastructure as a Service (IaaS) | Delivery of infrastructure on demand, usually billed per amount of resources consumed.

Injection flaw attack | Enables an attacker to bypass an application's access controls and create, change, delete, or read any data the application can access. The end result is compromised data. One of the most common forms of an injection flaw attack is the SQL injection attack.

Input validation | The verification of all data that is received. This helps prevent malicious data from entering an application. Input validation is a form of filtering in which unexpected or unwanted input is automatically rejected and the underlying database remains inaccessible.

Instant messaging (IM) | A program that allows users to exchange messages in real time.

Insufficient data breach response | One of the OWASP Top 10 Privacy Risks, this refers to the risk someone runs by failing to take adequate corrective steps after a data breach.

Insufficient deletion of personal data | One of the OWASP Top 10 Privacy Risks, this refers to failure to remove sensitive data from a computer after its intended purpose has ended.

Insufficient Transport Layer protection | Refers to the lack of security when data is in transit.

Integration testing | A software testing method in which individual software modules are combined and tested as a group. Integration testing typically occurs after unit testing.

International Information Systems Security Certification Consortium (ISC)² | A nonprofit professional and certification body that provides related programs for information security professionals.

Internet Key Exchange (IKE) | A protocol that manages the SA negotiation process for IPSec connections.

Internet Message Access Protocol (IMAP) | A TCP/IP protocol designed for downloading, or pulling, e-mail from a mail server. IMAP is used because although the mail is transported around the network via SMTP, users cannot always read it immediately, so it must be stored in a central location. From this location, it needs to be downloaded, which is what IMAP allows you to do.

Internet Protocol Security (IPSec) | Secures communication between systems within a network as well as communications transmitted outside a LAN; can be used to encrypt, authenticate, and verify the integrity of communications.

Internet Relay Chat (IRC) | An early form of synchronous online conferencing.

Interprocess communications (IPC) | A tool designed for developers to allow communication and sharing of data between applications.

Intrusion detection system (IDS) | A security mechanism that monitors data packets traveling across a network, comparing traffic against parameters of known threats. An IDS is a passive security measure in that it only monitors the network and doesn't take steps to mitigate the risk.

Intrusion prevention system (IPS) | A security mechanism that monitors and reacts to data packets traveling across a network. An IPS is an active security measure because it not only monitors but also blocks suspect traffic identified by the device.

ISO 17024 | The international standard for accrediting schemes that certify personal competences.

J

JavaScript | A scripting programming language most commonly used to add interactive features to Web pages.

L

Lack of binary protections | Refers to an attacker's ability to gain access to the underlying code of an application, analyze it, reverse-engineer it, and then modify the program.

Latency | A delay. Can apply to the sending, processing, transmission, storage, or receiving of information.

Least privilege | *See* principle of least privilege.

Lightweight Directory Access Protocol (LDAP) | A protocol that provides a mechanism to access and query directory services systems. Directory services include systems such as Novell Directory Services (NDS) and Microsoft Active Directory, database servers, Web servers, and Web application servers.

Local area networks (LANs) | Computer networks covering a small physical area, such as an office or the floor of a building.

GLOSSARY

M

Macro virus | A type of virus designed to infect, corrupt, and damage Microsoft Office documents.

Mainframe | A high-performance computer usually used by large businesses requiring large-scale processing and availability.

Malicious code | An umbrella term for Trojan horses, viruses, worms, and the like.

Malicious software | Software designed to damage or disrupt the operation of a system. Also referred to as malware.

Malware | Software designed to damage or disrupt the operation of a system, such as a Trojan horse, worm, or virus. Also known as malicious software.

Malware hoax | An illegitimate announcement of new malware.

Mandatory access control (MAC) | An access control mechanism in which access is controlled and dictated by the network administrator.

Man-in-the-middle attack | An attack that involves eavesdropping on communication between a sender and a receiver. Attackers use their position to listen and perhaps redirect or alter communication.

Microblogging | A form of blogging using limited content, such as Twitter.

Minicomputer | A computer of medium size with less processing capability than a mainframe, but more than a PC.

Missing function level access control | A security concern closely related to incorrect authorization assignment. It arises if users can access additional resources or application features beyond what their roles require. They sign in as authorized users but gain access that they don't need, because access controls have failed, or not been properly set up in the first place.

Missing or insufficient session expiration | One of the OWASP Top 10 Privacy Risks, this refers to the privacy issues arise when sessions on these sites are not properly closed or discontinued. This is an issue primarily for users of public computers or shared computers in a home or workplace.

Mobile broadband | The ability to communicate at broadband (cable modem/DSL or faster) speeds while being connected to a cellular network.

Multimedia Messaging Service (MMS) | A service provided by cellular networks that allows the sending and receiving of multimedia messages between users. MMS content includes audio, video, digital images, ringtones, and more.

Multimedia Messaging Service Encapsulation Protocol | A specification from the Open Mobile Alliance. The specification details implementation requirements for any organization interested in providing Multimedia Messaging Service.

Multiple points of presence (MPOP) | Presence information is aggregated from several devices to a single presence status. The reported status is provided to other users.

N

Network Time Protocol (NTP) | A protocol within the TCP/IP protocol suite designed to synchronize clocks of computer systems over packet-switched networks.

Non-transparent policies, terms, and conditions | One of the OWASP Top 10 Privacy Risks, this refers to the difficulty of reading and understanding the long policy documents typical of Web sites.

O

Open source | A copyright or licensing system that, compared with conventional commercial licensing schemes, allows wide use and modification of the material.

Open Web Application Security Project (OWASP) | An organization that researches and publishes known security threats to Web applications and Web services.

Operator-sided data leakage) | One of the OWASP Top 10 Privacy Risks, this refers to the accidental or neglectful release of personal information, typically by individual users themselves.

Outdated personal data | One of the OWASP Top 10 Privacy Risks, this refers to the risk that outdated personal information could be harmful to someone's reputation and a breach of privacy.

Output handling | The way applications control their output data. Output data from an application may take the form of logging, printing, coding, error messages, or raw data to be passed on to another application.

Outsourcing | Sending information to third-party service providers for storage, processing, or transmission.

P

Packet switching | A method for moving data over a network. Data is split into chunks (packets), and each packet contains destination details. The packets of the original entity being transmitted are recomposed at the destination. Packets may travel though different paths from the source to the destination in the network.

Password | A secret word used for authentication.

Path traversal attack | An attack in which the attacker attempts to circumvent acceptable file and directory areas to access files, directories, and data located elsewhere on the server. This is accomplished by changing the URL to point to other areas on the server.

Payment Card Industry Data Security Standard (PCI DSS) | A set of standards designed to help organizations that process credit card payments prevent fraud by having increased control over data and its exposure.

Penetration testing | An attempt to circumvent various layers of a system or application's security controls for the purpose of seeing how far into the system the attacker can get.

Performance testing | A software testing method that provides an accurate view of how applications perform in a large-scale deployment in a variety of production environments. These tests determine responsiveness under various workloads to ensure that the application works well under normal operational circumstances.

Personal identification number (PIN) | An authentication method that validates a user.

Phishing | A scam in which an impostor pretends to be a legitimate entity and tries to lure customers into divulging confidential information.

Physical security | A type of computer security that includes tangible protection devices.

Ping sweep | The act of sending TCPIP packets to various IP addresses and determining which of those addresses are active based on the responses that are received.

Platform as a Service (PaaS) | Delivery of a computing platform as a service.

Podcast | A podcast is a recorded audio program available for download from a Web site.

Point-to-Point Tunneling Protocol (PPTP) | Protocol used to establish and secure VPN connections.

Policies | An organization's documented basic requirements supported by senior management.

Poor authorization and authentication | A very common threat; where this condition exists, an adversary can anonymously execute functionality within the mobile app or back-end server the mobile app uses.

Portals | Single points of access to a collection of resources.

Presence | The state or availability of a remote object.

Presence and availability | The ability and willingness of an end user to engage in communication. The information is controlled by the end user and gives real-time confidence that the user is accessible. Delivery is not automatic, but relies on technology or applications being enabled to provide it.

Pretexting | A common social networking attack in which the attacker pretends to be someone else to gain the trust necessary to get personal information.

Principle of least privilege | The concept of providing users with as few privileges as possible, just enough to fulfill their network needs. It is a security measure that ensures users are not granted more permissions than needed.

Privacy | The protection of individual rights to nondisclosure.

Procedure | A task or set of tasks performed to implement a process.

Process validation | The correct sequence of steps in a transaction or online process.

Production environment | A real-world practical environment in which applications are used for business purposes. Compare with a development environment.

Protocols | Defined policies or standards that users adhere to. Protocols are well-defined and accepted procedures. In computer networking, the term refers to algorithms for exchanging various types of data and their interpretation at origination and destination.

Q

Qualified Security Assessor (QSA) | A person trained to conduct PCI DSS Security Assessments.

GLOSSARY

R

Ransomware | Refers to an attack whereby all the files and folders on a computer system are encrypted and held for ransom.

Really Simple Syndication (RSS) | A family of standardized Web feeds used to publish changes in recently updated work, such as news.

Real-time communication | An immediate exchange of information.

Real-time processing | A credit card transaction in which processing is immediate.

Real-time Transport Control Protocol (RTCP) | The protocol for the purpose of managing and maintaining the quality of RTP.

Real-time Transport Protocol (RTP) | The protocol used for streaming audio or video in packets over an IP network.

Recovery testing | A software testing method that gauges the recovery capabilities of an application in the event of failure. Recovery testing determines whether an application can recover from a crash or hardware failure.

Reflected XSS attack | Uses social engineering to initiate an XSS attack. A reflected XSS attack uses a malicious script that is embedded in a URL link to target a single victim.

Regression testing | A software testing method that checks for additional errors in software that may have been introduced in the process of upgrading or patching to fix other problems.

Regulations | Legal restrictions with legal consequences. Regulations are not set by an organization but by applicable laws.

Regulatory compliance testing | A software testing method that ensures an application meets and adheres to appropriate standards.

Relational database | A database in which the information is organized into tables related to each other by specific rules.

Request for Comments (RFC) | A formal document from the Internet Engineering Task Force (IETF) that is the result of committee drafting and revision of a technical document.

Resource Description Framework (RDF) | A framework for conceptual modeling.

Rivest Cipher | A family of secret key cryptographic algorithms from RSA Security, Inc. The family includes RC2, RC4, RC5, and RC6.

Role-based access control | An access control mechanism in which access decisions are determined by the roles that individual users have as part of an organization.

Routing detour attack | A form of man-in-the-middle attack in which an intermediary attacker reroutes data to an alternate location.

Rule-based access control | An access control mechanism in which access to objects is controlled according to established rules.

S

Sandbox | A strategy for separating programs and running them in their own virtual space.

Sanitization | Inspection of user input for potentially harmful code and modifying the code according to predetermined guidelines. Sanitization often involves identifying and disallowing specific characters and syntax sequences.

Secrecy | Protection from inadvertent information disclosure.

Secure Sockets Layer (SSL) | The standard security technology for establishing an encrypted link between a Web server and a Web browser. This link ensures that all data passed between the Web server and browsers remains private and intact. SSL is an industry standard and is used by millions of Web sites to protect their online transactions with their customers.

Security association (SA) | A security agreement between two systems on a network that enables the secure exchange of data. For communication to occur, the sending system and receiving system must agree on the same SA.

Security decisions via untrusted inputs vulnerability | Refers to making security decisions on potentially untrusted sources.

Security misconfigurations | Actions such as failure to change default settings for passwords, to patch for known flaws, or to secure data properly.

Security testing | A software testing method that checks the security of an application. This includes testing for injection attacks, path traversal attacks, and if the software is vulnerable in other ways. Vulnerabilities need to be addressed before the software can be released.

Sensitive data exposure | Exposure of information such as credit card numbers, research secrets, medical records, or banking data. Most companies have some such sensitive data and thus some risk of sensitive data exposure.

Server | Combination of hardware and software intended to provide services to clients, usually over the Internet.

Server-side include (SSI) injection | An injection attack that occurs on the server and not on the client system. In an SSI attack, malicious code is placed in a Web application that is then stored on the server. When the Web application is executed locally on the Web server, the malicious code carries out its function. The SSI injection attack is successful when the Web application is ineffective in filtering user-supplied input.

Service set identifier (SSID) | A unique client identifier sent over a wireless network as a simple password that is used for authentication between a wireless client and an access point.

Session | The tracking of requests and communications between a Web server and a user. Because HTML is "stateless" by design, Web applications and Web sites must create a session to pass information and authentication from page to page.

Session hijacking | The exploitation of a valid computer session to gain unauthorized access to information and services within the targeted computer system.

Session ID | Identifies previous users to a Web site and stores user-specific information about a session.

Session Initiation Protocol (SIP) | An Application Layer protocol designed to establish and maintain multimedia sessions.

Session management | Defines how systems handle and manage user sessions.

Sharing of data with third party | One of the OWASP Top 10 Privacy Risks, this refers to the risk that a Web site will share with another company for money the data users assume will be kept private. Typically this is done to target advertising.

Short Message Service (SMS) | A service provided by cellular networks that allows the sending and receiving of short messages between users. SMS is more popularly known as "texting."

Simple Mail Transfer Protocol (SMTP) | Protocol used for e-mail exchange.

Simple Object Access Protocol (SOAP) | A common protocol used to establish a session between a Web server and mobile app; it is stateless by design.

SIP user agent (UA) | A network endpoint that is enabled to function as a either a SIP user agent client or user agent server.

SIP user agent client (UAC) | A SIP user agent that makes requests and receives responses.

SIP user agent server (UAS) | A SIP user agent that acts as a proxy between two SIP user agent clients for the purpose of facilitating a SIP session. The UAS acts as both client and server to receive and forward session control requests and responses.

Skype | A software application that allows the user to make video and audio calls over the Internet.

Social engineering | The practice of obtaining confidential information by manipulating users in social communication.

Social media | A blanket term that describes social applications, including forums, message boards, blogs, wikis, and podcasts. Social media applications include Google, Facebook, and YouTube.

Social networking | The use of online services designed to establish friendships and find like-minded people.

Software Configuration Management (SCM) | The mechanisms used to track and control changes in software.

Software Development Life Cycle (SDLC) | The process of planning, designing, creating, testing, deploying, and maintaining software.

Software stress testing | A software testing method that pushes an application to its limits to see where the breaking points are. Stress tests go well beyond normal, real-world scenarios trying to find the limits of an application.

Software as a Service (SaaS) | A model of software deployment or service where customers use applications on demand.

Spam | Unwanted and unsolicited e-mail.

Spyware | A form of malware that covertly gathers system information through the user's Internet connection without his or her knowledge.

SQL injection attack | A type of attack designed to break through database security and access the information. A SQL injection attack "injects" or manipulates SQL code.

Standard | An established and proven norm or method. A standard provides a means of ensuring quality by setting a uniform expectation for development.

Store-and-forward communication | The technique of relaying communications between two or more users by intermediate storage. Delivery from sender to a central storage is immediate, but the final transmission to the recipient depends upon availability and a request for the stored information.

Stored XSS attack | An attack that embeds malicious script into a Web page that permits and stores user-supplied content, such as a social networking site or an online forum, where it will be accessible to multiple potential victims. The victim retrieves the malicious script from the Web server when it requests the stored information. Also known as a persistent XSS attack.

System testing | A software testing method that combines all components that have successfully passed integration testing and assesses the system as a whole. System testing tests combined components to determine their interoperability.

T

Telnet | A protocol for synchronous access to a remote machine.

Transport Layer Security (TLS) | As the successor to Secure Socket Layer (SSL), TLS provides secure communications at the Transport layer from end to end.

Triple Data Encryption Standard (3DES) | An encryption method that uses three 56-bit encryption keys.

Trojan horse | A form of malware application hidden within another application that introduces backdoor access.

U

Unified collaborative communications (UCC) | Integration of voice, video, and Web or data conferencing. *See also* unified communications.

Unified communications | The combination of real time and non-real time into a single communication strategy. *See also* unified collaborative communications (UCC).

Unified messaging (UM) | The storage of fax, e-mail, and voice communications in a single location.

Unintended data leakage | What can occur when sensitive data is stored on a device and accessed by a malicious user using malware or other means.

Unit testing | A software testing method in which a programmer verifies that individual units of source code are fit for use. A unit is the smallest testable part of an application.

Unix-to-Unix Copy Protocol (UUCP) | A protocol that emerged prior to high-speed Internet connections, which permitted the exchange of e-mail and Usenet news over dial-up link speeds.

Unsecure data storage | Keeping sensitive data on a mobile device, where it is at risk of being lost or stolen. This a significant concern and can lead to identify theft and financial loss.

Unsecure data transfer | One of the OWASP Top 10 Privacy Risks, this refers to the serious but manageable threat to online privacy that arises when data is sent over unsecured public wireless networks.

Unsecure direct object reference vulnerability | A threat that occurs when an administrator fails to secure directories and folders in a Web server. Enables an attacker to traverse through a Web server's directories, leading to the access of sensitive resources and information leakage. Also referred to as directory traversal.

Unvalidated redirects and forwards | Links from trusted sites that take users to an unauthorized site to gain sensitive information from them or to install malicious software on their machines.

Usability testing | A software testing method designed to check the usability of an application. This may be done in a limited production environment to get a sampling of potential application users. The usability test helps ensure that the application is user friendly and provides an intuitive interface.

Usenet | The first Internet discussion service, started around 1980.

V

Veronica (Very Easy Rodent-Oriented Net-Wide Index of Computerized Archives) | A search tool used across the Gopher network.

Virtual private network (VPN) | A secure communication tunnel used to connect a remote client to a network.

Virtualization | The creation of a virtual version of actual services, applications, or resources.

Virus | Malicious software that cannot spread to another computer on its own, without human assistance.

Voice messaging | The storage of voice messages for later retrieval.

Voice over Internet Protocol (VoIP) | Technology allowing voice transmissions over the Internet.

Vulnerability management | The ongoing maintenance and management of existing Web sites and applications.

W

Weak server-side controls | Not directly related to a mobile device vulnerability but rather to a server-side vulnerability that can be exploited through a mobile device.

Web 1.0 | The infancy stage of the Web (1990–2003), based on presentation of information towards the users. Also referred to as the Static Web.

Web 2.0 | Web advancements between 2003 and 2010, where social networking activities and tools greatly improved. Also referred to as the Social Web.

Web 3.0 | The stage of the Web expected between 2010 and 2020. The focus will shift from documents and their relationships to data and its meaning, with services that are personally relevant to the user. Also referred to as the Semantic Web.

Web application | A software program containing computer scripts that interact with the end user. Examples include Web mail, shopping carts, portals, games, forums, forms, online auctions, and other interactive Web page elements.

Web Application Security Consortium (WASC) | A nonprofit group dedicated to improving application security practices.

Web application vulnerabilities | One of the OWASP Top 10 Privacy Risks, these are data leaks resulting from out-of-date or unpatched applications.

Web Ontology Language (OWL) | A collection of languages used for describing ontologies.

Web site defacement | A type of attack in which the attacker changes the appearance of a Web site. The attacker might replace a company's home page, for example, with a Web page that displays messages from the attacker.

White box testing | A software testing methodology that examines the code of an application. This contrasts with black box testing, which focuses only on inputs and outputs of an application.

Whitelist | A practice to define what is acceptable, excluding all others as unacceptable.

Wide area networks (WANs) | Data communications networks that encompass a large geographical area and travel beyond the boundaries of a local area network.

Wi-Fi Protected Access (WPA) | A data encryption method used on 802.11 wireless LANs.

World Wide Web | Commonly called the Web, a collection of HTML documents, audio, and video that resides on the Internet, which is accessible by browsers using the HTTP protocol.

Worm | Self-replicating malware designed to infect systems.

X

XML Path (XPath) language | Used for navigating XML documents and for retrieving data from within them. User input and queries are used with XPath to access XML information.

XPath injection attack | An attack in which the attacker injects data into an application so that the application executes user-controlled XPath queries. When successfully exploited, this vulnerability may allow an attacker to bypass authentication mechanisms and access XML information without proper authorization.

XSS attack | An attack in which malicious scripts are saved to a Web server but run in a client browser. If the script code is executed, the attacker gains access to personal data on the Web server or the victim's personal computer.

References

"About Licenses" (Creative Commons, n.d.). http://creativecommons.org/about/licenses/ (accessed May 12, 2010).

"About the Security Content of iPhone OS 3.0.1," article HT3754 (Apple Support, July 31, 2009). http://support.apple.com/kb/HT3754 (accessed May 16, 2010).

Alberts, Christopher, and Audrey Dorofee. *Managing Information Security Risks: The OCTAVE Approach*. Boston: Addison-Wesley, 2003.

Alhadidi, D., M. Debbabi, and P. Bhattacharya. "New AspectJ Pointcuts for Integer Overflow and Underflow Detection." *Information Security Journal: A Global Perspective* 17, no. 5/6 (2008): 278–287.

"An 'Apples to Apples' Comparison of the Top Providers of Online Fax Services" (FaxCompare .com, 2010). http://www.faxcompare.com/ (assessed May 5, 2010).

"Anti-phishing vigilance." *eWeek*, October 17, 2005.

Applegate, Scott D. "Social Engineering: Hacking the Wetware!" *Information Security Journal: A Global Perspective* 18, no. 1 (2009): 40–46.

Auger, Robert. Threat Classification wiki. http://projects.webappsec.org/Threat-Classification (accessed April 22, 2010).

Bell, Mary Ann. "Celebrating Communicating: Email Is Still the Killer App." MultiMedia&Internet@Schools, November 1, 2007: 35–37.

Benediktsson, O., D. Dalcher, and H. Thorbergsson. "Comparison of Software Development Life Cycles: A Multiproject Experiment." *IEE Proc. Softw.* 153, no. 3 (2006): 87–101.

Bennett, Shea R. "Minimum Age Requirements: Twitter, Facebook, Instagram, Snapchat, WhatsApp, Secret," Advertising Week/Social Times, September 29, 2014. http://www .adweek.com/socialtimes/social-media-minimum-age/501920 (accessed June 17, 2015).

Berners-Lee, Tim, and Mark Fischetti. *Weaving the Web: The Original Design and Ultimate Destiny of the World Wide Web*. San Francisco: Harper, 2000.

"Black-box vs. White-box Testing: Choosing the Right Approach to Deliver Quality Applications" (Redstone Software, 2008). http://www.testplant.com/download_files/BB_vs_WB_Testing .pdf (accessed May 18, 2010).

Boberski, Mike. "A Guide to Building Secure Web Applications and Web Services" (OWASP Guide Project). http://www.owasp.org/index.php/Category:OWASP_Guide_Project#tab=Project _Details (accessed May 30, 2010).

Brazil, Jody. "PCI DSS Compliance for Firewalls: It Doesn't Have To Be Complex" (*SC Magazine*, April 28, 2009). http://www.scmagazineus.com/pci-dss-compliance-for-firewalls-it-doesnt -have-to-be-complex/article/131543/ (accessed May 1, 2010).

© Rodolfo Clix/Dreamstime.com

"Business Transaction Processing—How Does It Work?" (Trasactmoney.com, 2009). http://www.transactmoney.com/transaction-articles/business-transaction-processing.htm (accessed May 1, 2010).

C++ Institute. "Certification Program," n.d. http://www.cppinstitute.org/?p=5 (accessed April 26, 2015).

Chandra, Pravir. "Software Assurance Maturity Model: A Guide to Building Security into Software Development" version 1.0 (The Open Web Application Security Project, 2009) http://www.opensamm.org/downloads/SAMM-1.0.pdf (accessed May 12, 2010).

Chong, Leonard, Siu Cheung Hui, and Chai Kiat Yeo. "Towards a Unified Messaging Environment Over the Internet." *Cybernetics and Systems* 30, no. 6 (August 1999): 533–549.

Citrix Systems Inc. "The Industry's First End-to-End Virtualization Certifications Are Now Here," 2015. http://training.citrix.com/cms/education/certification-links/ccee-and-ccia-for-virtualization/ (accessed April 27, 2015).

Curphey, Mark, Joel Scambray, and Erik Olson. "Improving Web Application Security: Threats and Countermeasures" (Microsoft, June 30, 2003). http://www.cgisecurity.com/lib/Threats_Countermeasures.pdf (accessed May 13, 2010).

CVE Top 25, CVE-2008-2249, "Integer Overflow in GDI," http://www.cve.mitre.org/cgi-bin/cvename.cgi?name=CVE-2008-2249 (accessed May 22, 2010).

"Data Protection" (European Commission, November 23, 1995). http://eur-lex.europa.eu/LexUriServ/LexUriServ.do?uri=CELEX:31995L0046:EN:HTML (accessed March 1, 2010).

Deal, Walter F. 2008. "Communication Technology: The Magic of Touch." *Technology Teacher* 68, no. 2 (October 2008): 11–18.

Descy, Don E. "Web Hosting Services: Finding Your Place on the Web." *TechTrends: Linking Research & Practice to Improve Learning* 49, no. 6 (2005): 4–5.

"DoD 8570.01-M: Information Assurance Workforce Improvement Program," Change 2 (Washington DC: U.S. Department of Defense, April 20, 2010). http://www.dtic.mil/whs/directives/corres/pdf/857001m.pdf (accessed May 12, 2010).

Dunham, Ken. "The Problem with P2P." *Information Systems Security* 15, no. 2 (2006): 5–8.

Egan, Matt. "How to Turn Out the Lights and Access the Dark Web (and Why You Might Want To)." PC Advisor News RSS, January 12, 2015. http://www.pcadvisor.co.uk/how-to/internet/3593569/what-is-dark-web-how-access-dark-web/ (accessed April 29, 2015).

"Electronic Communications Privacy Act of 1986" (U.S. Department of Justice, Justice Information Sharing, February 27, 2009). http://www.it.ojp.gov/default.aspx?area=privacy&page=1285 (accessed March 1, 2010).

Enck, William, Patrick Traynor, Patrick McDaniel, and Thomas La Porta. "Exploiting Open Functionality in SMS Capable Cellular Networks." Presented at the 12th ACM Conference on Computer and Communications Security. The Pennsylvania State University, 2005. http://www.smsanalysis.org/smsanalysis.pdf (accessed May 16, 2010).

"E-Warfare." *Wilson Quarterly* 34, no. 1 (2010): 69–70.

"Facebook Patches Security Hole That Exposed Users' Instant Messages" (*Los Angeles Times*, May 5, 2010). http://latimesblogs.latimes.com/technology/2010/05/facebook-patches-security-hole-that-exposed-users-instant-messages.html (accessed May 19, 2010).

Federal Bureau of Investigation (FBI). "Internet Social Networking Risks." March 13, 2012. http://www.fbi.gov/about-us/investigate/counterintelligence/internet-social-networking -risks (accessed April 1, 2015).

Flew, Terry. *New Media: An Introduction*. 3rd ed. Melbourne: Oxford University Press, 2007.

Gallo, Alessandro, and David Barkol. *ASP.NET Ajax in Action*. Greenwich, CT: Manning, 2008.

Gawade, Prashant. "HTTP Request Smuggling." *Palisade Magazine*, 25, September 2006. http:// palisade.plynt.com/issues/2006Sep/http-request-smuggling/ (accessed April 22, 2010).

Geach, Neal, and Nicola Haralambous. "Regulating Harassment: Is the Law Fit for the Social Networking Age?" *Journal of Criminal Law* 73, no. 3 (2009): 241–257.

Google, Inc. "Analytics," n. d. http://www.google.com/analytics/ (accessed March 16, 2015).

Gordeychik, Sergey, et al. "Web Application Security Statistics 2008" (Web Application Security Consortium, October 2009). http://projects.Webappsec.org/f/WASS-SS-2008.pdf (accessed May 12, 2010).

Government of Canada. "Cyber Security Risks," March 3, 2015. http://www.getcybersafe.gc.ca/ cnt/rsks/ (accessed March 7, 2015).

Harwood, Linda. Personal communication with Linda Harwood, professor of English of Selkirk College, British Columbia, Canada, regarding best practices for creating professional e-mail. March 1, 2010.

Hashkiller.co.uk. "Hash a Password—Hash a Password into Multiple Hash Types," 2015. http://www.hashkiller.co.uk/hash-a-password.aspx (accessed April 13, 2015).

Heartbleed Bug. "The Heartbleed Bug," April 29, 2014. http://heartbleed.com/ (accessed March 15, 2015).

The Hindu Business Line. "Google Must Remove Outdated Personal Data from Searches: EU Court," May 13, 2014. http://www.thehindubusinessline.com/features/smartbuy/tech-news/ google-must-remove-outdated-personal-data-from-searches-eu-court/article6005021.ece (accessed March 13, 2015).

"HTML 4.01 Specification" (World Wide Web Consortium, December 24 1999). http://www .w3.org/TR/html4/interact/scripts.html#h-18.2.3 (accessed May 12, 2010).

InfoSec Institute. "Exploiting Unintended Data Leakage (Side Channel Data Leakage)," April 29, 2014. http://resources.infosecinstitute.com/android-hacking-security-part-4-exploiting -unintended-data-leakage-side-channel-data-leakage/ (accessed April 11, 2015).

———. "Securing the Software Development Environment," Aug. 27, 2012. http://resources .infosecinstitute.com/securing-the-software-development-environment/ (accessed March 16, 2015).

The International Society of Forensic Computer Examiners—ISFCE. "CCE Certification," n.d. https://www.isfce.com/certification.htm (accessed April 27, 2015).

Jackman, Michael. "Can Mid-Market Merchants Comply with PCI Standards In Time?" (*CIO*, December 6, 2007). http://www.cio.com/article/162900/Can_Mid_Market_Merchants _Comply_with_PCI_Standards_In_Time_?page=5&taxonomyId=3089 (accessed May 1, 2010).

James, Stephen. "The Self-Hack Audit." *Information Systems Security* 5, no. 4 (1997): 49.

Keary, Eoin, ed. "OWASP Code Review Guide" V1.1 (OWASP Foundation, 2008). http://www .owasp.org/index.php/Category:OWASP_Code_Review_Project (accessed May 12, 2010).

Klein, Amit. "The Insecure Indexing Vulnerability: Attacks Against Local Search Engines" (WASC article, February 28, 2005). http://www.webappsec.org/projects/articles/022805 .shtml (accessed April 22, 2010).

———. "A Refreshing Look at Redirection" (WebAppSec mailing list posting, November 2, 2006). http://www.webappsec.org/lists/websecurity/archive/2006-11/ msg00003.html (accessed April 22, 2010).

———. "HTTP Response Smuggling" (WebAppSec mailing list posting, February 20, 2006). http://www.webappsec.org/lists/websecurity/archive/2006-02/msg00040.html (accessed April 22, 2010).

Krantz, Matt. "The Guys Behind MySpace.com" (*USA Today*, February 13, 2008). http:// usatoday.com/money/companies/management/2006-02-12-myspace-usat_x.htm (accessed March 2010).

Kurzweil, Ray. Foreword to *The Intelligent Universe: AI, ET, and the Emerging Mind of the Cosmos*, by James Gardner, 11–16. Franklin Lakes: New Page Books, 2007.

Larkin, Erik. "Don't Let Bad Guys Pose as You." *PC World* 25, no. 4 (2007): 36.

Leiva-Gomez, Miguel. "Everything You Should Know About Your IMEI Number." Make Tech Easier, September 30, 2013. http://www.maketecheasier.com/imei-number/ (accessed April 13, 2015).

Lewis, Bob. "The Distinction Between Distributed Computing and Client/Server Is Essential." *InfoWorld*, July 21, 1997.

———. "Turn the Definition of Client/Server Computing Into a Useful Business Tool." *InfoWorld*, July 28, 1997.

"Licenses by Name" (Open Source Initiative, n.d.). http://www.opensource.org/licenses/ alphabetical (accessed May 12, 2010).

Lueg, Christopher, and Danyel Fisher. *From Usenet to CoWebs: Interacting with Social Information Spaces.* London: Springer-Verlag, 2003.

Malik, Om, Matthew Schifrin, Joshua Solan, Emily Manzo, Ben Berentson, Adit Nathan, and Adam Leitzes. "Message Boards." *Forbes* 164, no. 6 (1999): 52.

Mamis, Robert A. "Voice Mail Versus Voice Messaging—Here's the Difference." *Inc.* 16, no. 8 (August 1994): 110. (Academic Search Premier, EBSCOhost). http://www.inc.com/ magazine/19940801/3068.html (accessed February 24, 2010).

Manes, Stephen. "Ounces of Protection." *Forbes* 175, no. 5 (2005): 70. Academic Search Premier, EBSCOhost.

McDermott, Irene E. "All A-Twitter About Web 2.0: What Does It Offer Libraries?" *Searcher*, October 1, 2007.

Meier, J. D., Alex Mackman, Michael Dunner, Srinath Vasireddy, Ray Escamilla, and Anandha Murukan. *Improving Web Application Security: Threats and Countermeasures* (Microsoft MSDN Library, June 2003). http://msdn.microsoft.com/en-us/library/aa302420.aspx (accessed May 3, 2010).

Meucci, Matteo, ed. "OWASP Testing Guide" V3.0 (OWASP Foundation, 2008). http:// www.owasp.org/index.php/Category:OWASP_Testing_Project (accessed May 12, 2010).

Meyer, David. "SpinVox Uses Humans For Voice-To-Text Conversion" (ZDNet UK, July 23, 2009). http://www.zdnet.co.uk/news/networking/2009/07/23/spinvox-uses-humans-for-voice -to-text-conversion-39692521/ (accessed May 20, 2010).

Microsoft Corporation. "Advanced Security Audit Policy Settings," July 3, 2013. https://technet .microsoft.com/en-us/library/dn319056.aspx (accessed March 15, 2015).

Microsoft Learning. "Find the Right IT Certification," 2015. https://www.microsoft.com/ learning/en-ca/certification-overview.aspx (accessed April 26, 2015).

———. "MTA Certification & Exams | Microsoft," 2015. https://www.microsoft.com/learning/ en-ca/mta-certification.aspx (accessed April 25, 2015).

"Mission Statement" (United States Secret Service, 2010). http://www.secretservice.gov/ mission.shtml (accessed May 13, 2010).

"Mobile Cellular Subscriptions per 100 People" online report, 2003–2008 (International Telecommunications Union, n.d.). http://www.itu.int/ITU-D/icteye/Reporting/ ShowReportFrame.aspx?ReportName=/WTI/CellularSubscribersPublic&ReportFormat =HTML4.0&RP_intYear=2008&RP_intLanguageID=1&RP_bitLiveData=False (accessed May 16, 2010).

Mulliner, C. and Vigna, G. "Vulnerability Analysis of MMS User Agents," University of California, Santa Barbara (CiteSeerx, n.d.). http://citeseerx.ist.psu.edu/viewdoc/download ?doi=10.1.1.103.4803&rep=rep1&type=pdf (accessed May 20, 2010).

"Multimedia Messaging Service Encapsulation Protocol" (Open Mobile Alliance, March 2005). http://www.miniware.net/docs/OMA-MMS-ENC-V1_2-20050301-A.pdf (accessed May 10, 2010).

National Institute of Technology and Standards. "NIST Selects Winner of Secure Hash Algorithm (SHA-3) Competition," October 2, 2012. http://www.nist.gov/itl/csd/sha-100212.cfm (accessed June 17, 2015).

———. "The United States Government Configuration Baseline (USGCB)," April 22, 2015. http://usgcb.nist.gov (accessed June 17, 2015).

"Nessus: the Network Vulnerability Scanner" (Tenable Network Security, 2010). http:// www.nessus.org/nessus/ (accessed May 27, 2010).

"Network Security Policy: Best Practices White Paper," document ID 13601 (Cisco Systems, July 9, 2007). http://www.cisco.com/en/US/tech/tk869/tk769/technologies_white _paper09186a008014f945.shtml (accessed May 18, 2010).

Nmap, http://nmap.org (accessed May 27, 2010).

"Open Handset Alliance Android SMS WAP Push Denial of Service, android-smswappush -dos (53655)" (IBM Internet Security Systems, October 5, 2009). http://xforce.iss.net/xforce/ xfdb/53655 (accessed May 16, 2010).

Open Web Application Security Project. "OWASP Mobile Security Project," April 20, 2015. https://www.owasp.org/index.php/OWASP_Mobile_Security_Project#Top_Ten_Mobile_Risks (accessed June 17, 2015).

———. "OWASP Top 10 Privacy Risks Project," June 16, 2015. https://www.owasp.org/index. php/OWASP_Top_10_Privacy_Risks_Project (accessed June 17, 2015).

Oracle Corporation. "1 The Oracle Database Administrator," 2002. https://docs.oracle.com/cd/ A97630_01/server.920/a96521/dba.htm (accessed April 24, 2015).

OWASP Foundation. OWASP Developer Guide, n.d. Retrieved from https://github.com/OWASP/
DevGuide/tree/dc5a2977a4797d9b98486417a5527b9f15d8a251/DevGuide2.0.1
(accessed March 15, 2015).

"OWASP Top 10—2010: The Ten Most Critical Web Application Security Risks" (The Open Web
Application Security Project, April 19, 2010). http://owasptop10.googlecode.com/files/
OWASP%20Top%2010%20-%202010.pdf (accessed May 12, 2010).

Paulk, Mark C., Charles V. Weber, Bill Curtis, and Mary Beth Chrissis. *The Capability Maturity
Model: Guidelines for Improving the Software Process.* Boston: Addison-Wesley, 1995.

Payment Card Industry Security Standards Council. "PCI SSC Data Security Standards
Overview," 2006–2015. https://www.pcisecuritystandards.org/security_standards/ (accessed
March 15, 2015).

———. "Welcome to the PCI Security Standards Council," 2006–2015. https://www
.pcisecuritystandards.org (accessed March 15, 2015).

"PCI Compliance Made Easy." TraceSecurity, August 2007. http://www.tracesecurity.com/
docs/PCI-DSS-Compliance.pdf (accessed May 1, 2010).

"PCI DSS Security Audit Procedures, Version 1.1" (PCI Security Standards Council,
September 2006). https://www.pcisecuritystandards.org/pdfs/pci_audit_procedures
_v1-1.pdf (accessed May 1, 2010).

"PCI DSS: 5 Guidelines for Gaining PCI Compliance" (PCI Compliance Guide, n.d.). http://
www.pcicomplianceguide.org/merchants-20071022-gaining-pci-compliance.php
(accessed May 1, 2010).

Phithakkitnukoon, Santi, Ram Dantu, and Enkh-Amgalan Baatarjav. "VoIP Security—Attacks
and Solutions." *Information Security Journal: A Global Perspective* 17, no. 3 (2008): 114–123.

"Plaintiffs' Petition For Damages" letter from the law offices of Al Robert Jr. (*Wired*,
November 2009) http://www.wired.com/images_blogs/threatlevel/2009/11/radiant
-petition.pdf (accessed May 1, 2010).

Poremba, Sue Marquette. "Risky Business: Managing the Email Security Risk." *EContent* 31,
no. 7 (2008): 40–44.

Poulsen, Ken. "The Littlest Security Pro" (*SecurityFocus*, December 21, 2001). http://www
.securityfocus.com/news/301 (accessed May 12, 2010).

Racid, Radmilo, Denys Ma, and Hao Chen. "Exploiting MMS Vulnerabilities to Stealthily
Exhaust Mobile Phone's Battery," University of California, Davis (TechRepublic, n.d.). http://
whitepapers.techrepublic.com.com/abstract.aspx?docid=310218 (accessed May 20, 2010).

Rosenblum, David. "What Anyone Can Know: The Privacy Risks of Social Networking Sites."
IEEE Security and Privacy (IEEE Educational Activities Department) 5, no. 3 (May/June 2007):
40–49.

Sarno, David. "Twitter Creator Jack Dorsey Illuminates the Site's Founding Document.
Part 1" (*Los Angeles Times* Business section, February 18, 2009). http://latimesblogs
.latimes.com/technology/2009/02/twitter-creator.html (accessed March 2010).

Sarrel, Matthew D. "Web Site Analytics." *PC Magazine* 26, no. 20 (2007): 84.

"Secure Coding Guidelines for the Java Programming Language, Version 3.0" (Oracle, 2010).
http://java.sun.com/security/seccodeguide.html (accessed May 12, 2010).

"Security Policies and Procedures" wiki (Internet2, August 6, 2009). https://wiki.internet2.edu/confluence/display/secguide/Security+Policies+and+Procedures (accessed May 18, 2010).

Schiller, Kurt. "Phishing Scams Edge Into Social Networks." *Information Today* 26, no. 10 (2009): 46.

———. "Virtualization: Appealing in a Tough Economy." *Information Today*, January 1, 2010.

Seacord, Robert, and Martin Sebor. "Top 10 Secure Coding Practices" (CERT, February 23, 2010). https://www.securecoding.cert.org/confluence/display/seccode/Top+10+Secure+Coding+Practices (accessed May 12, 2010).

Shiflett, Chris. "Security Corner: Session Fixation." Reprint of article from *php|architect*, February 16, 2004. http://shiflett.org/articles/session-fixation (accessed April 22, 2010).

Siddharth, Sumit. "Five Common Web Application Vulnerabilities" (*Symantec Connect*, April 27, 2006). http://www.symantec.com/connect/articles/five-common-Web-application-vulnerabilities (accessed May 13, 2010).

Sima, Caleb, and Liu, Vincent. "Implementing Effective Vulnerability Remediation Strategies Within the Web Application Development Lifecycle" (Toolbox for IT, 2010). http://hosteddocs.ittoolbox.com/CS0815072.pdf (accessed May 18, 2010).

"Staying a Step Ahead of the Hackers: The Importance of Identifying Critical Web Application Vulnerabilities," white paper (IBM Service Management, June 2008). ftp://public.dhe.ibm.com/common/ssi/sa/wh/n/gmw14021usen/GMW14021USEN.PDF (accessed May 12, 2010).

Strassmann, Paul A. "40 years of IT history." *Datamation*, October 1, 1997.

———. 2001. "Secure the Internet." *Computerworld* 35, no. 40 (2001): 23.

Symantec Corporation. Norton: Your Security Resource: "Top 5 Social Media Scams," n.d. http://ca.norton.com/yoursecurityresource/detail.jsp?aid=social_media_scams (accessed March 13, 2015).

Tajfel, Henri, and John Turner. "An Integrative Theory of Intergroup Conflict." In *The Social Psychology of Intergroup Relations*, by William G. Austin and Stephen Worchel, 94–109. Monterey, CA: Brooks-Cole, 1979.

"Technical and Operational Requirements for Approved Scanning Vendors (ASVs)," version 1.1 (PCI Security Standards Council, 2006). https://www.pcisecuritystandards.org/pdfs/pci_dss_technical_and_operational_requirements_for_approved_scanning_vendors_ASVs_v1-1.pdf (accessed May 12, 2010).

Thompson, Samuel T. C. "Policies to Protect Information Systems: Building Barriers to Intrusion from Social Engineering Attacks." *Library & Archival Security* 19, no. 1 (2004): 3–14.

Tomayko, David. "Software Configuration Management," SEI Curriculum Module SEI-CM-4-1.4 (Carnegie Mellon University, Software Engineering Institute, December 1990). http://www.sei.cmu.edu/reports/87cm004.pdf (accessed May 12, 2010).

Tressler, Colleen. "Consumers Told It to the FTC: Top 10 Complaints for 2014." Federal Trade Commission Consumer Information, Feb. 27, 2015. http://www.consumer.ftc.gov/blog/consumers-told-it-ftc-top-10-complaints-2014 (accessed March 31, 2015).

Wagley, John. "Printer Vulnerabilities Exposed" (*Security Management*, June 2008). http://www.securitymanagement.com/article/printer-vulnerabilities-exposed (accessed May 13, 2010).

"Web Analytics Association" (Web Analytics Association, n.d.). http://www .Webanalyticsassociation.org/ (accessed May 18, 2010).

Weinstein, Lauren, and Peter G. Neumann. "Internet Risks." *Communications of the ACM 43*, no. 5 (2000): 144.

"What Are Standards?" (ETSI, 2010). http://www.etsi.org/WebSite/Standards/ WhatIsAStandard.aspx (accessed May 18, 2010).

"What Errors Are Included in the Top 25 Programming Errors?" (SANS, 2010). http:// www.sans.org/top25-programming-errors/ (accessed May 12, 2010).

"What Is Revision Control?" (Klariti, n.d.). http://www.klariti.com/technical-writing/What -is-Revision-Control.shtml (accessed May 12, 2010).

Wickr. "WickrTop-Secret Messenger Free Download Now!" 2015. https://wickr.com/ (accessed April 12, 2015).

Wong, David. "Secure Coding" (Symantec Connect, June 19, 2002). http://www.symantec.com/ connect/articles/secure-coding (accessed May 13, 2010).

Zeadally, S., F. Siddiqui, and P. Kubher. "Voice over IP in Intranet and Internet environments." *IEE Proceedings—Communications* 151, no. 3 (June 2004): 263–269.

Zeichick, Alan, Ed Scannell, Cathleen Moore, Paul Krill, et al. "The six myths of IT." *InfoWorld*, August 16, 2004.

Zettner, Kim. "Restaurants Sue Vendor for Unsecured Card Processor" (*Wired*, November 30, 2009). http://www.wired.com/threatlevel/2009/11/pos/ (accessed May 1, 2010).

Index